I0759499

Islamic China

Islamic China

AN ASIAN HISTORY

Rian Thum

HARVARD UNIVERSITY PRESS

Cambridge, Massachusetts, & London, England

2025

Printed in the United States of America
First printing

EU GPSR Authorised Representative
LOGOS EUROPE, 9 rue Nicolas Poussin, 17000, LA ROCHELLE, France
E-mail: Contact@logoseurope.eu

Library of Congress Cataloging-in-Publication Data

Names: Thum, Rian Richard, author.
Title: Islamic China : an Asian history / Rian Thum.
Description: Cambridge, Massachusetts : Harvard University Press, 2025. | Includes bibliographical references and index. | English; some words and phrases in Chinese.
Identifiers: LCCN 2025011885 (print) | LCCN 2025011886 (ebook) | ISBN 9780674976801 (hardcover) | ISBN 9780674302273 (epub) | ISBN 9780674302273 (epub) | ISBN 9780674302266 (pdf)
Subjects: LCSH: Muslims—China—History. | Islam—China—History. | Muslims—China—Intellectual life. | Chinese—Ethnic identity—History. | China—Ethnic relations—History. | China—Religion.
Classification: LCC DS731.M87 T53 2025 (print) | LCC DS731.M87 (ebook)
LC record available at https://lccn.loc.gov/2025011885
LC ebook record available at https://lccn.loc.gov/2025011886

Contents

Islamic China

Introduction

A Bird's-Eye View

> The *Huihui* [Muslims] were formerly all in the Western Regions,
> who would know that they would reside in China forever?
>
> —*Huihui yuanlai* 回回源來 [The origins of the Huihui], c. 1700

> Are they really Muslims?
>
> —Raphael Israeli, *Islam in China,* cover text, 2002

THE GOAL OF THIS BOOK is to reach an understanding of Islamic Chinese history that makes the Muslims of China unsurprising, even ordinary. Over the last 1,200 years, an astonishing diversity of communities have considered themselves at once Muslim and, in one way or another, Chinese. A comprehensive accounting of their interlocked histories is impossible in a single volume, but this book offers a bird's-eye view of that diversity from roughly 1640 to 1920, pieced together from a range of interconnected and sometimes intimate stories, many of which bleed into the present day: a Ningxia village that gathers daily to chant Arabic histories of the future; borderland Muslims who worked to restore the toppled Ming dynasty; a Chinese educationalist who published Confucian Islamic philosophy in India; a contrarian scholar from Nanjing who rewrote the five pillars of Islam; a valley in Yunnan that became saturated with Persian woodblock books; and an Indian mystical movement that penetrated all major Chinese Islamic sects, only to have its name forgotten. Until these stories become unremarkable, we will not have understood China or Islam.

To discuss these varied histories as part of a larger whole, called here Islamic China, is to entangle ourselves in thorny debates about the construction of both social groupings and the concepts we use to understand them. Because the histories of Islamic China fit uneasily within widely accepted categories, upending common expectations of both "China" and "Islam," they have an unusual potential for clarifying such problems. This book therefore seeks insights from Islamic Chinese history that can be of use to the study of communities beyond China and Islam. These include interventions on the persistence of origin-focused thinking in historical analysis, the interplay of ordinariness with controversy, and the mechanisms by which concepts we reject in the abstract, notably essentialism, continue to suffuse our scholarship. I have attempted to write the book in such a way that these questions emerge organically from the historical material, as they did for me in the course of the research.

Ordinary and Extraordinary

Without a basic understanding of a community's self-perception, we can arrive at only the most limited understanding of that community, if for no other reason than the fact that self-perception strongly informs decision-making. This book thus aims to bring us closer to understanding China's Muslims in light of their own views. To do so I focus on their writings about the meaning of Islam and about the place of Islam in China; on the lives of those who wrote such texts; and on the cultural, technological, economic, and mobile contexts that made their textual production possible. But "Chinese" and "Muslim" are controversial categories, and they are, in many cases, categories of unequal salience from one community to another. For some they are even irrelevant. By seeking a bird's-eye view of a diverse terrain, we busy ourselves in linking together self-perceptions that are often at odds with one another. In any case, to speak of even a small community is already to take a bird's-eye view, because no two individuals share an identical conception of their community.

Bruno Latour admonished "sociologists of associations" that their "duty is not to stabilize—whether at the beginning for clarity, for convenience, or to look reasonable—the list of groupings making up the social. Quite the opposite: their starting point begins precisely with the controversies about which grouping one pertains to, including of course the controversies among social scientists about what the social world is made of."[1] Such controversies are woven throughout the chapters of this book. Some are outlined more explicitly (if less organically) later in this introduction. "Controversy," as used by Latour, implies an intentional, considered, and openly communicated argument, including controversy about which social grouping a person pertains or belongs to. Many of our historical sources are precisely that.

My goal—making the Muslims of China unsurprising—involves also attending to what was uncontroversial, which I describe as ordinary. The study of "the ordinary" has a long history, particularly in cultural anthropology, and yet definitions of the ordinary are scarce. This is likely because the concept's close cousin, "the everyday," has attracted careful attention from an illustrious array of thinkers across the second half of the twentieth century, to the extent that we can even read a history of theorization of the everyday.[2] With good reason, scholars tend to treat "the ordinary" and "the everyday" as roughly interchangeable, allowing them to draw from the substantial scholarship of "the everyday." There are, however, cases in which "the ordinary," and especially "ordinary" as an adjective, can be different from the "everyday." We can attend an ordinary funeral or peruse an ordinary introduction to nuclear engineering, without taking these to be aspects of everyday life.

A recent ethnographic study, tracing the effortful construction of ordinariness in Mussolini's hometown, offers an overview of anthropological engagements with both the concrete designation of things as ordinary and the abstraction of "the ordinary." The author, Paolo Heywood, does not settle on a definition of either concept. However, a key quality of concrete ordinariness (my concern in this book) emerges in Heywood's description of an elderly woman setting out to buy groceries. As she passes a Fascist monument along the way, "Valentina will pay no attention to this," and as she passes another, "Valentina will pay it as little attention as she paid to" the first. The author is primarily interested in the special case of what happens when abstract ordinariness becomes a community's aspiration and thus an explicit, emic category. But the repeated appearance of inattention points to something that is shared across most discussions of what is ordinary.[3]

Things described as ordinary (as opposed to the abstract "world" or "context" that is "the ordinary") tend to be those that are not noticed, not remarked on, and / or do not require explanation. Because ordinary phenomena are, in most cases, literally unremarkable, we cannot expect to find these phenomena described in our historical sources as "ordinary." The presentation of a behavior, a book, or a language as ordinary is inexplicit. It is marked by a lack of open controversy.

Attention to ordinary discourses, which come down to us in texts that present themselves as uncontroversial, is crucial to making the Muslims of China unsurprising. This is true, not just in the more general sense that anthropologists have advocated when placing "the ordinary" at the center of their ethnographies, but also as a counterbalance to a century-long focus among scholars of "Islam in China" on extraordinary and controversial (in Latour's sense) sources, a focus that has continually constructed the Muslims of China as surprising.

Two historiographical habits have contributed to this scholarship of the extraordinary. The first is a lack of interest in sources that do not obviously spark or reflect historical change. Compilations of prayers, legal commentaries, grammars, guides for orthopraxy, abbreviations, and works composed outside China together made up the majority of written works that, in China before the twentieth century, circulated exclusively among Muslims. I am not sure that many specialists in the history of Muslims in China would recognize these texts in the wild. Vanishingly few studies of works from this textual core have appeared.

The second habit has its roots in a long-standing assumption that East Asian and Near Eastern cultures are distinct and inherently incompatible. Ulrich Brandenburg has shown that early Euro-American and Japanese engagements with Islam in China were rooted in orientalist divisions of Asia into two zones, with names such as "Western or Mohammedan Asia" and "Eastern or Buddhist Asia."[4] When, in the late nineteenth century, Europeans became aware of the millennium-long presence of substantial populations of Chinese Muslims, the resulting challenge to the orientalist ordering required explanations of this category-busting fact.

Early scholars found an overlap between their desire to explain the presence of Muslims and a particular subset of Chinese-language Islamic texts that aimed to justify Islamicness in a Chinese context, sometimes even with a sense of surprise, as in the epigraph from the *Huihui yuanlai* above. These works, most of which are now known by the problematic term

"Han Kitab," were extraordinary, controversial texts, which argued that Muslims and Islam were, in fact, ordinary in the Chinese context. Anti-Muslim condescension, discrimination, and barbarization inspired these authors and made their texts appealing to Muslim readers.

The essentialist assumption of an incompatibility between China and Islam has persisted into the current century, as the above epigraph from Raphael Israeli shows: "Are they really Muslims?" The orientalist bifurcation of Asia persists too, most troublingly in Western capitals, where Samuel Huntington's contemptibly simplistic "clash of civilizations" argument is still commonly cited with approval, despite the fact that every one of its predictions has proven false.[5] In China, Han nationalist imaginings have fueled a parallel essentialism, sorting China's Muslims into those whose practices are more "Chinese" and those that are more "foreign," valorizing the extraordinary texts of the Han Kitab in the process. This is visible in both government policies and much Chinese-language scholarship on Islamic China.

Most specialists in the history of Islamic China have endeavored to move away from essentialisms. Nonetheless, we write in a historical context that is profoundly shaped by the myth of incompatibility. Because our work is always in conversation with previous scholarship, the focus on extraordinary texts that directly address the question of compatibility, especially the so-called Han Kitab, has maintained an outsized place in the history of Islamic China. And because we write for audiences that are very often surprised by the presence of Muslims in China, we find ourselves addressing that history from a similar perspective. As a result, the history of pre-twentieth-century Muslims in China is almost entirely based on the kinds of sources I have characterized as explicit, controversial, and extraordinary. The resulting scholarship abounds in concepts that address the relationship between Muslims and non-Muslims in China, such as accommodation, assimilation, vernacularization, and syncretism. Among scholars both inside and outside China, language bias in source selection—especially the elision of Persian and Arabic sources—has further fueled the scholarship of the extraordinary, a topic addressed in more detail below. My bird's-eye view of Islamic China aims to re-entangle Muslim self-perceptions that are implicit and explicit, uncontroversial and controversial, ordinary and extraordinary.

Origins

There is another uncanny parallel between the academic scholarship of the extraordinary and those historical sources that explicitly address the boundaries of Chineseness and Muslimness: a fixation on origins, especially the instinct to explain by origins.[6] China's extraordinary Islamic texts return constantly to the discussion of origins, from the given name of the historical figure treated in Chapter 1 (Lianyuan 聯元, "connecting to the origin"); to the theology of the oldest substantial Islamic book in Chinese, with its two-hundred-plus appearances of the words for origins; to the community histories that invariably seek group origins. At the same time, attention to origins lies at the heart of the outsider's "surprise" at Chinese Muslims. Despite their thousand-plus years of history in China, they are defined by their purported ultimate origins in Arabia. Though China and Islam existed as mutually isolated phenomena for only a few decades in the seventh century CE, scholars have continually attempted to disentangle them, interpreting the ensuing millennium of entangled history in light of that brief moment of separateness. Introductions to the topic usually begin with an origin story of China's Muslims.

Western philosophers have problematized the concept of origins in various, often unconnected ways. Jacques Derrida, to take a famous example, aspired to an "interpretation of interpretation" that "is no longer turned toward the origin."[7] As far as I can tell, there is no unified lineage of thought on the role of origins in shaping our understanding of the world we inhabit, though the problem emerges often. Derrida's work is among the most direct diagnoses of origin-focused thinking as an obstacle to understanding. Anthropologists, folklorists, and scholars of religion have attended to origins in a different way, noting the prominence and ubiquity of origin stories across cultures and times, subjecting them to close readings, and posing them as keys to the understanding of various societies. Sociologists of identity have been particularly critical of origin-as-explanation, as when Stuart Hall writes that "there is always a politics of identity, a politics of position, which has no absolute guarantee in an unproblematic, transcendental 'law of origin.'"[8]

What interests me is the interaction between origin thinking in our historical sources and origin thinking in the analytical approaches that historians apply to those sources. Because origin stories are a ubiquitous element of group identity construction, they provide crucial data about how people see themselves in relation to communities. As we will see, origin stories can also preserve data about the historical transmission of ideas and the transregional mobilities that have shaped communities. In these senses, historians and the historical actors we study are natural allies in our attention to origins.

But historians also have the duty to reject the analytical approaches of historical actors where they create distortions. We can see this clearly in the case of essentialism: It is all but universally rejected by humanists and social scientists, but it is central to most humans' understanding of identity groups, be they religions, nations, ethnicities, or hometown affiliations.[9] Academic historians usually write in a different genre from their historical subjects, for a different audience (albeit one that includes the descendants of our historical subjects), and for different purposes from those who produced our primary sources. What I write can only ever be a product of both my own emic assumptions and those of the historical actors I engage.[10] I cannot lightly dismiss the arguments and insights of humanistic scholarship from outside Islamic China, especially while the distortions of essentialism and origin thinking fuel the current Chinese state's repression of Muslims, a topic discussed at the end of the book.

Chapter 8 uses the case of the so-called Han Kitab to demonstrate how misplaced or incautious attention to origins can lead to misunderstandings of the communities we study. Specifically, some kinds of origin thinking can smuggle essentialism into analyses that aim to provide nonessentialist accounts. One basic contribution I hope to make with this book is to encourage a heightened awareness of and wariness about origin thinking in historical writing. Like essentialism, it has often been critiqued. And like essentialism, origin thinking has ways of subtly (sometimes not so subtly) creeping into historical scholarship, especially when the primary sources are themselves origin-focused. But I also want to take a page from the extraordinary texts of Islamic China and explore the opportunities that origin-seeking analysis might offer. The community histories examined in this book all ask the question "where do we come from?," but some also ask "how did we get here, now?," thereby seeking an account not just of origins but of transmissions. Chapters 6 and 9 explore the opportunities that lie in attending to both origins and transmissions.

Some scholarly approaches I discuss are directly tied to essentialism. Most notable among them is the concept of syncretism, which contrasts a supposedly mixed tradition (e.g., Chinese Islam) with the *original* forms of its purported components. In confronting these approaches, my point is not simply that essentialism is inaccurate and distorting—that argument is already widely accepted. The point instead is to find the places where elements of essentialism have managed to stick around, sometimes in transformed states under different terminologies or discursive patterns, often piecemeal, and to develop some approaches that can starve those essentialist impulses.

Orderings: A Bird's-Eye View of What?

Origin stories are the products of social categories, and category construction is an unavoidable task for the historian, whether it is undertaken deliberately or not. To write history is to delimit the object of study, if only in the act of deciding what will and what will not be covered. Regardless of where it started, a history that followed any and all connections (causal relationships, movements of people, etc.) would end up addressing every knowable corner of the past, across the planet and for all time. So we draw lines around our subject matter. Doing this with intellectual consistency, and without collateral distorting effects, is complex and frustrating, perhaps impossible. The potential logics of delimitation are infinite.

The idea that the intersection of the categories "Muslim" and "China" could determine the scope of a history is a relatively new one. The earliest surviving history to focus on the topic of Muslims in China was written around the beginning of the eighteenth century by a Chinese-speaking Muslim. The goal of that work, *Huihui yuanlai* (The origins of the Huihui), seems to have been to justify the presence of Muslims and to tie their arrival in China to the state, in the form of the emperor.[11] However, most histories that Muslims in China wrote about their own communities did not frame their subject as Muslims in China. Some are presented as histories of Islam, others as histories of the leaders of Sufi orders, and still others as genealogies. Outsiders' histories of Muslims in China first appear in the second half of the nineteenth century, when European missionaries and orientalists took interest in China's Muslims as they related to the goal of making China a Christian land. These histories appeared as part of larger works surveying the demography and religious situation of China's Muslims at the time of writing. The first academic history of Muslims in China in monograph form was arguably the 1935–1936 general history by Jin Jitang, a Chinese Muslim himself.[12] The first effort at an academic monograph on the topic in a European language appeared in 1978, followed by Donald Leslie's brief but well-researched monograph in 1986.[13] Since then, fewer than a dozen monographs on the history of "Chinese Muslims," "Muslim Chinese," or "Islam in China" have appeared in English.

From among these histories and others at the intersection of "Muslim" and "China," we do not yet have many explicit arguments about where to draw boundaries around our subject matter. If we work from political boundaries and lump together all Muslims within the boundaries of the People's Republic of China or the Qing Empire, we find ourselves reading across communities engaged in very different conversations with very different rules, notably the Turki speakers of Eastern Turkistan (Xinjiang) and the Chinese-speaking Muslims spread across China proper (*neidi* 内地). And we exclude the diasporic communities of Chinese Muslims in places like Thailand, Central Asia, and Arabia. If instead we project backward from the current Hui ethnic group, or go slightly narrower to Chinese-speaking Muslims, we find a diversity that frustrates most generalizations. If we narrow our scope to a particular sect, such as the Jahriyya, we encounter conversations that are not fully understandable without the study of texts and ideas circulating between multiple sects. Following those connections, we find ourselves reading much of the madrassa curriculum of the Uyghurs and, to a lesser degree, the Muslims of Bukhara or Lucknow.

This book takes a subjectivist approach, letting historical actors' perceptions of themselves and others delimit the subject matter: communities that considered themselves at once Muslim and Chinese (though they often thought the intersection of the two unworthy of mention). In this, I follow the strain of scholarship touched off by Fredrik Barth's 1969 work on ethnicity and since elaborated and refined for other types of "groupness."[14] While this approach usefully delegates the contradictions and ambiguities of social classification (Latour's "controversies") to the historical contexts in which they were situated, it does not eliminate all classificatory problems for the historian. It is not always clear, for example, what exactly it means to "identify" as "Chinese" or "Muslim." The case of China's Muslims is particularly fruitful for exploring these challenges, because many Muslims in China did not use terms that are etymologically connected to the terms "Islam" and "Muslim," opting instead for terms such as *Qingzhen* (the pure and true) and *Huijiao* (teachings of the Hui people). Moreover, the application of the subjectivist or ascriptive approach to religious identities is still under debate. The case of "China" is just as messy, with a host of Chinese-language terms glossed in English by that lone word.

Chapter 9 addresses these complexities, drawing on insights from Islamic China's origin narratives to engage debates about "Islam" as a category. However, my interest in category-making is trained on the habits of historical actors, rather than an effort to settle on final boundary-making criteria for the historian. In Chapter 9 I examine the case of "Islam" as a category in order to draw generalizable lessons on the interaction between the category-making strategies of Muslim Chinese authors in the past and those of humanistic scholars today. Systematic treatment of all relevant category questions, including "what is China?" and "what is Huihui?," would depart from the central goal of the book. In delimiting my subject matter, I therefore take an open approach to what counts as self-ascription to such categories. For the thorny question of what counts as a "Chinese" self-identification, I cast my net widely, including, for example, communities that identified as subjects of the Qing. At the same time, I reserve most space in the book for communities with strong commitments to indisputably Chinese categories, such as "Zhongguo" and "ṣīnī" (the Arabic equivalent of the English "Chinese").

There are good reasons to attend to the history of people who were at once Muslim and Chinese. As the short historiography above suggests, they have been the focus of very little scholarly attention. More significantly, they receive scant attention in most general histories of China, as well as most general histories of Islam. In terms of relative numbers alone, this near absence is striking. Today there are more Muslims in China than in Syria, Malaysia, or Tunisia. This puts China well ahead of Russia and far behind India in terms of Muslim population, placing it among the nation-states with the largest Muslim minorities. The history of Islamic China is thus crucial to a full understanding of both Islam and China.

China-based states, including the Ming and Qing empires, the Republic of China, and the People's Republic of China (PRC), have all adopted policies targeted specifically at Muslims. The current government of the PRC considers Islam to be a "foreign" religion that poses a potential threat to the Chinese nation. It evaluates the diverse forms of Islam within China on a spectrum of "Chineseness," praising supposedly syncretic traditions and openly calling for the "Sinicization" of Islams that the state deems too foreign. This understanding of Islamic China's cultural terrain is expressed in repressive policies that vary across ethnic groups, with harsher treatment for ethnic groups seen as less fully Chinese. Among the Hui, most of whom are Chinese speaking, these policies include the closing of Arabic-language courses and the removal of mosque domes. When it comes to policy toward the Uyghurs, PRC understandings of Islam have contributed to the decision to forcibly control Uyghur birth rates, place children in assimilationist residential schools, and round up a large portion of the adult population in internment camps, detention centers, and prisons. The essentialist logic behind these policy choices crumbles quickly in the face of a nuanced history of Islamic China.

The political salience of Chinese Muslims extends to the international context. China-based states have often employed Muslim subjects to facilitate interactions with distant powers, whether through the fifteenth-century Indian Ocean voyages of Zheng He; the early twentieth-century diplomatic missions to the Middle East; or the contemporary PRC efforts to engage Chinese Muslim diaspora communities across Asia. The presence of Muslims in China has also drawn China into the politics of the US-led "War on Terror," which framed Islam as a religion uniquely likely to inspire violence, a view that has largely been internalized among PRC officials.

The Muslims of China thus represent a category of significance for both the members of that community and the wider world. Despite the diversity of Muslims in China, political actors and popular media outlets continue to discuss them as a coherent unit of political significance. The unexamined conceptual approaches in these discourses have effects on Chinese Muslims themselves and on relations between states. Similarly, the nature of Chinese Muslims and Chinese Islams shapes relations between various Chinese Muslim communities and diaspora ties back to China. All of this calls for increased scholarly attention to both the controversies and ordinaries of people who have been categorized as Muslim and Chinese. This book aims to contribute to that effort, but by moving away from categorization to thinking about what allows something to pass as ordinary in one place and time.

Sources

In 1925, a protestant missionary by the name of Isaac Mason published a list of 318 texts by Chinese Muslims, providing summaries of many of the works. Mason's extensive list would go on to influence much of what Western scholars viewed as the range of book-length sources on the topic. But the final sentence of his short introduction to the list has received little attention: "Books entirely in Arabic, though printed in China, have been omitted."[15]

Thus, at a seminal moment in the development of the field, an entire category of sources was made invisible. Mason, who does not seem to have distinguished between Persian and Arabic, would have in fact encountered many texts in those languages. For example, my surveys of mosque and antique traders' holdings suggest that Chinese-language texts accounted for less than half of the Islamic books in circulation in a county near Dali, Yunnan, at the beginning of the twentieth century. Many of the Chinese texts Mason described cite Arabic and Persian texts almost exclusively among their own sources. The famous Sinophone authors of the Yangzi delta, such as Liu Zhi, tell us that the majority of the Islamic texts they read were Persian and Arabic works. Yet few historians have directly engaged these works, the notable exceptions being Sachiko Murata, William Chittick, Nakanishi Tatsuya, Dror Weil, Masumi Matsumoto, and Florian Sobieroj.[16]

This linguistic bias, which has also shaped the work of Chinese historians (though for different reasons), has distorted the discovery and preservation of sources on the history of Chinese Muslims. Most scholarship on the topic has, in effect, worked from only half of the source base. Despite a few exceptional publications based on these elided sources, the sources themselves remain largely unread and unavailable.

Another archival bias has compounded the problem. As empires and dynastic realms gave way to nation-states in the nineteenth and twentieth centuries, Chinese Muslims across Central Asia, South Asia, Southeast Asia, and China found themselves in the unfamiliar position of national minorities. In many cases, the hardening of national borders severed or muted their global Islamic connections. Books and documents that had been central to inter-Asian Muslim communities became afterthoughts in the archival preservation and cataloging projects of new nation-states like China, India, Thailand, and Myanmar. In China itself, the state has in the last few decades treated sources in non-Chinese languages as "politically sensitive" items that it holds in secret.

Nonetheless, sources in Arabic, Persian, and Chaghatay have survived in mosques and antique dealer stocks across Chinese Muslim networks, both inside and outside China. Many of the primary sources for this book come from these alternative archives. One goal of the book is to reintegrate these sources into our view of Islamic China, which involves both analyzing the Perso-Arabic sources themselves and reappraising the Chinese-language sources in light of the Perso-Arabic context in which they were produced.

Because this book aims to recover Muslims' own ordinaries and controversies, it draws mainly from sources written by Chinese Muslims. State records almost invariably reflect outsider perspectives of non-Muslim Chinese officials, usually discussing Muslims when they are foreign interlocutors or sources of domestic conflict. They thus appear most commonly as rebels or parties to local disputes in pre-twentieth-century state documents.[17] Western missionary and imperialist sources sometimes provide useful information about Muslim communities, reporting on educational systems, language abilities, the circulation of texts, and demographic patterns. But the richest portraits of Islamic Chinese experiences come from books written by Chinese Muslims themselves.

The authors of those books are not widely representative of the Chinese Muslim communities from which they emerged. To begin with, they are exclusively men. Despite extensive searching and consultation with expert colleagues, I have not located a single text composed or copied by a Muslim Chinese woman before the twentieth century. Even the so-called women's classics, a curriculum of five Persian-language texts that formed the basis of specialized women's education, appear to have been all authored by men.[18] An exception to the rule may yet be discovered, but the consistency of the pattern makes clear that writing was highly gendered. This is all the more striking because, by the late nineteenth century, Muslim women in many parts of China were commonly taught to read in Persian and sometimes Arabic. Nonetheless, for the period before roughly 1910, we have no access to women's own representations of themselves and their communities.

The act of writing for a public readership made the men in this study exceptional. The complex of distinct skills that make up literacy was unevenly distributed across space, time, language, class, gender, and community. Writing was a specialized skill that did not necessarily follow from the ability to read. Most of the texts that have survived were written for a public or semipublic readership, because these are the texts that were reproduced in large enough numbers to encourage survival. Writing for a public audience required highly refined linguistic skills and expert knowledge. It also required the ambition and self-regard to add to a canon that was widely regarded as already complete. The total number of Muslim Chinese men who composed *new* texts or produced new versions of preexisting texts in the period of this study probably numbered in the low to mid-hundreds.

This book therefore reflects the outlooks of a small number of highly educated and unusually ambitious men. However, their texts have implications for a much wider swath of their communities, because they were consumed by the far larger population of Muslims who read but did not write books. We can only guess at how large that population was. In Yunnan, the area for which we have the best understanding of educational systems in the Ming and Qing periods, authors promoted a normative expectation that, in general, Muslims should be able to read basic texts in some combination of Chinese, Arabic, and / or Persian. We still have little research to indicate how successfully this ideal was put into practice, though it is clear that teachers were trained and books printed in substantial numbers.

Education was largely about reproducing Muslimness in a Chinese context. Educational texts are therefore particularly rich sources for notions of ordinariness and controversy. While the numerical reach of Islamic education is unclear, community leaders in the form of imams were drawn from among those who had achieved success in the schools. They went on to manage community finances and taxation, further propagate behavioral norms, mediate disputes, and, in a few cases, write their own texts. The continuity between the sources of any one community across the centuries testifies to the significance of these texts in both reflecting and continuously creating community self-perceptions.

Time and Place

The history of Chinese Muslims has often been told as the history of Islam *in* China. This book, by contrast, poses Islamic China as the sum of the networked communities of people at once Muslim and Chinese, wherever they are found. Today these communities stretch across the Hijaz, former-Soviet Central Asia, Southeast Asia, and China. Individuals and smaller parties have at various times resided in other places, notably Yemen and India, engaging in inter-Asian Islamic discourses that continually reshaped Muslim communities back in China.

Transregional connections have featured prominently in work on modernist Islamic reform in China. At the same time, Chinese Muslim history before modernist reform tends to be written with less attention to connections beyond the Qing borders (with notable exceptions, such as the work of Joseph Fletcher), sometimes even presenting that history as characterized by relative isolation. It is easy to come away from a reading of the scholarship on Islamic China with the impression that after the influx of Muslims to China in the Yuan dynasty (1279–1368 CE), inter-Asian networks are insignificant until the twentieth-century reform movements, with the story of other Chinese expressions of Islam appearing primarily as a domestic, even isolated development, shaped by rare injections of external influence but largely self-contained between those moments of rupture. This book shows the importance of the steady hum of inter-Asian circulation throughout the Ming and Qing, powered by what Engseng Ho has called "mobile societies."[19] And it explores the effects of increased transnational connection in the late nineteenth and twentieth centuries on those Muslim communities across China that stood aside from modernist reform movements.

The point is not to valorize transregional connection. Localism and even isolation are fascinating topics in their own rights, and they played their own parts in shaping Chinese Muslims' ordinaries and controversies. Even the products of interconnection often underwent transformations to make them appear appropriately local. While communities often boasted about the distant "Western" origins of key texts, they just as often reproduced works from India, Persia, and Central Asia in forms that erased obvious signs of "foreign" origins. Nonetheless, an examination of the most widely taught texts of the Ming and Qing shows that Chinese Muslim students were largely consuming works composed and taught in Central Asia and India.[20] This alone demands a close investigation of the inter-Asian networks that linked Chinese Muslims to fellow believers in far-flung locations. One of the main empirical contributions of this book is to recover the importance of India in the development of Islamic

China. Another is to expand our understanding of the role of transethnic connections, such as Chapter 6's account of a two-century-long conversation between the ancestors of the groups known today as Uyghur, Salar, Dongxiang, and Hui.

The 1630s and 1640s mark a turning point in the history of Islamic China. It was during these two decades that the earliest *surviving* Islamic texts composed in China were produced. These were woodblock-printed books in Chinese. In the ensuing hundred years, new works and translations of older Perso-Arabic texts appeared in growing numbers. There may have been earlier compositions, now lost, but it was from roughly 1640 that locally authored Islamic texts became unexceptional in China. Before this watershed moment, Persian and Arabic texts authored outside of China circulated in manuscript form (Arabic and Persian woodblock industries did not develop until the nineteenth century), undergoing continuous but subtle transformations as they were copied. Until more archives open in China, they will remain largely inaccessible in their original forms, but they were frequently cited and translated in printed Chinese works. The 1630s and 1640s thus represent the beginning of a period in which the discourses of Chinese Muslims first become accessible in a meaningful way.

Changes in the early twentieth century draw a second, rather porous, chronological boundary for this book. At this time reformers began not just to add to the canon of Islamic texts that were shared across the communities of Islamic China, but to try to remove books from the canon, declaring that they had diverged from the essence of Islam. They may be responsible for a rise in interest in Arabic-language learning, at the expense of Persian. A parallel linguistic change unfolded around the same time. Amid the rise of vernacular, rather than classical, Chinese, an increase in functional literacy, and educational reforms, Islamic books and pamphlets in Chinese proliferated in numbers previously unimaginable, as did the new medium of journals. Many of the new works were summaries, adaptations, or translations of older texts, but others reflected new discourses flourishing amid a sharp increase in inter-Asian connectivity. In many communities Persian and Arabic learning began a slow retreat as a larger proportion of China's Muslims were educated in non-Islamic contexts. The question requires more research, but the surviving texts suggest that the early twentieth century saw the first rise of a substantial monolingual reading public for Islamic texts in Chinese. The multilingual, inter-referential, textual world depicted in this book began a long process of shrinking to traditionalist contexts of specialized religious education.

The period from 1640 to 1920 is crucial to the arguments of this book in part because it was a time when Muslims were tightly integrated into Chinese society (some would say "assimilated"). It is also the period for which scholars have done the most work to maintain the boundary between a "real China" and a "real Islam," quarantining the most Chinese-seeming Islamic traditions as "syncretic" or "assimilated" to protect the pure essences of China and Islam as mutually foreign. This book aims to bring Chinese Muslims out of quarantine, to show their normalcy within their own communities, the ordinariness of their diversity, and the mechanisms by which they claimed simultaneous authenticity as Muslims and as Chinese. These characteristics apply equally to those Muslims who best meet stereotyping expectations of Chinese culture and to those who maintain artistic, linguistic, and theological attributes in common with the Muslims of the Middle East—often the very same people. I hope this will encourage the rewriting of Muslims into popular imaginations of China as a transhistorical community, and the rewriting of China into the history of Islam, in ways that avoid the essentialism and surprise that continue to project Chinese Muslims as perpetual outsiders.

1

Two Ordinary Books

Ma Lianyuan and Nūr al-Ḥaqq

JUST OFF OF India's Grand Trunk Road, a few hours' drive from the Pakistani border, stands the shrine complex of Aḥmad Sirhindī (d. 1624), the Renewer of the Second Millennium. The tomb itself is reached through three monumental gates, each smaller than the last. The first gate opens onto a dusty parking lot, the second onto neat pavement with long white lines to organize worshippers in prayer. The last gate is the smallest but also the most ornate, a white marble arch engraved with floral volutes and sweeping Arabic calligraphy. The domed shrine beyond it towers above. This low archway leads to a courtyard, which the pilgrim enters under a magenta cascade of bougainvillea. Here rose-scented smoke wafts from the incense sticks that pilgrims stop to burn in one of two vessels: a rough, sheet-metal tray—the more frequently used of the two—or a ponderous, cast-bronze urn in tripod form (Figure 1.1). The urn bears a bold, ungainly inscription that begins with this two-character word: 中国.

Sharing the urn's raised platform are three anonymous graves, marked by long and low lozenges of concrete. Across the walkway are more graves, and beyond them more, crowding three sides of the shrine itself. The rumble and diesel of the road are now far away, but the graveyard hush is punctuated by a distant car horn, along with wisps of sung prayer from the shrine's inner crypt. To reach this crypt the pilgrim must ignore the broad staircase leading to the main elevated floor of the shrine, with its airy verandahs. Instead, pilgrims enter a low, barrel-vaulted ground floor, where apprentices and relatives of the saint are buried. As the prestige of the graves increases, so do the pilgrims' offerings: fine thread, bracelets, and necklaces; flower petals; green cloth with the talismanic number 786 or

FIGURE 1.1 Pilgrims and incense urn at the shrine of Aḥmad Sirhindī. Sirhind, India, July 2018. *Credit:* © Rian Thum

Quranic inscriptions printed in yellow, purchasable from a nearby shop. The cheap synthetic cloth coverings stack up on popular graves. On one of them, the grave of a certain Shah Muhammad Farrukh (d. 1707), genuine green silk protrudes from below one of the cheap synthetic sheets, bearing a different marking: 88.8 元. This is the price of the cloth, in Chinese currency. The number, 88.8, is considered auspicious because its Chinese pronunciation sounds like "get rich."

A Link to the Origin and to the Future

We are fortunate that when Ma Lianyuan (1842–1903) left home on the final journey of his life, determined, as his grandson reported, to "not look back," he stopped along the way to compose a preface for his latest book.[1] We do not know where this stop was. Likely possibilities are southwest Yunnan or Burma, perhaps some caravaneer's inn along the so-called Tea Horse Roads that Ma was following, a network of paths for the mule trains that moved tea to Burma and cotton to China. Or perhaps he wrote from Burma's former royal capital, Mandalay, where a robust community of Chinese Muslims had taken root.[2]

Not all of Ma's twenty-plus books included introductory remarks. Where they do appear, those remarks are supremely laconic, offering a brief account of the book's content and purpose but few hints about the author / editor himself. This book was different. On this occasion he wrote for an absent audience. He would never see the preface in print, as the book was intended to be published in the home he was leaving behind, to which he indeed never returned.[3] When he finished, the preface included typically brief comments about the book itself, but also nearly two thousand words reflecting on his life and his place in the history of Islam in China. Without this absentee preface we would know very little about the details of Ma's extraordinary life.

Ma's biography and works are an ideal entry point into the history of Islamic China. They foreshadow many of the developments of the twentieth century, and they are intimately connected to the deep past, engaging with thinkers of nearly every century of Muslim presence in China, from the ninth century CE onward. Ma even traced his ancestry back to the first Muslims in Yunnan and ultimately to the Prophet Muhammad himself, a claim that seems to be reflected in his given name, which means "connecting to the origin."

He does not figure prominently in English-language scholarship on Chinese Muslims, and he appears in no overview of Islam in China.[4] In China itself, scholars are more attuned to Ma's legacy, especially in Yunnan. One scholar claims that the great historian Bai Shouyi named Ma Lianyuan as one of the five principal Islamic thinkers of early modern China.[5] However, the Chinese-language *Chinese Encyclopedia of Islam* has no entry for Ma in its 773 densely packed pages.[6] Until 2018, no comprehensive catalog of his publications had appeared in print in any language.[7] Nonetheless, his influence was enormous. In his own day, Ma's publications were probably the most numerous of Islamic books in circulation in northwestern Yunnan, home to one of China's great concentrations of Muslims. Among the books from Ma's lifetime and earlier that I surveyed in three village accumulations north of Dali, Ma's works accounted for over half of the domestically produced books.[8] Since his death they have been reprinted and translated across the geographical breadth of China—in Yunnan, Beijing, Tianjin, Shanghai, and Guangdong—from the 1910s to as recently as 2018.[9]

In recounting his life story, Ma situated himself very precisely on one of the three main routes by which Muslims first entered the various parts of what is now China. The earliest of these was likely the maritime route connecting Arabia to China's east coast via the Indian Ocean. Arab and perhaps Persian Muslims arrived in Quanzhou (known to the Arabs as Zaytun, meaning "olive") within a few generations of the Prophet Muhammad (570–632 CE), though probably not, as Ma would have it, in the lifetime of the prophet himself.[10] By the eighth century, Quanzhou had permanent Muslim residents, and by the ninth we see a Muslim earning the prestigious *jinshi* degree in the Tang state examination system. The second route was the robust overland trade from Central Asia, widely known today under the rubric of the "Silk Roads." This vector, which once stretched across the lands of the medieval Uighurs (Chinese: *Huihu*), is probably responsible for the modern Chinese term for Chinese-speaking Muslims, *Hui*. The third route is the one claimed by Ma: the Mongol conquest of China, which played out across the thirteenth century. The Mongol conquerors, distrusting the subjugated Chinese officials, relied heavily on Muslims from outside of China as administrators. This was particularly true in the southwestern borderland of Yunnan, where Ma claimed his ancestor was a Mongol-era official.

As later chapters of this book will emphasize, a focus on origins can be deceptive. Origin narratives tend to freeze traditions in time and buttress essentialisms, as they certainly have for the history of Islamic China. They also blind us to continuing transformations. In the succeeding centuries, new Islams and new Muslims continued to enter China by all the original routes but also along new paths (for example, from India), which had equal and sometimes greater effects on the shape that Islamic China would take. Those continuing arrivals and transformations are the subject of much of this book. But origins were important to Ma, and so they are crucial to his biography. Moreover, in the Yunnan of Ma's time, origin stories proliferated in the form of genealogies, most sharing themes with Ma's narrative, especially the focus on the Muslim officials of the Mongol Yuan era.[11]

Ma traces his ancestry to a thirteenth-century "Sultan" of Bukhara, the great Central Asian center of Islamic learning. This king, a certain ʻAbdallah (or ʻAbd al Malik, according to another edition) ibn ʻAbd al-Jalīl, supposedly fled to China with five hundred men when his younger brother attempted to take the throne.[12] The Mongol emperor of China employed him as an official and sent him to govern Yunnan. There, Ma says, he was given a new title, Sai Dian Chi. It is a title that is well known among Muslims in Yunnan today, where it serves as a metonym for the origin of Yunnanese Muslims in general. When I was detained in Ma's hometown in 2017 for asking questions at a mosque, a local official regaled me with the history of Sai Dian Chi as we waited for plainclothes security forces to arrive in their shiny SUVs. And a grave for Sai Dian Chi still stands in the provincial capital of Kunming. But these memorializations refer to a different Sai Dian Chi, albeit one with a very similar history to that of Ma's ancestor: the Mongol-era governor of Yunnan named Sayyid Ajall Shams al-Dīn (1211–1279), also a Muslim with Bukharan roots. While this Sai Dian Chi is a historically attested figure[13] and the general phenomenon of Mongols appointing foreign Muslims to administer Chinese localities is well documented, I have not been able to corroborate Ma's own descent claim and his story of Bukharan usurpation. Nonetheless Ma's autobiographical genealogy served to claim for his family a central role in the origins of Yunnan's Muslim community.

Ma's final trip was not the first time he had left China. When he was in his twenties, a wave of rebellion swept Yunnan, ultimately leading to the establishment of an independent, Muslim-ruled "Sultanate," which would last until 1873. Scholarly consensus today holds that the rebellion was a multiethnic movement against the ruling Manchu Qing dynasty,[14] but Ma saw it as the "war of the Muslims and the unbelievers."[15] He was thrilled by the rebel victories, which he attributed to God's divine will. But these very successes sowed seeds of disenchantment for Ma. Born into a scholarly family, with his father an imam at a mosque in his hometown, Ma was horrified to see religious scholars leaving to pursue worldly careers as officials in the new government. They "forgot God almighty, . . . entered into negligence, accepted official posts, and fell away from learning and religion. They became haughty and displayed their power, position, and riches, turning away from religion."[16] Ma left the Sultanate in disgust, following the trade routes toward Burma with a few companions. He traveled via India to Mecca, where he completed the Hajj and studied with renowned scholars.

According to Ma, he returned in 1873 to an unrecognizable world. Cities were destroyed. Muslims had been massacred and dispersed. Mosques were turned into temples. The system of Islamic education that Ma knew was, by his account, virtually eradicated. The Sultanate had fallen and the Qing were in charge again. Ma resolved to revive the Islamic educational system of his youth: "amid the echoes of discord I set up the banner of education and the religion." In the words of one of his followers, Jin Hanqing, Ma aimed to "revitalize the Dao of the teaching" [振興教道] (i.e., the Dao of Islam).[17] But what was the true Dao of Islam, and how could it be revived?

The Story of Two Ordinary Books

Over the last thousand-plus years, China's Muslims have left behind an uneven historical record. Rarely entrusted with the affairs of the state after the fall of the Yuan, they appear irregularly in chronicles and official histories, often as rebels. Little in the way of letters, contracts, or account books can be linked to Muslim communities before the twentieth century. But Chinese Muslims have left their words on tombstones, in architectural inscriptions, and in a fascinating body of their own books now scattered across the holdings of mosques, shrines, antique dealers, and scholars' personal libraries. As with so many important figures in the history of Islamic China, the only written sources we have about Ma Lianyuan are his own books and those of his students, as well as his tombstone.

A book can tell a lot about its author. This book's hundred thousand words represent at least as many authorial choices, many unthinking, some painstaking. The possible permutations in a book might not be infinite, but they are enough to support a few academic disciplines and, for the most successful authors, libraries of interpretive work—Shakespeare's *Hamlet* or Cao Xueqin's *Dream of the Red Chamber* come to mind, not to mention foundational religious texts like the Qur'an. But the choices an author doesn't make are just as interesting. Very few authors have had transformative influence on the genres to which they mold their words. Far fewer have chosen the calligraphic forms of the letters that present those words. As I write this I have no idea what font the press will choose for my text. I can be reasonably sure that it will be reproduced by offset lithography, because that technology dominates the print industry today. The authors who have *chosen* the technology that disseminates their work are scarce, and they are often not remembered for their word choices. Language is almost as rarely chosen. These seemingly mechanical predestinations spiral out into subtler systems—jargon, tone, epistemology, shared assumptions.

Two books, one ordinary in China, the other ordinary in India, speak eloquently to the interplay between authorial choices and social imperatives (Figures 1.2 and 1.3). Together they tell us a great deal about Ma Lianyuan, and, in turn, Islamic China: what was unique to Chinese Islams and what was not, how ideas moved in spite of differing social imperatives, how scholarly minds were shaped, and how they saw themselves. The first book is Ma's annotation of an older Chinese text, which unfolds Islamic strains of thought at the root of Ma's education, as well as Chinese Islams more generally.[18] The second, by a scholar named Nūr al-Ḥaqq bin al-Sayyid Luqmān, was published in India in 1902 / 1903.[19] It too is an annotation (though on a very different text), one that offers a stark contrast and highlights the distinctive characteristics of the first book. Though they depict two radically distinctive Islamic discourses, they have an intimate connection. Together they throw the problems of understanding Islamic China into stark relief. They also suggest that these problems may not be as formidable as they first seem.

The first book (Figure 1.2) is Ma Lianyuan's edition and annotation of an eighteenth-century work by Liu Zhi 劉智, called *Islamic Three-Character Primer* (*Tianfang san zi you yi*). It is a short introduction to the Islamic faith combining Confucian ethics and Sufi mysticism. Ma's annotation was published in Yunnan around the end of the nineteenth century. It follows the norms of China's most widely read Confucian genre of the

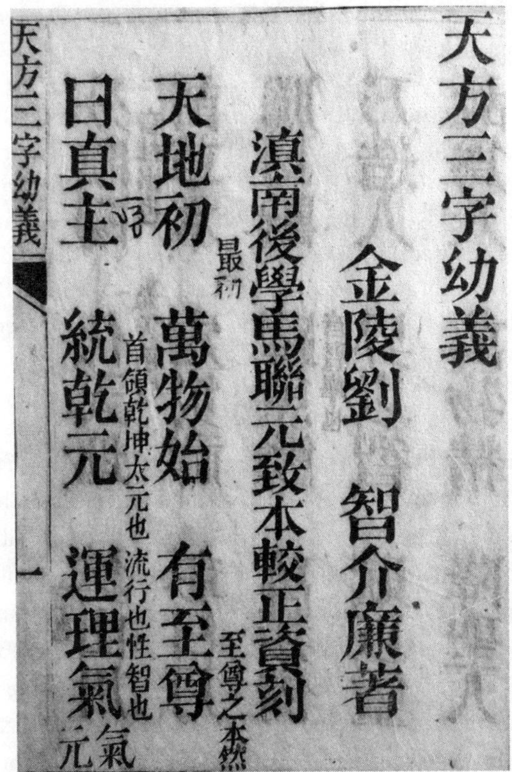

天方三字幼義

金陵劉 智介廉著

滇南後學馬聯元致本較正資刻

最初 至尊之本然

天地初 萬物始 有至尊

首領乾坤太元也 流行也性智也

曰真主 統乾元 運理氣 元氣

天方三字幼義 一

FIGURE 1.2 Title page of *Tianfang san zi you yi,* by Liu Zhi, annotated by Ma Lianyuan. Kunming, China, late nineteenth century. *Credit:* © Rian Thum

medieval and early modern periods: the three-character classic, used in elementary education. Three-syllable verses convey cosmology and worldly duties in pithy, memorable rhymes that hint at philosophical sophistications the student will explore in future studies.

In many ways, it is a perfect example of Chinese Islamic discourse as it has been stereotyped by both foreign and Chinese scholars. These have tended to see the embrace of Chinese Confucian, Buddhist, and Daoist concepts as salient elements of a Chinese Islam defined by its purported "syncretism": a melding of ideas from two distinct traditions into a new hybrid entity. This framing has severe distorting effects, which are discussed in Chapter 8, but concepts common to Confucianism and Daoism are certainly prominent in the *Islamic Three-Character Primer.* The opening passage is illustrative.

> At the beginning of heaven and earth, at the origin of the Ten Thousand Things, there was a supreme majesty called the Real Lord. It wove the creation, moved principle [*li*] and vital energy [*qi*], divided *yin* and *yang,* developed heaven and earth, settled mountains and rivers, germinated grasses and shrubs, defined disaster and blessing, displayed the sun and the moon. It animated the birds and the beasts, infused life into the fishes and shaped the ten thousand species. Only then did it create mankind.[20]

Because this creation story finds the origins of our world in the labors of a lone divinity, it is easy to align it with much of the Qur'an and the Bible, both of which had important but relatively small audiences in China when this text was printed. But there are aspects that would also resonate with the vast majority of non-Muslim Chinese readers, who were unfamiliar with those texts, reflecting textual traditions from periods before the monotheist movements reached China in the first millennium CE. Compare for example, a passage from China's most famous Daoist text, the *Daodejing:* "The Dao gave birth to the one; the one gave birth to the two; the two gave birth to the three; the three gave birth to the Ten Thousand Things; the Ten Thousand Things carry *yin* and *yang,* and created harmony through *qi.*"[21] Both the *Islamic Three-Character Primer* and the *Daodejing* trace the origin of all things to a process of division, ultimately manifesting our familiar world through vital energy (*qi*) and the contrasts of *yin* and *yang* that give character and variation to all existence. But this Islamic text is not directly engaging with the *Daodejing* or even Daoism in particular. The comparison is useful for demonstrating that Liu Zhi and Ma Lianyuan were using cosmological categories widely employed across Chinese systems of thought. However, the concept of "principle" (*li*) gives away a more direct intellectual genealogy of this Islamic text: the Neo-Confucian synthesis of the Song dynasty (960–1279 CE).

Even in this primer directed at young students, Neo-Confucian thought, in the form that came to dominate Chinese scholarly discourse for many centuries, maps neatly onto the work of Liu Zhi, a phenomenon we will revisit in Chapter 8. As for Ma Lianyuan himself, his knowledge of Liu Zhi's deeper philosophical work, with all of its Neo-Confucian subtleties, is evident in Ma's annotations (not included in the above translation). This is clear, for example, when Ma uses the word *benran* (本然), or "root suchness," to explain the "supreme majesty."[22] Liu's primer distilled his two longest and most revered works, a metaphysical text and a text on rituals and norms. By ascribing "root suchness" to God, Ma shows his familiarity with these more elaborate works, in which Liu applied this term. Sometime after this annotated primer appeared, in the last year of his life, Ma even published an extensive exegesis of Liu's metaphysics.

To be sure, most highly educated, mainstream Confucian scholars would have found Liu and Ma's text somewhat curious, perhaps even heretical, in its details. A century earlier, in an imperially sponsored survey of China's scholarship, a Confucian scholar had judged Liu's longer work on ritual with these words: "Islam is fundamentally far-fetched and absurd. However, (Liu) Zhi has extensively studied Confucian texts, so he intermingled various ideas from the classics in order to embellish his discourse. His literary style is actually rather elegant. However, the premise is at its root untrue . . ."[23] Nonetheless we can still call this text ordinary in its Chinese context insofar as its underlying concepts, its jargon, its tone, and many of its unexamined assumptions fit neatly into the wider body of Chinese philosophical texts. Its premise may be "absurd" but the text, in its presentation, passes as elegant for a critical non-Muslim reader.

It is also typical of Chinese book production of its time. Like any nineteenth-century Chinese book, and indeed nearly all Chinese printed books from at least the ninth century onward, this edition is produced by woodblock, a printing technology in which the entire text of each two-page leaf is carved onto a single slab of wood. Woodblock printing, or xylography, is particularly well suited to the Chinese writing system, with its tens of thousands of distinct characters. And the calligraphic form of Chinese that came to dominate from the Han dynasty onward, with its square, angular forms, can be quickly rendered in wood by an experienced block cutter,[24] to such an extent that Christian missionaries in Malacca, after careful study, concluded that xylography, not movable type, was the most economical means of reproducing their holy book for dissemination in Chinese.[25]

The Second Ordinary Book

The second book (Figure 1.3), by Nūr al-Ḥaqq ibn Sayyid Luqmān, is an Arabic-language legal commentary published in Kanpur, India, in 1903.[26]

إن لكل جديدة لذة

الجزء الأول

من شرح الوقاية المسمى بالتوضيح

لصاحب التصانيف الباهرة والتاليف البديعة الشاهرة عمدة اساتذة العصر ورحلة تلامذة الدهر

بدر علماء الصين بل نبراس علماء المتبحرين مقياس علماء المتاخرين العلامة الحبر

المحقق الفهامة البحر المدقق مولانا الحاج السيد محمد نور الحق بن

السيد لقمان الصيني اليناني السهيني لا زالت شموس افاداته

طالعة الذي التقطه من كتب ائمة الملة الحنيفية

واختص من دفاتر ائمة الحنفية ثم

عرضه للتصحيح على اجلة العلماء

في الاقطار الهندية ثم اشاروا الى الطبع

ليعم نفعه طلبة العلوم الفقهية

في البلاد الصينية جزاه عنا

وعن جميع المستفيدين

رب البرية

آمين

و سعى في طبعه المفتقر الى الله الغني السيد محمود علي الحنفي

في مطبع الذي كان سمي بمحمود المطابع الواقع بكانفور الهند

FIGURE 1.3 Title page of *Explication* by Nūr al-Ḥaqq ibn Sayyid Luqmān. Kanpur, India, 1903. *Credit:* © Rian Thum

More precisely, it is a commentary on a thirteenth-century reworking of a twelfth-century commentary on an Islamic legal manual (*furū*ʿ *al-fiqh*).[27] Such multilayered attempts to understand the *shari'a,* God's own sacred law (fully knowable only to God himself), were extremely popular in turn-of-the-century northern India. Many of these texts were ostentatious about the layers of commentary, placing a main text (the *matn,* sometimes itself a commentary on an absent book) in the center of the page, surrounded by a second, larger rectangle of commentary (*sharḥ*), and then a third rectangle of super-commentary (*hashiyah*) outside of that, running right up to the edge of the page (Figure 1.4). Some scholars never presumed to publish anything more central than a *hashiyah.* In this regard Nūr al-Ḥaqq did something unusual: He wrote both *sharḥ* and *hashiyah.* This particular book reveals only two of its layers visually. The original thirteenth-century abridgment known as *Wiqāyah* is absent. The central text is an abridgment of *Wiqāyah* interspersed with Nūr al-Ḥaqq's explanatory text (some taken from yet other legal works). Around the main text and between the lines is Nūr al-Ḥaqq's super-annotation. He named the finished product *The Explication* (*al-Tawḍīḥ*).

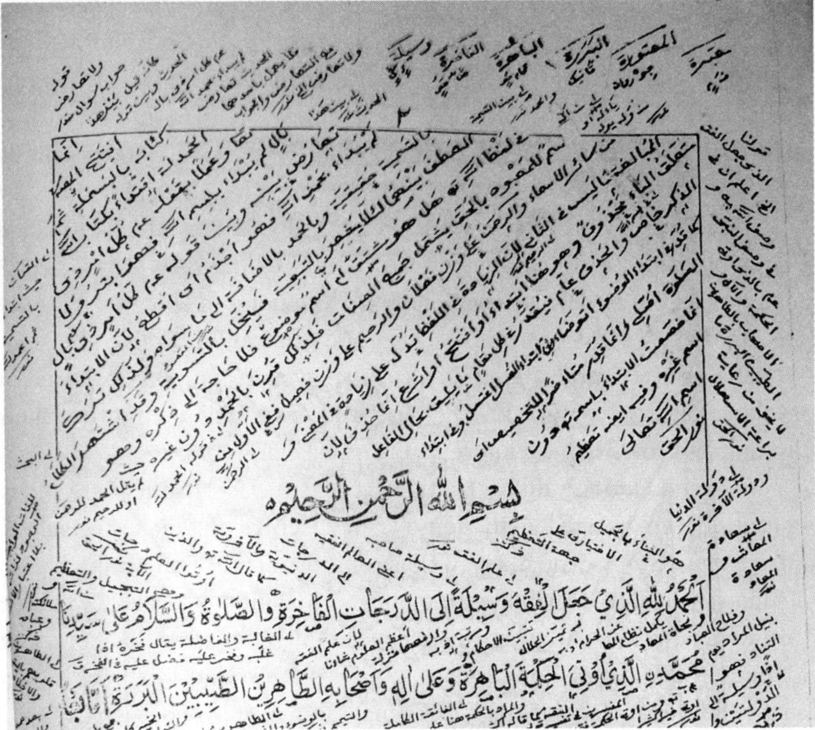

FIGURE 1.4 Detail of the first page of *Explication.* The largest writing, in the center, is the phrase "In the name of God the most gracious, the most merciful," with Nūr al-Ḥaqq's commentary above this and between the lines that follow. *Credit:* © Rian Thum

The multiple centuries of abbreviation and commentary were aimed in great part at making the Islamic legal tradition accessible to students (in this case, the Hanafi tradition of legal interpretation, one of the four predominant legal "schools" among Sunni Muslims worldwide). At the extremes this could result in stultifying pedantry. Nearly every Islamic book begins with the same phrase, *bismillah*—"in the name of God" (Ma Lianyuan's primer is an exception). Often the *bismillah* follows the full phrasing of the Qur'an, *bismillah al-Raḥman al-Raḥīm:* "in the name of God, the most gracious, the most merciful." What almost always follows is some kind of praise for God, the prophet, and often the prophet's companions. Nūr al-Ḥaqq begins his commentary by explaining this most ordinary of openings: "He begins his book with the *bismillah,* then *al-ḥamdullilah* [praise be to God], following the example of the Book of Allah the Almighty and working with the Hadith of the prophet, who said, 'Any matter of importance which is not begun with *al-ḥamdullilah* remains defective.'"

After further discussion of the role of praise for God, Nūr al-Ḥaqq goes so far as to point out the grammatical forms of *al-Raḥman* (the most gracious) and *al-Raḥīm* (the most merciful), without noting that these forms are conventional, used in exactly the same form, countless times, from their appearance in the Qur'an in the seventh century down to Nūr al-Ḥaqq's own day. No author would dare to adjust them, but Nūr al-Ḥaqq points out that *"al- Raḥman* is on the pattern of the verb *faʿlān* and *al-Raḥīm* is on the pattern of the verb *faʿīl."* The point of the work was not originality, but rather, as its title suggests, explication. Arabic grammar was seen as utterly indispensable for the analysis of complex questions of law, theology, and much else. The reader of this text could improve their grammatical knowledge while learning its legal precepts.

As excruciatingly dull as this kind of text may feel to outsiders, many of its kind were bestsellers in their own day. Genres that make bestsellers attract new authors, and many of those authors never break through. Nūr al-Ḥaqq probably did not make his publisher, Maḥmūd ʿAlī Ḥanafī, wealthy; despite extensive searching I have traced only two surviving copies of Maḥmūd's print run. Nonetheless, it makes sense that Maḥmūd took a chance on Nūr al-Ḥaqq. The big profit-making publishing houses in Kanpur had similar offerings. Legal commentaries in turn-of-the-century northern India were as popular as bone-dry, standardized test-preparation books are today.[28]

Nūr al-Ḥaqq's expansive and explicit glossing is the antithesis of Liu Zhi and Ma Lianyuan's three-character primer, which packs the subtleties of thousands of pages of philosophical and ritual thought into laconic, enigmatic poetry. Ma's annotations gesture at other pregnant ambiguities, like "root suchness." The *Islamic Three-Character Primer* opened vistas by smuggling a vast philosophical tradition in a handful of gnomic verses. The legal commentaries of northern India, by contrast, opened a well-marked path into a forest of legal interpretation by explaining the narrow choices (or nonchoices) behind each word.

The flourishing Islamic publishing industry of northern India at this time produced books in Arabic, Persian, and Urdu. Each language aligned with particular genres, and Arabic was the standard for legal works like Nūr al-Ḥaqq's. All three languages employed the same alphabet, the written form of the language that God chose for his final prophetic message to humankind, the Qur'an. The letters of the Arabic script thus had their own sacredness. And their curving, connected forms were challenging to reproduce by some printing technologies, but easy for others. The late nineteenth century was a time in which Eurasia saw wide use of an unprecedented variety of printing technologies. This did not involve much authorial choice, because within most communities the author was subject to a complete monopoly of one printing technology. The woodblock dominated China. Moveable type had long been king in Europe and had recently made inroads in Egypt, despite its tendency to butcher the Arabic letterforms. In India, where more elaborate forms of Perso-Arabic calligraphy like *nasta'liq* were in fashion, the lithograph held sway.

So, like nearly every Islamic book printed in India at the time, Nūr al-Ḥaqq's commentary was produced by lithograph, a process that turned hand-executed calligraphy into acid-etched stones. Those stone plates, some of which are still piled in the courtyard of a former publishing house in Kanpur, can be washed with ink to impress the text of books onto paper. The technology of lithography was invented in Europe in the late eighteenth century. There it filled a niche for printing illustrations and maps yet never competed with movable type for text. But in India, lithography conquered most of the Islamic publishing industry. The reasons for its dominance in a profit-driven printing industry are complex,[29] but one of its strengths was the ability to easily accommodate not just the sacred forms of the Arabic script but also creative embellishments, such as the elaborate vegetal motifs on the cover of Nūr al-Ḥaqq's book. Lithography worked by reproducing individual handwriting and drawing, as opposed to standardized, repeatable forms. Despite this freedom, fashions were as powerful as genres and technologies, and Nūr al-Ḥaqq's book ended up looking like pretty much everyone else's in turn-of-the-century Kanpur.

There are connections as well as differences between the two books in this story, the *Islamic Three-Character Primer* and *The Explication*. One is that both are difficult, if not impossible, to locate or access in any public archive.[30] After searching libraries in India, China, Europe, and North America I finally encountered copies of these two books a few kilometers away from each other, in a valley near Dali, Yunnan. I found the *Islamic Three-Character Primer* in the home of an antique dealer, who kept a hoard of old Islamic books in a tattered suitcase. The prices he quoted me were astronomical, and I negotiated a flat fee to photograph the books for two hours. He timed me strictly, while his wife loudly complained that I was taking too many photos per hour. I found *The Explication* in the library of a nearby mosque, where the caretakers allowed me to photograph freely. They even helped to hold the books open flat and made sure that a group of curious children didn't block the sunlight coming in through the library window. But the relationship between the two books is far more intimate than even this geographical coincidence would suggest.

The Road to India

Ma Lianyuan and Nūr al-Ḥaqq ibn Sayyid Luqmān were the same person.[31] When I give public lectures using the example of these two books, the revelation that the two authors were the same person elicits audible gasps of surprise. This sense of surprise is instructive, and I will return to the notion of surprise later in this chapter—the overarching goal of this book is to reach an understanding of China in which Ma / Nūr is *un*surprising. But first, the practicalities of Ma / Nūr's seamless move between the textual worlds of Yunnan and northern India are also instructive.

"Nūr al-Ḥaqq" is Ma Lianyuan's "scripture name" (*jingming* 經名), which he used when writing in Persian and Arabic and which he had engraved on his personal seal (Figure 1.5).[32] Many of his publications bear

FIGURE 1.5 Seal of "al-Ḥājj Muḥammad Nūr al-Ḥaqq," dated 1288 AH (= 1871–1872 CE), from Ma Lianyuan's *Tianfang fen xin pian*. *Credit:* © Rian Thum

both his Chinese name and Arabic scripture name. Arabic "scripture names," as they are called today, are still common among Muslim scholars in China.[33]

Ma's final trip along the Tea Horse Roads led him through Burma and onward to Kanpur, India, most likely taking the sea route via Calcutta.[34] It is not clear exactly when Ma left China, but his last publication there was in 1900.[35] By June 1902, *The Explication* was in preparation with his publisher in Kanpur.[36] It had not taken him long to adapt to the local environment.

Ma's early education paved the road to easy integration in the northern Indian scholarly world. He tells us that he studied Arabic from a young age, and, as a product of Yunnan's mosque education system, his Persian was surely learned early, too. In his schooling he would have likely encountered legal texts helpful in writing *The Explication.* Indeed, one of the most widely circulated and cited texts among Chinese Muslims from at least the seventeenth century was the Arabic-language *Wiqāyah,* the book upon which *The Explication* is a commentary. Today, the *Wiqāyah* remains one of the most common Islamic texts in China, both in the original Arabic and in a twentieth-century Chinese translation, spread across the length and breadth of China, among Muslims of every ethnic group, sect, and language community.

The *Wiqāyah* was also one of twenty-four representative "Arabic works, of which there are many in the mosques in Peking and throughout the country," according to the missionary Henry Blodget, who sent the list of books from Beijing in a letter dated 1863.[37] Ma would have been about twenty at the time. The other twenty-three books include at least two additional legal texts, several Quranic exegeses, and Sufi philosophy. Many of the books in the list are identifiable from their titles as famous Persian works, such as the *Gulistān* of Sa'adī. All of the listed books that are identifiable were written before 1500. Approximately half of them were extremely popular in northern India at the time of Ma's arrival.[38]

All of this means that *The Explication* was not only ordinary in northern India. It was also ordinary in China. Indeed, at the end of the book, Ma Lianyuan / Nūr al-Ḥaqq says that he wrote the book with a Chinese audience in mind. He laments that the students he taught for thirty years rarely went beyond the *Wiqāyah* in their studies of Islamic law, and even the *Wiqāyah* was extremely difficult for them. He wrote *The Explication* for them, to ease their understanding, and he planned to send the book to Yunnan. The extreme rarity of the original in China suggests limited success in this goal, at least initially. Eventually the book was republished in Yunnan in 1989, with a facing-page Chinese translation.[39] As we will see in Chapter 7, *The Explication* also played an important role among the Chinese Muslims of Thailand.

Many highly educated Muslims across China—the kind of people whom Blodget said "read, write, and speak the Arabic, but are not well versed in Chinese"—would have been able to make their way in northern India, but Ma Lianyuan had an additional advantage. When Ma left China the first time, sometime around 1868–1870, he went to Mecca, where he stayed for over one year and studied with several teachers from among Mecca's cosmopolitan gathering of scholars. From an Indian scholar he learned the book he called "*Shāmī,*" using a common nickname for an early nineteenth-century legal (*furu'*) super-commentary, *Radd al-muḥtār.*[40] Ma would later cite this book in *The Explication.* Under an Egyptian scholar he studied the proper recitation of the Qur'an (*tajwīd*).[41] And he studied Sufi ritual (*dhikr*) under a certain 'Abd al-Ḥamīd al-Turkī of the Naqshbandī order.[42] It was a varied curriculum that presumed the student was already deeply educated in the cosmopolitan Perso-Arabic scholarly tradition that stretched from the Balkans to Bengal—and, as Ma shows, further on to China.

We should not only ask how Ma managed to fit in once he arrived in India. There is another skill he employed during the longer period of his life spent back home in Yunnan: mastery of written Chinese. Scholars have sometimes presented the writing of Islamic texts in Chinese as a vernacularization of Islam. But written Chinese in Ma's day was not a vernacular. Ma spoke some form of Chinese from his youth. The written Chinese of his time, however, was distant from spoken forms. Its mastery required not only the memorization of thousands of characters but also training in a different grammar and vocabulary. In many ways, learning written Persian, with its alphabet and highly regular grammar, was easier for a Chinese-speaking Muslim than learning written Chinese. Indeed, Ma's son, Ma Jianzhi 馬建之 Muḥammad Ḥusayn, was, for a time, one of the scholars Blodget had talked about, who could "read, write, and speak the Arabic, but are not well versed in Chinese."[43] As a young man he mastered Islamic canons in Persian and Arabic, but it was only in middle age that he decided to study the (written) Chinese language.[44] It is unclear whether Ma Lianyuan himself learned written Chinese early in life or late. Of his three Chinese-language publications, the two that are dated (1899 and 1900) are from the last years of his life, as are his translations from Chinese.[45] Whenever it was that Ma studied the foreign language that was written Chinese, it is important to remember that the Persian and Arabic skills he took with him to India and Mecca were no more hard-won or exotic than the written language that dominated non-Muslim discourses back home in Yunnan.

Ma's travel to Arabia was part of a larger pattern. The traffic of Chinese Muslims to Mecca had increased in the middle of the nineteenth century. This moment of increased connection has been seen by many historians as a turning point in the story of Islamic China, suddenly bringing relatively isolated Chinese Muslims back into connection with their coreligionists, and eventually ushering in a host of modernist reform movements.[46] Certainly new ideas spread along this vector. But Ma's career suggests a more complicated relationship between China and Mecca. When he returned to Yunnan he determined to restore the true Islam in his home through an ambitious educational and publishing program. The details of that program, to which we now turn, gives us some idea both of what that true Islam was for Ma and of the relative significance of his early education and his time in Mecca.

Ma Lianyuan's Project of Restoration

> Today . . . nothing remains of Islam but its name, and nothing of the religion but its formalities, for most of our scholars are mired in dissension [*fitna*] and they do not have the learning or teaching of Allah.[47]

Taken out of context, this complaint of Ma Lianyuan's might seem like a modernist reformer's call to arms: Wayward scholars have obscured the original truth of Islam; a return to rigorous analysis of "original" core texts is the only window on God's plan for humankind. But Ma did not share these concerns. His worries were more basic. People weren't even praying regularly. His first concern was simply reestablishing the system he had been raised in, a system now smoldering in the ashes of war. He began by teaching.

Upon his return to Yunnan, Ma settled in his hometown in Xinxing 新興 county (today's Yuxi). His father, the imam at the village mosque, was ailing, and within a year or two, Ma took over his position. Ma began to teach, and, slowly at first, his reputation spread. Before long he was attracting students from all over war-ravaged Yunnan. But, he wrote, the turmoil of the times made study difficult. Many students were forced to abandon their studies for practical reasons. This was especially troublesome, Ma said, because of the difficulty of the Arabic language, which required many years of sustained study. He needed a way to serve those students who could not afford the long study that mastery required. He could not put the Muslims of Yunnan on the right path by teaching alone.

Ma's first dated publishing effort appeared in the summer of 1891. In the ensuing twelve years he would write, edit, or oversee the publication, via woodblock printing, of at least twenty-two books.[48] Most were aimed at people like the students who could not afford to continue studying with Ma. They included the following:

- The annotated *Islamic Three-Character Primer* of Liu Zhi (Chinese)
- Arabic grammars (Persian, Arabic)

- A Persian grammar (Arabic)
- Handbooks of doctrine and correct belief (Persian, Arabic)
- Sayings of the Prophet Muhammad (Arabic)
- A handbook of ritual and social obligations (Persian)
- Texts on substantive law (*furūʿ al-fiqh*) and commentaries (Persian, Arabic)
- The Qur'an (Arabic, Chinese)
- A beginner's guide for reciting the Qur'an (Chinese)
- Instructions on praying for rain (Arabic)
- Translation and explanation of the Sufi-Confucian metaphysics of Liu Zhi (Arabic)
- Refutations of Christianity (Arabic, Chinese)

What these books share is a pedagogical motivation. Ma was engaged at a sophisticated level with the fields he covered, but most of the books he brought to print were basic. Rather than equipping the reader to analyze Islamic legal findings, his books report the results of those findings, so that the reader can live according to *sharī'a*-based norms. Instead of delving into debates on correct beliefs, another book presents basic dogma for uncritical consumption.

Three of the books may reflect the influence of Ma's time in Mecca, to one degree or another. The "*Shāmī*" text he had studied in Mecca was a super-commentary (from the nineteenth century) on a commentary (from the seventeenth century) on a sixteenth-century legal text. Ma published that original legal text.[49] And his two anti-Christian polemics may have been partly inspired by his Indian teacher in Mecca, Rahmatallah Kairawani, who had written one of the most prominent texts of the genre. However, according to Ma himself, his own polemic texts had more to do with the situation on the ground in Yunnan, where Protestant missionaries were targeting Muslims for conversion. And there was already a local precedent. The prominent Yunnanese scholar Ma Dexin had published a similar work a generation before Ma Lianyuan.

The more important source for Ma's publishing spree was the canon of texts that had been circulating among Muslims in China for two centuries. Ma brought out the first printed edition of the original Persian *Basic Requisites for Muslims* (*Muhimmat al-Muslimīn*). The same text had circulated in the seventeenth century and was first published in Chinese translation in 1678.[50] Another of his editions, the *Four Sections* (*Chahār faṣl*), a popular text in India and Central Asia, had been translated into Chinese circa 1653.[51] The *Pillars of Islam* (*ʿUmdat al-Islām*), also in Persian, is mentioned in a manuscript circa 1719.[52] Together, these three Persian-language works were the foundation of the classical Islamic educational curriculum known as *jingtang jiaoyu* (classics hall education), which could be found throughout China by the seventeenth century.[53] And, of course, there was the *Islamic Three-Character Classic* (*Tianfang san zi jing*) of Liu Zhi, which Ma published as the *Islamic Three-Character Primer* (*Tianfang san zi you yi*). There are further examples, but these illustrate the pattern. Ma's renewal of Islam was mainly a revival of the Islamic truth he had been raised in, based on books that had been used in China from the seventeenth century, the time of our earliest sources on the reading habits of Muslims in China.

Ma's work to make basic texts available was successful. They represent a large portion of the nineteenth-century books in circulation in Yunnan (see Chapter 2). But they also traveled to other parts of China and beyond, even though manuscript copies were already scattered widely. Take, for example, *Pillars of Islam.* The Fude mosque library in Beijing holds six manuscript copies.[54] But Ma's printed edition made its way to Northwest China, namely Gansu province, where a copy is preserved by an *ahong* at the Huasi shrine in Linxia. This *ahong* wrote an introduction to a translation of *Pillars of Islam* published around 2003, by translators working in Inner Mongolia.[55] In his efforts to show the importance of *Pillars of Islam,* the *ahong* notes in his introduction that the work has received an important endorsement. It was recommended as crucial reading by Aḥmad Sirhindī, the Renewer of the Second Millennium, whose tomb is mentioned at the beginning of this chapter. Indeed, if we look to Sirhindī's most famous work, a collection of his letters published in 1616, we find the recommendation in letter number 193.[56]

The Surprise of Islamic China

If we are surprised to find that Ma Lianyuan and Nūr al-Ḥaqq are the same person, it is because for even the most sophisticated among us, the notions of China and of Islam that we rely on are ultimately rooted in essentialism, the idea of a transhistoric core reality to these two concepts that is immediately recognizable, one that makes it difficult for us to imagine the *Islamic Three-Character Primer* as a part of Islamic history and equally difficult to imagine *The Explication* as a Chinese text. Our sense of surprise is a reminder that, no matter how fervently scholars may reject essentialism at an abstract level, it maintains a tight grip on us as we make our own sense of the world's cultural and intellectual diversity. One of our fundamental tools for understanding and describing that diversity is the creation of categories: civilizations, religions, societies, cultures, and so forth. By means of such categories we disentangle complexity, sometimes usefully, but always at a cost.

Ma's story is important because many scholars have fashioned the same kind of confections that I did in my story of two ordinary books: of a typical Chinese Islam, with its "accommodation" to essentially Chinese concepts like *yin* and *yang,* and a typical Islam, Arab and legalistic. This tendency is particularly visible in scholarship that focuses on the story of one category of books: Chinese-language texts that present Islamic knowledge, as Ma did in his annotation of the *Islamic Three-Character Primer.* Ma Lianyuan's / Nūr al-Ḥaqq's full story makes this limited view untenable. Using the *Primer,* it would be easy to present Ma as an example of Islam's "adaptation" to a supposedly distinct entity called Chinese culture, and indeed he has recently been presented as a paragon of the "Chinafication of Islam" at a conference in Yunnan.[57] But when Ma described Islam using Arabic or Persian, rather than Chinese, the texts he produced bore little distinction from those circulating in Kanpur, India.

Ma's case asks us to look more carefully at the signals that trigger our essentializing assumptions about China and Islam. Language, be it Confucian-tinged Chinese or Qur'an-rooted Arabic, bears some resemblance to the printing plates, stone or wood, used to reproduce it. It certainly influences the meaning of the text, but it does not dominate. A text can be translated between vocabularies, just as it is translated between physical media. Wood responds better to the angularity of Chinese characters than to the curved Arabic forms. Chinese characters resist phonetic transcription of unrelated languages like Arabic. Not all of Ma's annotations to the *Islamic Three-Character Primer* were further additions of philosophical subtleties. Many of them were aimed at bridging vocabularies of Islamic communication. The "supreme majesty" is identified, in Arabic, alongside the Chinese characters, as "Allah."

Ma's work engaged many strains of Islamic thought, which, if we analyze them with a focus on their diverse and distant origins (Mujaddidī Sufism from India, Arabian legal discourse, Neo-Confucian metaphysics, philosophical concepts traceable to ancient Greece), might at first blush suggest contradictions in need of accommodation. But in Ma Lianyuan they were entangled in such a way that made him ordinary in his local contexts of Yunnan and northern India, rather than alien. Ma's entanglement was not amalgamation, accommodation, or compromise, but a coherent whole that appeared seamless and unremarkable.

The differences I have highlighted in my story of two ordinary books tempt us to disentangle them, to file them into categories of traditions, societies, cultures, religions, and sects. The identity of Ma Lianyuan and Nūr al-Ḥaqq shows the costs of such an approach. The remaining chapters aim to reentangle Islamic China, to show how ordinariness was continually produced among Muslims in China, and to show this without resorting to essentialism. There is, however, no real escape from disentanglement. In Chapter 9, I take a brief look back to inspect the categories that shaped the book you are reading: "Islamic" and "China."

China and the Renewer of the Second Millennium

The Indian shrine that appeared at the beginning of this chapter points up another lesson from Ma's biography: India played an important role in the history of Islamic China, one that has gone largely unrecognized. There were good reasons for Ma to choose northern India as a place to settle for the remainder of his life. The China-Burma trade along the Tea Horse Roads provided an infrastructure for travel to the Indian Ocean. From there, the main route for the pilgrimage to Mecca proceeded onward by sea, stopping at Indian ports along the way. Ma almost certainly saw India on the pilgrimage of his youth, and, in his final departure from Yunnan, he may have originally intended to make the Hajj again, settling instead in India. One of the Persian-language texts of the local tradition that Ma spent his career reviving was of Indian origin (*Pillars of Islam*). In Mecca Ma studied with a northern Indian teacher, and he learned the Sufi *dhikr* practice from another teacher who was affiliated with the Mujaddidī Sufi path, which took shape in Mughal India.[58] And the "*Shāmī*" text that Ma studied in Mecca was written by an author initiated in the Mujaddidī path.[59] That path (*ṭarīqat*), which spread throughout the Middle East, Central Asia, and China, is the reason that so many pilgrims burn incense at the shrine in Sirhind, where the Mujaddidī founder, Aḥmad Sirhindī, also known as Imam Rabbani, the Renewer of the Second Millennium, is buried.

Given Ma's important role in transmitting the Indian text, *Pillars of Islam,* recommended by Sirhindī himself, and his probable education in Mujaddidi *dhikr,* we might expect a direct connection between Ma and the incense urn in Sirhind. Indeed, there is a connection in the diffusion of Aḥmad Sirhindī's thought and Ma's studies in Mecca. However, the full text of the inscription on the incense urn leads to a more direct connection elsewhere. It reads, "Halu *Ahong* of Linxia's Mingde Mosque, China; Shrine of Imam Rabbani, India." Pilgrimage reveals the practical effects of such entangled intellectual genealogies, which otherwise tend to be most clearly expressed in the textual artifacts of educated elites. A wealthy businessman might not know why Sirhindī's ideas are superior but, under the guidance of scholars like Ma Lianyuan, still travel to Sirhindī's grave in India.

The urn itself is the donation of one of the clerical elites, who hailed from Linxia, sometimes called China's "Little Mecca," far from Ma's Yunnan. From Linxia we can pick up more directly connected historical threads leading back to Sirhind. They lead us not along the Tea Horse Roads of Yunnan and Burma, but through Chinese Central Asia and Afghanistan. But before chasing down this extraordinary thread in Chapter 3, we will pause to examine in more detail the textual world that Ma inhabited in nineteenth-century Yunnan—the context which made both his books and his Indian travels ordinary.

2

The Matrix of the Ordinary

The Textual World of Nineteenth-Century Yunnan

When the grassroots radicals of the Great Proletarian Cultural Revolution (1966–1976) began destroying much of China's cultural heritage, the residents of a village near Dali, Yunnan, took steps to protect a local treasure: their mosque library. According to a mosque official who lived through that turbulent period, the library's books were divided into packets of a few volumes each and parceled out among the community. Each recipient hid their own packet. When the danger finally passed, the mosque's old wooden teaching hall still stood, and the villagers reconstructed its library from their caches.

The result is an extraordinary rarity in China: an Islamic library that has been used and expanded since the nineteenth century, albeit with a brief pause during the Cultural Revolution. Owners' seals show the development of the collection and the passing of books from one hand to another. The earliest identifiable stamps belong to Ma Lianyuan, whose seal graces two of the books. Many more seal impressions belong to Ma Lianyuan's son and most successful student, Muḥammad Ḥusayn Ma Jianzhi (馬建志, 1875–1955); to Ma Jianzhi's son, Ma Ruitu (馬瑞圖, 1896–1945), who taught at the mosque; and to Ma Ruitu's students and successors. This was where I photographed Ma Lianyuan's *Explication,* originally published in Kanpur, India.

In 2016, in a nearby village, I met an antique dealer whose home was his warehouse and showroom. The courtyard house was crammed with an enormous but organized accumulation of old objects. A mound of wooden pack frames for mule caravans sloped down precariously from the rafters to the courtyard floor. Stacks of old cabinets, tables, and chairs climbed toward the ceilings. Assortments of intricately carved doors, a leopard skin, and old beams punctuated the hoard.

The owner brought out a worn green suitcase and opened it to reveal stacks of books, including everything from woodblock prints to manuscripts to mostly empty notebooks to magazine issues. Here, I found the copy of Ma Lianyuan's edition of the *Islamic Three-Character Primer*, described in Chapter 1. The next year, I found another home-based antique dealer with a small hoard of old books in the same valley. He let me photograph freely, and I purchased from him Ma Lianyuan's woodblock edition of selected and translated Quranic verses, which I gave to Yunnan University before leaving China.[1]

Together, the two types of collections—a nineteenth- / twentieth-century mosque library and the antique dealers' twenty-first-century accumulations—offer an unprecedented window onto the circulation of books in a single county in turn-of-the-century Islamic China. They form the main source base for this chapter. Through them we can arrive at a rough understanding of the intellectual context in which Ma Lianyuan's books circulated. We can also gain some insights into larger questions about the textual world of Islamic China around the turn of the twentieth century, not least because the corpus of works represented in these collections has striking overlaps with the less complete evidence that we have for other parts of Islamic China, in the form of book citations in other primary sources.

To call something ordinary is to make a claim about its relationship to a wider environment. The ordinary books of Ma Lianyuan would have been extraordinary in, say, nineteenth-century Peru. But in his home province of Yunnan, Ma's publications conformed to a norm established partly through the books that were already available. As we have seen, many of Ma's editions were printed versions of texts already circulating as manuscripts, in which form they supported the region's traditional Islamic education. Ma also elaborated on the norm, commenting on preexisting texts and composing new works that both addressed long-standing questions and found places for newly arrived ideas within the dominant discourse. Because Ma's publications eventually came to dominate the textual sphere, his conception of normativity became constitutive of the ordinary in much of Muslim Yunnan, while remaining reflective of a wider circulation of texts and ideas both across and beyond China.

But for many of Yunnan's Muslims none of Ma's books, indeed no books of any sort, were ordinary. There were multiple forms of literacy, a knotty concept that encompasses a wide array of skills in various combinations; the ability to recite, write, or read in one genre versus another, or read unfamiliar texts versus known texts—all of these are distinct skills that constitute various forms of literacy.[2] A large number of Yunnan's Muslims possessed none of them. Books may also have had some significance as sacred objects or at least as objects worthy of respect, but I have not yet seen evidence that books were commonly carried or held for talismanic value, certainly not in the way that they were for the Turkic Muslims of the Qing colony in Eastern Turkistan. And books were relatively expensive, even the woodblock editions. For many an impoverished tenant farmer, a book would have been an inscrutable, respected, and extraordinary object.

Nor would the non-Muslim literati of Yunnan, accustomed as they were to books, have found Ma's works ordinary. Most were in Persian or Arabic, inferior languages of the barbarian in the eyes of the non-Muslim scholar. Ma's Chinese-language works bordered on the heterodox, a judgment that had in fact been passed on Chinese-language Islamic books in earlier times. Nonetheless, for the substantial number of Yunnanese who were Muslims and, in one form or another, literate, most of Ma's publications were perfectly ordinary.

The textual matrix that suspended Ma's books in ordinariness required substantial infrastructure. Books had to be physically produced and distributed. Schools taught students to read them. Mosques called worshipers to pray and to recite from books. Mosque leaders assembled collections of books and passed them on to disciples. These institutions and enterprises left traces on the books, giving us clues about Yunnan's Islamic textual ecosystem at the end of the nineteenth century. This chapter begins with a short survey and analysis of the texts preserved in the mosque library and antique-dealer accumulations from Dali Prefecture, before working to reconstruct parts of Yunnan's textual ecosystem and exploring its connections to other places.

The Texts

The mosque library and antique-dealer stocks emerged from very different collecting habits. The former is largely the work of a single lineage of scholars, some of the most well-known Muslim intellectual figures of their times. Ma Ruitu was the most influential among Ma Lianyuan's descendants. He founded and edited an Islamic journal in Guangdong, and he produced the standard Chinese translations of two key modernist texts, Muhammad Abdu's *Risālat al-tawḥīd* and Muhammad Rashid Rida's *Al-waḥī al Muḥammadī* (The revelation to Muhammad).[3] The Ma scholarly lineage collected both basic texts for teaching and sophisticated, specialized works on topics such as Islamic law, theology, and Sufism. Many of their books were imported from Egypt or Istanbul, and these were added to the collection over several decades. For example, thanks to specimens on which records of acquisition have been inscribed, we can see that pre-1915 Egyptian publications were added continuously from at least 1892 to 1945 / 1946.[4] Alongside these works, the library also houses a substantial number of local woodblock books, especially Ma Lianyuan's publications. The collection thus reflects at once the availability of domestically produced books, the circulation of books across Eurasia, and the intellectual interests of a particular (and powerful) lineage of Islamic elites.

The antique-dealer stocks, by contrast, represent an omnivorous accumulation of old books, many of them purchased individually from villagers in the same valley, according to the dealers. Both dealers were unable to read much of what they had amassed, written as they were in Classical Chinese, Arabic, and Persian. They acquired their books for their age and aesthetic properties, with little attention to the particular titles or contents. Nearly all of these books were printed in China, though a few texts from India, Egypt, and elsewhere were present. The collections tended toward the introductory and the didactic, as well as texts for ritual use. Despite some differences between the two antique dealers' accumulations (for example, one amassed Republican-era periodicals, while the other did not), both accumulations are dominated by domestically printed works aimed at readers with a basic level of Islamic knowledge, and they demonstrate a similar balance of Chinese, Persian, and Arabic works. Both the omnivorous acquisition of books based primarily on their age and the similarities between the two accumulations suggest that the resulting corpus is roughly representative of the body of available books in the region as of the late nineteenth and early twentieth centuries.

Caution is nonetheless in order. Like any archive, these collections have been shaped by the decades that intervened between the books' printing and the present. Some books may have been singled out by governments for destruction, for example. A dealer may reject books of a certain type as unprofitable. One book in the mosque library contains an accounting of purchases of several Chinese-language books that are not present in the collection today; were they present, the proportion of Chinese-language books at the mosque would be higher. And the sample size is small, so overly precise statements about the proportions of one kind of text versus another could be deceptive.

For reasons that varied from one collection to another, my time with these books was limited. In all three cases, I managed to photograph at least the identifying pages of all books that appeared to have been published before 1915, regardless of whether I already had access to other copies. Based on this data, I produced the following charts, which present what I believe to be the most balanced picture yet of a local textual landscape for any part of Islamic China in the period of woodblock and manuscript publication.

My cutoff date of 1915, a dozen years after Ma Lianyuan's death, is arbitrary in its specificity but designed to roughly reflect several changes in the textual landscape around that date. It was around that time that many of the forces upholding Ma's textual world began to fade. Woodblock texts started giving way to moveable type in China, while in Egypt, where moveable type already predominated, book aesthetics were shifting away from a style that had reigned for several decades. In the realm of ideas, reformist movements were beginning to take hold in China. While Persian maintained a prominent place in many education systems across the country well into the 1940s, increasing numbers of elite scholars were focusing exclusively on Arabic and Chinese. Put simply, the Yunnan of 1910 was similar to Ma's context in ways that the Yunnan of 1920 was not, to the extent that one can usually guess on which side of the line a book lies from a momentary glance.

The charts (see Figure 2.1) illustrate two notable points of difference between the scholars' library in the mosque and the omnivorous accumulations of the antique dealers: language and place of publication. The scholars' library is dominated by imported texts, with only a third of the fifty-five pre-1915 texts published in China. And the scholars' library contains very few Chinese-language texts from this period (three), whether domestic or foreign. Arabic dominates and Persian or Persian-Arabic bilingual texts represent a fifth of the collection. Of the fifty books in the dealers' accumulations, on the other hand, nearly all were produced in China. The language proportions are more balanced in the dealer accu-

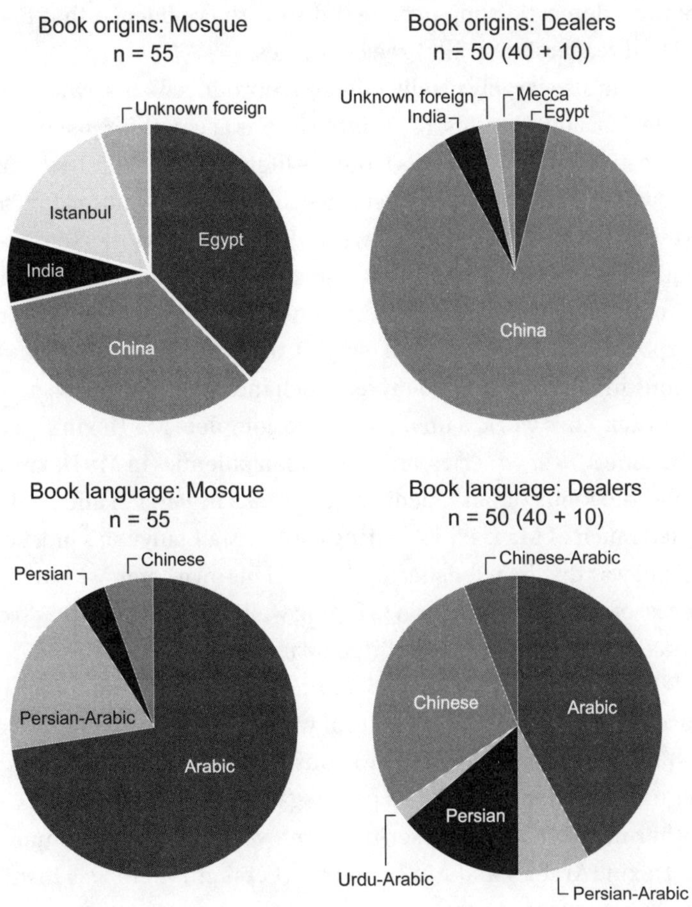

FIGURE 2.1 Origins and languages of books held by one mosque and two antique dealers in a valley near Dali, Yunnan. *Credit:* © Rian Thum

mulation: Chinese, 29 percent; Arabic, 42 percent;[5] Persian and Persian-Arabic, 22 percent.

In this context, the linguistic dexterity that Ma Lianyuan demonstrated in his publications looks entirely unsurprising. Those who produced, read, and preserved the Islamic texts that have continued to circulate in Yunnan did so in Chinese, Persian, and Arabic. And the more specialized scholars associated with the mosque library were collecting books from India, Egypt, and Istanbul. Even before Ma left China for the first time, he was likely well read in genres that flourished in those places. And when he wrote for a domestic audience, he did so with confidence that his books would find readership in all three languages.

But Ma also largely produced—and reproduced—his own context. In the dealers' accumulations, Ma's publications account for just over half of the domestically printed works from his lifetime or earlier. In the mosque library, where Ma's descendants studied, his works accounted for closer to two-thirds of domestic books.[6] If we look only to the works that predated Ma's publications, we are left with a much smaller, and thus less informative, sample size. In the dealers' corpus nearly all of those are the works of his purported teacher, Ma Dexin (seven), or Liu Zhi (five). Their influence is obvious in Ma Lianyuan's oeuvre, which includes translation and explication of Liu Zhi's work, a final volume to complete Ma Dexin's envisaged four-volume *Muttasiq* series, anti-Christian polemics in Ma Dexin's tradition, and the kinds of basic pedagogical books in Persian and Arabic that occupied much of Ma Dexin's writing career. Ma Lianyuan's most notable departure was that he published far fewer of his own compositions than his predecessors, focusing more on bringing well-known older texts from the Islamic school curriculum to printed form.

Both mosque and dealer collections bear witness to another important aspect of Islamic China's textual world: the manuscript. It was this technology that passed down the various Persian and Arabic works across the centuries in which woodblock printing was reserved for texts in Chinese and other non-Perso-Arabic scripts. Even with the printing innovations of Ma Dexin (Arabic) and Ma Lianyuan (Persian), there was insufficient demand or resources to create printed editions of more than a fraction of the Persian and Arabic works that China's Muslims consumed.

Islamic manuscripts circulated throughout China, but they are quite rare today and are mostly isolated behind bureaucratic barriers. An Iranian scholar visiting Beijing in 1977 encountered one of the largest documented collections, approximately sixty manuscripts at the Dongsi mosque.[7] The oldest dated specimen was completed in Beijing in 853 AH (1400–1401 CE): Najm al-Dīn Rāzī's classic Sufi treatise, *Mirṣād al-ʿibād,* which was still taught in Ma Lianyuan's day. Many more manuscripts have made their way into the holdings of state archives and libraries, but they are poorly documented and largely inaccessible. China's current state institutions tend to regard historical texts in languages such as Persian as too politically "sensitive" to show to foreign scholars, and very few of China's own scholars of

Islamic China read Persian or Arabic. I have encountered lone manuscripts at religious sites in Sichuan, Gansu, Ningxia, and Qinghai. And Islamic manuscripts appear on the Chinese book-trading site, kongfz.com, with some frequency, usually with no information about their contents. Unfortunately, manuscript copyists in China rarely recorded the date of copying. We must generally rely on mentions of manuscript texts in other, dated, woodblock works to vouch for the presence of those works that didn't make it into print.

Manuscripts are not particularly numerous in the mosque library, where I found six volumes. The two antique dealers held a combined total of five. It is no surprise that such handmade books should be drowned out by the printed works, which were, after all, mass produced. Their small numbers remind us of the preciousness of these books, which could only be produced by copyists who could write in languages that were not their mother tongues.[8] Despite their smaller numbers, the manuscripts effectively transmitted many texts across centuries. We have seen that several of the books Ma published were mentioned centuries before they reached print.

The eleven manuscripts I documented in Dali Prefecture can be divided roughly into two types: sophisticated scholarly works on the one hand, and texts for recitation, such as prayer compilations, on the other. The former account for all manuscripts in the mosque library. It seems that demand for difficult Sufi philosophical tracts was too limited to support printing, so scholars created their own copies. One of the manuscripts in the mosque library is signed by the copyist: Ma Lianyuan's grandson, Ma Ruitu, who completed the Persian Sufi text, *Haqāʾiq al-lamaʿāt,* in 1333 AH (1914–1915 CE). The five texts in the dealers' stocks were all recitational texts in Arabic, some quite crudely produced. Prayers did not require comprehension, only pronunciation, and the pronunciation of the Arabic script was the first, most widely taught lesson in Islamic schools. Such texts seem to have enjoyed wider demand, as they also appear in printed versions such as the book we turn to next, which was funded by villagers' donations.

Producing Books

While the printed Islamic books of late nineteenth-century Yunnan shared many technical characteristics with non-Islamic books from other parts of China, the Islamic publishing industry differed in two important ways from the wider popular book trade. First, book production was largely a charitable endeavor, rather than a profit-making enterprise. Second, book production was centered on a single prominent mosque, rather than diffuse private workshops.

For example, in the summer of 1894, fourteen believers in the village of Dabai 大白, near Yuxi, Yunnan, pooled their resources to publish a book of Arabic prayers. The title page says the book was "published relying on funding [資] from the co-religionists [教親] of Dabai." The last page of the book specifies the nature of this funding, describing it as *gongde* 功德, meritorious donation, and lists names and amounts, much like the signboards common at Chinese mosques (and temples) today, which list donor contributions for renovations or construction (Figure 2.2). With donations ranging from 0.3 to two taels of silver, these fourteen individuals amassed a total of at least 12.6 taels to support the carving of the woodblocks and,

並將大白邑刻經捐掛功德姓名開列於後
馬良標 捐銀貳兩
沐應甲 捐銀貳兩
沐開甲 捐銀壹兩伍錢
馬臣林 捐銀壹兩
馬占星 捐銀壹兩
馬自有 捐銀壹兩
馬東受 捐銀壹兩
沐金安 捐銀壹兩
馬聯恩 捐銀伍錢
馬中玉 捐銀伍仟
馬明輔 捐銀伍錢
合富祥 捐銀伍錢
馬登霄 捐銀叁錢
張萬喜 捐銀叁錢

استغفر الله العظيم الذى لا اله الا
هو غفار الذنوب

FIGURE 2.2 Donor list (*left*) and first page (*right*) of *Tawbah al-aghyār; Tawbah al-ʿjāʾib; Khwājah khatm; Barāt shaʿbān* (Dabai, Yunnan: Muslims of Dabai Village, 1894). *Credit:* © Rian Thum

likely, the other production costs, such as paper, ink, and labor.[9] The wood plates were stored at the Nancheng 南城 Mosque in Kunming, a fact inscribed on the title page for the benefit of any future benefactor who might wish to produce a second printing.[10]

Ma Lianyuan financed at least three of his publications through similar community donations: "the families in and around the Xinping 新平 county center"; "the co-religionists of Taoguoyuan 桃果園 village, Qiyang 棋陽"; and "Teacher Li Guozhu 李國住 and the Muslims of Heyang 河陽 County."[11] More often, his publications were backed by a single wealthy patron or business, such as the Xing Shun He 興順和 Company. In all cases where the title page gives a location for the printing plates, it is the same Nancheng Mosque of Kunming where the Dabai villagers deposited their plates. Today the mosque still preserves an enormous collection of plates, though most scholars, domestic and foreign, have not been given access to the collection.

In at least one case, the funder of Ma Lianyuan's publications linked his project financially to Yunnan's cross-border trade. The Xing Shun He Company, founded by Ma's uncle, Ma Youling 馬佑齡, began importing indigo or indigo-dyed cloth from Chiang Mai (in today's Thailand) via Burma in the 1850s. By the 1890s, when Xing Shun He began funding Ma Lianyuan's books, the company had branch offices in multiple provinces across China.[12] Xing Shun He ultimately funded at least three publications, among them Ma's largest project, the Qur'an.

We have little data on how the products of charitable publishing were distributed. Some editions from Ma's plates have printed prices, which may mean that the donations functioned as subsidies to keep prices reasonable and large projects feasible. On the other hand, these could be later editions from original plates, undertaken either by underfunded charitable publishers or profit-seeking entrepreneurs. An earlier charitable publisher, writing in 1828, complained about profit-seekers undermining his efforts to make Islamic texts widely available. He lamented that, after he spent great effort fundraising for printing expenses, some individuals sold their copies at high prices.[13]

The Islamic publishing industry in late nineteenth-century Yunnan shared much in common with other regions of China. Two recent studies of Islamic printing across Qing China, while restricted exclusively to Chinese-language texts, show a similar dependence on donations, though mixed with some profit-seeking publishing at the end of the nineteenth century.[14] The involvement of mosques in publishing, specifically in the storage of plates, is documented for many cities, including Chengdu,[15] Guangzhou,[16] Zhenjiang,[17] and Yongchang (Gansu).[18] In Sichuan, we see individuals who, like Ma Lianyuan, took up publishing, according to their own accounts, in order to spread Islamic knowledge. One of these was Zhou Mingde 周明德, who began publishing by 1894. He wrote that he engraved and printed "for the common good" and explained that he wanted his publications to address widespread religious ignorance among Muslims.[19] While such statements of motivation likely omit other incentives, such as status-seeking, they do seem to point to a lack of profit motive that aligns with other evidence. At the same time, the Sichuan printing industry also shows some differences from Yunnan. Another publishing entrepreneur, Yu Zhaowen 余昭文, seems to have created a successful business out of printing Islamic works, which he named Baozhentang 寶真堂 (Precious Truth Hall). And Sichuan's publishers printed many more Chinese-language works than their Yunnanese counterparts. However, the relative prominence of various languages is impossible to judge, because studies of Chengdu publishing have limited their research to Chinese-language works.[20] An Arabic book in the stock of a Chengdu antique dealer shows that at least one such volume was printed by woodblock in 1870.[21] Whether there were others printed in Chengdu remains to be seen.

The role of the mosque in Islamic printing calls to mind China's Buddhist monasteries, which have for centuries served both as a safe place to deposit woodblock plates and, in many cases, as organizing institutions for charitably funded editions of Buddhist canonical texts. By the late nineteenth century, however, such works were drops in an ocean of profit-driven publications aimed at non-Muslims. As Cynthia Brokaw has described in rich detail, small private publishing ventures competed to churn out cheap editions of in-demand texts, ranging from the Confucian classics upon which the imperial exam system was based to fortune-telling handbooks.[22] This booming business created a class of itinerant woodblock carvers who were well practiced at carving the angular Chinese characters with precision and speed. Undoubtedly, the presence of a skilled woodblock carving trade also benefited the less-common charitable publishing projects, which could tap a market of efficient artisans.

This did not apply to Islamic publishing projects in Yunnan that aimed to produce works in Arabic or Persian. The carving of the curved, connected Arabic letters would have represented a distinct skill, for which there was little to no market support. This is not to say that carvers were entirely unable to produce Arabic letters—there are copious examples of woodblock text with figural engravings, and Liu Zhi included examples of each of the Arabic letters in his 1710 treatise on the alphabet, *Tianfang zimu jieyi* 天方字母解義—but carvers would not have been practiced at producing these letters quickly and thus economically. The Qing court faced a similar obstacle in its promotion of the Manchu language through printed works, but the vast resources of the state seem to have dwarfed the startup costs of woodblock publication in a new script. For Ma and others who wished to publish woodblock books in the Arabic script, the obstacle would have loomed much larger. Despite the fact that both Arabic and woodblock printing had been used separately in China for a millennium by the turn of the nineteenth century, the earliest Arabic woodblock book so far identified was only published in 1863, by Ma Dexin.[23] The first Persian book printed in China would have to wait until Ma Lianyuan's 1894 woodblock edition of *Chahār faṣl*.[24]

This is not to say that Persian and Arabic books were absent in China before the woodblock editions. On the contrary, they played an important role for Muslims across many communities for centuries. *Chahār faṣl* itself was already present in the mid-seventeenth century at the latest, a fact we know because Zhang Shizhong 張時中 translated it into Chinese and printed his translation by woodblock circa 1653. The original Persian work continued to circulate in manuscript form, such that Ma Lianyuan had access to a copy when he prepared his woodblock edition more than two centuries later. The roles of various languages will be discussed in more detail in Chapter 8, but it is important here to emphasize that the late appearance of the first *printed* Persian book produced in China does not indicate any absence of *manuscript* Persian books, which were clearly available in substantial numbers from the first moment when we have evidence of what kinds of books China's Muslims were reading.

The world of books in late nineteenth-century Yunnan also owed some of its shape to the decades before Ma Lianyuan's return, during which widespread rebellions led to the political empowerment of several prominent Muslims. Each of the three most prominent leaders in the Yunnan rebellions of 1856–1873 engaged in publishing.[25] The ruler of the new Dali Sultanate, Du Wenxiu (杜文秀), printed the Qur'an in Arabic in 1862–1863.[26] Ma Lianyuan's teacher, Ma Dexin, wielded military power through another of his students and was even, for a short time, declared the King of Pingnan at Kunming. His substantial political power may account for the funding of his numerous publications (thirty-seven, by one count) between 1858 and 1868.[27] For some of this period Ma Dexin's publications may perhaps best be considered as state products, given the military and political resources at his command. A well-funded, state-supported publication program may also account for Ma Dexin's ability to surmount the challenges of cutting woodblock plates in Arabic. Ma Lianyuan's own publishing program was in many ways a continuation of his teacher's efforts. Without the state and military backing Ma Dexin had enjoyed, Ma Lianyuan turned to community donations. Whether any of Ma Dexin's carvers of Arabic-script woodblock survived the violence of the Qing reconquest is unknown, but their works continued to circulate and demonstrate the viability of woodblock publishing in the Arabic script.

Cultural and generic factors also exerted great force. When Ma Dexin and Ma Lianyuan managed to bring Arabic and Persian works to print, cross-pollination between the forms of Chinese and Arabic-script books remained limited. While title pages were common for Chinese texts, Arabic title pages were rare. Where an Arabic or Persian woodblock book has a title page, it is almost always primarily Chinese. Prefaces from scholars other than the author are also common for texts in Chinese, but unusual for Perso-Arabic works. Even author prefaces are far less common in the Perso-Arabic texts. Nor did Chinese-language texts adopt much in the way of book tradition from the Perso-Arabic manuscript tradition. The tradition of beginning a book with praise of the prophet and his companions never approached the same universality in Chinese-language Islamic book culture. The maintenance of separate conventions for book forms in the two scripts suggests that language was never fully extricable from form.[28] The convention of producing Chinese books in woodblock and Perso-Arabic books in manuscript had its own inertial power, which may have been as significant an obstacle to Ma Dexin's and Ma Lianyuan's publication projects as the difficulty in finding skilled woodcarvers for Arabic letters.

Producing Readers

Books are not made without readers. And like books, readers are produced through community effort. In Yunnan's Muslim communities, this task fell mainly to privately funded and operated Islamic schools, normally housed in mosque compounds. Children from well-off families sometimes enrolled instead in non-Muslim private schools, and in rare instances they advanced far enough in Confucian learning to pass the state exams at various levels and earn official positions. These cases were, however, exceptional. Most of the Muslim children in nineteenth-century Yunnan who undertook formal education did so through a Perso-Arabic curriculum at the mosque.

The history of Islamic education in China has enjoyed an enormous amount of attention from Sinophone scholars.[29] These scholars refer to the Perso-Arabic educational system, variants of which were widespread across China from at least the Ming, as "classics hall education" (经堂教育), and they have identified regional "schools" with variations in curricular emphasis. Unfortunately, their detailed portraits of mosque-based education often provide only limited citation of primary sources, and scholars sometimes present their subject as an unchanging, timeless, "traditional" education. Nonetheless, where primary sources can be located, they tend to confirm the prevailing understanding among China-based historians of Islamic education as it stood before the modernist reforms of the twentieth century.

The standard depiction can be summarized as follows. Mosque-based education served two main goals. First was the moral education of children, women, and the elderly, aimed at producing good Muslims capable of fulfilling basic ritual duties and meeting the norms of the community. The second role was to develop a smaller number of students into Islamic scholars who could guide the community and perpetuate the educational system. Both functions were funded by the charitable donations of the community.[30] By Ma Lianyuan's time, these institutional arrangements had assumed some regularity across China, with an increasing professionalization encouraged by a trend of hiring teachers from outside of the communities in which they taught.[31]

For children, the more general, or "universal," education (普及教育) began at age four. The first task was to learn to pronounce the Arabic alphabet, with an eye toward reciting the Qur'an. This was followed by instruction in basic religious duties using three reasonably straightforward texts in Persian: *al-Faṣl* (The chapter); *Muhimmāt* (Essentials); and *ʿUmdat al-Islām* (Pillar of Islam). These three works formed the introductory curriculum not just in Yunnan but in mosque schools across China, from at least the early Qing through the twentieth century. The Muslim scholar Zhao Can 趙燦 of Jiangsu, writing in 1719, reported that his master recommended these three texts as the starting point in an Islamic education.[32] In 1945 Pang Shiqian reported that they still constituted the standard foundational curriculum of "old-style" education across China.[33]

Curiously, despite much attention to the writings of both Zhao and Pang among historians of Chinese Islams, the foundational role of Persian-medium education has rarely been remarked on. A notable exception is the work of Masumi Matsumoto. Her history of the process by which reformers in the twentieth century uprooted Persian education confirms its ubiquity at that time. The words of a Hunanese reformer writing in 1925 (also cited by Matsumoto) neatly capture both the role of Persian and the attitude of those trying to relegate the language to an ancillary position:

> Persian language is the speech of the Persians. It is an indirect way to transmit the meaning of the classic(s) for the understanding of today's Chinese people. When transmitting indirectly, students and readers expend excessive skills in translating. Moreover, those who have not studied Persian learn with difficulty and forget easily. How is this worth the trouble? If we encounter someone from another province and they speak with an incorrect accent, we find it very funny. Don't we think it is very funny to teach Chinese children the meaning of the classics using Persian?[34]

For Chinese-speaking Muslims before the modernist educational reforms of the twentieth century, the most common initial experience of learning to read for comprehension was in Persian, not Chinese or even Arabic. The nature of specialized women's education further emphasizes the role of Persian as a foundational medium of basic education. In many parts of China, women's education followed an abbreviated version of the curriculum outlined by Zhao and Pang, consisting of five texts that came to be known as "the women's classics." All five of these texts were Persian texts (authored by men), and all seem to be texts mentioned by Zhao.[35]

This "universal" education rooted in Persian was not the only option for Sinophone Muslims. The many dozens of Muslims who achieved the highest rank in the imperial examination system throughout the Ming and Qing dynasties demonstrate that a substantial number of Muslims received their education outside of the mosque system, in the private Confucian schools, where they would have learned to read and write first in classical Chinese. This was the case not just in the coastal provinces but in areas with large Muslim populations, including Yunnan, Shaanxi, and Gansu.[36] Nonetheless, despite the steady flow of some Muslims through the Confucian education system, Muslims who could read Chinese beyond "primer literacy" probably remained a rarity.[37]

In exceptional cases, individuals pursued education in both systems. It was this rarest educational path that produced the most respected authors of Chinese-language Islamic texts: Liu Zhi, Wang Daiyu, and Ma Zhu. In the case of Wang Daiyu, Islamic education came first, followed by the study of Confucian and Buddhist classics in adulthood. Ma Zhu, by contrast, studied in a Confucian school in his youth, before traveling throughout China in search of Perso-Arabic learning later in life. Ma, a native of Yunnan, advocated a version of his special educational experience for all Muslims in China, writing that children must learn the teachings of both Confucianism (儒) and the Qur'an, but should be careful not to confuse the two systems of thought.[38] While he mentions mosque schools and the recruitment of teachers, he provides little detail about curriculum or institutional arrangements. Texts by Ma Zhu and other dually educated scholars would eventually open Islamic education to those students who studied in the Confucian schools. In particular, Liu Zhi's *Three-Character Classic* and the other verse primers it inspired brought Islamic cosmology within reach of children at the earliest stages of Chinese-language education.[39]

Nonetheless, observers' writings from the turn of the twentieth century suggest that the classical mosque education remained the most common type of formal education for Sinophone Muslims. Western Christian missionaries were particularly interested in Muslims' education, either because they viewed China's Muslims as more open to conversion than non-Muslims or because they saw Islam as a competitor to their proselytizing mission. Marshall Broomhall solicited observations on Muslims' education from missionaries posted throughout China and compiled them in his *Islam in China: A Neglected Problem.* He concluded that "schools are connected with most of the mosques throughout China," effectively placing a Perso-Arabic school in most Muslim communities.[40]

How ordinary were books? Complaints about low rates of literacy (in any language) abound in the writings of both Chinese and foreign observers of China's Muslim communities. But books can be useful even to those with partial literacy or none at all. It is notable that in the tiny rural village of Dabai, a dozen individuals were willing to contribute to the printing of a recitational compilation. Their anthology of prayers in Arabic would be useful to anyone who learned to pronounce text, even if they could not understand it. The skill of Arabic recitation (not comprehension) was the first subject taught at the mosque schools, immediately followed by reading of the three Persian introductory texts.

Still, the number of people who could understand the literal meaning of the texts in Yunnan's books was limited by steep linguistic challenges. None of the languages in which these works were printed were vernacular. No Yunnanese Muslim could have the experience of encountering a written representation of the language they were raised to speak. To read the available Islamic texts they would need to learn at least one of three alien grapholects: Classical Chinese, Persian, or Arabic. In the case of Classical Chinese, they would have the advantage of a familiar set of phonemes and numerous words with familiar meanings, though these were mixed with *faux amis.* However, as was noted in Chapter 1, they would also face a very different grammar, a large vocabulary of entirely unfamiliar words, and the necessity of memorizing a different written character for (virtually) each word. Today, Chinese speakers literate at the highest levels cannot understand Classical Chinese texts without special training. Persian may have been slightly easier, with its alphabet, familiar word order, and regular, lightly inflected grammar, though it required learning a larger stock of wholly new vocabulary. Arabic offered access to the most authoritative texts of all, Qur'an and *hadith* collections, but was more grammatically demanding. Ma Lianyuan singled out that language as one that presented students with a particular challenge.[41] It is difficult to know whether Ma succeeded in his stated goal of producing texts that people could read even if their studies were broken off for practical reasons.

Language preferences varied across space and changed over time. As of the late 1920s, it appears that Persian and Arabic were still the main media of Muslim literacy in most of Yunnan, while Muslims in the provincial capital were more likely to read Chinese. This situation surprised Ma Lianyuan's son and main scholarly successor, Ma Jianzhi, who had only learned written Chinese in middle age. He wrote about the experience of moving to Kunming to take up a teaching post that he held circa 1927–1930: "In the provincial capital I saw that there were many Muslim [回民] readers of Chinese (華文), and the traditional religious scholars were few. I started to realize that translation is an urgent task of the present, so I concentratedly delved into the study of Chinese."[42]

The linguistic and educational terrain of Islamic Yunnan was clearly complex and dynamic, as it was throughout China. Through at least the middle of the nineteenth century, all scholars who published Islamic texts in Chinese were well versed in Persian and Arabic (see Chapter 8). Other Muslims seem to have passed the Confucian exams, entered the civil service, never learning Persian or Arabic, and never producing any written work on Islam. Yet, as Ma Jianzhi's "realization" in Kunming suggests and the corpus of surviving books confirms, engagements with Islamic text in Yunnan at the dawn of the twentieth century were more likely to take place in Persian or Arabic than in Chinese.

Ma Lianyuan's Publications in Context

On his sixtieth birthday, Ma Lianyuan received a gift fit for a scholar of the highest repute: a woodblock-printed booklet of twenty-one pages commemorating his birthday and his life's work, specially printed on celebratory red paper. Among its praises, the text lists the names of sixty-nine students who went on to serve as headmasters at Islamic schools in Yunnan, Sichuan, Guizhou, and Burma.[43] This list lends some credence to Ma's own claim, in his farewell address, that most of the teachers in Yunnan's mosques were his students. Thanks to his decades recruiting and teaching students for the network of schools he helped revive, by the end of his life, Ma already witnessed his ideals of knowledge transmission spreading among Chinese-speaking Muslims over a substantial stretch of territory. Ma's restoration and subtle reshaping of the ordinary in Islamic learning would continue to expand after his death, taking root across the breadth of China and even expanding, as we will see in Chapter 7, to Thailand.

Most of what Ma promoted through his twenty-plus printed editions was ordinary in Ma's community even before he began his own education. His earliest dated publication (1891) was a basic introduction to the Arabic alphabet in Chinese, accompanied by exercises and essential passages from the Qur'an. Ma's Chinese-language explanation of the alphabet gives some insight into the earliest stage of Islamic education.[44] The brief text uses relatively simple Chinese, with rhyming, rhythmic couplets that would have allowed the student to memorize Ma's instructions (with the aid of a Chinese-literate teacher). The text emphasizes the importance of pronouncing Arabic correctly when reciting the Qur'an as part of worship. This was clearly a work directed at the first stage of "universal" mosque-school education, equipping students to recite Arabic sacred texts.

Over the following seven years, Ma produced his editions of the three Persian texts that completed the first stage of education. However, during the same period, Ma published several other texts aimed at more advanced learners. These included a complete edition of the Qur'an, three grammar textbooks on Persian and Arabic, a simplified exposition of Islamic doctrine, a legal text, and a short *hadith* selection.[45] He was as concerned with advanced students—those aiming for teaching roles of their own—as he was with general education.

Most of the original texts that Ma authored were elaborations of the Perso-Arabic tradition in which he had been raised. *Explication* was, as we saw, an annotation of perhaps the most widely circulated book in Islamic China, the *Wiqaya.* His *hadith* book, *Sermons,* borrowed an earlier selection of sayings of the prophet and expanded them, interpolating additional words and phrases to expound upon what he regarded as the original intent of the prophet.[46] In his farewell address, Ma summarized his writing and publishing career as an effort to make standard works accessible to students living through challenging times, with a focus on explanation, abbreviation, and language instruction.

However, Ma also gently reshaped the tradition he had inherited. One of his more interesting departures was an effort to bring insights from Chinese-language Islamic scholarship into Perso-Arabic learning. In 1898–1899 he published an Arabic translation of the core text from Liu Zhi's famous Sufi philosophical text, *Nature and Principle in Islam* (*Tianfang xingli* (天方性理), as well as a version with his Arabic-language commentary. After his arrival in India, he published a lithographed super-commentary on his own commentary, using the same press that produced *Explication.* In his introduction, Ma wrote that Liu Zhi's core text "perfectly explains everything about the two worlds. Therefore, I ordered my followers to memorize it. But some of the meanings were unclear to them, so, I have explained it in Arabic."[47] For the first time, scholars educated solely in the Perso-Arabic curriculum could access what was perhaps the most famous Islamic text produced originally in Classical Chinese. Ma's publication of the *Islamic Three-Character Primer* suggests that he also may have introduced some of Liu Zhi's ideas at the earliest stages of education using Chinese.

In addition to learning from his father, who was an imam, Ma Lianyuan is said to have studied under Ma Dexin, one of those rare authors proficient in both Chinese- and Perso-Arabic-language scholarship. This may account for Ma Lianyuan's abilities in Classical Chinese, which appear to have been prodigious, given his engagement with the complex philosophy of Liu Zhi in that language. The overwhelming majority of his published works focused on the Perso-Arabic scholarly tradition. However, when he wanted to connect with Muslim readers across the educational divide, he was well equipped to do so. Thus, he published his refutations of Christianity in both Chinese and Arabic.[48] Despite his own linguistic prowess, though, Ma did not envision the learning of written Chinese as a norm, directing his sons to an education first and foremost in the Perso-Arabic tradition, as we have seen in the autobiographical comments of his son Ma Jianzhi.

There are also hints in Ma's writings of an increased prominence for Arabic, despite Ma's publication of Persian educational staples. He notes in his farewell preface that students were particularly keen to learn Arabic. And he penned his own primer on faith in Arabic, *Tafṣīl al-Īmān,* covering basic material that was already delivered in the Persian textbooks he published. He also stated that this text was aimed at both "boys and girls," hinting at a possible expansion of Arabic-language education to women, who often studied only Persian.[49]

None of Ma's publications seem to have aroused controversy during his lifetime. He was an extraordinary scholar in his organizational efforts, his dedication to teaching, his ability to marshal community resources, and his mastery of a wide range of scholarly works. His project was ambitious in scale, and he must have garnered some enemies in addition to admirers.

Indeed, in one text he briefly railed against the leaders of "innovator" (Ḥadūthiyyah) sects, probably the Jahriyya, who he claimed departed from orthodox beliefs.[50] But his publications ultimately differed little from the books that were in circulation in Yunnan during his lifetime. Nonetheless, at the end of his life Ma still sought external certification of the orthodoxy of his life's work. As he undertook his failed final journey to Mecca, he wrote instructions in his farewell address that his publications should be forwarded to Mecca should he die before reaching the holy city. And he proudly appended a letter of praise from a Medinan scholar who had already seen his abbreviated work on doctrine.[51] Ma aspired to normativity not just in Yunnan or even India, where he died, but at the origin point of Islam.

Nūr al-Ḥaqq / Ma Lianyuan was not alone in his concern for origins and connections leading beyond China. In Chapter 3, we turn to texts presented not as ordinary, but extraordinary. Through them, the wide range of origin preoccupations that characterized many of China's Islamic self-conceptions will become apparent, along with the inter-Asian circulations that fueled them.

Implications for the History of Chinese Islams

Historians of Islam in China have long placed importance on booklists and bibliographies as sources for understanding the nature of Islamic knowledge, beliefs, practices, and identity in China. These lists range from Liu Zhi's citation of his sources in the eighteenth century,[52] to a list of books shown to the Qianlong emperor,[53] to Christian missionaries' lists of books in the mid-nineteenth to early twentieth centuries,[54] to modern surveys of mosque libraries.[55] Ma Lianyuan's publication efforts, aimed at reviving Islamic learning after the destruction of the Yunnan rebellions, offer an extremely valuable source for understanding what the preeminent Chinese scholar of his day thought was the traditional Islam that needed bringing back to life. Ma's publications then went on to determine the contours of nonsectarian (*gedimu* 各地木) Islam for succeeding generations, not just in Yunnan but in much of the Northwest, where Ma's texts continue to be republished, and in parts of the Southeast, where Ma's grandson, Ma Ruitu 馬瑞圖, taught and edited the Islamic magazine *Tianfan xueli yuekan* 天方

學理月刊, as well as in northern Thailand, where the Chinese Muslim community comprises the descendants of exiles from Yunnan.

The picture that Ma's textual corpus paints does not fit neatly with common depictions of Chinese Islams either within or outside of China. Much attention has been devoted by both Chinese and foreign scholars to the Chinese-language Islamic classics composed in the late Ming and early Qing, with their fascinating deployment of Confucian and Daoist terminologies. In some accounts of Chinese Islam, these texts, often anachronistically labeled with the mid-nineteenth-century moniker of "Han Kitab," appear as the main textual basis of a generalized Chinese Islamic tradition. However, Ma Lianyuan's attempt to restore the educational system of his pre-rebellion youth through publishing shows that the Chinese-language texts played a secondary role in Yunnan's Islamic knowledge production during the late Qing. Only two of Ma's twenty-two printed editions were in Chinese. He did bring two of Liu Zhi's Chinese-language texts, one a primer and the other in Arabic translation, to print. But his educational mission only aimed to give students a basic familiarity with Liu's ideas. The rest of the works Ma worked so hard to fund, edit, and print were Arabic and Persian works that would not look out of place in Central Asia or northern India. Indeed, many of them were editions of Central Asian and Indian works.

One of the most notable characteristics of Ma's corpus is continuity. While we have vanishingly few Islamic manuscripts from the seventeenth and eighteenth centuries, almost none of them readily accessible to scholars, we do have some idea of what manuscripts were circulating and being read in China at that time. In his monumental dissertation, Dror Weil identified more than one hundred Persian and Arabic texts in circulation during that period.[56] Weil's work is based on mentions of these books in the Qianlong list and the works of various Muslim authors from the period, which often show significant overlap.[57] At least ten Persian and Arabic works were also translated into Chinese and printed in the seventeenth and eighteenth centuries, ensuring their survival through sheer numbers.[58] Thanks to these sources, we can identify five of Ma's Persian and Arabic editions as works that were circulating in China in the seventeenth and / or eighteenth centuries. Two others, *Mukhtaṣar sharḥ al-ʿaqā'id* and *Min sharḥ al-wiqāyah al-masmi bi-al-tawḍīḥ,* are abbreviations or commentaries of texts documented from that earlier period. Of course, Ma could not have produced these printed editions without access to manuscripts in the original languages. This suggests that a large number of manuscripts circulating in the seventeenth and eighteenth centuries continued to be copied and read into the end of the nineteenth century, even in large enough numbers to survive the destruction of the Yunnan rebellions and reconquest.

The continuous production of the Perso-Arabic literature casts doubt on a common characterization of the development of Islamic knowledge in China, which sees the emergence of Chinese-language Islamic texts in the late Ming and early Qing as a sign of a turn not just toward the use of Chinese, but *away* from the use of Persian and Arabic. Students in Ma's educational network, it seems, had less contact (though not zero) with Chinese-language texts than with Persian and Arabic books, and many of those were the same works that had featured prominently in the very period in which the Chinese-language canon was created. We should not be surprised, then, to see that Ma integrated Liu Zhi's Chinese-language philosophical texts with a Persian and Arabic corpus rooted in India and Central Asia; Ma was reading many of the same Perso-Arabic texts that Lui had access to.

The continuity apparent in Ma's work stands out even more because of his connections to the wider Muslim-majority world. His teacher, Ma Dexin, had spent four years studying and traveling in the Middle East, with additional time in India and Singapore. Ma Lianyuan studied with masters from Mecca, Egypt, the Turkic world, and India before returning to Yunnan and taking up his educational mission. As we saw in Chapter 1, the marks of this period of study are barely perceptible in his choice of texts for publication (though his experience no doubt helped him to better understand and elaborate the texts he was teaching).

For these reasons, I have described Ma Lianyuan's project as a "restoration" of the ordinary, rather than a revival or a reform. The latter terms are widely used to describe movements that aim for a break with recent or existing forms of Islamic knowledge, often hearkening back to a golden age in the distant past when Islam was thought to be pure and authoritative. But Ma's golden age was his own. He did not aspire to bring back an earlier form of Islam, uncorrupted by centuries of mistaken Islamic elaborations. Instead, he regarded the Islamic education of his own youth as authoritative, and it only needed restoration because a decade of war had destroyed its physical and human infrastructure. It did not need any reform. Ma was, of course, not untouched by the changes we call modernity. Steam travel facilitated his Hajj; increased commercial activity fueled the businesses that funded some of his publications;[59] and Western colonialist missionaries inspired him to write his apologia. But both the body of texts he produced and his autobiographical writing show that Ma's project was an effort to ensure continuity, to boost the existing tradition of Islamic thought and transmit it to the next generations, to reproduce the ordinary.

3

Extraordinary Books

Wang Daiyu and Long Ahong

On the Tibetan Plateau's northernmost edge, in Qinghai's Haidong Prefecture, the tomb complex of ʿAbdallah Qādir preserves a small and unusual manuscript from the first half of the nineteenth century.[1] The caretakers of the tomb cannot read the text because it is written in a language no longer used in this region. If anything, this archaism makes the text more sacred. Indeed, as a non-Muslim, I was not allowed to touch the book when I visited in 2015. For an anxious fifteen minutes I examined the manuscript and scribbled notes while a somewhat impatient caretaker turned its pages. It was not enough time. I will likely never see the book again. It is one of several important manuscripts at the core of this study that I encountered at sacred sites I can no longer visit, due to the current Chinese government's repression of Muslims across ethnic groups.

The text is written in Eastern Turki (a form of Chaghatay), a language that was widely used in Altishahr, the southern part of what the Chinese government today calls Xinjiang, from the late seventeenth to the early twentieth centuries. But the nearest place where Eastern Turki was written is a thousand kilometers away from Haidong Prefecture. The caretakers of the tomb today are members of the Salar ethnic group and speak both Salar and Chinese. While Salar is a Turkic language, it is not quite close enough to make reading an Eastern Turki manuscript possible.

This was the first and only time in my research among Muslim communities in the People's Republic of China that I was forbidden from touching a book due to my religious status. The phenomenon is uncommon throughout the Muslim-majority world, but in China I had thought it was nonexistent. There are secret books, whose contents cannot be divulged.

The Persian-language original of *al-Rashḥat al-sharīfat,* a sacred history of the Jahriyya Sufi order, was until recently kept unavailable to all but a few adepts.[2] The Arabic text of *Minshār,* a liturgy of the Resplendent Mosque (Huasi) community in Linxia, was once supposed to be kept secret, though copies occasionally surface in Islamic bookshops in various parts of China. I would not have been surprised if the caretakers of this tomb wanted to keep their text a secret, too. But they were willing to share the text, or at least allow me to skim it. Instead, it was the physical object itself that could not touch an unbeliever.

On my arrival, I had asked the caretakers if they kept any old books. Their response explained the value of this little manuscript. Yes, they told me, they had an "*ijaza.*" This is the Arabic term for a type of license, the formal permission that a learned master grants a student. Depending on the tradition, an *ijaza* can be granted to teach a particular text or it can authorize the transmission of an entire mystical path of spiritual development. During my short perusal of the manuscript, I could find no internal evidence that the book served as an *ijaza.* It consisted of a *rāhnāma* (guide) to a Sufi path and a *silsila,* a record of the transmission of that Sufi path through a succession of masters, beginning with the Prophet Muhammad, and in this case ending with a man who died in the eighteenth century.[3] The caretakers said that this *ijaza* had been given to the tomb's occupant, but neither he nor his teacher were listed in the *silsila.* The book thus performed its authorizing function as an object, a phenomenon that has been documented for at least one other Sufi order in China, which preserves various relics of previous leaders as *ijaza.*[4]

This manuscript, which exercised its power through physical presence rather than textual content, is one of two types of extraordinary books treated in this chapter: those composed with the intent of leaping boundaries and setting new rules; and those, like the *ijaza,* that acquired talismanic power as physical channels of authority. Both types have left deep imprints on Islamic China.

For Ma Lianyuan, the author of the ordinary books discussed in Chapter 1, ordinariness was hard earned. Whether Persian, Arabic, or Classical Chinese, the languages of Islam were difficult to master. Ma often lamented that many students were not up to the task. For them he published his many abridgments and handbooks—crib sheets for achieving ordinariness in multiple discourses.

For the outsider historian studying communities that are commonly framed as exceptional, exotic, or syncretic (of which Chinese-speaking Muslims are a notable example), attention to the production of ordinariness is crucial. But ordinary books are not always what are called for. For all his success at fitting in across languages, geographies, and intellectual traditions, Ma Lianyuan also had to face, from time to time, special burdens of being multiply ordinary. To his non-Muslim Chinese neighbors in Yunnan, Ma's connections to distant lands and unfamiliar languages might make him heterodox, threatening, a native outsider. To his co-religionists in Kanpur, India, he would have been alien in other ways, ultimately Chinese. To be at home in multiple places is to be a stranger in all of them. Perhaps this is what Ma felt when he wrote in his farewell preface, his most extraordinary text, "I am the most foreign among foreigners."[5]

The extraordinary books in this chapter helped Chinese Muslim scholars not only to resolve the tensions of local rootedness and far-flung attachments but to capitalize on them. In the first example, a seventeenth-century scholar named Wang Daiyu abandoned predominant Islamic genres to address his place in a world dominated by non-Muslims. His argument was that Islam alone offered an answer to the key question of origins—origins of the universe and of humanity. The second example brings us back to the incense urn at Sirhind. Its author, popularly known as "the Deaf Cleric," lived in a locality where Muslims were and are the majority: Linxia, China's "Little Mecca." In the twentieth century, when reformists called into question the authenticity of established Islams and religious leaders like the Deaf Cleric were forced to bolster their authority, he called to his defense the story of an ancestor and the physical bestowal of a powerful book. Extraordinary books such as these shed light on consequential ruptures and on efforts to maintain continuity in the face of change, and they reveal what Islamic Chinese community leaders saw as the most effective resources for advocating their ordinariness.

An Extraordinary Composition

The world's first Islamic book to reach print at the behest of a Muslim author was probably produced in China, in the first half of the seventeenth century. It is difficult to assign this transformative moment to a particular book, because it occurred at an extraordinary time in the history of Islamic China: in the 1630s and 1640s, at least four different authors wrote Islamic works in Chinese. After eight centuries during which none of China's Muslims seems to have written a sustained treatment of their faith in the Chinese language, a half dozen texts suddenly appear in the historical record. As the very late appearance of Arabic-script printing in China suggests, composition in the Chinese language seems to have been a key factor in Islamic texts jumping from manuscript to print.

The authors who produced these first Chinese-language works took widely varying approaches. There was a four-page explanation of the Islamic profession of faith, *Explanation of the Kalima* (*Kelimo jie* 克理默解).[6] A man named Zhang Xin 張忻 compiled knowledge about Muslim-majority lands across Asia in his *Investigation of Islam*.[7] An undated text called *Avoiding Perplexity about the Real Origin* (*Sheng mi zhenyuan* 省迷眞原) provided an overview of Islamic cosmology, history, and ritual duties.[8] Most famously, Wang Daiyu produced three polemical works arguing that Islam is at once compatible with Confucian teachings and ultimately superior to them.

Which of these works was first, and which was first to appear in print, is unclear. Several have dated prefaces or postfaces from the 1630s or 1640s, but none have clear publication dates. Two of them are known only from late nineteenth or early twentieth-century editions. Some may have circulated only in manuscript form.

Whichever of these writers was the world's first Muslim author to send a book to the printer, it is unlikely that he knew it. Printed books in Chinese were widely available in the early seventeenth century, even if none treated Islam. The author would have been unaware of the early interconnections of Islamic sacred texts and printing that had preceded him in other parts of the world. Short, woodblock-printed talismans, though not books, had been produced for centuries in the Middle East.[9] European Christians began printing Islamic books for study soon after Gutenberg's time, notably a Qur'an in 1530. The Jewish Nahmias brothers produced the first printed book in the Ottoman Empire in 1493 (in Hebrew), but the Ottoman emperors prohibited the printing of Islamic texts.[10] At the turn of the seventeenth century, lively manuscript traditions flourished across the Muslim-inhabited parts of Eurasia and Africa, but it seems no Muslim had yet endeavored to print a book.

Among these pioneering authors, the one we can be most certain was *not* the first to write Islamic texts in Chinese is the most famous, Wang Daiyu. That is because Wang criticized two of the other works in his *Real Commentary on the True Teaching* (*Zhengjiao zhenquan* 正教眞詮), published in 1642 or shortly thereafter.[11] However, Wang is the only author we can be certain used print to disseminate his work. That is because first-edition copies of his *Real Commentary on the True Teaching* have survived.[12]

For Wang, the woodblock technology he used to disseminate his book would have been unremarkable. By the time his book went to press, Wang had read countless printed Chinese books across the Daoist, Buddhist, and Confucian canons. He lived amid one of China's explosions of printing, during which books became even more accessible than they had been in the earlier printing boom of the eleventh and twelfth centuries. Wang had also read numerous Persian and Arabic Islamic books in manuscript form. He never mentioned the technological chasm between the Chinese and Perso-Arabic realms of knowledge production. This gap, as we have seen in Chapter 2, would persist in China for two centuries and have strong effects on both the academic study of Islamic China and on Chinese Islams themselves. After Wang's book, the printing of Islamic texts in Chinese became common, while the publication of Arabic and Persian texts in China continued in manuscript form.

Although Wang was silent on printing, he did have something to say about writing in Chinese and about writing Islamic philosophy for audiences steeped in Daoist, Buddhist, and Confucian thought. This is another sense in which his books stand out from the other texts of his time: Wang self-consciously understood his work as extraordinary, and he explicitly addressed the issue, justifying both the fact of his writing and the novel approaches he adopted. Answering a question about his use of Buddhist and Daoist expressions, he said:

> There is nothing lacking in the classical canon of Islam [清真], but there is no one outside the teaching [i.e., outside of Islam] who knows this. This is because our languages [文字] are different. I wrote and discussed using these [Buddhist and Daoist] expressions precisely to make our teachings comprehensive. All the borrowed expressions I used were because of my concern to show how the principles work. The expressions do not carry the same meaning, but if I had not bor-

> rowed them, how could I make clear that these two doctrines [Buddhism and Daoism] are different from ours?[13]

Wang is gesturing here to the extraordinary nature of his project, explaining Islam in written Chinese, with only a handful of contemporary authors to offer precedents, all of them working in different genres. As Wang suggests, the task was difficult. In Classical Chinese there were no words for crucial Islamic concepts, including "prophet," "angel," or, for that matter, "Islam." As a nonphonetic script, Chinese is notoriously poorly suited to transliteration, and in any case using foreign terms would probably have worked against Wang's goals. For "prophet," he settled on "Ultimate Sage" (*zhi sheng* 至聖), parting ways with the earlier *Avoiding Perplexity About the Real Origin,* which used simply "sage" (聖人). For "Islam" he chose the "Pure and True" (*qing zhen* 清真), a term that is absent from *Avoiding Perplexity* but central to *Investigating Islam.*[14] No one has yet undertaken a comprehensive study of Sino-Islamic terminology's historical development, but a brief comparison of early works shows that much of this vocabulary was in flux when Wang and his contemporaries pioneered Islamic writing in Chinese. Their specialized lexicon would grow over the succeeding centuries, eventually flowering into to a whole genre of bilingual Chinese-Arabic Islamic dictionaries.[15]

In an autobiographical preface, Wang explains his purpose in writing the *Real Commentary:*

> Sometimes I met with scholars face to face, and many discussions sprouted from that. They usually did not compete with me in my reasoning. The gentlemen who were gladly convinced all regretted that they had no ability to read the books of the true teaching [Islam]. . . . Someone also said that the books of Islam are seldom seen by Confucians. My book is incomplete, so perhaps later scholars of noble aspiration will add to it, expanding on the teachings and going further. So I will probably be the opener of the field. Just as my ancestor gained the pleasure of the sage ruler by editing and correcting astronomy, perhaps I, though I lack in eloquence, may be able to open up and put forth the Ultimate Way [Islam].[16]

But what led Wang Daiyu to debate with non-Muslims in the first place? Why would Wang knowingly set out to write an extraordinary book, becoming "the opener of the field," rather than an ordinary book that, through its mastery of the inconspicuous, could place Wang within the unconsidered norms of his environment? Here it is useful to turn to the opening sentence of the book: "My ancestor was a native of Tianfang [Arabia, the Heavenly Abode]." Wang provides a short account of his ancestor's arrival in China and service to the emperor, concluding, "For three hundred years my ancestors became habituated to the customs of this land. I trace back the roots and investigate the origins so that I will not venture to forget about them."[17] This last sentence is not as tautological as it first appears, and we will return to it below. But Wang continues:

> I did not study the Confucian learning at a young age. By the time I became an adult, I could read the language [Classical Chinese] only roughly, no more than for purposes of social intercourse and letter writing. When I reached the prime of life I was ashamed of my simple and rustic knowledge. I began to read the books on Nature and Principle and the histories, reading widely in the writings of the scholars of the various schools. When I penetrated a little into the general meaning of those books, I became aware that their arguments are strange and their ways different and mutually contradictory. If I measure them in terms of Islam, the differences and distinctions are like those between heaven and earth. Regardless of my own ability, I dared use my words to clarify the utmost principle.[18]

In short, Wang Daiyu was troubled first by his outsider status, his "simple and rustic knowledge" among the elites of his age. Wang was trained in Persian and Arabic scholarship, reading the Qur'an, *hadith,* and mystical philosophical texts, but when he found himself in "the prime of life" he could not engage the philosophical and religious traditions that governed the wider society in which he lived. Then, upon mastering non-Islamic scholarly discourse, he was struck by the gap between his worldview and those of the scholars he respected. As so often happens when belief systems meet, the gap appeared to him as the clear superiority of his own tradition.

There is some disagreement about whom Wang intended as his audience. Sachiko Murata, whose excellent translation I have used in the quotations above, believes that "Wang was addressing Chinese-speaking Muslims of the seventeenth century." In the text, Wang only ever explicitly addresses *non*-Muslims, often in answers to their hypothetical or reported questions. Murata points out that the text is often highly polemical, a fact that she says makes sense because Wang is "not engaged in an outward dialogue with representatives of other traditions."[19] Her argument is that a work actually designed to convince outsiders would not be so aggressively polemical. Certainly, it is plausible that Wang hoped his text would be of value to Chinese-speaking Muslims, perhaps strengthening their faith in the face of competing philosophies, or even arming them for disputation with followers of those traditions. Indeed, in the succeeding centuries, Wang's work has been read far more widely by Muslims than non-Muslims, and it came to be seen itself as a "classic," the earliest work in what grew into a large body of Chinese-language Islamic texts.

However, I am more inclined than Murata to take Wang at his word when he says he is giving access to Islam for people outside of the faith. He laments that adherents to other teachings have limited access to books about Islam. He tells us that he discussed with non-Muslim scholars and bested them with his arguments. In a later work he quotes extensively from debates he says he had with Buddhists and Daoists.[20] Perhaps we need not doubt Wang when he tells us that he tried to convince non-Muslims of the superiority of his philosophy, Islam, and that this book was a part of that project. Polemic was not uncommon in late-Ming philosophical writing, and it was a prominent element of the tensions between various schools even within Confucianism, not just between the "Three Teachings" of Confucianism, Daoism, and Buddhism.

Nor was an attempt to convert people through argument an unthinkable task for a Chinese Muslim in the seventeenth century. Reliable biographical information on Wang is scarce, but we know that later in the same century the Chinese Muslim author Ma Zhu invested considerable time and effort to get the Qing emperor to read his own polemic on the superiority of Islam and its compatibility with Confucianism. This episode is perhaps our best concrete evidence for authorial action, as opposed to just words, that indicates a seventeenth-century Chinese Muslim's intended readership.[21] Wang Daiyu himself also valued the emperor's stamp of approval, boasting that "the Emperor's heart rejoiced and thought that if my ancestor had not received a real transmission of a true learning, he could not have reached this level."[22]

In any case, Wang likely had multiple goals and thus multiple audiences in mind. These goals may have included convincing non-Muslims to take up his philosophy (Islam), gaining respect for his faith among the

Confucian scholars who controlled so much of life in China, shoring up the faith of Chinese-literate Muslims (a much smaller group of people), and equipping his fellow Muslims to defend their faith, not to mention promoting his own standing within both Muslim and non-Muslim scholarly circles. What unites these goals is an effort to address the place of Muslims in Chinese society, with their local rootedness and distant attachments, along with Wang's own sense of outsider status. He knew what it meant to be highly educated (in Perso-Arabic thought) and still regarded as "rustic and simple." He responded with an extraordinary book, one that had a profound effect on Chinese-speaking Muslims in the ensuing centuries.

The Origin of the Universe

Wang's book made a double argument: Islam does not diverge from the values and ideas of Confucianism, and Islam is superior to Confucianism. More precisely, he suggested that, for those questions that Confucian thinkers have addressed, Islam is the same as Confucianism: "The way of Confucius and Mencius for cultivating the body, regulating the family, and governing the country is the same as our way."[23] But Wang believed that "our way," Islam, held a trump card: It fully explained the origins of existence. The Confucian thought that prevailed in Wang's time emerged from a great rethinking of ancient philosophy in the Song period (960–1279 CE), known today as Neo-Confucianism. One of its chief concerns was a question that Confucius never thought to address: the nature of the universe, of existence, which it ascribed to the interplay of principle, *li,* and energy, *qi.* However, the origin of these forces was discussed only briefly and, to Wang's mind, unconvincingly. Worse, the Confucians' lack of interest led to neglect of the Creator: "When we look at other teachings, all disavow the root and forget the fountainhead [源]."[24] Wang explained in an introductory passage that his book would only discuss what was different about Islam. More than anything else, for Wang, that was the question of origins.

Islam's clear and detailed account of the Creator and the origins of the universe was in Wang's view indispensable. How could the Confucians understand the nature or essence of anything without understanding its origin? He was similarly frustrated by the Buddhists, saying, "For all the questions they are asked, they have answers, but not for this one question, which inquires after the root and thoroughly investigates the fountainhead.

Responding to it is truly difficult. Their answer is elaborate, but in fact it is a forced explanation, not letting people ask again."[25]

Words for origin (*yuan* 元, *yuan* 原, *yuan* 源, *benlai* 本來) appear over two hundred times in the book. Related terms, such as root (*gen* 根, *ben* 本) and beginning (*shi* 始, *chu* 初), expand the count substantially. While Wang devotes a great deal of text to the act of creation, the uncreated Creator, and the metaphysical implications of these ideas, his presentation of other aspects of Islamic faith is also suffused throughout with references to origins.

Consider, for example, his explanation of the five pillars of Islam, normally summarized in English today as the profession of faith (*shahāda*), daily prayer (*ṣalāh*), almsgiving (*zakāh*), fasting during Ramadan (*ṣawm*), and pilgrimage (*ḥajj*). Wang presents these both as practical duties of Muslims and divine commands whose esoteric meanings give us clues to the nature of the universe. The profession of faith he calls "remembrance" (念), and he summarizes it thus: "When drinking water, you must think of the fountainhead and not forget the root. This is the humaneness of recalling and remembering the true teaching."[26] The duty of remembrance extends to the historical and genealogical heritage of the community and family: "Remembrance means to remember going home to one's homeland and to long for and look to Islam. Forgetting means to forget the memory of one's native place and to rebel against and disobey the original beginning."[27] In this light, Wang's explanation for beginning the book by discussing his ancestor—"I trace back the roots and investigate the origins so that I will not venture to forget about them"—looks less like a tautology and more like a religious duty. In the first pillar of Islam, two types of origin consciousness are folded upon each other: the origins of existence and the origins of one's own people. A vigilant consciousness of origins, a constant remembrance, is a command of God and a crucial act of devotion, extending even to one's own lineage.

Wang's emphasis on family origins was shared by many non-Muslims of his day, even if his interest in cosmological origins was not. But the non-Muslim reasons for knowing family origins were different. The foundational Neo-Confucian thinker Zhu Xi was often quoted in family genealogies, saying "if a family genealogy is not compiled within three generations, the descendants are considered to be unfilial."[28] Non-Muslim genealogical prefaces frequently provided explicit justifications for their endeavors, sometimes using language very similar to Wang's. A preface from the tenth or eleventh century, cited in Michael Szonyi's study of genealogies, writes of the compiler that "he wished to be able to distinguish close from distant relatives, and encourage the members of the lineage to do so as well. This can be called knowing one's roots and extending back to one's origins."[29] Here, the tracing of roots is aimed at regulating relationships between clan members and providing the information needed to fulfill filial duties. It is a common sentiment, even a cliché, among genealogies of the Song through Qing periods. A second commonly cited purpose, usually mentioned alongside the first, is the unification of clans. In these works, the origin refers to the creation or adoption of the clan surname. They are practical tools for maintaining lineage solidarity and encouraging proper filiality.[30] By contrast, Wang Daiyu's Islamic origin discourse frames the remembrance of family origins as a subset of remembrance of the origins of creation (i.e., God). Nonetheless, the non-Muslim genealogies may have provided Wang with language for his ideas.

Wang's fixation on origins is not exactly reflected in the broader Perso-Arabic intellectual tradition that China's Muslims inherited. There existed in both Arabic and Persian a genre (or at least a frequently borrowed book title) called "origin and return" (*al-mabda' wa al-ma'ād*).[31] A work that includes this phrase in its title is one of the main sources Wang refers to in his work: Najm al-Dīn Rāzī's (d. 1256 CE) *Mirṣād al-ʿibād min al-mabdaʿ ila al-maʿād.* But in view of the broad sweep of Islamic knowledge production, in which such discourses on origin ultimately occupy a limited role, Wang's choice to focus on origins when explaining his faith is not an obvious one. Rāzī, for example, despite placing origin and return in the title of his book, devotes very little space to the metaphysical origin question Wang weaves throughout his book.[32]

In much of Islamic writing outside of China, origin, while important, is not an obsession. Creation is central, philosophically, but usually not in need of much discussion, because it is agreed upon, presumed.[33] In the Chinese context, on the other hand, the basic underlying shared assumptions of so much Islamic debate appear extraordinary. No wonder Wang felt so frequently tongue-tied. Origins then rise to the forefront of philosophical and spiritual discussion.

Wang's prediction that he would be "the opener of the field" was correct to a great extent, though it elided the contributions of the two Islamic books in Chinese he cited and criticized. His book opened a path for many later Islamic books printed in the Chinese language. Soon after it appeared, other scholars published Chinese translations of Persian-language Islamic texts that were circulating in manuscript form. And in 1683, a scholar from Yunnan named Ma Zhu followed in Wang's footsteps and published an original composition explaining and defending Islam in Chinese. In his massive *Compass of Islam* (*Qingzhen zhinan* 清真指南), Ma Zhu offered his own version of Wang's origins argument. Wang and Ma would come to be seen, along with the slightly later Liu Zhi, as the three greatest luminaries of Chinese-language Islamic writing.

Wang's linking of origins, identity, and religious duty casts new light on the origin story we encountered in Chapter 1, in which Ma Lianyuan begins his farewell discourse with an account of his family origins. Ma's given name, Lianyuan 聯元, "connecting to the origin," likely reflects the duty of origin seeking and the outlook of his father, a cleric and scholar. At maturity Ma Lianyuan took as his courtesy name another origin-themed pair of characters, Zhiben 至本, which appeared on most of his books and means "reaching the root" or "ultimate origin."[34] His teacher Ma Dexin 德新 took the courtesy name Fuchu 復初, or "returning to the beginning." If we assume continuity between the writings of Wang Daiyu and Ma Lianyuan—and Ma's deep education in the Chinese-language Islamic theological tradition suggests we can—then Ma's engagement with origins should also be read as an intertwining of identity, religious duty, and metaphysics, one that suffused his many ordinary books.

A Claim to an Extraordinary Book

The inscription on the urn at Sirhind, with which Chapter 1 opened, leads us to our second extraordinary book. The inscription cites the Mingde mosque, named after an influential twentieth-century cleric, Qi Mingde (祁明德, scripture name Kamāl al-Dīn, 1898–1987), better known as the "Deaf Cleric" (Long Ahong 聾阿訇). Qi Mingde's eponymous mosque is in the town of Linxia, near the northeastern edge of the Tibetan Plateau, along the mountainous border of the Gansu and Qinghai provinces. The altitude is just high enough that in summer the evening air is cool, luring out diners, shoppers, and elderly men who sit outside to watch them walk by. Chinese is the most common language, but one might also catch the sounds of Dongxiang (a Mongolic language), Salar (a Turkic language), or Amdo Tibetan.

Anyone in China who has heard of Linxia can tell you that it lies in "the Northwest," though very few know that it is closer to the eastern coast of the People's Republic than to its western border. For most of China's history, this region was indeed a western borderland, but in the seventeenth and eighteenth centuries the Qing Empire annexed the enormous regions of Tibet and Eastern Turkistan. The People's Republic of China laid claim to that imperial heritage and eventually asserted control over both regions. They now constitute nearly 40 percent of the country's landmass, divided between several provinces and regions to the west of Linxia. By virtue of this colonial inheritance, Linxia, a quintessential "Northwest" town, now sits sixteen kilometers from a mountain that China's state media once called "the geographic center of China."[35]

Today Linxia is widely known as China's "Little Mecca" (中国小麦加),[36] positioning the town not just at the geographical center of the Chinese nation-state but also at the spiritual center of Islamic China. A remarkable diversity of Islamic communities maintains footholds in Linxia, representing most of Islamic China's sectarian landscape. Two of those communities, the Khufiyya and Qadiriyya orders, locate their founders' graves in Linxia, and these sites draw pilgrims from across sectarian identity groups.

At many points over the last three centuries, this diversity of Islamic denominations in Linxia has been reflected in conflict. In his own lifetime, Qi Mingde played a prominent role in defending against powerful, sometimes violent, attacks from reform movements that deemed his religious beliefs corrupted. In the 1930s, Linxia fell under the control of a Muslim general who supported Yihewani and Salafi reformists engaged in their own uncompromising pursuit of origins. They sought to return to Islam's earliest texts and shed intervening religious thought, which they saw as corrupting accretions. The state supported the replacement of long-standing imams in Linxia with Yihewani and Salafi imams. Thus empowered, the reformists pressed to uproot both the traditionalist Muslims known as Gedimu and the various Sufi orders, or *menhuan,* even attacking the sacred tomb-shrines of the orders' founders. Qi Mingde responded by engaging reformist leaders in public debate, quoting scripture and scholarship to refute their claims and keep a foothold for the forms of Islam that preceded the reformists.

When Qi Mingde died in the spring of 1987, seven years after founding the mosque that bears his name, he left several unpublished writings in Chinese. These texts, edited and published in 1996 as *Long Ahong* (The Deaf Cleric), outline the history of what Qi called the "correct transmission," or orthodoxy of Islam, with a focus on his own patrilineal descent from a line of Islamic scholars.[37] Much of the collection describes his struggles against the fundamentalist reform movements, which Qi names as Wahhabi, Ikhwani, and Salafi. But the authority that permitted Qi to represent the "old teaching" against these reformers is rooted in earlier events, including Qi's claims that his family transmitted an extraordinary book to China's "Little Mecca." That book was Aḥmad Sirhindī's most famous work, *Maktūbāt* (The [collected] letters). Qi's family history actually makes two claims of transmission of the *Maktūbāt,* one by bringing a copy of the original Persian text to Linxia, and a second, two centuries later, by arranging the publication of an Arabic translation. In both cases, an ancestor's receipt of the physical book is not just an acquisition of knowledge but a ritual bestowing authority.[38]

More generally, Qi's writings ground his authority both in his education—he had studied in Mecca, among other places, and was said to be a master of Islamic scholarship in Arabic and Persian—and in his lineage. Lineage claims remain a common source of religious legitimacy, and thus also of disputes, among both Sufi and non-Sufi Muslim scholars throughout China. In some cases, lineage-based claims are rooted in chains of teachers and students, but they are very commonly based also on blood lineage, with each link in the chain simultaneously representing both a father-son and teacher-student relationship. Qi's lineage followed this latter pattern. Today his family name denotes a neighborhood in Linxia, in addition to eponymous mosques. But not all ancestors are great figures. For lineage to bolster authority, one needs ancestors with authority. The Qi family makes no claim of descent from the prophet. Instead, it is the special relationship to the *Maktūbāt,* and the implied transmission of authority from the foreign holy men who bestowed the book upon them, that makes the Qi ancestors sources of authority.

Qi traces the first transmission to his ancestor Ibrāhīm Sunnī Qi Xinyi (祁信一; 1651–1742), whom the text describes as follows. Ibrāhīm completed his elementary religious studies in Linxia and then traveled to Yunnan to undertake advanced study with a teacher called Ḥajjī Yaʿqūb. There, he mastered Persian and Arabic. After completing his studies and receiving the robe and turban of a scholar (*ahong*), Ibrāhīm returned to Linxia and founded a mosque, known by his Chinese surname, Qi.[39] His reputation grew, and eventually followers in the neighboring province of Sichuan invited him to found a mosque there, where he taught until 1672.

Qi Mingde's recounting places his ancestor at a pivotal time and place for the history of organized Sufism in China. The two earliest of the "four *menhuans*" (Sufi orders) trace their origins to the arrival of foreign masters in the "Northwest" during the late seventeenth century: the Qadiriyya and the Khufiyya. Both of these outsiders—one from Arabia (purportedly) and the other from Central Asia—traveled and preached in Gansu and Qinghai, one in the 1660s and the other in the 1670s. In both cases the news of their presence spread widely, and local Muslim scholars traveled to find them and learn at their feet. Among those local seekers were the founder of the Khufiyya, whose tomb in Linxia is known as the Huasi shrine, and the founder of China's Qadiriyya, also buried in Linxia. Thus, key elements of Linxia's religious landscape took shape in Ibrāhīm Qi Xinyi's lifetime.

Ancestor Ibrāhīm is said to have learned at the feet of the Central Asian Sufi master named Afaq Khoja.[40] Afaq is perhaps best known in the English-speaking world for his role in the history of the Uyghur people—the indigenous, Turkic-speaking inhabitants of the region known variously as Eastern Turkistan, Altishahr, or Xinjiang. To many Uyghurs today, Afaq Khoja was a traitor who opened the doors to China's colonization of the Uyghur homeland. But in "Little Mecca," Afaq Khoja is better known as a twenty-fifth-generation descendant of the prophet, who brought the correct teaching of Islam to China. Qi Mingde claimed that Afaq bestowed a physical copy of the *Maktūbāt* upon his ancestor Ibrāhīm and gave with it the formal permission (*ijaza*) to teach the book.

Qi Mingde's story of the presentation of the *Maktūbāt* to his ancestor is in one way consistent with what we know from older historical sources about Afaq Khoja, but in another it is at odds with those sources. Afaq Khoja (d. 1694), along with his father, Muḥammad Yūsuf, is widely credited with transmitting Naqshbandi Sufism to Gansu and Qinghai. Nineteenth-century Turki- and Persian-language hagiographies written in Eastern Turkistan by followers of Afaq Khoja repeatedly depict the bestowal of a book as part of Afaq's ritual for designating *khalifas,* followers who are licensed to transmit his teaching and authority.[41] However, in these Afaqi manuscripts the book presented is not the *Maktūbāt* but instead Rumi's

Masnavi.[42] It appears from this that the Qi lineage inserted the *Maktūbāt* into the widely known tradition of Afāq's Naqshbandī missionizing at some later point.

Qi Mingde's narrative skips over the life stories of the succeeding seven generations of Ibrāhīm's descendants, merely listing their names, before picking up the narrative thread again with his father, Yūsuf Qi Huantang (祁焕堂 1852–1933), the ninth-generation descendant of Ibrāhīm. After a few lines outlining Qi Huantang's deep education and pilgrimages to Mecca, the narrative turns to his study with a descendant of "Yimamu Ranbani" (伊玛目 冉巴尼), a title of Aḥmad Sirhindī, as well as Qi's purportedly central role in facilitating the translation of the *Maktūbāt* from Persian into Arabic. At the age of forty-three, Qi Huantang learned that a certain "Mulaji Afanji" (穆拉吉阿凡吉, Murad Effendi),[43] a descendant of Yimamu Ranbani, was visiting Eastern Turkistan (by this time part of the Qing Empire) from "Central Asia." As his ancestor had done, Qi Huantang walked to Eastern Turkistan and found the teacher he was seeking. Mulaji Afanji gave Qi Huantang copies of *Rashāḥat* and *Tafsīr Husaynī,* both in Persian. Qi Huantang told Mulaji Afanji the story of his ancestor receiving the *Maktūbāt* from Afaq Khoja. The teacher was impressed and "praised the ancestor's *Dao* [way, *ṭarīqat*], saying: he attained the Dao early, was of high quality, and successfully sought the Faith—it is a true rarity."

Qi Huantang then pleaded with Mulaji Afanji to translate the *Maktūbāt,* "which his [Qi's] family had kept for nine generations," from the original Persian into Arabic. Mulaji Afanji replied that he would need the permission of his master. Qi Huantang traveled with Mulaji Afanji to "Indonesia" to meet the master, identified as Zewawei (则瓦为), who in turn said he could not permit the translation without permission from his own master in Mecca, Haimiji Afanji (海米吉 阿凡吉). The two then went with Zewawei to Mecca, where Haimiji Afanji gave approval for the translation. The group then visited "Shaykh Maʿsum of the Khāfiyya order," who informed them that they would need the king's permission to publish the book. This they obtained, and the translation was published in 1316 AH (1898–1899 CE).

The interaction between Qi Huantang and Mulaji Afanji follows the pattern of the earlier ancestor and Afaq Khoja in a general way, lending authority to the lineage through pilgrimage to a master in Eastern Turkistan. However, it is not quite as momentous: Mulaji Afanji gives books to Qi

Huantang, but he does not give an *ijaza*. There is no clear bestowal of formal authority, though the narrative clearly presents Mulaji Afanji as an authoritative shaykh and purported descendant of Sirhindī, whose praise of Qi Huantang is a credit to the lineage.

The details in this story are numerous and precise enough to locate the historical figures involved. Zewawei must refer to Abdallah al-Zawāwī, a Meccan *sayyid* who traveled widely and resided for some time in Pontianak, Borneo, during the 1890s. Before his exile from Mecca, Zawāwī, along with his father, had already transmitted the Naqshbandī Mujaddidī path to a large number of Muslims of the Dutch East Indies. The reference to a Mujaddidī shaykh by the name of Zawāwī residing in what would come to be known as Indonesia thus indicates that the narrator had specific knowledge of Mujaddidī networks in the late nineteenth century. This level of accuracy also suggests that, despite the errors in other parts of the narrative, notably the presentation of Afaq Khoja as a Mujaddidī, Qi Huantang probably did visit Indonesia on the way to Mecca.

There is only one historical figure who fits the description of Mulaji Afanji: a translator of the *Maktūbāt,* student of Zawāwī, and visitor to Eastern Turkistan. This was Muḥammad Murād Ramzī al-Qazāni al-Manzilāwī (1855–1934 / 1935), a well-known and well-traveled scholar from Tatarstan, at that time part of the Russian Empire. Manzilāwī studied in Bukhara, spent many years in Mecca, where he studied under Mujaddidī masters, and spent the final fifteen years of his life teaching in Chuguchak, in Eastern Turkistan. Manzilāwī's translation of the Maktūbāt was the first into Arabic, and to this day it has not been superseded. Notably, Manzilāwī also translated *Rasḥāhat ʿayn al-ḥayāt,* one of the books he supposedly presented to Qi Huantang.

What is known of Manzilāwī's biography presents some chronological problems for the account in *Long Ahong.*[44] It is likely that the *Long Ahong* narrative conflates separate incidents in the biography of Qi Huantang, as Qi made multiple pilgrimages to Mecca. By connecting the meeting with Manzilāwī to the translation of the *Maktūbāt,* the narrative squeezes the historical material into the common Hui Sufi trope of an ancestor meeting and receiving authority from a foreign Sufi master, while at the same time giving the Qi lineage further claims to a second special connection to the *Maktūbāt.*

There is one more important figure to identify from *Long Ahong:* Zewawei's own master in Mecca, Haimiji Afanji. This scholar can only be ʿAbd al-Hamīd al-Shīrwānī al-Dāghistānī, whose role as a teacher of Abdallah al-Zawāwī is well documented.[45] (Ḥamīd is also an excellent fit for the Chinese transliteration Haimiji.) We have, in Chapter 1, already encountered an ʿAbd al-Hamīd who taught the Naqshbandi path in Mecca: ʿAbd al-Hamīd Turkī, who taught *dhikr* to Ma Lianyuan. The *nisba* (name of origin or relation), Shīrwānī, indicates an origin in the town of Shirvan, in today's Azerbaijan, where most of the inhabitants were, in fact, Turkic speakers. Given that there is only one known Naqshbandī shaykh by the name of ʿAbd al-Hamīd who was active in Mecca at the time, the "Haimiji" shaykh that Qi Huantang claimed to have met was almost certainly the same individual who taught Ma Lianyuan.

The receipt of a book from a foreign master serves as a legitimating story in other Sinophone traditions as well. The Xianmen (鲜门) founder is also said to have received books from Afaq Khoja.[46] Ma Laichi, regarded as the founder of the Khāfiyya order, received an Arabic text called *Minshār* from his teacher, Shaykh "Aqil" in the Yemen, which is central to the identity and rituals of the order.[47] And the Jahriyya founder, Ma Mingxin, is said to have brought back from Yemen *Mukhammas* and *Madaʿih,* the two central texts upon which the Jahriyya have elaborated their distinctive rituals.[48]

The Qi lineage tradition presents the extraordinary book as a powerful force. the *Maktūbāt* was and is venerated across most of the sects that hold sway in Linxia, including the Ikhwanis whom the Deaf Cleric fought so persistently.[49] The claim to a special copy of the book and the transmission from foreign Muslims that it represented may very well have bolstered the lineage's influence. But the extraordinary book wielded its own influence. As we will see in Chapter 6, the Qi lineage investment in the *Maktūbāt* ultimately brought the Deaf Cleric's son back to India and a full embrace of the Mujaddidī identity—and with him his community of followers. The story of the Qi lineage suggests that this kind of extraordinary book always holds within it the potential for reconnection to distant communities, and with it a course change in community identity and practice.

Conclusion

In Chapter 1 we saw how phenomena that look extraordinary from a distance can appear ordinary at the local level. It may seem surprising from afar that Ma Lianyuan, proficient commentator in the Confucian-tinged

Sinophone Islamic tradition, could be the same person as Nūr al-Haqq, an expert in Arabic legal texts. But in his own local context Ma had achieved ordinariness, even if it was marked by a certain scholarly excellence. Ma lived, wrote, taught, and published in a region with a large population of fellow Muslims, including countless Muslim-majority villages. He achieved high status in this community, and he endeavored to return it to its prewar religious affluence, to reinstate norms in which cultivated adult men could navigate Arabic legal treatises, Persian faith handbooks, and perhaps some Chinese philosophy. None of them needed the kind of explanation or justification that Wang Daiyu offered in his work. As Ma departed Yunnan for the second and final time, he expressed some misgivings, but in his home region his place was secure; his excellence in the normative was a model for others.

When, on the other hand, Muslims in China have felt the need for something extraordinary to justify their place in the local community, they have often reached for origin stories of one kind or another. At the Sufi tomb in Qinghai's Haidong Prefecture, they prove their connection to authoritative origins with a physical book, not to be touched by nonbelievers, which they explicitly name as a license to transmit the true teachings. The Deaf Cleric reports his ancestors' receipt of similarly transformative book transmissions, as do many Sufi orders. In every case these books are extraordinary for their powers to connect people with holy men and scholars who curate the true teaching. They also share a more mundane characteristic: They are all books composed outside of China proper. This centrality of foreign texts testifies to a shared feature of nearly all Chinese Muslim origin stories: They trace community roots to places outside China.

On the opposite end of China, Wang Daiyu faced a very different situation. There, in Nanjing, where Muslims were a minority, Wang labored to justify his tradition to the outsiders (from his perspective) who dominated the politics and culture of the region: non-Muslim Chinese. To do so, he too appealed to the authority of his ancestors, but he went further, claiming that his tradition had the keys to the origin of the universe. To present these arguments to people outside of his community, Wang was forced to abandon the established genres of his community, to be an "opener of the field." In doing so he began his text with family history, noting his own ties to a foreign land.

Chapters 4 and 5 address phenomena that these extraordinary books (in the eyes of their authors and readers) show to be powerful historical forces across Muslim communities in China. One of these is the deep concern for origins, which ties stories of community or family origins to authoritative knowledge of the ultimate origin, God. We will return to this topic in Chapter 5. But, first, we turn to another phenomenon that we have seen in these extraordinary books: pervasive and self-conscious connection to the world outside China. In order to better understand this phenomenon, Chapter 4 explores the geography of interconnection as it played out in Muslims' travel, trade, politics, and pilgrimage.

4

The Matrix of the Extraordinary

Inter-Asian Muslim Networks of the Seventeenth Century

THREE CENTURIES before Ma Lianyuan slipped seamlessly into the North Indian world of Islamic publishing, a parallel arrival unfolded at the court of a Mughal ruler. Sometime in the mid- to late 1600s, a scholar from China arrived in Hindustan (modern India / Pakistan). Our lone source for this arrival tells the story as follows. The Hindustani ruler invited the scholar, Wang Mingyu 王明宇, to his court, where he and his courtiers were astonished to find that the Chinese scholar was knowledgeable in the courtly language of Persian, as well as Arabic and Turki. Together they discussed various fields of Islamic learning, including law, Arabic rhetoric, theology, and logic. The ruler asked Wang if he would enter his service as an official, but Wang was on his way to Mecca and politely declined, saying that they could discuss the matter after he completed his pilgrimage.

According to the story, Wang was true to his word and returned to the ruler's court after five years. While there he received a letter from his father-in-law, informing him that his wife in China had died. The ruler commanded his daughter to marry Wang, but soon she too died of an illness. After Wang declined to marry the ruler's second daughter, the ruler instructed him to establish a religious school, where Wang taught thousands of disciples. When the lone account of this event was written (1697 or 1714 CE), Wang still had not returned home to "the East."[1]

The historical source for Wang's travels is vague in its details and shows signs of exaggeration. It does not tell us where in "Hindustan" it took place or what the "ruler's" position was; he may have been a local official.

The manuscript is a "genealogy" of famous Muslim scholars of China, completed in 1714 and incorporating earlier sections completed in 1697.[2] The short biographies that occupy most of its pages often verge on hagiography, but where the figures discussed are known from additional sources, the "genealogy" has proven remarkably reliable. The hagiographical tone is apparent in the account of Wang's travels, where the ruler's regard for Wang is suspiciously excessive. According to the source, the ruler not only married his daughter to Wang, but also sent him off on the Hajj with a retinue of five hundred guards. The latter treatment is not out of line with the hospitality that the Mughal emperor Aurangzib showed to emissaries from foreign courts, but Wang had no connection to any state. And if Wang had not returned to China when the text was written, one has to wonder how the author had so many details about his travels, even if an exchange of letters was possible, as the story claims. Nonetheless, the source shows a solid geographical understanding, and its detailed engagement with a large number of Persian and Arabic texts that circulated in India suggests that the basic premise of the story is likely true, that is, a Chinese scholar did in fact pass through Hindustan and found that his education made intellectual exchange with the local elites not just feasible but rewarding.

The route attributed to Wang was an unusual one for the second half of the seventeenth century. He passed beyond the borders of the Great Qing Empire by a typical route, exiting at the famous Yumen gate in what is today western Gansu. The route must have veered south soon after, because the source tells us Wang was captured in Tibet and forced to live as a servant for two years. He made his escape when he met a visiting Muslim scholar from Egypt, who was revered by the Tibetans as a "living Buddha." The Egyptian requested that he be allowed to take Wang to Egypt as his student. They departed southward into Hindustan, where they parted ways.

The story of Wang's journey highlights the diversity and variability of routes through a geography I will refer to by the archaic name of Serindia. In this chapter we follow the travels of individuals along four of the most common Serindian routes in the period from 1640 to 1680. Wang's route is not among these main roads. Instead, it serves as an example of the vulnerability of individual travel channels to political vicissitudes and the resilience of Serindian networks in the face of that vulnerability. For every typical journey, there were improvised routes. Wang's story also suggests that even sporadic connection—the arrival of a Chinese scholar was, after all, unusual enough to elicit a special invitation from the Mughal official—was sufficient to maintain a shared discourse and shared norms across vast distances separated by alien cultures.

Together, Serindian circulations and the Hajj undergirded both the ordinary and the extraordinary texts of Islamic China. The authors of the extraordinary texts in Chapter 3 attributed their extraordinariness to arrivals from distant lands. The Deaf Cleric grounded his lineage's authority on ancestral meetings with shaykhs beyond the Yumen gate, bearers of books that originated in Hindustan. Wang Daiyu, descendant of foreigners, reappropriated his outsider status by asserting that his tradition had a special connection to the origins of existence, tied as it was to Tianfang, Arabia, the center of the world. But Serindian circulations and Arabian pilgrimage did not only shape extraordinary texts. They lay behind more quotidian efforts, such as Ma Lianyuan's program to resurrect the local Islamic learning of his youth in Yunnan. His project owed much to both the continuous circulations of Serindian trade and the stochastic exchanges of the Hajj. His textbooks, designed for daily use among the largely rural Muslim populace of the Qing Empire's southwestern provinces, were built in part on Siamese indigo and the authority of his discipleship in Mecca. As this chapter will show, these circulations may have accelerated in Ma Lianyuan's day, but they were by no means new. From the moment at which Islamic textual production first becomes visible in China (c. 1640–1690), Serindian interconnection was integral to the continuous negotiation of both the extraordinary and the ordinary.

Serindia

My use of the rare geographical term "Serindia" is intended to call attention to geographical relationships that have been omitted from most histories of China, in no small part due to the lack of attention to Muslims' roles in China over the last thousand years. The term was created after the rediscovery of a lost civilization. The Hungarian-British archaeologist M. Aurel Stein coined the word to describe the cultural geography of Eastern Turkistan during the first millennium CE, when Buddhism had a prominent and sometimes dominant position in the region. Because Eastern Turkistan appeared to Stein's archaeological gaze as a place where the cultures of China and India merged, he created the portmanteau of Seres, a

Latin word for China, and India. But Stein's Serindia was more than just a geography of China and India, because the terrain across which their entanglements stretched included Central Asia, highland Inner Asia, and the sea route around Southeast Asia. Stein's archaeological interests found their chronological limits at the Muslim conquest of the region in the eleventh century, and that is where his application of the geographical neologism ended too.[3] In this chapter I trace a similar though not identical geography by extending the Serindian concept into the period of Islamicization. In doing so I also include territories that had only an implicit presence in Stein's formulation, such as the seas and coasts along the maritime route from India to China, as well as newer (to Muslims) land routes through Southeast Asia that developed alongside the growth of substantial Muslim communities in China and India.

When we think of long-standing exchanges between the South Asian subcontinent and East Asia, perhaps the biggest one, the kind of thing that makes it into world history textbooks, is the transmission of Buddhist traditions in the first millennium CE. What has not penetrated our image of Asian history is the fact that land-based connections between the subcontinent and East Asia did not end with the fading of Buddhist practice in the subcontinent. It turns out that these land-based connections have continued into the present. After the waning of Buddhism, the mobile societies that nurtured these links were often made up of Muslims. And if we look at the body of Islamic texts consumed all over China today, we see the imprint of those South Asian connections on the shape of China's Islamic canons.

In the last decade, Tansen Sen has done important work excavating the significance of China-India connections, much of it summed up in his book *India, China, and the World: A Connected History.* For the Yuan and Ming, Sen centers the maritime exchanges that entered the historical record thanks to state projects dispatching emissaries to South Asia, most famously the missions of Zheng He. From there Sen turns to another important phenomenon in China-India interactions, the arrival of European colonial powers.[4]

In the current chapter I trace a slightly different geography, which has largely managed to slip through the cracks of a rising interest in the history of China-India connection: the interconnections maintained by Muslims in the seventeenth to nineteenth centuries.[5] The following pages show how trade, politics, and cultural forces encouraged Muslims to reproduce the circulations and transmissions of Stein's Serindia. Stein focused on overland connections via Eastern Turkistan and the Tibetan plateau, but the maritime route also figured into the earlier, Buddhist geography of Serindia, as Stein would have been the first to admit. At least two of the Chinese monks who traveled to India in the fourth through seventh centuries CE used sea routes, with Faxian (c. 337–c. 422 CE) traveling overland on the outward journey and returning by the maritime route to China's east coast. Like Stein, I will expend more ink on the overland linkages, partly because they appear more frequently in the sources, and partly because so many accounts of global connection tend to shift toward sea routes from the sixteenth century onward. It is at that time that the Silk Routes are often supposed to have atrophied in the face of rising maritime activity. Debate on that point continues, but it is certain that land routes persisted, and the case of Islamic China's overland circulations shows that they deserve serious attention.

Shared linguistic heritage smoothed the circulation of ideas and people across the Muslim societies of Serindia, be they in coastal China, northern India, Kashmir, or Eastern Turkistan. In each place there were readers of Persian and, perhaps to a lesser extent, of Arabic. The individuals whose stories are outlined below—Zhang Shizhong, Ma Zhu, Afaq Khoja, and Sufis of highland Inner Asia—all engaged and transmitted Persian texts.

The geography of Muslim Serindia overlapped with other geographies and linked to them. Its routes were others' routes, in many cases extending beyond Serindia and drawing in merchants, romances, natural histories, and much more. We have already seen that the intersection of Serindian circulations and the Hajj had powerful effects, with each facilitating the other. But the prominence of India in the Chinese Islamic cultural landscape suggests that attention to the Serindian portion of global interconnection offers its own insights.

Chronology

There is one part of Islamic Serindia's story that has not been forgotten: the voyages of Zheng He, China's most famous Muslim. With a crew that included many fellow Muslims, Zheng He led Ming imperial fleets on several voyages of diplomacy and trade in the early fifteenth century, plying the Indian Ocean all the way to Arabia and East Africa. He was an excellent choice for the admiral to navigate the politics of the Indian Ocean. The merchant ships that sailed that ocean were steered by Muslims, as were many of the most powerful coastal kingdoms that surrounded it. And some of Southeast Asia's Muslims were likely the descendants of fourteenth-century refugees from coastal China.[6] In Mecca, Zheng He and many of his crew members performed the Hajj. Among the many treasures they brought back to Beijing were descriptions of the holy city and a giraffe presented by the Muslim Sultan of Bengal. But these journeys were no acts of exploration. They were the product not of ignorance but of knowledge, an effort to project Chinese power in a region that was already known to Chinese authors and sailors. The selection of a Muslim admiral may very well have been intentional, a reflection of the knowledge that the Indian Ocean world was dominated by people who shared something with the Chinese people known as Huihui.

After the voyages of Zheng He, Islamic Serindia disappears from modern histories of the world. The Ming rulers attempted to close their borders to the outside world, with mixed success. The impact of this isolationist effort on Muslims under Ming rule is difficult to discern from our limited sources. With no state-sponsored voyages, Muslim travelers were less likely to appear in the state-dominated sources. And without the Islamic publishing that would appear in the mid-seventeenth century, we are left with few Muslim sources beyond tombstones and mosque inscriptions. Our only substantial Chinese account of Muslim engagement with the wider Serindian world for this period comes much later, in the same source that reported Wang Mingyu's adventures in Hindustan. It tells us that the seminal Muslim teacher Hu Dengzhou made the pilgrimage to Mecca in the mid-1500s. It has been assumed that Ming China's Muslims were "cut off in terms of contact with the Islamic world," but there is as little concrete evidence for this as there is for continued connectivity.[7] The question of whether and how much Muslim circulation across the Ming borders was curtailed will have to await further research, and it may well depend on increased source availability. But this question falls outside the chronological scope of the present book.

It was in the middle of the seventeenth century that Chinese Muslims began producing printed books discussing their communities and their beliefs. This shift, described in more detail in Chapter 8, has bequeathed to historians a rupture in the historical record. Before Chinese Muslims' adoption of printing, we have only the most limited evidence of what members of the community thought about their place in the mundane and spiritual worlds. Before the seventeenth century they were producing manuscripts in Arabic, Persian, and Chinese, but to date vanishingly few surviving specimens have been documented, much less become available to researchers, with the exception of Qur'an copies. Inscriptions in all three languages survive on grave markers and a handful of commemorative steles at mosques, testifying to the flourishing of Muslim communities, but these short texts give a very limited window on the thought-worlds of Islamic China.

With the adoption of printing, Chinese Muslims were able to reproduce long texts in numbers large enough to ensure substantial survival into the present. As a result, the historical record of Islamic China lurches from the sparse and laconic at the end of the sixteenth century to dense and prolix by the second half of the seventeenth century. At this moment, the cultural effects of Serindian circulations on Chinese Muslims suddenly come into historical view.

Interestingly, this moment of textual florescence coincided with the chaos of dynastic change as the Ming Empire crumbled. In moments of dynastic transition, borderlands take on new roles. Challenges to new dynastic powers—not just rebellions but also attempted restorations—frequently operate from the borderlands. As would-be successors to the throne of the crumbling dynasty take refuge beyond the reach of upstarts in the capital, center and periphery become inverted. The core of the Chinese polity, in our case the Ming court, finds refuge in the periphery, and cosmopolitan machinations become entwined with the zones that lie between empires. The exiled court participates in these in-between societies not as a distant would-be overlord but as a naive new local player. The lives explored here show that Muslims, who were frequently found among the borderland brokers of Chinese empires, were often caught up in the high-stakes machinations of dynastic change. This interesting phenomenon, however, is incidental to the chronological delimitation of this chapter. Here, the period of c. 1640–1690 is most important for showing that, at the moment when a rich source base for Muslim communities in China first appears, Serindian entanglements are extensive and significant.

The Maritime Route to India

In the waning years of the Ming dynasty, a mystic from India appeared at the empire's auxiliary capital, Nanjing. He had been wandering for thirteen years. The locals dismissed him as an uncivilized monk, but, for reasons lost to history, he chose to settle in the city. Sometime around 1640, a local Islamic scholar recognized that the Indian wanderer was a Sufi sage. One of that local scholar's students,[8] Zhang Shizhong 張時中, would spend three years as a disciple of the Indian master. Zhang's writings call him simply ʿĀshiq (Ashige 阿世格), Arabic for "lover," a name that reflects the Sufi love of the Real, the all-encompassing truth that is God.[9]

Zhang kept a written record of ʿĀshiq's oral teachings, of which only part survives. His discipleship drew to a close around the time that the Manchus, calling themselves the Qing, were conquering China, pushing southward province by province. Nanjing surrendered in the summer of 1645. According to Zhang, ʿĀshiq managed to "return" (to India) before the transfer of power. Zhang went on to establish himself as a respected Islamic scholar, though he lost many of his records in the disorder that accompanied the Qing conquest. Nonetheless, based on the records that survived he eventually managed to publish ʿĀshiq's discourses on a particular statement of faith, called *Imān-i mujmal.* The introduction to this book, a Chinese-language woodblock edition printed in 1661, is today our only source of biographical data on ʿĀshiq.

The *Primer on Imān-i Mujmal,*[10] more commonly known today by the title *General Meaning of the Return to the True One* (*Gui zhen zongyi 歸真總義*), is a wide-ranging treatise encompassing mystical philosophy, theology, Islamic law, and dogma—an encapsulation of ʿĀshiq's (and Zhang's) understanding of Islam, all arranged as an explication of a single Arabic sentence: "I believe in Allah, as He is known by His names and attributes, and I accept all His commands." This phrase, known as *imān-i mujmal,* is a distinctive form of profession of Islamic faith, common in South Asia and China, but rare elsewhere.[11] Zhang calls the formula the "original classic" (*benjing* 本經), following a tradition common to Chinese philosophical works, in which an older, authoritative text is expounded upon.

In all likelihood, Zhang's record of the Indian master's teaching is the reason for the *imān-i mujmal* formula's continued presence in Chinese Islamic discourse over the succeeding centuries. *Primer on Iman-i Mujmal* was reprinted in 1878, 1908, 1922, and 1932 and given an extensive exegesis in 2016.[12] The formula has been analyzed in a long Arabic treatise on faith by Ma Anyi (馬安義, son of Ma Lianyuan), published in 1905.[13] It remains a staple of basic religious observance among many Muslims in China, appearing in introductory texts and manuals such as *Required Readings for Muslims* (穆斯林必读 *Musilin bidu,* 2011).[14]

Zhang does not tell us where in "India" (*Xindu 欣度*) ʿĀshiq called home or how he reached China (or, more accurately, as Zhang calls it, the "Ming"). Two routes seem most likely: the maritime route from the Indian Ocean to the southeastern coast of China, and the overland route through Burma. It is not impossible that ʿĀshiq's thirteen years of wandering included the long trek from the Burmese border on the empire's far southwestern border. That route is discussed in more detail further below, using the life of Ma Zhu as a point of entry. Nonetheless, the fact that Zhang encountered ʿĀshiq in one of China's most important port cities makes the maritime route a more obvious choice. Zhang's mention of "sailing the sea" among the tribulations ʿĀshiq endured, while not fully conclusive, also weighs in favor of the maritime route to the eastern coast.

The fact that interactions like the one between ʿĀshiq and Zhang were ongoing at the moment sources become plentiful makes it difficult to date the arrival of other South Asian influences that are apparent in the late seventeenth- and early eighteenth-century sources. Notable among these are translations and mentions of books that were staples of South Asian Islamic literature. For any one of these works, we can only speculate as to whether they were recent arrivals of the seventeenth or eighteenth centuries or had been circulating in manuscript form for centuries. For example, *Pillars of Islam,* written by an author called "Dihlāwī" (of Dehli), mentioned in the late seventeenth-century Chinese translation of *Muhimmāt,* and later published in the original Persian by Ma Lianyuan, may have already been present or may have been introduced at this time.

After studying with ʿĀshiq, Zhang published a translation of another work that may have arrived from South Asia, though it was a text popular in both South and Central Asia, another region with which China's Muslims had long-standing ties.[15] This work was the *Chahār faṣl* (The four chapters, also called *Bedān*) a section from a longer text known as *Chahār kitāb* (The four books) or *Kulliyāt.* This also found a lasting readership in

China. The translation was reprinted in 1872, and Ma Lianyuan wrote that the book was "famous in China" when he printed his own edition of the Persian original in 1894.[16]

Neither of the works that Zhang helped introduce to Sinophone Muslims have been seen by China's Muslims as works that need domesticating beyond translation. The texts and the concepts they expounded took on new names, which placed them in conversation with non-Islamic Chinese discourses, such as Confucian thought. *Primer on Imān-i Mujmal* became *General Meaning of the Return to the True One. Chahār faṣl* underwent a more subtle transformation, becoming *Four Chapters on the Essential Way.* The profession of faith known in India as *imān-i mujmal* continues to be used in almost its precise form in China, and the ritual norms of *Essentials* are still taught with little alteration.

The Burma Route

If ʿĀshiq instead took the overland route to China via Burma, he would have passed near the residence of a contemporary, Ma Zhu 馬注, a scholar who would go on to write the influential, Chinese-language *Compass of Islam.* Ma Zhu was one of those elite, state-entangled Muslims who received their education in Classical Chinese, an education aimed at shaping a good Confucian subject and preparing him for the civil service exams. In late Ming China, these exams were the most famous and widely pursued paths to status and wealth for men. In the best of circumstances, an aspiring scholar-official could dream of passing several successive exams, taking him to the county seat, the provincial capital, the imperial capital, and, ultimately, the palace itself.

Ma Zhu rose to an official position in the emperor's court by a more surprising route. He began, like other scholar-officials, with the exams, passing the local tests in the remote region of Southwest Yunnan. He was raised near Baoshan, on the edge of the contested borderland zone where Ming China faded into tributary Shan states and the Burmese kingdom of the Taungoo dynasty. Even for a successful candidate on the local exams, Beijing was as distant as the stars.

But in 1656, the capital came to Ma Zhu. Emperor, courtiers, eunuchs, bureaucrats, generals, and the imperial family all moved to Yunnan, pursued by the invading Manchu-led armies of the Qing. This was the court of the Yongli emperor, a prince from the Ming royal family, around whom resistance to the Qing conquest coalesced in China's Southwest. Ma Zhu joined the relocated Ming bureaucracy, where he was quickly promoted to a high position.

His success as an official was short-lived. Just before the third anniversary of the court's move to Yunnan, Qing armies forced the Yongli court to flee further southward in disarray. By the time the emperor reached Burmese territory, his entourage had been robbed more than once by its own armed escort. The Yongli court eventually found refuge at the Burmese capital, Ava, but never regained control of its remaining military force. In 1661 a new Burmese king took the throne and massacred most of Yongli's officials. In the same year, pursuing Qing armies reached the outskirts of Ava, where the Burmese king delivered to them the captive Yongli emperor.[17]

Specialists in Hui history disagree as to whether Ma Zhu followed the Ming court to Burma or remained in Yunnan.[18] Decades later, in an (auto) biographical chapter of his masterwork, *Compass of Islam,* Ma Zhu (or one of his followers) recorded his rise to Ming officialdom in just a few terse sentences. The author was by that time working under the rule of Qing conquerors, so there would have been no benefit in elaborating on his former loyalty to the Ming emperor. The text leaves his departure from the Ming court vague, merely stating that the Qing conquered Yunnan and he retired to a life of reading, studying, and teaching.[19]

Whether Ma Zhu accompanied the Ming court to Burma or not, borderland flows shaped the community in which he came of age. The Qing pursuit of the Ming armies into Burmese territory was only one episode in a long history of military movements across the Yunnan-Burma region. Nearly four centuries earlier, Naṣr al-Dīn, a Muslim governor of Yunnan under the Mongol Yuan dynasty, invaded the Burmese kingdom of Pagan. The goal was probably to prevent the Chinese Southern Song court from fleeing to Burma as the Ming would do in Ma Zhu's time. The Ming, in its own heyday, and later the Qing, competed with Burma's Toungoo state for influence over tributary Shan and Tai statelets located between them, sometimes escalating disputes to armed conquest. In times of peace, officials visited each other's capitals.

Trade provided a more regular circulation of people and ideas. C. Patterson Giersch has detailed elaborate and robust trade connections across the Qing-Burma frontier, which increased in intensity and complexity across the sixteenth to nineteenth centuries. By the sixteenth century there was a Chinese marketplace called the "Great Ming Market" in the Burmese town of Katha, situated on the Irrawaddy upriver from Ava, and a traveler from London reported the presence of Chinese traders in Chiangmai when he visited the town, then part of the Taungoo Empire, in the 1580s. We have few sources for Taungoo's trade in the seventeenth century, but a 1746 Qing document describes a robust movement of cotton from Burma flowing north, and metals from Yunnan's mines flowing south. Large numbers of Yunnanese farmers would travel to northern Burma for seasonal work in cotton production, suggesting a strong integration of southern Yunnan and northern Burma's economies.[20]

Southern Burma had its own distinctive political and trade entanglements. As the Ming emperor-claimant Yongli was spending his last days at Ava, another imperial exile arrived on the western coast of the Burma region: the Mughal emperor-claimant Shah Shuja', who found shelter in the Mrauk U kingdom in Arakan. Just as upper Burma was intertwined with China, lower Burma was inextricable from the Muslim-ruled societies around the Bay of Bengal, most notably the Mughal Empire. Mrauk U was itself a Muslim-dominated kingdom that adopted much of its political culture from the Mughals. In both Mrauk U and its next-door neighbor Taungoo, Muslim traders were prominent. Roughly forty kilometers from Arakan's coast, the Bassein River, a branch of the same Irrawaddy River that watered Taungoo's capital, flowed to the sea. By the late fifteenth century, the ports of Bassein and Pegu had become "major rendezvous points for Muslim . . . traders."[21]

In the lifetimes of Ma Zhu and ʿĀshiq, it is unclear how much the movement of goods and people across the Taungoo state linked the Muslims of Yunnan with the Muslims who frequented Taungoo's southern coast. Records from the period are sparse, and I can find no mention of Muslims in the heart of the Taungoo state, or any specification of which among the many ethnic groups in Burma / Yunnan dominated various commercial activities. When such specifications first appear in the late eighteenth and nineteenth centuries, Chinese Muslims are prominent or even predominant figures in the caravans that moved goods overland between Yunnan and Burma. Whether this was a new phenomenon or the continuation of an older trend is unknown.

Ma devoted a substantial chapter in his *Compass of Islam* to a polemic against "foreign" Muslims he believed were heterodox. Ma's condemnation of the group's nighttime congregations involving chanting, music, and intoxicants sounds very much like complaints about Sufis common across Islamic history. Modern scholars have often surmised that the offending foreigners were from India, presumably based on Yunnan's strong connections to South Asia via Burma.[22] A competing hypothesis attributes their origin to Central Asia.[23] Whatever the case may be, it is clear that the presence of people from outside of China were shaping many Muslims' religious lives and affecting Ma Zhu's thinking. Whether this connected arena of Islamic dispute was directly linked to the Burma-inflected environment in which Ma passed his youth remains to be seen.

One hundred fifty years later, the connection between the Burma route and Islamic knowledge becomes much clearer. Ma Dexin, teacher of Ma Lianyuan, left Yunnan for Mecca via Burma in 1841, later describing his journey in his *Account of the Hajj Route* (*Chaojin tuji* 朝覲途記).[24] By Ma Dexin's day the Yunnan-Burma trade had intensified greatly. Nonetheless, as Ma Dexin traced the trade routes on his way to the Bay of Bengal, many particulars reflect what we know of earlier economic flows. He traveled overland to Burma and made his way to the same Ava that had hosted the Yongli emperor. There he counted some three thousand households of Muslims, most of whom spoke "Hindustani." From Ava he traveled down the Irawaddy on a boat hauling metals from Yunnan's mines, though in this case it was copper, which had come to rival silver among Yunnan's exports. He continued on to Rangoon, whence he departed by sail to Calcutta in 1842.

It has been argued that Ma Dexin exemplifies a new era of transnational connectivity enabled by the rise of steam travel and print.[25] However, Ma's description of his ocean voyage—forty days to Calcutta due to difficult winds—rules out steam travel.[26] Indeed, steam service would not arrive in Burma until the 1850s, after British annexation. In all, Ma Dexin's journey through Burma looks much more like a continuation of the same general patterns of connectivity that had prevailed in Ma Zhu's day, though encouraged by the intensification of trade. It was only when Ma Dexin's student, Nūr al-Haqq / Ma Lianyuan, left for his second Hajj in 1901 or 1902 that the forces of steam and (nonwoodblock) print would directly touch a prominent scholar on the Burma route.

Central Asian Routes

While Ma Zhu was fretting over foreign Sufis near the Burmese border, another foreigner was successfully converting Muslims to his own Sufi practice along the Central Asian and Tibetan frontiers. Afaq Khoja, whom we encountered bestowing an extraordinary book on the Deaf Cleric's ancestor in Chapter 3, would leave a profound impact on multiple forms of Islam in China. He was born in Qumul, an oasis kingdom just outside the Qing Empire's northwestern borders, in what would centuries later become the Xinjiang Uyghur Autonomous Region.

Stories of Afaq's visits to Tibet, Salar country, and Hezhou (today's Linxia, China's "Little Mecca") have appeared across a remarkable geographic expanse, bridging cultures and languages. From the Ferghana Valley (in today's Uzbekistan), through Eastern Turkistan and into Gansu, his travels have been set down in Persian, Eastern Turki (Chaghatay), and Chinese. Many of the tales are replete with improbable miracles, meetings with the Dalai Lama or the Qing emperor, and other extraordinary claims. Were there only a single hagiography documenting Afaq's eastward missionizing, we might have good reason to doubt his peregrinations. But eastward travels, along with Afaq's ability to enlist followers, are agreed upon across the sources throughout their geographical and cultural range.[27]

At the same time, disagreements and ellipses among the sources leave the precise dates and routes of Afaq's journey(s) to China unclear. He most likely visited the Qing realm after his banishment in 1670 from the Khanate of Yarkand, which ruled most of Eastern Turkistan. The two recent historians who have given Afaq's travels the most attention, Joseph Fletcher and Alexandre Papas, argued from Turki sources that Afaq probably traveled via Kashmir into Tibet, thence toward Hezhou (today's Linxia).[28] This was not the most convenient route. A traveler from Yarkand to the Qing lands would normally have proceeded via Uighuristan (Hami, Turpan) to the Gansu corridor. There is a strong likelihood that Afaq followed this more common route, at least partly, on his eventual return to Eastern Turkistan. However, the lands of the Yarkand Khanate were off limits to Afaq in the 1670s, probably making the Kashmir / Tibet road his best option on the outward journey. Two decades earlier, he may also have traveled in the Amdo / Gansu region with his father, Muḥammad Yūsuf Ishan, though the source for this is a late one and Muḥammad Yūsuf does not seem to show up in Chinese sources from Hezhou or elsewhere.[29]

The political terrain along the Ming's and Qing's western borders shifted frequently, so much so that a slight shift in the dates of Afaq's travels could yield a dramatically different political landscape. Among the contenders for power in Afaq's birthplace of Qumul were the Ming, the Qing, the Yarkand Khanate, the Dzungar Mongols, and the local Turkic nobility of both Turfan and Qumul itself. Each of these powers controlled the oasis at least briefly at some point in the seventeenth century. For the most part, Qumul remained outside of Ming / Qing control, but this did not amount to a stable political environment. Populations flowed in the wake of wars, most commonly Muslims from Qumul and neighboring Turpan into Chinese territory. The numbers could be quite large. In the sixteenth century, the Ming welcomed tens of thousands of refugees from Qumul who fled the warfare between the Ming and Turfan. In 1732, by which time the Dzungars controlled Qumul and Turfan, a Turkic notable led ten thousand Turfani refugees into Qing territory, settling in the town of Guazhou, near modern Jiayuguan.

On the Ming side of the border, frequent economic and agricultural crises drove many Muslim communities to desperation. Some responded in a way that was also prevalent among non-Muslim Chinese communities of the period throughout China: They rose up in armed rebellion. Ming records for the first half of the seventeenth century document Muslim uprisings in the northwest at a rate of roughly two per decade. The rebellion of Li Zicheng, which ultimately toppled the Ming in 1644 (before quickly succumbing to the Manchu Qing invasion), also originated in the northwest. Some of Li's top advisors were Muslims, as were many members of his armies, though they were certainly a minority. Li himself was said to have been adopted by a Muslim woman and trained in the basics of Islam in his youth, though there is no evidence that he considered himself a Muslim.[30]

When the Qing displaced the Ming, two other Muslim leaders took up arms under a different banner. Mi Layin and Ding Guodong led tens of thousands of fellow Muslims in a movement that captured some of the main cities of the Gansu corridor. They proclaimed that they were restoring the Ming, complete with a would-be emperor from the Ming imperial family. Their Ming restoration lasted about as long as the Yongli "emperor's" court in Yunnan / Burma, and in 1649 their leaders suffered the same fate at the hands of the Qing.[31] Their movement does not seem to have produced any Muslim thinkers on the order of Ma Zhu.

The frequent political disruptions forced trade to shift often in route, volume, and nature. In some periods China-based states managed to minimize trade outside of formal tribute missions, while in others long-distance commerce flowed more freely. When the direct route through the Gansu corridor became difficult, some trade would divert upland through modern Qinghai. But there was no period in which trade, implicated as it was in power rivalries, was not significant enough to appear frequently in the contemporary accounts of political struggles.

The earliest record of Afaq's arrival in China, a hagiography from 1730, is similarly attentive to trade, describing in detail the moment that a caravan arrived at the Qing border with Afaq in its midst. *Hidāyatnāma* is a Persian text completed during the lifetime of Afaq's younger contemporaries. It states that Afaq arrived in China ("*Chīn,* of the province of *Khitāy*") from India ("*Hindūstān,*" probably Kashmir) as part of a magnificent caravan. At the walls delimiting Qing territory, the guards were suspicious of Afaq and his followers, as they carried no merchandise or any personal belongings of note. According to the text, the caravan was admitted but Afaq was made to wait outside the walls. The emperor grew sick, and his doctors determined that this illness had been caused by angering a Muslim (i.e., Afaq). The order was given to admit Afaq and his companions, and Afaq bestowed his breath upon a vial of water, which cured the emperor.[32]

In China, Afaq promoted his religious path and designated *khalifas,* deputies who would continue to spread his Sufi order after his return. He likely left by the more standard Central Asia route from the Gansu corridor into Uighuristan (the route is also mentioned in the *Hidāyatnāma*), and thence into the heart of Dzungar Mongol territory, before proceeding to Kashgar with the aid of Dzungar armies. That part of Afaq's story changed the fate of Eastern Turkistan, and indeed many Uyghurs today see Afaq's Mongol-assisted conquest as the first in a series of falling dominoes that eventually led to the Qing conquest of the region.[33] But here we are concerned with Afaq's effects on China proper. Those effects were epochal, ushering in patterns of religious and political organization that in many ways define the Islams of Northwest China today.

Alexandre Papas has neatly distilled what Afaq brought to China into four categories. The first, by no means unique to Afaq's brand of

Naqshbandi Sufism, was the veneration of saints' tombs. Second was the meditative practice called *dhikr,* the remembrance of God, which believers used to bring themselves closer to a mystical union with God. Third, Afaq frequently taught his path through the interpretation of Rumī's *Masnavī-ye ma'navī,* a thirteenth-century work of Sufi verse that has been called "the Persian Qur'an." This practice does not seem to have made a lasting mark. Finally, and most politically significant, Afaq spread the idea of the *silsila,* the chain of transmission by which spiritual authority was perpetuated. The notion that authority could be concentrated in a single master and passed down to a single chosen or inheriting successor developed into what became known in the nineteenth century as *menhuan* (门宦), Sufi orders that commanded the loyalties and frequently enmities of large parts of the Muslim population in the northwest. As competing claims to authority split some *silsilas* and innovators founded new authoritative chains, *menhuan* proliferated. Disputes between these groups often erupted into open warfare in the eighteenth and nineteenth centuries.

How much any of these developments can be credited to Afaq in particular is unclear. Afaq (or, if we accept the claims of the late hagiographies, his father Muhammad Yūsuf) is the earliest documented bearer of Naqshbandi Sufism in China. In all likelihood other Naqshbandis, now lost to history, preceded him. The Naqshbandi order was the most prominent Sufi path in Eastern Turkistan from at least the middle of the sixteenth century, and by the seventeenth century it had a wide popular following. Given the constant back and forth of Muslims between Eastern Turkistan and Northwestern China, the arrival of prior Naqshbandi adepts in the Gansu corridor is likely.

Nonetheless, in China, Afaq is remembered more vividly than any other Sufi shaykh. The vast majority of Sufi followers in China today are associated with one of many branches of the Naqshbandi transmission. Roughly half of Naqshbandi followers in China identify with *menhuan* that cite Afaq as the crucial transmitter. These include the Xianmen,[34] Mufti, Bijiazhuang, and the main Khufiyya order, the Huasi.[35] The founder of the Da Gongbei order, China's most prominent branch of the Qadiriyya, is said to have sought teaching from Afaq, who told him to seek instead his true (Qadiriyya) master. And of course the Deaf Cleric grounded his family's Gedimu authority in a founding ancestor's meeting with Afaq.

As we will see in more detail in Chapter 6, the Central Asian route continued to feed into China new notions of Islamic identity and practice in the eighteenth and nineteenth centuries. Even into the 2010s, for example, the leader of the Beizhuang *menhuan* regularly visited Yarkand, in Eastern Turkistan, reenacting an early nineteenth-century transmission to Gansu. The Chinese Muslims who traveled the Silk Routes also left their marks on the societies of Central Asia. When the Yarkandi author of the *Hidāyatnāma* penned his account of Afaq's caravan, he relied on the information of a Chinese adept named Mulla Yūsuf Chīnī.[36] In the nineteenth century, thousands of Chinese Muslims would flee to Russian Turkistan, founding what are today the Dungan communities of Uzbekistan, Kazakhstan, and Kirghizstan.

Completing the Circle Via Highland Inner Asia

Serindia was not just a bundle of links between China and outside regions such as India, Burma, and Central Asia. Those regions were connected to each other as well. While there is no space here to detail all the interconnections between them, one zone, highland Inner Asia, deserves treatment because it so often served as a conduit for circulations between China and South Asia. Afaq was able to take refuge in Hindustan / Kashmir, and then to travel from there via Tibet to China, largely because of the robust circulations between Eastern Turkistan and South Asia over the Karakorum Mountains. This route fills in the western portion of our map of Serindian circulations, bringing us back to Mughal India, home of the seafaring mystic ʿAshiq, who settled in Nanjing, and the exiled prince Shah Shuja', who fled to Burma. Put another way, highland Inner Asia linked Burma and Central Asia via India, completing the circle.

A little-known figure active in the 1640s, Mullā ʿAdil Kāshgarī, offers an evocative glimpse of the traffic over highland Inner Asia. Kāshgharī's name (*nisba*) indicates an origin in the heart of Eastern Turkistan. He would have completely escaped the historical record, had he not appeared in one of the most famous texts of the Mughal Empire: *Dabistān-i mazāhib* (School of religious doctrines), which describes the various religions of South Asia.

The author of *Dabistān,* probably a Neo-Zoroastrian of the Azar Kayvan school, traveled the breadth of India in the 1640s, learning about the various faiths he would describe in his book. For the Islamic faith he relied on two men he met in Lahore, both bearing the name Kāshgharī. One had roots in Badakhshan, while Mullā ʿAdil Kāshgarī was presumably from Kashgar itself. It is hard to draw conclusions about why the author would choose two men with origins in or connections to Eastern Turkistan for his main informants on the nature of Islam. However, we can say that the appearance of these individuals as the representatives of Islam in the *Dabistān*'s survey of South Asian religions reflects the numerous political, economic, and intellectual ties with Eastern Turkistan. Not only were men from Eastern Turkistan frequent visitors to South Asia, but they were embedded in local communities there.

The Mughal royals were distant relatives of the ruling family in Yarkand, capital of the Yarkand Khanate, which ruled most of Eastern Turkistan in the seventeenth century. From the 1640s onward they maintained close connections, and the Mughals frequently provided refuge to nobles who fled dynastic infighting in Eastern Turkistan. The two states occasionally invaded the Sultanate of Kashmir, which lay between them. That state managed to remain independent for most of the seventeenth century, but it succumbed to the might of the Mughal emperor Akbar as the century drew to a close.

As it did along the Burma route, trade provided the infrastructure for movement between Eastern Turkistan and South Asia. In Ladakh, a mountain kingdom just to the east of Kashmir, entire meadows were reserved for the feeding of caravan horses from Eastern Turkistan.[37] They needed fattening up after the arduous climb from the lowlands. It was the merchants' horses, along with yaks, that carried religious and sometimes political figures to the top of the great mountain range dividing India and Turkistan, just as a tribute caravan had brought Afaq to China.

The trans-Karakoram trade was, however, entirely different in nature from the exchanges the powered the other routes discussed here. Whereas the China-Burma trade, for example, moved bulk commodities like cotton and eventually copper, the Karakoram trade focused on smaller, high-value items. The mountain passes were so treacherous that the transport of bulk goods only began after the opening of the Karakoram highway in 1978. The bones of dead horses, yaks, and merchants famously littered the snow-draped gorges along the perennially shifting routes. But precious items such as silver, *charas* (a cannabis product), *tus* (a wool-like fiber finer than cashmere), and musk spurred traders, their scarcity in part a product of the danger of travel. When people of other professions wanted to travel for other purposes these luxury goods meant that caravans were available.

Holy men were frequent passengers. Mullā ʿAdil Kāshgharī was probably among their number, though he may have been a trader, too. Eastern Turkistani names flicker across the Sufi hagiographies of Kashmir.[38] And Sufis from Kashmir took the reverse path. The Kubravi order, so prominent in Kashmir, never found much purchase in Eastern Turkistan, but it wasn't for lack of effort. In the period of Ismail Khan (1670–1677), the ruler who exiled Afaq Khoja, a South Asian Kubravi master named Tirmizi arrived in the court at Yarkand. The hagiographical account of this mission claims a warm welcome, but Tirmizi was soon on his way back to India, where he found richer patronage at the Mughal court.[39] Islamic texts moved in the caravans' saddlebags, too, making their way into citations by Eastern Turkistani authors.[40]

The highland routes were more numerous than can be accounted for here, moving through other zones, such as Tibet in the east and Badakhshan (Afghanistan) in the west. In Chapter 6 the Badakhshan route will play a crucial role in explaining how the Chinese urn arrived in Sirhind. As with the other routes we have examined, they often shifted in response to political changes or the drifting threat of banditry.

Conclusion

I have traced these Muslim lives to explore their entanglements across the breadth of Serindia. The biographical approach helps us think past the category-making phenomena of states, ethnicities, religions, civilizations, and the like. The humans we have followed here certainly engaged in their own category-making. Ashige was an "Indian" (欣度国人) in Zhang Shizhong's eyes and was a "barbarian" (胡) to the populace of Nanjing.[41] Ma Zhu disdained certain Sufis as "foreign." Afaq's biographer spoke of "infidels" (*kāfir*).[42] Wang Mingyu is identified as a "Chinese person" (我國華人) in "Hindustan."[43] Following these travelers and thinkers as they crossed category boundaries brings other geographies into view, tangles of interconnection that frustrate territorial parceling out of subjectivities and solidarities. It also shows how one form of category-making—religious self-identification—can lead people to cross the boundaries of other identity forms. So it was that self-identified Muslims such as Wang Mingyu and ʿAshiq found hospitality and community in far-flung regions and assistance, even rescue, along the way.

Biography privileges routes over territory. Human relations with land and space are often described territorially. "India" and "China" are said to interact. But territory is the preserve of states and vaguely defined collectivities such as "civilizations." Routes, by contrast, are the concern of all scales of human endeavor, from individuals to nations to religious movements to companies. Routes always entangle chronology and geography. Territory can be synchronic, a slice in time. Routes cannot be. They are produced by the diachronic act of travel. While territory expresses suprahuman social forces and the indifference of nature, routes can express individual human intention as it is channeled by those forces.

Individual lives also resist reductive analysis. This selection of Muslim circulations in mid-seventeenth-century Serindia thus serves as a reminder of phenomena that lie outside the scope of most chapters in this book: Muslims engaged in activities not marked as specially Islamic. While this book focuses mostly on Muslims in their engagements with Islams, such engagements were only one part of Muslims lives, and for many a very minor part. Many engaged China's broader politics. Ashiq returned to India when the dynastic wheel turned, but other Muslims were directly involved in the political turmoil. As we have seen, Muslims played high-profile roles in both the Ming overthrow and two Ming courts in borderland zones. Muslims also played prominent, sometimes predominant, parts in trade on both the Burma route and the so-called Silk Routes to Central Asia. Ma Zhu, one of the foundational Sinophone thinkers on Islam, was invested—and successfully so—in the Confucian civil-exam system. We have also seen hints of another widespread phenomenon that lies outside of this book's focus: Muslims and Islam influencing China's non-Muslims. Li Zicheng, whose attempt to found a new "Shun" dynasty in the Confucian tradition opened the way for the Qing conquest, had been educated in Islamic knowledge.

Through these lives, economic forces reassert themselves in the story of Islamic China. Trade is perhaps the steadiest engine of circulation. Circulation creates the infrastructure, social and physical, upon which one-way migrations, mobilities, and transmissions are possible: guest houses, roads, markets for fresh animals, fields reserved for caravan fodder, kinship networks, and so on. The case of Islam in China has often been presented as a case of one-way migration and dissemination. Authors ask, when did Islam come to China? In how many "tides" did it arrive? But Serindian exchange hitched a ride on the backs of circulatory travelers and through circulatory channels. The repeating mule trains of the Burma route, the maritime trade, and the trans-Karakoram / Pamir paths made it possible for scholars and shaykhs to bring *imān-i mujmal* from Hindustan to the Ming Empire and to bring Wang Mingyu's teaching to Mughal Hindustan.

The mobile lives traced here show Islamic China to be thoroughly entangled in Serindian and Hajj circulations at the very moment when the earliest Islamic literature of China comes into historical view. The extraordinary texts of Chapter 3, with their emphasis on interventions from afar, tempt us to view Islamic China as something stable and distinct from the Muslim communities that surrounded it. The vision they conjure is similar to the island societies that the anthropologist Marshall Sahlins described, whose cultures clicked along within a stable structure until confronted by natural disasters or the arrival of strange humans from far away.[44] But the Serindian circulations that produced these texts were not interruptions in the structure of Muslim communities. They were instead integral to the perpetuation of the ordinary. Ma Lianyuan replanted the fallow fields of Islamic education in Yunnan, restoring them to their former state, after the interruption of war. He did so on the back of both stochastic and continuous interconnection: his own pilgrimages (two in the course of sixty years) and the international trade of his uncle's Xing Shun He Company, which funded his work. And most of the ordinary texts he made available once more had their roots in Hindustan, Central Asia, or other parts of Serindia. These circulations helped constitute ordinariness for Muslims in China, both those who were self-consciously aware of ties that exceeded the bounds of Chinese empires and those who were not.

In Chapter 5 we examine how Muslims in China have made sense of their local rootedness and distant connections, as well as experiences of difference and solidarity, through narratives that disentangle and simplify, as all histories do. We have already seen in our examination of ordinary and extraordinary texts a focus on origins. As we turn now to Muslims' community histories, to their efforts to justify and authorize their ways of life, we will find that complex Serindian circulations were resolved into the stories of simple arrivals and one-way transmissions that the present chapter has deemphasized. These idealized arrivals take the form of origin stories.

5

Origins Identify

Lan Xu, Manṣūr Ma Xuezhi, Muḥammad Yūsuf, and Ma Qirong

At Lanzhou the Yellow River makes a turn to the north, striking out toward the edges of Mongolia. For much of this six-hundred-kilometer northward run, the river divides the Gobi Desert from the Ordos Desert. On this riverine boundary sits the Hong Le Fu 鸿乐府complex of mosque, graves, and recitation hall, where a ritual enactment of community origins unfolds daily, connecting worshippers to a foundational teacher in Yemen.

The dramatic geography of Hong Le Fu's surroundings is masked by a millennia-old engineering project: the diversion of Yellow River water into canals. Despite the arid climate, the canals have transformed the surrounding wind-deposited soil into a fertile agricultural plain. It has long been a valued part of China's economy and a strategic linchpin for relations with nomadic peoples to the north. When Ming dynasty (1368–1644) officials expanded the network of fortifications we call the Great Wall, they included a special diversion of the walls, turning up north dramatically along the Yellow River and surrounding this finger of farmland jutting into the Mongolian deserts.

The air at Hong Le Fu is dusty but the landscape is green, with the enormous deserts on either side lurking just out of sight, beyond a flat expanse of nonnative trees and crops. Hong Le Fu sits close by one of the larger canals, and the edges of the compound are thick with gardens, evergreen trees, and weeping willows. But the center of the compound is reserved for two broad, stone-paved plazas, sharing the mostly featureless aesthetic of modern squares such as Tiananmen, versions of which are found in virtually every Chinese city today. A building with an orange-tiled roof and sweeping, curved eaves dominates the far end. It both flaunts its newness with crisp concrete columns and gestures to an imperial past, its roof and stone balustrades looking very much like those in Beijing's Forbidden City.

The bare main square was empty even of humans when I visited one July in the mid-2010s. But the vast space was full of voices. Some forty worshippers, men in front and women in back, were gathered in the main hall to sing a sacred Arabic-language text, *Madā'ih.* They sang in a studied disunison, starting lines at subtly different moments and striking notes of slightly different tuning. The variation was subtle enough that it generated a rich, multilayered sound rather than cacophony. As Ha Guangtian has argued in his ethnography of the Hong Le Fu community, this accentuated polyphony is an expression of the community's long history of migrations and pilgrimages.[1]

The text they sang, *Madā'ih,* plays a central, even identifying, role for one of China's largest Islamic affiliations, the Jahriyya Sufi order. Those who profess loyalty to the Jahriyya order can be found from Jilin in the far northeast to the Burmese border in the southwest and Uzbekistan in the west. Hong Le Fu, which boasts the tomb of the order's fourth Chinese leader (Ḥaqīqallah, d. 1849), is one of a handful of communities with claims to leadership of the Jahriyya.

In their recitation of *Madā'ih,* Jahriyya worshipers have adopted a type of text common among Muslim communities across the world—a *mawlid*—and put it to entirely new purposes. The words of the text would look familiar to many Muslims from Southeast Asia to North Africa, but the Jahriyya have given *Madā'ih* social functions and meanings that the text's authors could never have imagined. The *mawlid* genre is a category of texts that commemorate the birth of the Prophet Muhammad. These works are popular among many Muslim communities throughout the world and are frequently read during the birthday celebrations of the prophet. As with other *mawlid* texts in other communities, the Jahriyya recite *Madā'ih* to mark the birthday of the prophet, but they also sing sections of the text at numerous other occasions, ranging from weddings and funerals to pilgrimage rituals at the tombs of past Jahriyya leaders.

Madā'ih traces the prophet from his existence before creation, through various ancestors (beginning with Adam) who transmitted his being in the form of a beam of light called the Light of Muhammad, to his birth and early life. The sixteen sections each contain prose and verse sections, interweaving tales from the prophet's life with elaborate praise. Aside from *Madā'ih*'s unusual silence on the prophet's later life, the text is similar to other popular *mawlids*, to such an extent that Ha Guangtian has suggested it "draws inspiration and narrative exemplars" from earlier *mawlid* works.[2]

Over time, the Jahriyya community has folded multiple new layers of significance onto *Madā'ih*. On the one hand, it functions as an extraordinary text in the same sense that the *Maktubāt* did for the Deaf Cleric, discussed in Chapter 3: Its bestowal upon the founder of the Jahriyya is seen as a talisman of authority and a license to spread the true teaching. Sometime around 1730, Muḥammad Amīn Ma Mingxin (馬明心) set out from his home in Gansu and followed the Hajj routes west. Eventually he settled in Yemen, where he studied for two decades with a shaykh of the Naqshbandi order. This teacher bestowed on Ma Mingxin the two books that would become central to the lives of Ma's followers after his return to China, both for daily recitation and as liturgy for special occasions such as holidays, pilgrimages, and funerals. One was called *Madā'ih*, the other *Mukhammas*. By the nineteenth century, Jahriyya followers viewed Ma Mingxin's transmission of these works as a pivotal moment in their community's formation, as well as the proof of that community's inheritance of the true path. Recitation of the two texts—daily, in the case of *Mukhammas*—constantly created and re-created the community.[3] *Madā'ih* is thus an originary text, not just an artifact but the very stuff of the Jahriyya's beginning.

For the purposes of this chapter, the more important function of *Madā'ih* is as history, weaving the account of Jahriyya origins and transmission into the life cycles of community and family. Remarkably, many Jahriyya followers believe that this text, compiled before the early seventeenth century, narrates the history of the Jahriyya leaders who came *after* the composition of the text. They believe the text unfolds the trials and achievements of the Jahriyya saints in the two centuries from Ma Mingxin's delivery of *Madā'ih* to China down to the death of the fifteenth Jahriyya shaykh in 1960. In its own day a history of the future, it has become an account of the past. As we will see, it has also served at many times to shape its various presents. *Madā'ih* is a history foretold at the origin, an origin story whose composition *is* the origin.

Madāʾih and, to a greater extent, its sister text *Mukhammas,* are also interesting for their ability to collapse the ordinary and the extraordinary. These extraordinary texts are of the sort that the Deaf Cleric's *Maktūbāt* was: They were bestowed to a founding figure by a foreign teacher in distant lands, granting special authority and distinguishing the founder's new community from its neighbors. At the same time, they are recited frequently (*Madāʾih*) or even daily (*Mukhammas*) by the community, embedding the extraordinary origination in the rhythm of everyday life and the ritual cycles of calendars and lives. In this sense, the two texts achieved a goal common to many community histories consumed in Islamic China, making claims at once to extraordinary authority and the normativity of ordinariness.

Today we are fortunate to have several rich academic studies of Islamic Chinese approaches to history. In Anglophone scholarship, the historical writings of the early Confucian-inspired Muslims (*Huiru*) and the Jahriyya Sufis have benefited from multiple analyses.[4] We also have valuable studies of a Qadiriyya Sufi community by Tiffany Cone and of nineteenth-century historical writings in Chinese by J. Lilu Chen.[5] Some of these works have asked their specific material to stand for "the Muslim position" in China,[6] while others have presented their subjects as representative only of narrower communities. None, however, provide a view of historical practices across the range of Islamic traditions in China. Building on this scholarship, this chapter brings together the works and lives of four history writers of the period from 1850 to 1933, to give a sense of the diversity of approaches to the past that have been seen as both Islamic and Chinese. Their texts, whether despite or because of the controversial claims within them, became widely consumed within their communities. The four authors are representative of an interest, we might even say a fixation, that was shared by almost every Chinese Muslim who wrote about their own community's histories, an interest that has already appeared several times in earlier chapters of this book: origins.

In the Anglophone scholarship on Islam in China, it has been common to introduce a chapter, an essay, or an entire book with a tale from the seventeenth century, *The Origins of the Huihui* (回回原來 *Huihui yuanlai*), in which the Prophet Muhammad appears to the Tang emperor in a dream.[7] In his seminal study, Zvi Ben-Dor Benite called it "the ultimate Chinese Muslim source on their own origins."[8] This widely repeated origin story, popular across China's numerous Islamic denominations, would offer a fitting introduction to the present chapter, in which I examine a range of accounts that Muslim authors have produced and consumed about their own pasts. But because this chapter emphasizes the diversity of such histories, I chose to begin with a historical practice that is exclusive to a particular Sufi order, the recitation of the *Madā'ih,* an originary text simultaneously seen as an origin story. In surveying the various self-histories of Muslim communities in China, we will find more divergences than commonalities. Across this diversity, the intersections that appear offer insights on the complex relationship between social categories on the one hand—from clan identities to sects to high-order concepts like China or Islam—and the drive for origins on the other. They suggest that categories create origins, perhaps more even than origins lead to categories, not just metaphorically, but through the historical practices of community members.

From a global perspective, it is difficult to argue that any one community has had an unusual concern with origins. It would be easier to argue that every community is origin obsessed, citing creation narratives such as Pangu in the classical Chinese tradition, Oduduwa among the Yoruba, the book of Genesis for Jewish and Christian traditions, and so on. But the recurrence of origins among Chinese-speaking Muslims is indeed remarkable in frequency and emphasis. I am not the first person to note it. J. Lilu Chen pointed out the centrality of origins in her important book on nineteenth-century Chinese-language Islamic historical traditions.[9] From this chapter's survey of various ways that Islamic Chinese authors have dealt with community history, intense origin concerns emerge as a connecting artery amid confounding diversity.

A Chinese Genealogy of Sages

When the post of county magistrate in Xingzi (星子), Jiangxi, opened up in the mid-1860s, a middle-aged official jumped at the chance. A native of neighboring Hunan, the scholar Lan Xu (1813–c. 1890) had served in low positions in several regions across the territory of the Great Qing. Magistrate was a position with very real, if localized, power. When the post became available, Lan Xu was serving in a modest administrative role in the suburbs of Beijing, where his mother had moved following his father's death. Perhaps Lan Xu wished to return to a post closer to his childhood home, or perhaps he was simply seeking a higher position. In 1866 he officially put his name forward for the magistrate post, submitting a résumé of his career that would make its way into the Qing records.[10] By 1867 he had taken up the position.

One of the first tasks he set himself was history writing, overseeing the compilation of the Xingzi gazetteer. The gazetteer, as *difangzhi* (地方志) is known in English, is a quintessential genre of Chinese-language history writing, perhaps best described as a local chronicle of encyclopedic scope, documenting the landscape, industries, demography, culture, and, of course, major events of a single location. Lan Xu's personal views are said to shine through briefly in two short entries on Confucian philosophy, but by all accounts, Lan Xu's gazetteer (which I have been unable to access) was unremarkable. Except for the occasional history researcher over the last century and a half, few have paid any attention to the work. A few years later, in 1874, he annotated a *Complete Explanation of the Book of Changes,* one of the "five classics" of the Confucian tradition, but this effort is also long forgotten. In 1876, Lan Xu was demoted from his post as magistrate under vague circumstances, and he never again appeared in Qing official records. His death date remains unknown.[11]

But Lan Xu *is* famous in some quarters—not for his entirely ordinary official career or Confucian scholarship, but for another Chinese-language text he wrote, over a decade before his posting to Xingzi. Lan Xu gained fame among Muslims literate in Chinese thanks to his *Correct Learning of Islam* (*Tianfang zhengxue* 天方正學) of 1852, which, among other topics, takes up the same task as the Jahriyya order's *Madā'ih:* tracing the transmission of the Light of Muhammad from the beginning of time to the prophet's day.[12] Despite this shared topic, however, Lan Xu's approach to Islamic history differed in numerous ways from the Jahriyya text.

Lan Xu's history is embedded in a larger work. It is the last of seven chapters in a comprehensive guide to Islam, ranging from an explanation of the Arabic alphabet to commentary on Wang Daiyu's work to mystical philosophy. The history chapter, which he named "The Epitaphs of the Perfected Beings," covers the history of the world in fifty-two short biographical notices, from Adam, the first human, down through the ages to Lan Xu's own parents (*Madā'ih,* by contrast, does not explicitly discuss figures after the Prophet Muhammad).[13] While not a genealogy, Lan Xu's stringing together of lives across time, ultimately leading to the author, shares much in common with that genre, which was extremely widespread in the Chinese-speaking territories of the Great Qing. The use of Chinese allows Lan Xu to refashion Sufi categories from their common meanings in Persian and Arabic. Lan Xu makes a distinction between prophets (大聖 = Great Sage) and other holy figures (真人= Perfected Being), with several later figures given the Sufi title Pole of Guidance (固土補奧師, *qutb al-irshād*). These nonprophetic titles are applied much more liberally than in the Persian traditions Lan Xu is drawing upon. He lumps together Sufi shaykhs, the Yuan governor Sai Dianchi, the author Wang Daiyu, and his own mother under the term "Perfected Being."[14] Confucian terms and philosophical notions are integrated throughout.

Time also operates in an entirely different manner from the Jahriyya historiography. Whereas the Jahriyya followers map recent events onto the prophetic past in a recursive and resonant chronoscape (described in more detail below), Lan Xu offers a mostly linear progression from one figure to the next. In one case, he places a saint (Uways Qaranī) before other figures we know to be born earlier, but the pattern is otherwise a present-ward movement through time. This is not, however the "homogeneous, empty time" of modernity;[15] most figures are not given dates, and the time between personages is elided entirely. Instead of empty time, it operates in deeply meaningful time. As Chen points out, progress forward in time is accompanied by degeneration. Lifespans decline, people become shorter in stature, and natural disasters increase in frequency. In a second form of chronological meaning-making, the deaths of prophets and saints, while not assigned to specific years in most cases, are each given a different week, appointing them patrons or matrons of particular moments in the agricultural cycle.

Lan Xu lived a very different life from the Jahriyya readers and writers of Hong Le Fu. He was deeply educated in Confucian texts, excelling sufficiently in the state examinations to occupy a post with real power. He wrote in Chinese rather than Arabic. He was probably not a member of a formal Sufi order, and the power struggles that touched him played out in the bureaucracy, rather than amid branching sects. If he publicly performed any Islamic worship, it would have been the daily prayers, not the collective chanting of *dhikr* or *Madā'ih.* And unlike members of the Hong Le Fu community, he spent most of his life in social contexts that framed Muslims as a minority.

Nonetheless, beneath these differences lie shared inheritances. While *Madā'ih* probably did not circulate extensively outside of Jahriyya contexts, other *mawlid* texts did. Particularly common throughout China was the *mawlid* popularly known as "Barzanjī," after the author's name.[16] Chen argues that Lan Xu was influenced by the *Qiṣaṣ al-anbiyā'* (Stories of the prophets). This is quite plausible, as Persian versions of this text circulated among China's Muslims in Lan Xu's day.[17] Both Barzanjī and *Qiṣaṣ al-anbiyā'* discuss the Light of Muhammad, though the latter is more explicit about its transmission. *Qiṣaṣ al-anbiyā'* is also an inspiration for a different Jahriyya text described further below (*The Briefest Treatise*), as were other biographical compendia. In sum, Lan Xu was working from the same Perso-Arabic biographical tradition as the Sufi writers of the Jahriyya.

How was it that an official educated in the Chinese Confucian system could be so fully in touch with this Perso-Arabic biographical environment? Another work by Lan Xu suggests that he had substantial education beyond the Confucian system. Eight years after his demotion, Lan Xu returned to publishing in the Islamic realm. In 1884 his *Dictionary of Islam* (*Tianfang Erya* 天方爾雅) appeared. It is a Persian dictionary, focused on religious terms. The most likely explanation is that Lan Xu received the kind of education that Ma Zhu had recommended, learning both the Confucian classics in Chinese and the Islamic classics in Persian.[18] In this sense he also followed in the footsteps of the most famous Chinese-language author of Islamic texts, Liu Zhi, whose work is discussed in Chapter 9, and indeed all authors who had written Islamic texts in Chinese down to Lan Xu's own day.

For Lan Xu, as for Muḥammad Nūr al-Ḥaqq / Ma Lianyuan, Ma Zhu, and Wang Daiyu, there was no essential difference between Confucian knowledge and Islamic knowledge, and nothing un-Chinese about Islam. This extended even to history, wherein, according to Lan Xu's account, China and Islam were interwoven from deep antiquity. Lan Xu could not have helped but notice that most books in Chinese described a very different selection of historical figures than books in Persian. But his own life demonstrated that figures from both textual traditions could be ancestral to a single human or a whole community. His placements of the ancient mythical emperor Shennong next to the prophet Abraham and of Sai Dianchi next to Abu Hanifa, founder of the Hanafi school of Islamic law, were significant acts that resolved two bodies of texts. They united the origins of the Confucian political-philosophical-religious project, which Lan Xu joined as an official in the Qing state, with the political-philosophical-religious project that he learned about in Persian and advocated in *Correct Learning of Arabia*. As with Ma Lianyuan, Lan Xu expressed no difficulty in being simultaneously Confucian and Muslim, or Chinese and Muslim. After all, the histories of the Confucian sages and the Islamic prophets—both groups categorized as sages (聖)—were simultaneous and interwoven. They were interwoven in his own life and ancestry, culminating in the epitaphs of his parents. In a sense, Lan Xu used autobiography as method, tracing origins that were bifurcated between Chinese- and Persian-language sources and uniting those origins in his *Correct Learning of Arabia*.

An Arabic Folding of Time

No record from Manṣūr Ma Xuezhi's (马学智, c. 1860–1933) early life seems to have survived, though he later said that he had studied with a teacher named Muʾadhdhin al-Fannī al-Shansī and had read Jamī's sophisticated Sufi philosophical text, *The Rays of the Flashes*, originally written in Persian.[19] By the time Manṣūr entered the historical record, he was already a high-ranking adept in the Jahriyya order, and by the time of his death he was second in command of the suborder, the "vizier" of the Jahriyya's seventh leader, or *murshid*. He became known as the "second grandfather" (al-Jidd al-Thānī), probably the most prestigious in a lengthy string of names and sobriquets by which he has been identified: Muḥammad Manṣūrallah Burhān al-Dīn, al-Jidd al-Thānī, al-Jisr al-Farisī, Ma Xuezhi. Hailing from the canal-fed lands around the Hong Le Fu complex (where this chapter opened), Manṣūr described himself as Muslim, Chinese, and a follower of the Jahriyya—in that order.

Sometime around 1930, he set to work on a project he had long postponed: a history of the Jahriyya order. He was concerned about certain "liars" who attacked his order with claims that practices like *Madā'ih* recitation were un-Islamic. His refutation would be an account of the miracles and wisdom of the seven successive *murshids* (guides) who had led the order since it was transmitted to China from Yemen in the mid-eighteenth century. Manṣūr, who wrote with exaggerated modesty, blamed his own "laziness" for a long delay, during which two fellow scholars wrote books that seemed to make his work unnecessary. But one day, according to him, the *murshid* himself convinced Manṣūr to write the book anyway.[20]

Although Manṣūr died before the book was fully completed, his text would not only survive but continue to grow. In its most recent form, it speaks to two distinctive but interlinked approaches to history. One is the neat, chronological account of the succession of Jahriyya leaders, which documents the unbroken transmission of the Jahriyya way (*ṭarīqat,* or dao) from its origins, an account which, for all its narrative streamlining, also emerged from a messy layering of authorship. The other is the mapping of this chain of transmission onto the sacred recitational texts of the Jahriyya (*Madā'ih* and *Mukhammas*), transforming those pre-Jahriyya texts into prewritten histories of the order.

Manṣūr generously presents in the first pages of his book a categorization of his own identity, as he wanted it to be understood. He introduces himself as "the most contemptible among Muslims, the most despicable of the Chinese [Ar: Ṣīnī] scholars, the weakest of lovers of the Jahriyya, Muḥammad Manṣūrallah Burhān al-Dīn."[21] The self-deprecation is a convention of the genre. The rest of the phrase attests to the author's most salient affiliations: Muslim, Chinese, follower of the Jahriyya.

Near the end of the text, Manṣūr's modest self-presentation yields to glorification. The "despicable" author is now blessed with the "highest attributes" and "diligence of worship"; he is eloquent and handsome. But Manṣūr did not write this. Instead, his student Ibrāhīm has taken up the pen, completing the work within the year of his teacher's death. It is here that we learn that Manṣūr was the "vizier," or prime minister, to the *murshid,* as well as the lord (*sayyid*) of Jinjipu, the town to which Hong Le Fu belonged.[22] Manṣūr had been a companion of the two previous *murshids* as well. And he lent his nickname, al-Jisr al-Farisī,[23] to a school, in which Ibrāhīm taught. Clearly Manṣūr was not as insignificant as convention had demanded he portray himself. Manṣūr named his book *The Briefest Treatise on the Jahriyya Chain of Transmission* (*Risālah aqṣarayyah li-bayān al-silsilah al-Jahriyya*), a title that Ibrāhīm abbreviated to *The Briefest Treatise.*[24]

Manṣūr's *murshid,* Siddiqallah Ma Yuanzhang 馬元章, was a strong claimant to the title of seventh Jahriyya *murshid,* but his position was not uncontested. Manṣūr claims he was reluctant to write his history because he feared it was superfluous, but from Siddiqallah Ma Yuanzhang's perspective, one more history placing him firmly in chain of *murshids* could only bolster his claims. At the turn of the twentieth century, the order already boasted a written history, set down in the early 1800s, but it only accounted for the first three *murshids*. Although two other authors had already offered their own solutions to the problem, Manṣūr set about extending that earlier history (called *al-Rashḥat al-sharīfat*)[25] down to his present.

Manṣūr was familiar with hagiographical texts of at least three other Sufi authors who wrote in Persian: Farīd al-Dīn ʿAṭṭār; Muḥammad Maẓhar Mujaddidī; and Ismāʿīl Ḥaqqī Bursavī. As Ha Guangtian has shown, Manṣūr borrowed much of his introductory defense of Sufism from ʿAttar, lifting substantial passages word for word[26] (don't feel bad for ʿAṭṭar, who himself lifted from the hagiographer Hujwīrī;[27] such uncredited copying and recomposing was common across the Persianate world). For the early parts of his book, Manṣūr also copied sections from *al-Rashḥat al-sharīfat*, the earlier Jahriyya history in Persian and Arabic.[28] The text was thus, to a degree, a collective effort even before Manṣūr died, necessitating Ibrāhīm's completion of the manuscript.

Like ʿAṭṭar, Manṣūr divided his book into chapters, each devoted to a different saint. Within those chapters, which cover the seven *murshids* down to Manṣūr's time, the material is organized by anecdotes that are sometimes clearly chronological, sometimes not. This too followed ʿAttar's precedent. The anecdotes record the *murshid's* miracles, tribulations, and wise words. Some are pages long, others just a few lines. For example, one anecdote repeated from *al-Rashḥat al-sharīfat* relates:

> It is narrated that one day the literary scholar Shandongawī [i.e., from Shandong] asked His Holiness [*ḥaḍrat*, i.e., Wiqāyatallah Ma Mingxin, the first Jahriyya *murshid* in China], "Jesus, peace be upon him, was a prophet, and he said, 'arise, by the proclamation of God!' and His Holiness Shaykh Imām Rabbānī [Aḥmad Sirhindī], God protect his secret, was a friend of God [*wālī*, i.e., a saint and thus lower than a prophet], and he said 'arise, by *my* proclamation'" [emphasis added]. And he [Wiqāyatallah] answered, "do not be amazed by this, for the waves are higher than the sea."[29]

Like this passage, many of the anecdotes leave much to the reader's interpretation. It is clear that the questioner in this episode finds it odd that a saint would elevate himself to God's level of command, while a prophet would carefully issue commands in God's name. I leave the precise interpretation of the *murshid*'s answer to Sufi adepts. Such philosophical passages are mixed with accounts of the saints' discourses on proper ritual, educational habits, or Arabic pronunciation. Other passages document miracles or political strife, such as battles with Qing soldiers during the violence of the late eighteenth and late nineteenth centuries. The family members and associates of each *murshid* are also recorded, along with *murshids*' pronouncements regarding who should succeed them.

In this way Manṣūr's history is typical of the Jahariyya histories written *after* the order was established in China: Persian- and Arabic-language texts documenting the *manaqib*—miracles, words, and tribulations—of the successive leaders of the order. At least three such works survive (Manṣūr suggests that a certain Ṭayyib al-Dīn wrote a fourth).[30] Like *The Briefest Treatise,* they each offer a direct narrative of transmission, expressed as the succession of one legitimate *murshid* after the next, the collective channel through which the dao, or *ṭarīqat,* flowed from eighteenth-century Yemen to the China of their respective presents. They are divided into sections by *murshid,* in chronological order. Within each section they present anecdotes, much like the *hadiths* that provide so many Muslims with their biographies of the Prophet Muhammad. And they argue for the holiness of the *murshids* with citations from the Qur'an or *hadiths,* frequently likening them to the prophet. There are no gaps of the sort that lie between the lives of Lan Xu's "Perfected Beings." One *murshid*'s life leads to the next, one "axis of axes" at a time, bringing the *ṭarīqat* down to each author's present in an unbroken, orderly march across the centuries. They constitute a neatly bounded river of history, flowing in a single direction. Along the way, canals nurture excurses with useful teachings for Jahriyya followers, but the central channel flows inexorably to the present.

The river of Manṣūr's history flows to the reigning *murshid* of the author's own time. Anthony Garnaut has convincingly argued that both of the surviving histories written under the patronage of Manṣūr's *murshid,* Siddiqallah Ma Yuanzhang 馬元章, serve to bolster the *murshid*'s claim to succession.[31] It is likely that Siddiqallah Ma Yuanzhang's efforts to quell disputes over his status were a central reason for his encouragement of Manṣūr's authorial venture. Among those who identify as followers of the Jahriyya order, there is universal agreement that at any one time the order has had no more than one true leader, the *murshid,* who stewards the transmission of the Jahriyya *ṭarīqat*. However, for the period after 1890, when the universally accepted sixth Chinese *murshid* died, the transmission is disputed, with five main communities each recognizing a different line of *murshids.* Siddiqallah Ma Yuanzhang's claim to be the seventh Chinese *murshid* ultimately won far more followers than any of his rival claimants. Manṣūr's *Briefest Treatise* can perhaps claim credit for some part of this success.

With the passing of both Manṣūr and Siddiqallah Ma Yuanzhang, a historiographical vacuum confronted the next *murshid* and his followers. That gap was filled in 1983 by Muḥammad ʿAbd al-Ḥakīm, who added a new, eighth chapter to the *Briefest Treatise.* His new chapter tells the story of Siddiqallah Ma Yuanzhang's son and most widely followed successor, ʿAbd al-Jāmiʿ Ma Zhenwu 马震武. Neither this latest author, Muḥammad ʿAbd al-Ḥakīm, nor his master, ʿAbd al-Jāmiʿ Ma Zhenwu, fared well under the rule of China's Communist Party. In 1958 ʿAbd al-Jāmiʿ was killed and Muḥammad ʿAbd al-Ḥakīm was sent to prison for just over a decade. The Hong Le Fu community believes that the succession of *murshids* ends with the death of ʿAbd al-Jāmiʿ. Today they inhabit a world with no living *murshid.*

But the *murshids* of the past only grew in significance. It was in prison that Muḥammad ʿAbd al-Ḥakīm says he resolved to write his new, eighth chapter of Manṣūr's *Briefest Treatise,* should he ever be released, a goal he accomplished in 1983. His augmented version was published as a manuscript facsimile in the early 2000s under the Chinese title *Zheherenye shi* (哲合忍耶史; History of the Jahriyya). It is a work of at least four authors: (1) ʿAbd al-Qādir, whose *Al-Rashḥat al-sharīfat* provided many of the anecdotes about the first Jahriyya *murshid;* (2) Manṣūr, who extended the history through the time of the seventh *murshid;* (3) Ibrāhīm, the student of Manṣūr, who finalized Manṣūr's work; and (4) Muḥammad ʿAbd al-Ḥakīm, who brought the history forward to the eighth *murshid,* regarded by the community at Hong Le Fu as the last true *murshid.*

Before the 1990s, when Chinese translations of both *al-Rashḥat al-sharīfat* and *The Briefest Treatise* were published, few Jahriyya followers would have had direct access to these histories.[32] In Manṣūr's day literacy levels were low, and I have seen no evidence that the works were read aloud with any frequency. By the late twentieth century, literacy in vernacular

Chinese had become the norm, but reading knowledge of Arabic was relatively rare. However, there are accounts, both historical and ethnographic, of the oral trading of anecdotes about *murshids.*[33] Extracted from the larger narrative, these decontextualized narratives partly lost the chronological and sequential context through which they constructed a clear account of not just an authentic origin but an unbroken transmission between origin and present.

However, both *The Briefest Treatise* and the history it presents have been transposed onto another, more accessible, text, the *Madā'ih,* which so frequently enters the daily life of the Hong Le Fu community. The *murshids* themselves were also recontextualized in time by the recitation of *Madā'ih.* In the supplementary eighth chapter of *The Briefest Treatise,* we find a key to deciphering the *Madā'ih:* a chart, dividing the *Madā'ih* into sixteen sections, each indicated by its first word(s), with the name of one *murshid* written above each in smaller script (Figure 5.1). This supplementary chapter was written in 1983, but the same practice is already documented in the early twentieth century for the other main *Jahriyya* recitational text, *Mukhammas.* Ma Tong has suggested that the pairing of *murshids* with particular *Madā'ih* passages is a practice that emerged during the succession battles of the early twentieth century. The rich context of interreferential layering and discovery of prophetic meanings during

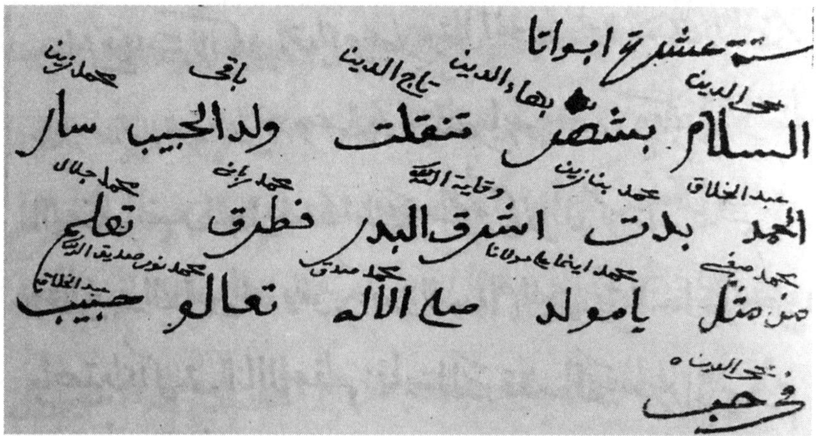

FIGURE 5.1 Key to correspondence between sections of the *Madā'ih* and *murshids* of the Jahriyya, from Muḥammad ʿAbd al-Ḥakīm's augmentation of *The Briefest Treatise.* *Credit:* © Rian Thum

this time, documented in fascinating detail by Garnaut, suggests that the practice has deeper roots.[34]

Whatever the precise age of the practice, the result is an embedding and constant re-instantiation of history in the lives of Jahriyya followers. The chronological sequence of *murshids* aligns with the sequence of sections of the *Madā'ih*. As ordinary Jahriyya followers proceed through the cycle of reciting the *Madā'ih,* they trace the history of succession of *murshids*. The decontextualized anecdotes about *murshids* that circulate orally are thus knitted back together into an unbroken transmission from origin to present. As the *Madā'ih*'s literal text unfolds the transmission of the Light of Muhammad from Adam onward, the prophetic prewritten succession of *murshids* marches along through both historical time and the lived time of the worshipper, superimposing the life of the worshipper, the *silsila* of *murshids,* and the Light of Muhammad upon each other. All of this plays out via the extraordinary recitational text that itself embodies the origin of the Jahriyya.

This is just one part of a larger system of rituals and recitations that tie Jahriyya followers to their history or, rather, permit them to continually instantiate their history, in what Ha Guangtian calls the "trinity of Muhammad, saint and ancestor." The deceased *murshids* themselves retain a presence in followers' lives. An empty seat is left for the *murshid* at feasts.[35] And when the life of the worshipper comes to an end, saintly leaders are present too: The names of the *murshids* are tucked into the shrouds at funerals.[36]

A Persian Hagiography

Muḥammad Yūsuf (c. 1802–1866) of Beizhuang, Gansu, was proud of his literary skills.[37] The work by which he wrote himself into the historical record, a Persian manuscript called *Delights of the Hearts* (*Nuzhat al-Qulūb*), records the teachings, biography, lineage, and miracles of his deceased father and Sufi master, Shāh Ḥamza Ma Baozhen (馬保真).[38] In the midst of this hagiography, in a passage describing Shāh Ḥamza's correspondence with his own *murshid,* Muḥammad Yūsuf does something unusual. He states that two of Shāh Ḥamza's letters were ghostwritten by none other than Muḥammad Yūsuf. Noting that his authorship is demonstrated by the style of exposition and the form of the blessings, Muḥammad

Yūsuf proceeds to present the text of these two letters in their entirety, filling two manuscript pages before returning to the task at hand: glorification and memorialization of his father.

Muḥammad Yūsuf likely wanted to show off his facility with elaborate, though not especially original, honorifics and blessings, as well as his competence in Arabic, the language in which the letters are written (the rest of the book is in Persian).[39] But the letters also serve to demonstrate the trust his father, founder of a major *ṭarīqat* branch, placed in him. Shāh Ḥamza had learned at the feet of a Sufi master in distant Yarkand, and he received from the master a license to spread his *ṭarīqat* in China. Muḥammad Yūsuf claimed that Shāh Ḥamza had initiated "thousands of thousands" of people "in most of the Chinese cities and cultivated regions" into "his secret of the truth," placing "the darkness of the Chinese country [*kishwar Chīnī*] in the light of the realm of enlightenment."[40] While the numbers are exaggerated, Shāh Ḥamza's *ṭarīqat* did spread. His deputies established communities in Linxia, Taozhou, and Xinjiang. Eventually Shāh Ḥamza's *ṭarīqat* became known as the Beizhuang *menhuan,* or order, named after his home village, where his tomb is located.[41] Across Gansu, Qinghai, and Xinjiang, followers of the order would eventually reach 100,000, according to a 1984 estimate.[42]

We can find some hints in the manuscript of Muḥammad Yūsuf's understanding of his place in the world. As we have seen, he wrote of his home region as a part of the "Chinese country." Elsewhere he describes it as "the familiar land" (*waṭan ma'lūf*). In both cases he makes clear that towns in Xinjiang, as the Qing called their recently conquered territory in Eastern Turkistan, are, in his reckoning, outside of the "Chinese country." When giving dates, he most often employs what he calls "the Chinese reckoning," which uses the regnal year of the emperor, and less frequently uses the Islamic calendar. It is, in effect, a recognition of his subjecthood in the empire of the Great Qing, and the subjecthood of his expected readership. To write these Chinese dates in Persian, Muḥammad Yūsuf uses calques: the Daoguang (brilliance of the Way) reign becomes *Nūr al-dīn* (light of the religion). His calque for the Qianlong emperor suggests some limits to his Chinese skills. He translates that reign title into Persian as "Dragon of Heaven," confusing two Chinese words that are both pronounced "long": 隆 (prosperity) and 龍 (dragon). His mother tongue was probably a form of Sarta, also known today as Dongxiang, as his descendants today speak this language, a little-studied language that includes Mongolic, Turkic, and Chinese elements.[43] His Qianlong calque, though mistaken, nonetheless required some knowledge of at least spoken Chinese. In sum, we can say that Muḥammad Yūsuf considered himself a native inhabitant of the land of China (Chīn), ruled by the emperors who called their dynasty the Great Qing.

He also presented himself as follower of the *ṭarīqat* he called *Naqshbandiyya Sirhindiyya.* (The reader might notice in this phrase the name of the town where Chapter 1 of the present book began, Sirhind. We will return to this connection in Chapter 6.) It was only later, though it is not clear when, that followers began to refer to themselves as members of a "Beizhuang" order.

Muḥammad Yūsuf's text became a foundational expression of Beizhuang teachings. When I visited a Beizhuang-order mosque in 2015, a student in the attached boarding school showed me his copy of *Delights of the Hearts,* which he said every student was required to study. At the time Muḥammad Yūsuf wrote the text, his older brother Ḥasan had succeeded to leadership of his late father's *ṭarīqat.* His book likely had the same authority-buttressing goal / effect for his brother as the seventh Jahriyya *murshid* sought from the *Briefest Treatise.*

Like Lan Xu, Muḥammad Yūsuf situated his historical writings in a larger composition that combined history with a comprehensive view of the true Islam. He divided his work into three sections. The first, and longest, is an exposition of the teachings of the order, both at the high philosophical level and at the practical level, for example, prescribing specific prayers for specific ritual situations. The second section is a combination of genealogy and *silsila,* or chain of transmission of the order. Records of *silsilas* are common among Sufi orders across the world. They function much like genealogies but are genealogies of teaching, in which successive individuals do not need to be related by blood. The third and final section is a narrative hagiography of Shāh Ḥamza. It follows many of the same genre conventions as the *Briefest Treatise,* providing a largely chronological sequence of events and anecdotes from the *murshid's* life. It differs in focusing on one individual, rather than stringing together the hagiographies of multiple *murshids.* Both approaches are common in the hagiographical traditions of Central Asia, which were influential in Yarkand, where Shāh Ḥamza had received his license to teach.

The centerpiece of the claim to authority in *Delights of the Hearts* is the second section. Muḥammad Yūsuf provides a particularly deep *silsila,* combining it with the (blood) genealogy (*nasab*) of the Prophet Muhammad to trace the origins of his order all the way back to Adam. This is quite distinct from the Jahriyya *Briefest Treatise,* which traces Jahriyya transmission only to as far back as the Yemeni master who taught the first Chinese Jahri *murshid.* In Muḥammad Yūsuf's work, the *silsila* section begins with the genealogy of Muhammad, then later documents the chain of teaching from Muhammad down to the *murshid* in Yarkand who transmitted the *ṭarīqat* to Shāh Ḥamza. Chapter 6 will offer more details on the roots of the Beizhuang order, tracing the originary claims of *Delights of the Heart* and cross-referencing them with other texts and lineages to uncover a broader movement among China's Muslims that has long gone unnoticed. For the moment, what is important is the approach to Islamic history that this key text in the Beizhuang order adopts, combining genealogy and *silsila* to link the community first to earlier masters from neighboring lands, from there back to the Prophet Muhammad, and then back to Adam and creation itself. And it does so, unlike Lan Xu, without any gaps. Each individual in the chain learned directly from the previous one, providing an unbroken and direct line to the origin.

The Origins of the Huihui Revisited

It would lead the reader astray if I were to omit *The Origins of the Huihui,* with its tale of the Tang emperor's dream of the Prophet Muhammad, from this sampler of Chinese Muslim community histories. This work and its variations were, among Chinese-language texts, probably the most widely consumed narrative of the history of Muslims in China from the eighteenth century through the early twentieth.[44] Certainly it saw the largest number of editions and variants.

With our fourth author, then, we return to the famous dream of the Tang emperor. Ma Qirong 馬啓榮 shared much in common with Ma Lianyuan / Nūr al-Ḥaqq: Both were raised in the small town of Yuxi, Yunnan, in the second half of the nineteenth century; both made the Hajj to Mecca;[45] both were teachers at mosque schools;[46] and both published versified primers aimed at imparting Islamic knowledge to children.[47] Ma Qirong, however, left Yunnan to teach in Eastern China, conducting classes at the

Huaisheng Mosque in Guangzhou, the city's most storied mosque. It was at this mosque that he published his history of the arrival of Muslims in China, *Genealogy of the Arrival from the West (Xi lai zongpu 西来宗谱),* around the year Guangxu 2 (1876–1877).[48] Two years earlier he had published a four-character religious primer at a mosque in Zhenjiang (near Nanjing), which may reflect earlier travel or teaching in that city.[49]

In his *Genealogy of the Arrival from the West,* Ma Qirong tells a history clearly derived from *The Origins of the Huihui* but written afresh and with substantial differences in the details. He offers no author preface, plunging directly into the historical narrative with no explanation as to why he decided to write it.[50] In explanation of his intent we have only a single sentence at the end of the first section of the narrative: "I specially gathered the old sayings and transmitted books so that my colleagues can also understand the meaning of drinking water and thinking about the source," a cliché that Wang Daiyu had used in explaining the Islamic duty of contemplating origins. The question of motive is interesting because the core story that he tells circulated widely, in numerous minor variants. There was no obvious need for a new version of this tale, written from scratch—unless, that is, Ma Qirong saw the differences between what he planned to write and what was already in circulation as matters of some significance.

Certain core details remain the same across the various versions of *The Origins of the Huihui:* In the reign of the second Tang emperor (626–649 CE), a turbaned man appeared in the emperor's dream. In all variations the dream includes some threat, be it a monster, a crashing roof beam, or the turbaned man himself. The emperor and his officials interpret the dream and decide to send an ambassador to a great Muslim leader in Qumul, just outside the westernmost pass of Jiayuguan, or in a nonspecific place in the "Western Regions." The king of Qumul sends three emissaries, only one of whom makes it to the Tang capital alive. There the emissary discusses Islam with the emperor, convincing him that Islam is in accord with Confucian teachings. The emperor asks for more Muslim men to be sent from abroad, and when they arrive, he encourages them to settle permanently and marry local women.

Ma Qirong's text retains all of these elements but has the Tang emperor's ambassador stop briefly in Qumul and then proceed all the way to Arabia, where he meets the Prophet Muhammad himself. The prophet sends three ambassadors, and the one who survives the trip is called Waqqas (as he is in some variants of *Origins of the Huihui*), a reference to one of the companions of the prophet attested in other, Arabic sources. Ma divides the migration of Muslims to China into two separate events. First the emperor invites a group of Muslim men to keep Waqqas company and help with his religious mission. Later, another Tang emperor invites foreign Muslim soldiers to help put down the An Lushan rebellion. As in the *Origins of the Huihui,* the emperor rewarded them with wives, permanent residence, and subjecthood (入籍). Ma also appends a second narrative, devoted to the details of Waqqas's life and with stories of his interactions with the prophet, including a return to Arabia for the prophet's burial. He concludes with an account of Waqqas's burial in Guangzhou.

The changes make sense in light of the history of Guangzhou's Muslim community over the eighteenth and nineteenth centuries, our knowledge of which Aaron Glasserman has recently expanded greatly. After a long period in which Guangdong's scholars were nearly all locals, in the course of the nineteenth century the community increasingly sought teachers from outside the province, especially Yunnan. These outside scholars probably offered a sense of greater access to authentic Islamic learning, and indeed, as Glasserman has pointed out, there are numerous scattered references to a weaker Islamic educational system in Guangzhou in the seventeenth through the early nineteenth centuries, documenting a situation in which most of the city's mosques did not have regular schools and scholars perceived a shortage of necessary texts for Islamic study.[51] The demand for nonlocal scholars also fits a larger nineteenth-century pattern that Zhang Shaodan recently documented for Central and Eastern China proper, in which communities sought to break the corrupting effects of inherited positions in their communities by institutionalizing the use of outsider scholars for imams and teachers.[52] Ma Qirong, arriving from Yunnan to teach at Guangzhou's Huaisheng Mosque in the mid- to late nineteenth century, fits both the local milieu of Guangzhou and the larger pattern.

The earlier *Origins of the Huihui* narratives, by omitting any substantial discussion of the lands from which the Muslims arrived, concentrated almost entirely on validating the presence of the Muslims in China and tying them to the state through the approval of the Tang emperor. Ma Qirong has added a new element of authentication by having the Muslim arrivals come not just from a vaguely described king on China's borders, but from the kingdom of the Prophet Muhammad himself. He continues to credit the Muslim arrivals with imperial endorsement, defending their legitimacy as residents of China, or, rather, "the Central Plains." But he is also invested in authenticating their Islamic bona fides, an interest very much in line with the efforts of the Guangzhou Muslim community to establish legitimate knowledge and practice of Islam in their city.

The focus on Waqqas may also reflect the changed sacred geography of Guangzhou. In the course of the eighteenth century, Waqqas was increasingly understood to have a tomb in Guangzhou, and in the nineteenth century this tomb seems to have grown in significance as a point of convergence for various local congregations, as well as Muslims from foreign countries and other provinces.[53] Whether through Ma's exposure to oral traditions in Guangzhou or from an interest in tying the "origin" of China's Muslims to the local landscape, it is fitting that Waqqas should have a larger presence in Ma Qirong's adaptation of the long-standing origin narrative.

Ma's history reminds us that origin stories, despite normally masquerading as fixed points of reference, themselves have histories, changing over time in adaptation to the evolving communities they serve. The *Origins of the Huihui* and *Genealogy of the Arrival from the West* have often been discussed as though, from the moment of the first text's publication in 1712, they were timeless expressions of a singular Chinese Muslim community's historical self-understanding, literally the *ultimate* Chinese Muslim origin story. As far as I am aware, no focused study on the numerous variations of this narrative tradition has been undertaken. The source material is rich and diverse, encompassing both printed works and manuscripts, and deserves further investigation. This transformation of an origin story across time (and in this case place) shares something with the *Briefest Treatise,* the current version of which was collectively authored across a century and a half.

It is worth briefly returning to the earliest version of *Origins of the Huihui,* because that text presents a highly distilled example of the focus on origins that can be seen across so many Muslim Chinese histories (a focus that Ma Qirong dilutes only slightly). As the title of the text so neatly summarizes, its purpose is to explain the people called Huihui (Muslims of China), by seeking an origin. This origin takes the form of a single moment, a first moment, in which Muslims set foot in China, with the assumption that this moment can bear the full weight of explanation for the nature and history of the Huihui. Ma Qirong, despite diluting the singularity of origin by adding a second migration later in the Tang, shares this impulse, ending one passage with the statement "the origin [由來] of the Hui teaching first arriving in the Central Plains lies in these [events]."[54]

In this kind of historical explanation, the events and transformations between the early origin and the present largely disappear, projecting the origin perpetually onto its purported heirs in their various presents. Indeed, today it is widely accepted among Hui of all sects that they are descendants of migrants from the time of the prophet who married local wives, as related in these texts. Ben-Dor Benite has noted that this focus on a single moment of origin sets up the history of the Huihui as a convergence of Islam and China as naturally separate elements, "convergence of the histories to which [Chinese Muslims] belong."[55] The disentanglement of the two histories is clear in the poem that is at the beginning of most versions of *Origins of the Huihui:*

> The Huihui were originally all in the Western Regions,
> How could one know that they would settle in China [中國]
> forever?[56]

The desire to find the earliest contact between a China-free Muslim and a Muslim-free China has yielded an interesting, perhaps ironic, depiction in this poem. According to all versions of the *Origins of the Huihui,* the first Muslims arrived in China during the lifetime of the prophet. For the emperor's dream, the 1712 edition gives the date of 629 CE, while Ma Qirong's text gives 628. According to Islamic traditions, the final *surah* of the Quran was not revealed until several years later, and the first revelation had only occurred at most two decades earlier. Ma Qirong makes this explicit, describing how Waqqas brings back to China only those parts of the Quran that had been revealed up to that moment. If we associate "Muslim" or "Huihui" with those who follow the revelations received by Muhammad, then the statement "The Huihui were originally all in the Western Regions" takes on a very narrow meaning. As of the printing of the *Origins of the Huihui* in 1712, the "former" period of separation had lasted at most two decades, while the period of China and Islam's interweaving had already lasted one thousand years. But the single-minded focus on an originary moment projects that moment onto the remainder of history. Here it preserves a China-free, "original" Islamicness that becomes associated permanently with the Huihui of China.

Genealogy of the Arrival from the West and *Origins of the Huihui* represent an extreme form of origin seeking, which is not universally present in the histories that Muslims wrote about their own communities in China. Jahriyya histories, such as the one that Manṣūr wrote, go to great lengths to show the unbroken transmission between a point of origin and the present, as does the Beizhuang hagiography by Muḥammad Yūsuf. Lan Xu leaves gaps between historical figures, but by no means does he abandon the long time span between origin and present. All emphasize origin, but they vary in their concern for the process of transmission.

What Is Shared

At first inspection it is the differences between the four authors above that draw attention. Two of them were members of Sufi orders and thus each recognized a community guide who sat atop a clear, if contested, hierarchical structure. Their histories emphasize both origins and the unbroken transmission of authority from the origin. The others wrote from within more diffuse communities lacking a clear leadership structure, in which religious and scholarly authority was spread informally. Their histories are less concerned with the continuous transmission of authority and are more tightly focused on origins. Some employed Confucian philosophical terminology extensively, while others made almost no use of Confucian concepts. Some wrote in Chinese, others in Arabic or Persian.

Across the varied cultural terrain of Islamic China, language choice and genre have a rough correlation. In the raw number of distinct books published with community histories, Chinese-language works dominate. This contrasts with the books on the various Islamic sciences and the textbooks in wide use in schools, which are more weighted to Persian and Arabic. As we have seen, this pattern did not hold in every community. Persian and Arabic treatments of community history have been of central importance in some important communities, namely the Jahriyya and the Beizhuang. Moreover, though I am aware of no community histories in Persian or Arabic in circulation among the non-Sufi communities before the late twentieth century, Perso-Arabic histories of the wider Muslim-majority world (for example, *Qisas al-anbiya)* were common.

Alongside the differences between these authors there are substantial connections and shared characteristics. All were men, as were the authors of all known Chinese Islamic histories written before the middle of the twentieth century. And all of them had substantial religious education. At least two were religious teachers. Lan Xu, who worked as a Qing official, embedded his historical treatise in a larger treatment of the fundamentals of his Islam, as did Muḥammad Yūsuf, a Sufi insider who may or may not have served as a teacher. While the Islamic character of their educations distinguished these historians from their non-Muslim Chinese counterparts, the close connection between moral education and history writing was shared by both groups. No one was educated outside of a system of moral teachings, be it Islam or Neo-Confucianism or both. Those with an interest in writing history tended also to write about moral systems. This was amplified by the fact that no one was writing in their vernacular, preventing potential writers from outside dominant educational systems from contributing to the written historical discourse.

Most importantly for our current aims, these authors all demonstrated an abiding concern with origins. They did this to establish a place for themselves and their communities, to explain the categories they inhabited. For authors attempting to defend the authority of a particular claimant to a leadership role, it was important to trace transmission, recording each link between that origin and the present. For others, the connection between distant origin and lived community was presumed. Regardless of this variation, in selecting which parts of the past to transform into history, all four authors focused on material that produced a compelling origin for their self-categorization. The search for origins is about cutting off and cutting out explanations. Any phenomenon has almost infinite origins. To choose one or two or five is to erase explanations, eliminate co-origins, streamline, and thus transform. In this sense, origin stories are invaluable maps of community values and self-identifying features.

But across the narratives the different approaches to origin seeking are worthy of consideration. Ma Qirong's *Genealogy of the Arrival from the West* shows the tightest origin focus, recounting a moment of category-forming arrival (in the Tang dynasty), and ignoring the subsequent millennium, superimposing the Tang past on the Qing present to explain the essence of the Huihui. In this way it parallels the recourse later historians have so often taken, when explaining the presence of Muslims in China, to suggesting a discrete moment of arrival. Lan Xu, in his *Epitaphs,* claims not one origin but two, pruning multiple roots of inheritances less completely than Ma Qirong did. And, though his chronological and genealogical coverage is fragmentary, he gives a sense of transmission, of the double inheritance moving forward (he would perhaps say downward) in time, even changing along the way. In the two Sufi texts we see full accounts of transmission. For each, an ultimate origin is significant, but there is reenactment of origination with each link in the *silsila.* Manṣūr's Jahriyya history provides the fullest accounting for each figure in his chain and, in the process, folds transformation into the identity of his community. The tragic martyrdom of the sixth *murshid* is nearly as foundational to the Jahriyya of Manṣūr's day as the first *murshid's* journey to Yemen. And through the recitation of *Mukhammas* and *Mada'ih,* it is woven into the fabric of the ordinary.

One final point of variation among these authors is worth noting: divergent approaches to time. It would be easy to assume that the notion of an origin includes within it a clear and linear temporal direction. The origin stories of the four authors described here show that origin obsession is not tied to homogeneous, empty time, or even to linear time. The Jahriyya histories, in particular, demonstrate that origins can be simul-present. Not only are origin stories possible in meaning-pregnant time regimes (rather than time regimes that are empty and measuring), but they flourish in those meaning-pregnant time regimes. Their meaningfulness folds back on itself repeatedly, multiplying resonance, mapping origins onto the present.

6

Origins Reveal

The Naqshbandiyya Mujaddidiyya

I FOUND MY WAY to the tomb of ʿAbdallah Qādir and the precious *ijaza* book described in Chapter 3 by following a thread that I began pulling two thousand kilometers to the west, in an oasis town of Altishahr (Eastern Turkistan) near the current Chinese border with Pakistan and Tajikistan. As we have seen, the manuscript at ʿAbdallah Qādir's tomb speaks to the role of extraordinary books in Muslim assertions of legitimacy. But at the time of my encounter with that little book, I was trying to answer a different question: What practices, sacred sites, and texts are shared by the Chinese-speaking Hui and the Turkic-speaking Uyghurs, two modern ethnic groups that tend to have stark cultural differences but together make up roughly 90 percent of the Muslim population of the People's Republic of China?

In pursuing this question I found myself engaged in a practice familiar to many of Islamic China's authors: seeking origins. My first step was a visit to a desert shrine far outside of the Uyghur town of Niya.[1] In 2007, while working on a book about Uyghur historical practices, I had been surprised to find Hui pilgrims at the holy site. Eight years later, it seemed like a good place to find Hui worshippers sharing in the Uyghur sacred geography. But by then the police had closed the shrine. I moved on to the oasis of Khotan, where I asked the advice of Hui imam. He pointed me to Yarkand. It was there that I acquired a book, *The Ninth-Ranked Transmission* (*九品乘传*), that claimed to reveal the origins of an Islamic network stretching across China and its colonial possessions, tying together Uyghurs, Salars, Dongxiang, and Hui. The text described a sacred center at

Yarkand, the last Qing-controlled city on the old trade routes to Kashmir and Afghanistan, called the Yarkand Daotang, or Hall of the Way. It told of seekers from China proper traversing thousands of kilometers to learn at the feet of the Daotang's master, after which they returned to spread the Way in their home territories. I resolved to trace these origins forward in time, leading me eastward.

This brought me to ʿAbdallah Qādir's tomb in Haidong Prefecture, Qinghai, a cultural center for the Salar ethnic group, and to Dongxiang, home to the Sarta (Dongxiang) people. Both places had purportedly sent seekers to Yarkand. To my astonishment, the claims in *The Ninth-Ranked Transmission* were corroborated by nineteenth-century manuscripts preserved in those places, one in Chaghatay and one in Persian. Continuing downstream chronologically, I pursued traces of the further spread of Yarkand's Dao into China proper. And heading upstream, I made my own pilgrimage to the Yarkand Daotang's self-professed point of origin: Sirhind, and the tomb of Aḥmad Sirhindī, where Chapter 1 opened. There, in Halu Ahong's urn, my two paths of origin exploration converged. I could reconstruct the spread of a network forward from its origin—Sirhind to Kabul to Badakhshan to Yarkand to Dongxiang—and, according to some claims I was encountering, onward to the Hui of China proper. And I could see the return to origins that pilgrimage represents, the closing of the loop, moving from Linxia, China's "Little Mecca," back to Sirhind. But I could not yet connect the two.

This chapter is inspired in part by the prominence of origin-seeking discourses in Islamic China. What opportunities lie in the investigation not just of origin stories, but of origins? What are its limitations? To answer this, I examine here a case in which pursuit of origins opens new understandings of Islamic China: the network that runs through the Yarkand Daotong. Readers familiar with the history of Sufism, often glossed as Islamic mysticism, will recognize in Sirhind and its famous son, Aḥmad Sirhindī, the father of a renowned Islamic movement, the Naqshbandiyya Mujaddidiyya. It is a movement that has heretofore been absent from synoptic depictions of Islamic China. This chapter is an extended tracing of origins, following the origin narratives of multiple communities to the points where they interconnect. Those interconnections tie nearly all of China's main Islamic traditions to the Naqshbandiyya Mujaddidiyya.

Naqshbandiyya Mujaddidiyya

Among the more notable characteristics of the Naqshbandiyya Mujaddidiyya is its wide geographical spread. By the late nineteenth century, the order had a substantial presence from Mozambique to Indonesia, stretching through the Ottoman Empire, Central Asia, the Russian Empire, and South Asia, leading Waleed Ziad to characterize it as "the most extensive Muslim revivalist network in Asia before the twentieth century."[2] In many parts of the world it was also the predominant Sufi order. However, China proper has long been assumed to lie outside of the zone of Mujaddidī expansion. Recent scholarship has shown that the Mujaddidī order also has a longstanding presence among the Uyghurs of Eastern Turkistan (Xinjiang), as well as Turkic and Mongolic groups living around the northern edge of the Tibetan Plateau (Qinghai and Gansu, China).[3] However, the roughly ten million Sino-Muslims, known today as the Hui ethnic group and spread throughout China proper, are absent from existing depictions of the Naqshbandiyya Mujaddidiyya.[4] The order also goes unmentioned in overviews and characterizations of "Chinese Islam," despite the fact that a handful of exceptional studies have spotted Mujaddidī connections in specific communities.[5] Through a pursuit of origins, this chapter links localized data points from secondary sources with new primary evidence, concluding that the Mujaddidī order has played a much more important role in the development of various Chinese Islams than previously recognized.

The Naqshbandi Mujaddidī order is an offshoot of the much older Naqshbandi order. The original Naqshbandi order traced its origin to Bahā al-Dīn Naqshband (1318–1389 CE), though it is unclear when exactly the movement coalesced into a formal order. The origins of the Naqshbandiyya Mujaddidiyya are much more distinct, resulting from the self-consciously reformist activities of Aḥmad Sirhindī (1564–1624), who encouraged the notion that he was the *mujaddid-i alf sānī,* the "renewer of the second [Islamic] millennium."[6] Sirhindī wrote extensively on both the failings of existing Sufi practices and on the flaws in anti-Sufi polemics offered by some juridical scholars. In his writings he proposed a unifying philosophy that explained how the mystical Sufi path and the *sharīʿa* (divine law), the esoteric and the exoteric, were not, in fact, at odds. He developed a clear plan of spiritual development for his followers, adapting and arranging existing Sufi techniques of meditation. And he designated a number of his followers as *khalifas,* successors who were licensed to spread the renewed Sufi path that he had developed, soon to be known as the "Naqshbandī Mujaddidī" path. Those successors went on to designate their own *khalifas,* and so on. Political instability of the mid-eighteenth century, including the 1763–1764 sacking of the order's center at Sirhind, accelerated the spread of the Mujaddidī network.[7]

The original Naqshbandi order was itself geographically expansive at the time of Sirhindī's intervention, with prominent branches throughout the Near East and Central Asia.[8] The older form continued to spread after the appearance of the Mujaddidīs, reaching Chinese-speaking Muslims in the late seventeenth century. But the Mujaddidī variant gradually eclipsed its progenitor in most places, including its original home of Central Asia, to the extent that most of today's Naqshbandi orders are Mujaddidī.[9] The Chinese Muslims described in this study were already exposed to, and in many cases followers of, the older Naqshbandi path when Mujaddidīs arrived to spread Aḥmad Sirhindī's vision. As this chapter will argue, in China proper the line between the two has become blurred over the last two centuries.

Important scholarship has already identified substantial Mujaddidī traditions among Turkic and Mongolic ethnic groups within the borders of the People's Republic of China, mainly the Uyghurs, Salars, and Dongxiang. The works of Thierry Zarcone, Alexandre Papas, and Waleed Ziad have been crucial in uncovering the transmission of Mujaddidī lineages and traditions among these Inner Asian groups in Eastern Turkistan and on the northern edge of the Tibetan Plateau, including parts of Gansu.[10] Nonetheless, the strong presence of the Mujaddidiyya among the Hui ethnic group, which accounts for the bulk of China's Sinophone Muslims, has not been recognized in English-language scholarship. Even individual Mujaddidī groups have largely escaped notice, with the notable exception of Leila Chérif-Chebbi's documentation that the Deaf Cleric's lineage began calling itself Mujaddidī by the early 2000s, a phenomenon also reported in Mathew Erie's 2016 Linxia ethnography.[11] However, as we will see in our pursuit of the Yarkand network, the Mujaddidī transmissions extended beyond Turkic and Mongolic groups to Sinophone Hui communities across China, giving the Mujaddidiyya a substantial role in the shaping of Chinese Islams. And the texts we traverse along the way, especially our sources on the Mujaddidiyya among Turkic and Mongolic groups, expand our understanding of both the Mujaddidiyya among those groups and the nature of transmission to the Hui and China proper.

Mujaddidī Shadows at the Heart of the Hui Autonomous Region

In August 2002, the Japanese geographer Takahashi Kentaro and 120 Muslims of Shanmen village climbed into a cargo truck normally used for transporting livestock and coal.[12] The truck was on loan, at no charge, from a local businessman, and it carried them roughly one hundred kilometers to one of the largest pilgrimage sites in the Ningxia Hui Autonomous Region: the Honggangzi (洪岗子) tomb shrine, or *gongbei* (拱北). The shrine complex features an eclectic accumulation of towers, domes, and spires: pyramids painted with green and white chevrons atop rectangular clock-towerlike structures; the upturned eaves of an octagonal pagoda; a conical spire ringed with blue stripes; and, until they were removed around 2020 under government pressure, green onion domes. The main ritual complex covers approximately eighteen thousand square meters, not including the industrial-scale cooking facilities and other support buildings, all of it painted in bold red, yellow, blue, and green.[13] Two hundred meters past the entrance is the tomb of the saint, Hong Shoulin 洪寿林 (1858–1937).

The villagers' pilgrimage took place two days before the anniversary of the saint's death, and the parking lot was full of trucks, motorcycles, tractors, and other pilgrims' vehicles. Takahashi estimated that twenty thousand people visited that day, but the pilgrimage festival stretched over multiple days. An online report by the Tongxin Compassionate Aid Society estimates that in 2016, the week-long festival saw two hundred thousand visitors.[14] Takahashi encountered pilgrims from as far away as Urumqi, Xinjiang, which has a substantial Hui population. Indeed, the Honggangzi death anniversary is among the largest Islamic pilgrimage events in China.

Inside the shrine complex, the pilgrimage group performed ritual ablutions, chanted *dhikr,* and presented alms. They touched the tombstone and rubbed their bodies, then they washed themselves in a special well. At the end they partook of a free communal meal in the cavernous cafeteria.

Due to political and security concerns stemming from my writings on the Chinese state's atrocities against the Uyghurs, I have been unable to visit Honggangzi to learn about the beliefs and practices of the pilgrims and their hosts. Fortunately, a locally produced volume of *Tongxin Historical Materials* details some of the beliefs and practices of the Sufi order for whom Honggangzi is a ritual center: the Hongmen order. Both Takahashi's ethnographic report and *Tongxin Historical Materials* identify the Hongmen order as a sub-branch of China's largest Sufi order, the "Hufuye" (虎夫耶, Arabic: Khāfiyya), as do all other Chinese scholars who have written on the subject.[15]

However, the practices documented in *Tongxin Historical Materials* show distinctive marks of Naqshbandī Mujaddidī spiritual exercises, especially in its account of *dhikr,* a "remembrance" of God that takes the form of meditative recitation, usually of short formulae such as the name of God. *Dhikr* is a common feature of various Sufi orders both within China and across the world, but the precise form of *dhikr* varies from one order to the next. In the Hongmen scheme, *dhikr* is divided into two categories: *yisimuzanti* (伊斯目咱提) and *naifeiyisibati* (乃非伊斯巴提).[16] The former is the recitation of "Allah," known elsewhere in the Persianate sphere as *ism-i ẕāt* (name of the Essence). The latter is a method of meditation on the phrase "there is no god but Allah," called in Persian *nafī-iṡbāt* (negation and affirmation). During the initiation of new followers, the shaykh presses his finger to three points on the initiate's body in succession to teach him where to direct his concentration during *nafī-iṡbāt.*[17] These points are the *laṭā'if* (subtle centers), rendered in the Chinese as *xuewei* (穴位). While versions of these techniques appear in the practices of various Sufi orders outside of China, the particular terminology and categorization reflect the Naqshbandī Mujaddidī discipline as it is still practiced in many parts of the world today.[18] The same source also presents general philosophical approaches that are hallmarks of the Mujaddidī tradition and Aḥmad Sirhindī's intellectual legacy. It says that the Hongmen order promotes the integration of *dao* (道: *tarīqa,* the Sufi path) and *jiao* (教: *sharī'a,* divine law): "like core and shell, *jiao* is the basis of *dao, dao* is the highest stage of *jiao.*" The follower should cultivate the Sufi path without escaping from practical life, a task enabled by the more general Naqshbandī practice of *khalwat dar anjuman.*[19] But how did these Mujaddidī practices make their way from Sirhind to the Hongmen followers in Ningxia?

A Short History of the Mujaddidiyya in China

Three questions raised so far in this chapter suggest a historical connection. How did an *ahong* from the Deaf Cleric's mosque in Linxia come to place an urn at the shrine of the Mujaddidiyya founder in Sirhind? Is the claim of *The Ninth-Ranked Transmission,* that the Mujaddidī path spread from Eastern Turkistan to numerous communities in China proper, true? Why does the Hongmen *menhuan* in Ningxia promote Mujaddidī spiritual exercises? These questions inspired me to investigate how and to what extent Mujaddidī affiliations, ideas, and practices spread from India across China. Elsewhere I have published a detailed account of the analysis and evidence I drew upon to answer that question.[20] What follows here is one product of that investigation: a brief, chronological narrative of the transmissions that account for the overlapping Mujaddidī origins that are shared by a broad range of Islamic China's communities.

In the decades following the sacking of Sirhind in 1763–1764, leading Sufis of the Mujaddidiyya order began to establish new centers of teaching, moving westward and northward quickly, such that by 1780 there were Mujaddidī communities in Lahore, Peshawar, Kabul, Badakhshan, Bukhara, and Khoqand.[21] In this period of rapid expansion, numerous Mujaddidī proselytizers arrived in Eastern Turkistan, which had recently been conquered by the Qing Empire. There was no single wave of Mujaddidī transmission to Eastern Turkistan. Numerous, often overlapping, transmissions resulted from more-or-less constant inter-Asian connection, which continuously transformed and diversified Mujaddidī communities in China proper, Eastern Turkistan, and Tibet. Of these three regions, Eastern Turkistan saw the earliest and most numerous arrivals of Mujaddidī proselytizers, and most Mujaddidī lineages in China proper and the Tibetan Plateau run through the orders that took root in Eastern Turkistan in the eighteenth century.

The spread of Mujaddidī orders in Eastern Turkistan can be traced in all cases to arrivals from outside the region, as opposed to travels of Eastern Turkistan's inhabitants to other regions. The proselytizers came first from South Asia (Hindustan and Badakhshan) and then Central Asia. The later, Central Asian, exchanges began in the early nineteenth century and continued through at least the 1930s. Thierry Zarcone and Alexandre

Papas have outlined these later branches in some detail, based on both written sources and fieldwork among members of their orders.[22] The earlier lines, with South Asia origins, seem ultimately to have had broader influence, generating substantial offshoots in China proper and supplying leaders in Eastern Turkistan's 1864 revolts.

Yarkand seems to have seen the largest number of the early Mujaddidī arrivals (late eighteenth century). One of them, a descendant of Sirhindī named Shāh Awlīyā', established the Yarkand Daotang, subject of *The Ninth-Ranked Transmission.* He came from Fayzabad, in Badakhshan, part of today's Afghanistan. It was probably around this time that another Mujaddidī proselytizer settled 350 kilometers north of Yarkand, in the village of Aykol, outside of Aqsu. It is difficult to date his arrival securely, because the only available sources are oral accounts recorded in secondary Chinese literature.[23] This "Indian" proselytizer was known as Ishan Muhammad Qari Akhund, and he is credited with establishing a *khanaqah* that would spread its teachings over the following century. His teaching lineage came to be known as the Aykol branch. Though Mujaddidī teachers would continue to arrive in Eastern Turkistan well into the twentieth century and some established their own followings, it was the Yarkand Daotang and the Aykol branch that would last longest and expand the farthest.

By the early nineteenth century, the reputations of both Shāh Awlīyā' and the second leader of the Aykol branch (a Huihui man named Ma Fang 马方) grew to such an extent that they were beginning to attract seekers from China proper and the northern edge of the Tibetan Plateau, men who traveled to Eastern Turkistan and studied the Mujaddidī path there. Among them were two figures we have already encountered. Shāh Ḥamza Ma Baozhen 馬保真 (1772–1826), the subject of the Persian hagiography explored in Chapter 5, arrived at the Yarkand Daotang in 1812 to learn from Shāh Awlīyā'.[24] From the Salar community in today's Qinghai came 'Abdallah Qādir, whose tomb holds the small Turkic *ijaza* that opened Chapter 2.[25] Both returned to the Gansu-Qinghai region and founded their own centers. The followers of Ma Baozhen would come to be known as the Beizhuang *menhuan.* Chinese-speaking Muslims also came in substantial numbers, from within Eastern Turkistan but also from China proper. Among them, individuals from Linxia and Lintao (Gansu) traveled to Yarkand, while others from Heilongjiang and Xining went to Aykol. These, too, returned to their home regions and established new branches that became *menhuans*. Within China proper, these *menhuans* spread further over the course of the nineteenth century. Today, the Hui *menhuans* that trace their roots to Yarkand or Aykol include the Dingmen (丁门),[26] Hongmen (洪门),[27] Jinggou (井沟),[28] Lintiao (临挑), and Beizhuang (北庄) orders.[29] Of these, all but the Beizhuang are considered today to be sub-branches of the Khāfiyya.

While formal Mujaddidī orders proliferated, another broader transmission was underway: the spread of the *Maktūbāt* (Collected letters) of Aḥmad Sirhindī, which serves as a foundational textual resource for the Mujaddidiyya's adherents around the world. Indeed, the impact of the Mujaddidiyya across Islamic China may have been more extensive outside of the formal orders than within them, because in textual form it reaches even beyond groups that consider themselves part of Sufi traditions. The *Maktūbāt* is widely read and taught among various Hui groups, playing a slightly different role in each.

The spread of Sirhindī's thought to non-Mujaddadī-affiliated groups appears in the historical record already circa 1830, when the classic Jahriyya hagiography, *al-Rashḥat al-sharīfat,* quotes Sirhindī, showing at least a familiarity with Sirhindī's reputation as a saint.[30] As the Mujaddidiyya gained influence across Asia in the nineteenth century, the growing numbers of travelers from Islamic China became ever more likely to encounter Mujaddidī scholars in their search for learning abroad. By the 1870s, the Sufi landscape in Mecca was overwhelmingly Mujaddidī. Chinese pilgrims who were not already affiliated with the Mujaddidī order would encounter its teachings as an authoritative discourse legitimated by a dense institutional presence in the sacred city. Thus, when Ma Lianyuan arrived in Mecca in 1870 / 1871 to acquire authentic learning, he appears to have turned to the Mujaddidī shaykh, ʿAbd al-Hamīd al-Shīrwānī al-Dāghistānī, the "Haimiji Afanji" of the Deaf Cleric's narrative, to study *dhikr*.[31] The Deaf Cleric's narrative concerning his father, Qi Huantang (1852–1933), is chronologically murky, but the names of the scholars Qi Huantang met in his travels clearly demonstrate interactions with Mujaddidī shaykhs in both Mecca and the Dutch East Indies in the late nineteenth century.

In the 1880s and 1890s, the Hajj brought Islamic China into contact with another, newer style of Islamic learning: modernist Islamic reform movements. Ma Wanfu, a Dongxiang man from just outside of Linxia, returned from Mecca after his 1888 pilgrimage to found the reformist Ikhwan movement. Though he renounced the Mujaddidiyya order into which he had been born (specifically the Beizhuang) for a textual literalist approach based in the Qur'an and *hadith,* he retained respect for the *Maktūbāt* and its calls for Islamic renewal. In his now-lost work *Buhualizande* (布华里咱德), he is said to have included portions of Sirhindī's foundational work, and his successors continue to study the work today. Ma's student, Hu Songshan, who would succeed Ma as the most prominent Ikhwanī leader, was also raised in a Mujaddidi family. Like Ma Wanfu, despite renouncing this heritage, even destroying his father's tomb, Hu retained a deep regard for the *Maktūbāt,* publishing an annotation of the text in 1940.

By the Republican era in China, the *Maktūbāt*'s penetration of Islamic China in the Northwest was so thorough that it became a common reference point in the intense sectarian struggles of the 1920s and 1930s. Several prominent *menhuans* regarded it as their core text on belief and practice. The Ikhwanī reformists, who pursued the destruction of the *menhuans* and the transformation of the nonsectarian Gedimu, kept the *Maktūbāt* as a core text themselves, with Hu Songshan wielding it as an "ideological weapon" in these sectarian battles, according to a study of Hu's writings.[32] And Qi Huantang, an *akhund* of the "old teaching" who led much of the defense against the reformists, had supposedly followed the *Maktūbāt* translation project to Mecca, an association that his son, the Deaf Cleric, would record as a central authorizing force in his lineage history. Because participants on opposite sides revered the same text, it became a common source of authority on which to base attacks and defense. In an ideological battle, there is limited value in citing a text or an authority source that your opponent doesn't recognize.

Availability of the *Maktūbāt* in China expanded when a prolific publishing house, Shanghai Believers' Classics, made a print edition available sometime in the middle of the twentieth century.[33] In the early 2000s two translations into Chinese appeared, one from the Persian original[34] and the other most likely from the Arabic.[35] The full history of the spread of Sirhindī's thought among Chinese Islamic communities unaffiliated to the Mujaddidiyya remains to be uncovered. But the outline history presented so far makes one of its outcomes entirely unsurprising: The *Maktūbāt* is commonly found in mosque libraries across the vast geographical terrain and sectarian variety of Islamic China. These include the Fu'ad library, formerly associated with the Chengda Muslim Teacher's Academy in Beijing; the library of the Banqiao Daotang, headquarters of one of the two main branches of the Jahriyya; the library of the Huasi Mosque in Linxia, the central mosque of the Khāfiyya *menhuan;* and the library of the Yangjiazhuang mosque in Xining, Qinghai. Today, with the possible exception of the Salafis, every major sectarian division of Islamic China is touched in some way by the Mujaddidī movement that Sirhindī initiated, continuously reshaped and reinvigorated by the movement of scholars and books to and from multiple parts of South, Southeast, Central, and Southwest Asia.

Transformations, Miracles, and Genealogies

The above narrative was driven by the question, which of China's Muslim communities have roots in the Naqshbandiyya Mujaddidiyya, and how were these inheritances transmitted? The product of these activities is a style of historical narrative that will be familiar to most readers of this book: an account of the origin and spread of a religious or intellectual movement, focused less on the meaning of the Mujaddidī path to those who engaged with it and more on determining which communities were touched by Mujaddidī influence and how those connections happened. As with any historical question, pursuing this one meant omitting whole worlds of meaning to which the sources give us access. In this section I want to give a few examples of what my story of origin and transmission ignored, both as a means to reflect on what origin accounts do and do not accomplish, and as a way of describing the diversity of Islamic China from a different angle, one that makes clear the interconnection of Islamic China's various communities, as well as the dynamic between local forces and the steady inter-Asian exchanges of the eighteenth and nineteenth centuries.

One question my short narrative should raise is, how has the Mujaddidī path transformed as it moved? The Hongmen order, with its Sirhindian spiritual exercises, shows that, for some practitioners, important parts of Sirhindī's message survived the four-century journey intact. In other cases, it appears that the transformation may have been so profound as to leave little in the way of recognizably Mujaddidī belief or practice, though we do not yet have enough sources to explore the changes in detail. One such example is the Dingmen *menhuan,* for which we have a short description of beliefs and practices outlined by a Dingmen leader in the 1980s.[36] What is most notable about the Dingmen as presented in this source is that, despite a clear, self-conscious identification with the order's origins in the Yarkand Daotang, none of the beliefs or practices described bear any distinctive marks of Sirhindī's renewal program. Without the Dingmen origin story, the *menhuan* is not recognizably Mujaddidī. It may be that the author intentionally omitted recognizably Mujaddidī practices, perhaps regarding them as secret. But if his representation is accurate, it would suggest radical transformations that are yet to be researched.

For a richer account, and a subtler transformation, let us turn to *The Ninth-Ranked Transmission.* The text includes a mix of material, ranging from a Chinese translation of a circa nineteenth-century hagiography to a compilation of online comments that followers left on the Yarkand Daotang's internet posts. While the online comments have much to tell us about recent transformations, the hagiography probably gives us more insight into the nineteenth-century localization of the order.

According to the hagiography, the Daotang's founder, Shāh Awlīyā', spent forty years traveling Eastern Turkistan, spreading his teachings and designating *khalifas* to further spread the *ṭarīqat.* In other areas of Eastern Turkistan he visited the shrines of local saints, for example, the tomb of al-Ḥasan al-'Askarī in Qaraqash, where he left behind a follower to continue teaching his *ṭarīqat.*[37] He also engaged in an activity commonly attributed to saints in Eastern Turkistan and especially Yarkand, the (re)discovery of the tombs of other saints. The two most prominent shrines in Yarkand, Chiltăn and Muhammad Sharif, are both associated with tales of miraculous shrine rediscovery.[38] Shāh Awlīyā''s hagiography credits him with discovering Terăk Mazar near Ghulja, which is described as the tomb of a local preacher whom Tughluq Timur Khān had met in the fourteenth century. Shāh Awlīyā' ordered a large tomb structure to be built there and appointed a follower to guard it and hold prayer sessions there.

In his travels, the hagiography says Shāh Awlīyā' promoted both silent and vocal *dhikr,* advocating that his followers practice different forms on different occasions. These included *dhikr* practices from the Qādirī, Kubravī, and Chishtī Sufi traditions. He also taught Mujaddidī doctrine familiar from manuals such as Khwāja Ṣafīallah Sirhindī's *Makhzan al-anwār,* including the mapping of subtle centers to parts of the body.[39] Upon deputizing *khalifas,* Shāh Awlīyā' would present them with a robe, a turban, prayer beads, and an engraved seal. No mention is made of the bestowal of a book in the manner we have seen in the case of the Qi lineage of Linxia or the Eastern Turki hagiographies of Afaq Khoja. At the age of 102, Shāh Awlīyāʿ passed the leadership of his order to his son, Mirza Shāh Muḥammad Sharīf, and returned Badakhshan, where he died two years later.

The narrative is replete with miracle tales, including some shared with another local Yarkand hagiography, the *Tazkira of the Seven Muhammads.*[40] The miracles range from transforming eggs into chickens to bringing a dead child back to life. Particularly interesting is an episode in which local notables attempt to shame the shaykh by hosting a feast for him and serving cat meat, a forbidden food. Shāh Awlīyāʿ sees through the ruse and begins crying. He caresses the meat and it transforms back into a living cat.[41] The same event, minus the tears and petting, occurs in the *Tazkira of the Seven Muhammads,* when Shāh Ṭālib Sarmast, who has rediscovered the tomb of the Seven Muhammads, is tested by the king of Yarkand with a meal of cat kebab and revives the cat.[42] Another tale from the Seven Muhammads finds a parallel later in *The Ninth-Ranked Transmission.* A Qādirī saint, whose son became a follower of Shāh Awlīyāʿ, was buried alongside his staff, and the staff grew into a tree.[43] In the *Seven Muhammads,* the titular saints carried a staff given to them by the Prophet Muhammad, and upon reaching their fated graves the staff turned green.[44] The Yarkand shrine to which the *Tazkira of the Seven Muhammads* is attached is much older than the tomb of Shāh Awlīyāʿ, appearing under that name in the Mirza Muhammad Ḥaydar's history of 1546.[45] The shared miracle of the cat meat, in particular, suggests that the author(s) of Shāh Awlīyāʿ's hagiography had been inspired by the local traditions and may have even attached them to their founding shaykh's biography in an effort to root his claims to sacred authority in Yarkand's prevailing notions of sainthood.

The hagiographical form in evidence here, combining aspects of South Asian Mujaddidī hagiography with the Eastern Turkistani hagiographical genre, is an ideal tool and vessel of transformation. As Shahzad Bashir has shown, hagiographies in the Persianate world can be dynamic texts, both reflecting their social contexts and constituting them.[46] The miracles (*barakāt*) that they report serve multiple functions, demonstrating the saint's proximity to God, promoting moral qualities (such as Shāh Awlīyāʿ's mercy toward the cat), and providing a shared sacred history that binds the community to each other (and to the local landscape, via the saint's shrine). Shāh Awlīyāʿs followers, among them the likely author(s) of this text, stood to benefit directly from the divine authorization these miracles claim as well as the community building they effect. But the author(s) must be conversant in the local vocabulary of *barakāt,* for some miracles are more compelling than others.

Further adaptation to local systems of sacred authority appears in another section of *The Ninth-Ranked Transmission:* the *silsila,* or chain of transmission. The *silsila* departs from standard Mujaddidī *silsilas* found throughout South and West Asia in several ways, but one will suffice as an example of the adaptation to the environment of Eastern Turkistan. This is the interpolation of Twelver Shiʿi imams, ten of which (all but Ali and the Twelfth Imam) are added to the *silsila.* At least five of the Twelver Imams have shrines in Eastern Turkistan, and several other shrines of "Imams" have hagiographies with genealogies that proceed through the eleventh Imam. The popular hagiography of Afaq Khoja also includes a genealogy passing through the first eleven Shiʿi imams.[47] In the case of Afaq Khoja, a Naqshbandi of the (non-Mujaddidī) line from Makhdūm-i Aʿẓam, this Twelver interpolation is similarly a deviation from standard *silsilas* of his branch known elsewhere in Central Asia. A Twelver genealogy also appears in the center of Yarkand itself, on the walls of the tomb of Muḥammad Sharīf.[48] In short, a spiritual (and genealogical) lineage proceeding through the eleventh Shiʿi imam was a widely claimed marker of sacred authority in Eastern Turkistan, even where it was at odds with other Sufi texts.[49] The Mujaddidī *silsila* in *The Ninth-Ranked Transmission* conforms to this pattern. It also interpolates figures from the local pre-Mujaddidī Naqshbandiyya, the Makhdhumzadas. By the nineteenth century the Makhdhumzadas had split and split again into several competing lineages, most of which were very politically active, for example, supporting Qing colonial rule or leading rebellions against it. The inclusion of the Makhdhumzada figure Isḥāq Walī was politically significant, aligning the *silsila* with a lineage supported by the Qing.

Silsilas, it turns out, can be just as dynamic and socially constitutive as hagiographies. While they often preserve important empirical data about who taught whom, creating a record of the *ṭarīqat*'s leadership over time, they also include markers of the order's commitments in the social context of the era in which the *silsila* was set down on paper. In this case we see a veneration of the Twelver Imams and the Makhdhumzadas peculiar to Eastern Turkistan, aligning the Yarkand Daotang with powers divine and earthly. All of these interpolations are placed before Aḥmad Sirhindī in the chain of transmission, preserving a more or less accurate record of the route of transmission between Sirhindī and Shāh Awlīyā', which is confirmed by comparison to the *ijaza* from the tomb of Abdullah Qādir. The latter part of the *silsila* worked to connect the Yarkand Daotang firmly to Sirhindī, while the pre-Sirhindī part aligned the Daotang with the local context.

Given that half of the Mujaddidī orders of China proper received their initiation from the Yarkand Daotang, the Daotang's adjustments of Mujaddidī historical production to Eastern Turkistan's discourses of authority and divine proximity must have, to some extent, transferred to these new communities. Both 'Abdallah Qādir's *ijaza* and the Persian Beizhuang hagiography, *Nuzhat al-qulūb,* include several of the Yarkand Daotang's *silsila* interpolations, documenting early movement of some Eastern Turkistani localizations to the Gansu-Qinghai region. But this would not be a one-off occurrence. The successive leaders of the Salar Mujaddidiyya and the Beizhuang *menhuan* continued to return regularly to the Yarkand Daotang to renew their learning and refresh their authorization. More on-the-ground research is needed to determine exactly how the Yarkand Daotang's integration in the Eastern Turkistani context left its mark on Mujaddidī communities of China proper, but we should expect the Mujaddidī traditions in China to be the product of their own local environments, the social contexts of intermediary communities, such as those of Eastern Turkistan and Badakhshan, and the interventions of Sirhindī himself.

Silences, Naming Practices, and Textual Authority

Another obvious question arising from my short historical narrative is, why have Mujaddidī connections been omitted from modern historical depictions of Islamic China? Formal Sufi lineages tracing their roots to Aḥmad Sirhindī are well documented in Chinese-language scholarship on the Hui. However, the connection between these communities and the global Mujaddidī movement has generally not been recognized. In most cases, the lineages are traced to "Yimamu Ranbani" or "Yimamu Rebani" (Sinicizations of Aḥmad Sirhindī's honorific, Imām Rabbānī) without identifying the figure as Aḥmad Sirhindī. With two exceptions, the terms "mujaddidiyya" and "Mujaddidī" do not appear in Chinese-language scholarship on these orders, which tends to categorize them instead as sub-branches of the Khāfiyya order, most notably in the influential work of Ma Tong.[50] The first of the two exceptions is Tan Wutie and Fu Yu's 1986 survey of Islam among the Hui of Eastern Turkistan, which they later developed into a book.[51] Through fieldwork with Hui religious practitioners, this seminal work identified links between various Hui groups and the lineage of Aḥmad Sirhindī. While they described Sirhindī's thought and placed several lineages of China and Eastern Turkistan in this category, they did not mention that Sirhindī's disciples and descendants spread the movement to other destinations beyond China, from Indonesia to Istanbul. Another chapter, by Chen Guoguang (陈国光), took the further step of recognizing that lineages traceable to Sirhindī are links to a global Mujaddidī tradition. Both studies focused on Mujaddidī orders in Eastern Turkistan, and while they listed the names of several orders from interior China that descend from Eastern Turkistan's Mujaddidī lines, they did not describe those orders in any detail. Nonetheless, their analysis of oral material among the Hui of Eastern Turkistan provided crucial data on the links between the region's Mujaddidīs and the Hui of China proper. Unfortunately, these researchers' scholarship has not been taken up outside the study of Hui Muslims in Eastern Turkistan itself.[52] Thus, the various groups identified in Chinese-language scholarship as descending from "Yimamu Ranbani" have not widely been recognized as historically connected to the Mujaddidī order, and they continue to be seen in studies of Islam in China proper as "Hufuye" (Khāfiyya) orders.

Much of the Mujaddidī erasure is a result of *ṭarīqat* naming practices specific to the Chinese context. Available primary sources from the Chinese Mujaddidī orders themselves use only the names of the sub-branches, such as Hongmen and Dingmen. Whereas suborders elsewhere in the world will often append a further name or names, for example, the "Naqshbandi Mujaddidi Aslami Arshadi" in the United Kingdom, the Chinese Mujaddidī orders have for several generations used only the narrowest sub-branch designation, dropping both "Naqshbandī" and "Mujaddidī" when referring to their own orders. In most sources, whether primary or secondary, the reader's only hint that a Sufi order is connected to the Mujaddidiyya is the inclusion of "Yimamu Ranbanni" in the spiritual lineage chain.

As we have seen in the case of the Jahriyya, succession struggles following the death of the shaykh could lead to a division of the *menhuan*. The division and subdivision of *menhuans* has been extremely common. Despite government efforts to end the phenomenon, such splits continue. When I visited the Beizhuang main mosque in the 2010s I found it abandoned. The community had split and established two new mosques. Over time, divided lineages sometimes developed into distinct *menhuans*. Another force behind the multiplication of *menhuans* was the product of community expansion; shaykhs would authorize students from distant regions to return to their hometown and found a new offshoot. As *menhuans* competed for resources, influence, and followers, communities found it useful to distinguish between various groups with distinctive names. Often they chose to name groups after the first leader of the new subgroup (e.g., Hongmen, Dingmen) or the place of its headquarters (e.g., Beizhuang, Jinggou). The Jahriyya and Khāfiyya are important exceptions in several ways. Their names refer to *dhikr* practices, and they are transliterations from Arabic. Moreover, their communities retain these designations even in the face of splits (e.g., the various Jahriyya subgroups all identify as Jahriyya). Had the Mujaddidī lineages followed the Jahriyya / Khāfiyya model, their connection to the global Mujaddidī history might not have disappeared. Based on the limited amount of data and scholarship currently available, we can only speculate as to why the Mujaddidī lineages consistently chose the founder / location approach to *menhuan* naming. However, we can say that this practice, which kept the Mujaddidī name and connections to Sirhind out of descriptions of Islamic China for so long, was also a part of the continuous transformation of the Mujaddidī movement as it developed in various parts of Northwest China.

The change in self-identification that comes with a new *menhuan* name is a socially significant act. Devin DeWeese, in his study of Islamic conversion narratives in Central Asia, has demonstrated that a change in name (in his case, the adoption of the name "Muslim") is anything but superficial, concluding that "to adopt a name is to change one's reality."[53] It brings with it a host of responsibilities and privileges, and in many Islamic traditions, self-ascription is itself a ritual act. When members of the Dingmen community identify themselves as such, they are demoting their responsibilities and allegiances to both the Yarkand Daotang and the global

Mujaddidiyya, drawing the circle of "us"-ness tighter and elevating their solidarity to fellow devotees of Sufi masters that trace their lineage to master Ding.

The demotion or even severing of Mujaddidī links has occurred not just in local naming practices but also in the treatment of texts. We have seen how extraordinary texts can serve to link communities in the cases of ʿAbdallah Qādir's *ijaza* and the Qi masters' receipt of authorizing books from foreign saints. The diffusion of the *Maktūbāt* in China provides interesting examples of how a text with strong sectarian implications can break free of its community-identifying functions. To accept the Mujaddidiyya path is to pledge oneself to a living master of Sirhindī's *silsila,* trusting him for guidance on the reformed path that Sirhindī set down in writing in the *Maktūbāt.* Yet the formative Ikhwān leaders, both of whom rejected the Mujaddidī paths in which they were raised, remained advocates and students of the *Maktūbāt.*

The case of the *Maktūbāt's* translation from Arabic to Chinese gives a small window on the dynamics of the text's liberation from its identitarian functions. The co-translator was the head of the Huasi *menhuan,* regarded as the leading branch of the Khāfiyya. Unlike the case of the Qi lineage, in which there is a claim to a formal transmission of the *Maktūbāt,* the Khāfiyya embrace of the *Maktūbāt* appears to be independent from the initiatic chain of the Mujaddidiyya, rooted instead in the ideas of the text as a theological and ritual resource.

The Khāfiyya *menhuan* is the older of the two main divisions of the Naqshbandiyya among the Hui. The founder was the son of Ibrāhīm Qi Xinyi's traveling companion, whom Afaq Khoja supposedly sent home while Qi Xinyi was invited to stay. According to Khāfiyya tradition, this companion, Ma Jiajun, received a blessing from Afaq, which alleviated his inability to have a son. After his return to Gansu, he married a non-Muslim woman according to Afaq's instructions, and she gave birth to the founder of the Khāfiyya order, Ma Laichi (马来迟). The order that emerged from Ma Laichi's teaching was, presumably, regarded simply as Naqshbandi for its first century. However, in the middle of the seventeenth century, another Chinese Muslim scholar, Ma Mingxin, returned from the Hajj with new ideas about Naqshbandi ritual practice, learned from a master in Yemen. Those ideas included the promotion of vocal or "loud" *dhikr*. The existing

Naqshbandiyya in China, by contrast, advocated silent *dhikr.* The ritual difference became the symbol and justification of contention over authority in Northwest China, conflict that burst into full, open, and deadly warfare that came to be known, misleadingly, as the "Muslim rebellions" of the late eighteenth and late nineteenth centuries. It also gave the two factions their names, with the Khāfiyyah order taking its name from the Arabic word for "silent" and the Jahriyya from the Arabic for "sawing," a reference to the sound of vocal *dhikr.* Like every large *menhuan* in China, the Khāfiyya has in turn divided into several branches, most of which coexist in competition but not conflict. The largest of these is the Huasi *menhuan,* which controls the most prominent mosque in Linxia and the tomb shrine of the Khāfiyya founder, Ma Laichi. As we have seen, several of the *menhuan* that consider themselves sub-branches of the Khāfiyya in fact place themselves in Mujaddidī *silsilas.* This is not the case with the Huasi branch, whose *silsila* proceeds through Afaq Khoja.

The translation was undertaken on the initiative of the late Hasan Ma Hongzhan (马鸿章), leader of the Huasi *menhuan* and descendant of the order's founder, Ma Laichi. Hasan Ma Hongzhan worked together with another translator to produce the Chinese version. In his introduction to the translation (dated 2005), Hasan Ma Hongzhan explains part of the *Maktūbāt*'s special value to his community: in one passage of the work, Aḥmad Sirhindī recommends that *dhikr* be carried out silently, rather than vocally. Thus, the core Mujaddidī text functions as an ideological asset in the dispute between the Khāfiyya and Jahriyya, rooted again in a presumed authority of Aḥmad Sirhindī, even outside the initiatic chain. This narrow sectarian concern probably does not fully account for Hasan Ma Hongzhan's interest in the work, the translation of which he called his "life's aspiration" and the "long-cherished wish" of his own master. But it provides another example of how Muslim scholars enlisted the *Maktūbāt* as "an ideological weapon," as the Ikhwani Hu Songshan is said to have done. The fact that the Jahriyya, the implied target of Hasan Ma Hongzhan's remarks on silent *dhikr,* hold Sirhindī and the *Maktūbat* in high regard makes it a particularly useful tool of critique. None of this provides a comprehensive explanation for why the *Maktūbāt* became so popular beyond its author's *ṭarīqat.* It does, however, demonstrate how texts could be put to new uses as they traversed the Islamic networks that linked Sirhind to China's "Little Mecca."

A Return to the *Tariqāt*

In the final example of this chapter, the *Maktūbāt,* having been separated from sectarian or *tariqāt* significance, comes to be seen once again as a Mujaddidī text. As the extraordinary book behind the authority of Qi Mingde, the Deaf Cleric, the *Maktūbāt* was more than just one philosophical and religious text among many. It was the central symbol of the transmission of religious authority for Qi Mingde and thus a representation of the religious identity of the lineage. Yet Qi Mingde gives no hint in his book that he identified with the Mujaddidiyya. Qi Mingde came to be regarded, instead, as one of the "three mainstays of the old teachings."[54] In his book he identified himself explicitly as follower of the Gedimu, which he explained as the "venerable ancient denomination" (古派) and the "old teaching" (老教), "in terms of doctrine, part of the orthodox Sunni sect, and in terms of law, Hanafi."[55] The Gedimu, he said, supports the [Sufi] *menhuans,* while the *menhuans* do not diverge from the Gedimu, and the two together are of one vein. He also called his father, Qi Huantang, an *akhund* of the "old teaching." There is no indication in Qi Mingde's memoir and family history of formal affiliation with the Mujaddidiyya, nor any place in a *silsila.* The *ijāzat* that the ancestor Ibrāhīm received from Afaq Khoja was never passed on, and no *ijāzat* from Manzilāwī is mentioned. Qi Mingde was not reluctant to express his support for the Sufi *menhuans,* and he records in his memoir his concrete actions to defend the *menhuans* from attacks by reformists and their government supporters in the Republican era. But he never claims in his writings membership in any *menhuan,* instead presenting his lineage's interactions with Mujaddidī figures as sources of learning and authority that strengthened his claim to be the defender of the Gedimu "old teaching."

Qi Mingde's son would later say that his father instructed him to seek out a Mujaddidī Shaykh Maʿṣūm in India. It is possible that Qi Mingde had always regarded himself as a follower of the Mujaddidī *tariqāt* but hid this identification for political reasons that are not clear, while remaining happy to praise Sufi orders in general. Another possibility is that his reverence for the *Maktūbāt,* together with regard for his father's interactions with Mujaddidīs abroad, led him and his son to learn more about the broader movement when the People's Republic of China opened up in the 1980s. Whatever the case may be, after Qi Mingde's death in 1987, his son, Qi

Jiequan (祁介泉, d. 2012), assumed leadership of the Qi lineage and its community. Qi Jiequan began an effort to reconnect with the figures to whom his lineage's authority was tied. Saying that his father had told him to seek out Shaykh Maʿṣūm, he made multiple trips to India, where he undertook pilgrimages to Sirhind.[56] In 2000, the order published a *silsila,* naming Qi Huantang, Qi Mingde, and Qi Jiequan as the most recent links in a Mujaddidī chain.[57] The chain passes through Shaykh Maʿṣūm via a successor named Abū Sharīf ʿAbd al-Qādir. This *silsila* is quite distinct from the Qi scholarly family lineage presented in *The Deaf Cleric.* Unlike the earlier work, which traces the Qi (genealogical and scholarly) lineage back to the seventeenth generation, in the *silsila* the Qi family appears only beginning with Qi Huantang in the twentieth century. Under Qi Jiequan's leadership, members of the community used the term "Mujaddidi" and made pilgrimages to Sirhind. Halu Ahong, donor of the urn at Sirhind, was one of them.

For Qi Mingde, writing in the 1980s, the *Maktūbāt* and the stories of its bestowal were foundations of the Qi lineage's claim to special, inheritable authority, but the community seems to have identified primarily as Gedimu. His son, who enjoyed the benefits of an increasingly open and prosperous China, was able to seek the roots of these authoritative texts and connections. The result appears to be a more formal association with the Mujaddidī order as an international movement, with authority rooted in the *silsila* as much as the older Qi family lineage.

Conclusion

If a *menhuan* doesn't call itself Mujaddidiyya and doesn't show any ritual or theological commitments that are distinctive to the Mujaddidiyya elsewhere, does it matter that its leaders trace their intellectual lineage to the Mujaddidiyya? What is the use of the origin story I presented above? One unsatisfactory answer is that it adds to the origin stories that already dominate the study of Islamic China. It is tempting to call the Mujaddidī transmission described in this chapter a new "tide" of Chinese Islam, following the prevailing scholarship on the history of Islam in China. The "three tides of Chinese Islam" framing is an excellent example of origin thinking's penetration of academic history, because it posits a series of discrete transmissions of various new-to-China forms of Islam over the last 1,400 years.

These are the first transmission of Islam, supposedly represented by the Gedimu; the arrival of the original Naqshbandi Sufi orders from Central Asia in the seventeenth century; and the modernist reform movements of the late nineteenth and early twentieth centuries.[58] The model has value as a heuristic framing, but the Mujaddidī example throws into relief what is lost in origin-focused simplification. There were multiple, overlapping transmissions of Mujaddidī texts, preaching, and organizations, into and within China. Given the regularity of pilgrimage to various sites of Mujaddidī significance, it might even be best to think of Mujaddidī transmission as a continuous process, one that is ongoing today in the pilgrimage of Hui followers to the tomb of the Mujaddidī founder in Sirhind, India. Moreover, the continuous transmission of the Mujaddidī movement overlapped and interacted with the Sufi and reformist "tides." In any case, the Mujaddidiyya have claims to both of these categories.

But there are more important lessons to be learned from the Mujaddidī transmissions. For the study of the Chinese Islams, the Mujaddidī case expands the catalogue of transregional connections, revealing yet another dimension of religious and intellectual exchange. India and Afghanistan are often omitted from accounts of Islamic China, but the Mujaddidī transmission show continuous interaction, from the mid-1700s down to today. It reminds us again of the importance of Persian, Arabic, and Turkic languages in the history of Chinese Islams, as media of connection to neighboring Muslim societies, and it further undermines the myth of Chinese Muslim isolation.

Where direct Mujaddidī transmissions to China proper can be traced, they almost always passed through Eastern Turkistan (although the Qi lineage also traveled to the Hijaz via Indonesia). The importance of interactions between the Turki, or *Musulmān,* people of Eastern Turkistan, whose descendants are known today as Uyghurs, and the Huihui, or Hui, was already well established in the work of Joseph Trippner and then Joseph Fletcher, who demonstrated the role of Afaq Khoja and his father in spreading Naqshbandī Sufism among the Huihui during the seventeenth century.[59] Afaq continues to be venerated as the origin point not only of the Qi lineage, as described above, but also of the Khāfiyya and Xianmen orders. More broadly, the canons of Islamic texts consumed in nineteenth-century Eastern Turkistan and much of Islamic China proper show substantial overlap, particularly among legal and Sufi philosophical texts. As recently as two decades ago, Hui pilgrims regularly made the journey from China proper to the Uyghur shrines of Tuyuq Khojam (near Turpan) and Imam Jă'firi Sadiq (near Niya), not to mention the Yarkand Daotang and its associated shrine.[60] The Mujaddidī transmissions effected by the Yarkand Daotang and Ayköl orders greatly expand the documented historical cases of circulations between Turki / Uyghur Muslims and the Huihui / Hui, widening our view of the long-term and varied exchange of Islamic thought that took place across this ethnolinguistic boundary and profoundly affected the Islams of China proper.

The case of the Mujaddidiyya in China also tells us something about the spiritual revolution set off by Aḥmad Sirhindī. It supports the arguments of Waleed Ziad, who noted that a combination of organizational, ideological, and textual characteristics made the Mujaddidiyya particularly suited to wide dissemination. Ziad documents accommodation of Mujaddidī outposts by various political orders and the localization of Mujaddidī techniques in varied cultural environments.[61] The Chinese case shows that Sirhindī's interventions, continuously and subtly reshaped by succeeding generations, had wide effects not just in spreading the formal order but in spreading ideas and texts among numerous Chinese Muslim sects.

While my brief history of Mujaddidi originations was necessarily reductive, it raised questions for me that I would not have otherwise considered. The power of Eastern Turkistan's hagiographical traditions to take root in a newly arrived religious enterprise, the systems of *menhuan* naming that have obscured Mujaddidī connections, and the process by which a text with strong sectarian functions becomes a cross-community locus of authority—all are issues that may yield valuable insights with further research. The range of Mujaddidī affiliations among Chinese Muslims is too extensive for a single researcher to address comprehensively. Every major Chinese Islamic tradition is touched in some way by Mujaddidī influence, from the Gedimu to the Jahriyya to the Ikhwani modernists. For scholars with access to Chinese Muslim communities, the scope for future research is vast. More *menhuan* will likely be discovered to be part of Mujaddidi lineages, especially among the *menhuan* that call themselves Hufuye (Khāfiyya). There is much more to be learned about the role of Sirhindī's *Maktūbāt,* along with other Mujaddidī texts, in various communities within China. In particular, the timing, routes, and mechanisms of *Maktūbāt*'s spread deserve detailed investigation. I hope that by identifying Mujaddidiyya ideas and identities as major components of Islams in the Chinese culture area, this chapter will encourage and facilitate such research. And by focusing on the great variation in the ways that Mujaddidī connections have affected Chinese Muslims, I hope this case can serve to remind us of the contingent, continuously emergent, and heterogeneous nature of even highly formalized solidarities, such as the Mujaddidī order.

These claims make a case for the scholarly value in seeking origins as one among many angles of analysis. The signs of China's Mujaddidī inheritance have been hiding in plain sight. As I noted above, some scholars have noted apparently isolated cases of Mujaddidī identity or practices. Many have reported on the importance of "Imam Rabbani" to various Muslim groups in China. But it is only through the tracing of origins that the connection between these cases becomes clear and the profound role of the Mujaddidī movement in shaping the landscape of Islamic China comes into view.

The notions of "transmissions" and "contributions" to Chinese Islams require some caution. Used carelessly, these terms might suggest a unidirectional outside "influence" on an essentialized, stable tradition of Chinese Islam. However, Muslims in China practiced a wide range of continuously transforming Islams—sometimes competing, frequently overlapping, and usually influencing each other. At the other, "foreign" end of the exchange in question here, the Naqshbandiyya Mujaddidiyya did indeed emerge in a clearly delimited place and time: Northern India in the sixteenth century. Many of its early leaders were committed to spreading their teachings, authority, and institutions to new territories. But it would be a mistake to equate the origins of the Mujaddidiyya with a transhistorical essence and neatly identify Mujaddidī phenomena in China with the movement's ultimate origins. The Mujaddidī traditions that arrived in Eastern Turkistan in the mid-eighteenth century were not quite the same as what Aḥmad Sirhindī had developed. Subsequent transmissions onward from Eastern Turkistan to China each took their own particular form, based partly on the constantly changing nature of the traditions in Eastern Turkistan and partly on the local needs of worshippers in the Chinese locales where they took root. In some cases these communities maintained the commitment to lineage and formal organization that had been present at the earliest manifestations of the Mujaddidī movement in Northern

India, even keeping the name. In other cases, the division of Mujaddidī lineages into sub-branches led to the coining of new lineage names and the forgetting of the term "Mujaddidi" as a lineage label, even where lineages and teachings were explicitly traced back to Aḥmad Sirhindī, *"mujaddid-i alf sānī."* In yet other examples, the Mujaddidī foundational text, the *Maktūbāt* of Aḥmad Sirhindī, gained reverence among leading Muslim intellectuals but without association to a formal order; the text was simply seen as a source of valuable teachings for people who trace their spiritual lineages to other origins. Finally, it is important to emphasize the shared agency of transmission. In some cases, the arrival of Mujaddidī traditions in new places was the work of proselytizers from abroad, while in others it was a result of Muslims from the Chinese interior traveling to seek learning (and authority) in foreign lands, whence they brought Mujaddidī associations back to China. Often it was a product of multiple journeys, reenacted across centuries, in both directions.

It has not always been the case that Mujaddidī transmission, even when direct and well documented, was clearly reflected in the beliefs and practices of the tradition's inheritors. The Dingmen, one of the communities that most clearly and formally traces its beginnings to the Mujaddidī order, does not show much evidence of investment in the teachings of Aḥmad Sirhindī. On the other hand, the Huasi Khāfiyya *menhuan,* which does not trace any connection to Sirhindī or his order, gives Sirhindī's *Maktūbāt* a prominent place in its teachings. In any case, a complete account of the role of Sirhindī and other Mujaddidī thinkers' teachings in the various communities discussed above would require long-term ethnographic fieldwork that has not been possible during the research for this chapter. Self-identification is also of limited use in tracing Mujaddidī links, because in most cases the term "Mujaddidī" does not seem to have survived. Rather than attempting to draw lines between "true" Mujaddidī communities or restricting this account to communities that literally self-identify as "Mujaddidī," I have presented here an account of evidence for a wide range of transmissions that are traceable to the movement begun by Aḥmad Sirhindī, be their linkages genealogical, textual, or organizational.

At an empirical level, I hope that this chapter can serve as a starting point for further research on the varying types of Mujaddidī presence among Chinese-speaking Muslims. Just as importantly, it shows that origin stories, be they genealogies, *silsilas,* or narrative histories, preserve special kinds of data across long time periods. Whereas Chapter 5 analyzed origin stories to uncover how authors understood their own communities in their own presents, the tracing of Mujaddidī inheritances shows that origin stories can lock information from earlier times into community memories, creating a record of travels, transmissions of ideas, and Muslim networks that crossed ethnic groups and religious communities and were otherwise lost to history. An investigation into origins has the potential to uncover much more than a single, category-constructing origin, especially with due attention to the continued transmissions across time. Moreover, even when origins have been forgotten or suppressed by political exigencies, they retain the potential to reemerge and reshape a community, inspiring new identities and new journeys. It is to this potential we turn next.

7

Origins Move

Diasporas of the Hijaz, Thailand, Malaysia, Taiwan, and Northwest China

Once in a lifetime you should pay a visit to the Heavenly Chamber [in Mecca], having given up what you treasure and departed from home. From antiquity until now this has continued so that people will not forget the first root.

—Wang Daiyu[1]

In 1948 a family in Azaq village, in Chinese-ruled Eastern Turkistan, decided to leave their homeland. They began making financial arrangements that looked very much like preparations to never return, transferring property to relatives and settling debts. The political turmoil of the time was probably the precipitating factor. Azaq was held by the Chinese nationalist party (Kuomintang), which was at war with the Soviet-backed Republic of Eastern Turkistan (1945–1949), and the front lines were not far away. Like so many Turkistanis at the time, when this family sought a route out of their homeland they turned to a type of travel deeply entrenched in their community, the Hajj. Over the centuries, this ritual return to the origin of Islam produced a thick network of knowledge and infrastructure for long-distance travel. Now, it provided fleeing Turkistanis with a well-trodden route, cross-border financial systems, and the promise of accommodation in distant Mecca.

So it was that in the summer of 1948 a fourteen-year-old Uyghur girl named Hajar Khenim left her home in Eastern Turkistan and headed for Mecca. She had no idea that the holy city would become her new home.

Today she remembers most vividly the sheer mountain defiles and shaggy yaks of the Karakoram Mountains, as well as a stormy sea passage to Arabia, but another turn of events had a more powerful effect on her life. After the Chinese Communist Party took control of her hometown, Hajar's parents decided to remain permanently in the environs of Mecca, where she lives to this day and where she is known not as a Uyghur, nor as Chinese, but as a Turkistani.

My colleague Huda Kashgary and I met Hajar Khenim at her house in Jeddah in 2016, nearly seventy years after Hajar's arrival from Eastern Turkistan. Despite the passage of so many decades, Hajar Khenim has vivid memories of her 1948–1949 journey from Eastern Turkistan to Mecca. When Dr. Kashgary asked Hajar what road she took, Hajar launched into an animated story of her adventures. She was young when they left, and it was the new and unfamiliar that left the deepest impressions on her. Hajar's family took the most common route, the extremely difficult but well-established path over the Karakoram Mountains, crossing passes more than four thousand meters in elevation between some of the world's highest peaks. Her party of a dozen or so horses rode along narrow paths hemmed by rock faces on one side and deep gorges on the other, and Hajar recounted brushing against the cliff face as their mounts pressed away from the defiles.

The Karakoram Mountains were a world not at all distant for Hajar—indeed, they could be seen from her home—but they were entirely alien. Azaq village, the center of Hajar's childhood world, is part of the Artush oasis, a patch of green—poplars, fruit trees, wheat fields—watered by streams from nearby the mountains and surrounded by a stony plain on the edge of the vast Taklamakan Desert. The mountains were the domain of nomads, the oasis-dotted plain the land of farmers and merchants. It was in this strange mountain world that Hajar rode an animal she had never seen before, the name of which she still does not know. She described it as a cow with long, black hair that she clutched to keep her balance as she rode. This was, of course, a yak, the hardiest of high-altitude domesticated animals. At night Hajar and her family slept in tents, another distinctive feature of the nomads' world.

Hajar's tale skipped over the more familiar lowlands on the other side of the mountains, moving on to Karachi, where her family boarded a boat bound for Mecca. Whereas Hajar remembered wonder in the mountains, she remembered terror on the seas. A storm tossed the ship, and in her quarters she heard loud clanging sounds she couldn't understand. She cried, fearing for her life. The ship arrived in Jeddah in the month of Ramadan, in the heat of the summer. The family found housing in a *ribat,* a pilgrims' hostel funded by a charitable endowment, and eventually settled in al-Safa, a neighborhood north of Jeddah's old city. Later they would move to the town of Ta'if, on the escarpment just east of Mecca.

Hajar says she was not aware that she was leaving her home for good, and she did not recall for us the moment when it became clear that her pilgrimage had transformed into exile. But soon she faced the difficult task of making a new home. The new environment was physically more similar to Azaq than many of the places en route, if drier and hotter. Culturally, however, the barriers were formidable. The local children did not accept Hajar, and they told her that her language was ugly. She cried often and longed for her home. And she stuck to her own people, who by this period were already numerous in the Hijaz. As for the Arabs, "we didn't mix with them." Even today, Hajar speaks very little Arabic. I asked about other people who, like Hajar, are called Turkistani today but who did not come from the Tarim Basin. In particular, I asked if Hajar's family interacted with fellow Turki speakers from Bukhara or Samarqand. Hajar grimaced and gave an emphatic "no!"

Hajar's memories convey well the emotional impact of experiences that are largely absent from the contemporary world: a childhood almost entirely ignorant of even neighboring cultures, suddenly interrupted by immersion in alien environments and ways of life; travel on a scale completely obviated by new technologies: eight months by horse, yak, and steamer, without international retail banking, formal identity documents, or telecommunication; as well as experiences that are all too common today: a sudden change in the political landscape that turns a respected member of one community into a dangerous or laughable outsider in another. But Hajar's memories are not the only evidence she has of her exile to the center of the world. She also keeps a packet of old documents, legal agreements that preserve another side of the story: the mundane arrangements that made her family's pilgrimage / exile possible. These reveal that Hajar's parochial childhood was enabled by a family that not only had their own small-scale international network but also knew how to harness the denser and more powerful global networks that enmeshed them, including, as we will see below, imperialist states and a globalizing capitalist economy.

Uyghur histories from the last two centuries tend to take markedly different forms from the varied approaches of Chinese-speaking Muslims. There is far less concern for family origins and genealogy in Uyghur historical writing, and even community histories place somewhat less emphasis on the origins of the Uyghur people.[2] But the Uyghurs and the Huihui shared one larger origin story: the birth of Islam. Virtually every Islamic account of the origin of the faith gives a central role to the Prophet Muhammad's reception of God's word, the holy Qur'an, which took place in the Hijaz in the seventh century. In this history, built into the Qur'an itself, Mecca is not just a place where things began, it is a place to which the believer must return. It is not only the birthplace of a founder, or the tomb, or a place in which enlightenment was achieved. It is framed as the destination, or at least the aspiration, of all Muslims, who are enjoined to make the Hajj at least once in their lives.

When Uyghurs, Huihui, and other Muslims under Chinese rule left their homelands as exiles, traders, or seekers of knowledge, they very often took advantage of the infrastructure of the Hajj, including transportation, financial systems, and, perhaps most importantly, community knowledge of routes and methods of travel to Mecca. In effect, the origin story of Islam became a script for action. When Hajar arrived in the Hijaz, there was already a long-standing community of fellow Uyghurs, known locally as Turkistanis. There was also a growing community of Huihui, who had become known as Sīnī.[3] This chapter presents cases in which origin stories led to a particular form of action: travel. Origin-seeking travels maintained connections between Islamic China and other Muslims throughout the rest of Asia, and they led to the establishment of Chinese Muslim communities from Southeast Asia to the Middle East to Central Asia.

The Hajj is an unusually clear example of an origin story creating movement and shaping diaspora. It neatly fits the widespread and misleading conception of Chinese Muslims as people defined by origins outside of China, the descendants of foreigners who arrived from beyond the borders and created new communities. But Chinese Muslims have also established new communities in various places outside of China. Thus, the last two centuries have seen the rise of another kind of origin story, in which Islamic China has become an origin. This chapter addresses both kinds of origin stories, as well as the phenomena that emerge from their interplay. By describing three diaspora communities whose history has not received enough attention, it aims to bring Chinese Muslims outside of China more firmly into the history of Islamic China. It also demonstrates that origin stories can have substantial practical effects, not only because they create socially constructed realities of identity categories and community bonds (as we saw in Chapter 5) but also because they inspire literal movement.

Eastern Turkistan to Mecca and Back Again

Hajar Khenim's exile to Mecca was inextricable from trade patterns. Her extended family's trade in textiles created intricate economic relationships with merchants spread throughout South Asia and the Hijaz, and when the time came to flee her homeland this network of credits and debts supplied a financial infrastructure for travel across multiple economies and financial systems. In the weeks leading up to their departure, Hajar's immediate family purchased debts owed to family members and acquaintances—debts owed by traders scattered along Hajar's route. After crossing the Karakorum Mountains, they could, for example, look for a certain ʿAbd al-Raḥmān Hajjim of Gilgit, whose debt they now owned. And upon their arrival in Mecca, they could attempt to collect a debt from Hajar's uncle, which they had also purchased.[4]

To prepare for this, they drew up brief legal documents recording the debt transfers. These they had signed by multiple witnesses and stamped with the ornate, round seal of an Islamic judge. They also sought the endorsement of a transnational authority: the British Empire. For the price of ten shillings per document, the British consulate in the neighboring city of Kashgar notarized the debt transfer documents, witnessing the signatures and fingerprints of the parties and witnesses. Hajar's family was not alone in converting debt transfer into a kind of traveler's check. One document in the trove is the product of a different family's debt purchase, marked as paid in Mecca by a member of Hajar's family. All were part of a larger flow of traders and exiles to the holy cities of Arabia.

Eastern Turkistan endured an unrelenting succession of political and economic hardships in the first half of the twentieth century, and from the 1930s the number of refugees fleeing to the Hijaz increased substantially. In the Hijaz, they were known as "Bukhari" or "Turkistani," terms that referred to anyone, Turkic or Persian speaking, who arrived from Central Asia. Those terms stuck, and most descendants of migrants from Eastern Turkistan today consider themselves to be at once Bukhari and Turkistani.[5]

Today, most Turkistanis in Saudi Arabia trace their families' arrival in the Hijaz to the 1930s–1950s. This was a time before the ethnonym "Uyghur" had wide purchase on the sensibilities of the settled Turki peoples of Eastern Turkistan. In the migrants' absence from Eastern Turkistan, the settled Turki people and the Chinese state have come to agree that they are all "Uyghurs." Among the diaspora in the Hijaz, this term is still new, and it remains less compelling than the "Turkistani" idea (which includes people with roots in former-Soviet regions of Central Asia). Meanwhile, some Uyghurs in Eastern Turkistan—a minority, to be sure—have come to see themselves as Chinese.[6] This identity remains alien to all or nearly all Turkistanis in Saudi Arabia. Its Arabic form, *Ṣīnī,* is applied instead to the smaller Hui diaspora community.[7]

No longer subjects of China, the Turkistanis of Saudi Arabia do not consider themselves Chinese in any way. However, they remain aware of and interested in their origins in Eastern Turkistan. Even before travel to China became possible, a Saudi Turkistani author nourished origin memories with a book, called *The Great Tragedy of Turkistan,* documenting Central Asian history since its conquest by Russia and China.[8] Following China's opening in the 1980s, many Saudi Turkistans contacted long-lost family members. Some have managed to travel to the region and discover their "homeland"—a region that second- and third-generation Turkistanis had never set foot in before. Hajar was among those who managed to return in the late 1990s. Now exiled to the center of the world, Turkistanis embrace another origin, in Chinese-ruled Turkistan.

Reconnection had lasting effects. From the 1980s through roughly 2015, family members in Eastern Turkistan have arranged for brides to travel to Saudi Arabia to marry Turkistani relatives there. The women who arrived from Chinese-ruled Eastern Turkistan to marry Turkistanis in Saudi Arabia experienced a gendered change in social roles that probably gives a glimpse of what Hajar and her family encountered. They moved from a context in which women were able to travel freely and independently outside of their homes to one in which they must be accompanied by a male family member. They were also subject to new dress codes, in which attire that was forbidden as "extremist" by the Chinese government was legally required by the Saudi state.

Hajar's collection of legal documents suggests women exiles also faced a dramatic change in economic roles. Among the eight documents, five name women as key participants in financial transactions. One woman sells a debt that she had acquired in the process of buying land from another. Two other women transfer parts of their inheritance in exchange for debt to be collected in India, while recording that they will keep certain land and houses for themselves. There are challenges in comparing this prominence of women in land transactions with the situation they encountered in Saudi Arabia. Hajar's documents cannot be assumed to be representative, and hard data on Saudi Arabia's economic situation in the late 1940s and 1950s is difficult to come by. However, the situation forty years later, when data on land ownership by gender becomes available, points to a stark difference. In 1999, only 0.8 percent of agricultural landowners in Saudi Arabia were women.[9]

Shifts in ethnic identification and women's roles were only two among many transformations that the exiles from Chinese-ruled Eastern Turkistan faced in Saudi Arabia. Surviving first-generation Turkistanis often mention language, foodways, and climate as memorable shifts. These have shaped the occupations and settlement patterns of the community. Many new arrivals made their livelihoods by selling Turkistani foods to locals. A substantial part of the community eventually moved from Jeddah to the town of Ta'if, some in search of a more familiar climate, establishing charitable hostels for the exiles that continued to arrive from their hometowns.

In most practical senses, the Hijaz does not look like an obvious choice for Muslims fleeing China's westernmost territorial possessions in the 1930s and 1940s. To begin with, it is four thousand kilometers away as the crow flies, over six thousand kilometers along standard routes. The Muslim-majority lands that exiles traversed on their journeys were more familiar in terms of culture and in some cases landscape. Indeed, some exiles settled in British India and Afghanistan, but most continued to the Hijaz.

The religious obligation to return to the origin point of Islam once in a lifetime had built an economic and social infrastructure for movement. In addition to the trade relations that made debt purchase an effective tool for moving money, pilgrimage infrastructure softened the hardships of exile. Pilgrims to the Hijaz found shelter in charitable hostels called *ribat* (plural *arbuta*), which were financed by charitable foundations (*waqf*, plural *awqaf*). In many cases a *waqf* was initially funded by a foreign ruler as a religious act, designating it for the support of pilgrims from his territory. One example involves the grandfather of Qi Mingde, the Deaf Cleric, who carried on his Hajj funds from the warlord Ma Fuxiang to establish a *waqf*.[10] Yaqub Beg, who ruled an independent kingdom in Eastern Turkistan from 1865 to 1877, is said to have established a *ribat* in the Hijaz as well.[11] Just as often, a *waqf* was founded by a wealthy pilgrim or émigré. As the number of Turkistani migrants increased throughout the twentieth century, so did the *ribats*, many of them dedicated to specific hometowns in Eastern Turkistan. Trade and pilgrimage infrastructure thus interacted with the force of origin stories in a mutually strengthening way, overcoming the enormous disincentives to choosing such a distant land as a place of exile.

By directing Turki exiles to the Hijaz, the tradition of returning to Islam's roots has radically altered the émigrés' lives, to the extent that they have developed a new sense of what is ordinary, including new ethnic identities and a wholly new delineation of gender roles. But swimming up history's stream has also produced new origin stories. As of the 1930s, vernacular local histories in Eastern Turkistan, known as *tazkira*, tended to frame the region as a destination. They chronicled the great deeds of sacred heroes who had arrived from far away (sometimes the Hijaz) and established Islam in Eastern Turkistan, leaving behind tombs that knitted together the regions' oases through local pilgrimage. Today, however, the Turkistanis, exiled to the center of the world, call the Hijaz home and have begun to see Eastern Turkistan as a point of origin. Reconnection with that newer origin—through the flow of brides, visits to relatives, and increasing connections with other exile communities in Turkey and Europe—is now cementing that origin and the identity that comes with it. More than ever before, the Turkistanis of the Hijaz are beginning to think of themselves in terms of the ethnonym that took hold in their absence: Uyghur.

Yunnan to Thailand and Back Again

The reader may have noticed a curious detail in Chapter 1, which I left unexplained. In discussing Ma Lianyuan's *Explication*, the Arabic-language legal text he published in India, I mentioned that the only copy I could locate bears the stamp of a mosque library in Thailand: the Attaqwa Library in Chiang Mai. Finding this book was the culmination of a long and wide-ranging search on my part, encompassing Ma Lianyuan's home province of Yunnan, as well as Kanpur, where the book was printed, and nearby Lucknow, where old Islamic lithographs are widely available. I did not expect that when I finally located a copy, it would come from Thailand. In search of an explanation for this small mystery, I traveled to Chiang Mai, where I encountered examples of movement patterns inspired by both kinds of origin story—those in which Mecca is origin, and those in which China is origin.

The specimen of *Explication* I located in China is a photocopy of the Indian lithograph, with an additional page recording that the reproduction was undertaken by the Attaqwa Islamic school in Chiang Mai, Thailand, called in Chinese the Jing Zhen School 敬真學校.[12] It also bears the rubber stamp of the Yunnan Mosque where I found it and a handwritten inscription, dated May 20, 1988, recording an individual's gift of the book to another school. It is not clear who was responsible for transporting the book from Thailand to Yunnan.

I visited the library at Attaqwa Mosque in Chiang Mai in hopes of locating the original from which the photocopy had been made, along with any other books that might shed light on movement between the two communities. The contents of the library were, by and large, disappointing in this respect, but the staff generously presented me with a copy of a locally produced history of the mosque's founding.[13] A group of Yunnanese Muslims had fled China in the 1950s, just after the Communist Party took power, and settled in Chiang Mai. The movement of this copy of the *Explication* suggested that they had brought with them elements of Ma Lianyuan's textual and educational program. I would later learn that the connection was deeper than this.

There is a larger and older Chinese mosque in Chiang Mai, the Ban Haw Mosque (王和清真寺). There I also asked after books, but I was told that the mosque had no library. A few years later I returned and learned that this was untrue. This time, in December 2022, I was given access to a substantial library, with several books dating back to the late nineteenth century. Among its holdings, perhaps the best represented author / editor is none other than Ma Lianyuan.

Both the founding of the Ban Haw Mosque and the educational curriculum of Ma Lianyuan have roots in the interlinkage of trade and Hajj pilgrimage. The story of a Yunnanese businessman named Ma Youling 馬佑齡 is both illustrative of the role of Chinese Muslims in the Yunnan–Chiang Mai trade and directly linked, in a generative way, to Ma Lianyuan's publishing career. Ma Youling's biography is recorded in a Yunnan local history from 1996 (a provincial *wenshi ziliao*), unfortunately without citations. Its author writes that as of 1855 Ma Youling had a stable but modest business based in Yuxi, Yunnan (the hometown of Ma Lianyuan). For nine years Ma Youling's business followed a simple pattern. He would travel to the provincial capital, Kunming, to buy yarn. Back in Yuxi, he would sell the yarn to local weavers. Then, he would purchase the cloth they produced, sell it in Kunming, and begin the process again. By 1855 he was wealthy enough to begin planning his pilgrimage to Mecca.

He set off that year along the Tea Horse roads to Burma. He did not, however, follow the Irawaddy to the Bay of Bengal as Ma Dexin had. Instead he traveled another well-worn route, overland through Chiang Mai. Indigo was a major crop in this region, and according to the local history, it was on his pilgrimage that Ma Youling encountered the dye that would greatly expand his business. He began arranging caravan shipments of the dye and integrated indigo dying into his cloth enterprise.[14]

Ma Youling's cross-border business would go on to play a significant role in the development of Islamic literature in China. In the late nineteenth century, one of his nephews would begin a publishing project that needed substantial funding. The business that Ma Youling founded, under the new name of "Xing Shun He," was prominent among many funders for that project. The nephew was Ma Lianyuan, and the name Xing Shun He is found on three of his editions, including the most ambitious project: the printing of the entire Qur'an in Arabic.[15]

We have seen in Chapter 4 that the presence of Chinese traders in Chiang Mai had already been documented in the 1580s.[16] As of 1890, according to the British colonial railroad engineer Holt Hallet, most of "the Yunnan trade" moved through Chiang Mai.[17] It is unclear when Muslims in particular rose to prominence among Chinese traders in the city, but as of the early twentieth century, the area of Chiang Mai known as the Yunnan quarter was informally led by a *hajji* named Zheng Chonglin 鄭崇林. It was this community that, in 1916, pooled its resources to build the Ban Haw Mosque.[18]

The oldest books in the Ban Haw Mosque library are Persian woodblock editions of Ma Lianyuan, namely *Pillars of Islam* and *Basic Requisites for Muslims* (see Chapters 1 and 2). The library shows substantial evidence that the interest in Ma Lianyuan's curriculum has continued into very recent times. Some of Ma's works are present in photocopied editions, including his Kanpur publication *Sharḥ al-Laṭa'if* and his woodblock *Basic Requisites.* The former is also represented in a 1983 translation into Chinese, another work I had sought for years in China without success.[19]

The work held in the largest number is none other than the *Explication,* Ma Lianyuan's explanatory commentary on the *Wiqaya,* the book that originally brought me to Chiang Mai. The half-dozen or more copies at Ban Haw Mosque demonstrate the continuous development of Ma Lianyuan's curriculum and the maintenance of connection between the Muslim communities of Chiang Mai and Yunnan. They include a second volume, authored by Ma's second son, published in 1924.[20] And they were printed in Yunnan between 1989 and 1993.[21]

Today the Chinese Muslim community of Northern Thailand has come to view not just Mecca but also China as a point of origin, inspiring regular travel. This sense of connection survived the long period of dislocation created by the communist seizure of power in China, between the exile of the Attaqwa Mosque founder in the early 1950s and the reopening of China's borders in the 1980s. The travel permitted by that reopening is memorialized in the 1988 inscription on the Attaqwa copy of *Explication* in the Yunnan Mosque. Across Northern Thailand, Chinese Muslims continue to nourish ties to their Chinese origins in Yunnan. When I visited communities in Chiang Mai, Chiang Rai, and Mae Sai, I encountered individuals who studied or visited Yunnan, and I heard that young men are often sent to study in China. The library at Ban Hao continues to host teaching sessions. For these Chinese Muslims of Thai nationality, Ma Lianyuan's curriculum, shaped by the intertwining of Hajj and trade, has played a prominent role in defining the nature of Islam. The founders, funders, and caretakers of the library have invested heavily in making Ma Lianyuan's texts ordinary on new soil. At the same time, China has become another origin, one that moves people to travel in the opposite direction of the Hajj.

From Quanzhou to Taiwan and Malaysia and Back Again

The Bao'an Temple (保安宮) in Lukang, Taiwan, is an impressive three-story structure, with an ornate altar and a historic statue of the god known as King Guang Ze, among other deities. The once-bustling port city has lost its commercial significance but retains much of its nineteenth-century architecture, which draws a steady flow of tourists. Among the many historic temples of Lukang, the Bao'an Temple cannot compete for tourists' interests, and on many days only a handful of local visitors stop by to pay their respects and burn incense. But on festival days the temple comes alive as worshippers parade the statues of the gods into the streets. There are no visible signs that the temple was once a mosque, as community leaders say it was.

Inscribed on pillars and plaques both inside and outside the temple are the names of prominent community members and donors. Nearly all of them share the same surname, Guo (郭), identifying them as members of the neighborhood's predominant lineage group, for whom the temple serves as ancestral hall. Genealogies and elders of the Guo lineage report that their clan descends from Muslims who settled in Baiqi, just outside of Quanzhou, the renowned mainland port that hosted a substantial number of Muslim traders from at least the Song dynasty onward. Today, none of the Guos of Lukang identify as Muslims, but Guo elders and scholars describe practices that reflect their Muslim heritage. Most notable is a taboo on pork during ancestor worship and funerary rites.

The Guo clan's historic engagement in maritime trades of fishing and commerce has spread its members widely over the last three centuries. In addition to their mainland home region and several cities in Taiwan, Guos of this lineage can be found in Malaysia and the Philippines. It is only in Baiqi that some, though only a minority, of the Guos continue to identify as Muslims. Across this geography the no-longer-Muslim Guos share the taboo on pork as an offering to ancestors.[22]

As their geographical dispersal suggests, the Guos once maintained frequent contact through trade and travel. For much of the last century, however, that contact was disrupted by political upheaval, including Japanese occupation, the Sino-Japanese war, and the isolationist polices of Mao-era mainland China. According to Oded Abt, who carried out groundbreaking anthropological research among the Guos, few young clan members in Lukang today are aware of their Muslim heritage.

In 1958, an *ahong* from Kaohsiung and another Muslim named Li Zhongtang preached to a gathering of Guos in Lukang and interviewed them about their practices and beliefs. At that time, any engagement with Islam beyond limited pork taboos was already confined to the distant edges of living memory. Elders told the interviewers that there were still a few people around who remembered a particular old woman who was able to recite passages from the Qur'an. This would probably place the last transmission of Quranic recitational practices in the nineteenth century. They also said that in the past the community would sometimes send to Fujian for an *ahong* to perform funerary rites, but war had put an end to the practice.[23]

When the People's Republic of China opened up in the 1980s, Guos from Taiwan began traveling to Baiqi to reconnect with their origins and their fellow Guos. Over the course of a few years, Taiwan Guos made repeated, substantial donations to economic and educational development in Baiqi, sometimes in cooperation with Guos from Singapore and Malaysia. They collected donations for a library, an auditorium, and the construction of a middle school. In 1990, they funded the construction of a hostel for future visitors from Taiwan and in 1992 the renovation of the ancestral hall in Baiqi.[24]

As these stories demonstrate, the Lukang Guo origin story spurred different reactions based on the commitments and identifications of the people who consumed it. To the Muslim visitors of 1958, the Islamic element of the origin story was most significant, making the Lukang Guos a particularly important object of proselytization. The Guos were a people who could and should be called back to their religious origins. In their 1958 interview with the Lukang Guos, the Muslims asked about the Guos' habits of worship, marriage practices, funerary rites, and dietary customs. At the end of the interview, they asked whether the youth of the community would be open to returning to Islam, to which young people at the meeting supposedly answered with an enthusiastic yes. Sixty-five years later, it seems that the offer did not lead to any permanent change—no Lukang Guo converts to Islam have been reported.

Outsiders of all kinds have tended to view the Lukang Guos primarily through their ancestral connection to Islam. Li Zhongtang, the visiting

Muslim, wrote that "as far back as 1938, I had heard that there were many Muslims in Lukang."[25] In a collection of reminiscences about his youth in Lukang, a member of the Ding lineage (which has its own ancestral link to Islam) wrote that most of the residents of the Guo neighborhood of Guo Cuo "believe in Islam."[26] A 2022 documentary about Lukang on Taiwan's public television interviewed a Guo community leader about "Taiwan's oldest mosque" and remnants of Islamic practices.[27] In the academic sphere, for example, in the seminal work of Dru Gladney (and now again here), the Guos of the People's Republic of China side have also been studied in terms of their relation to Islam.

As anthropologist Oded Abt has argued, and as the activities of the Taiwan Guos who returned to Baiqi in the late twentieth century demonstrate, the focus on Islam misses much, if not most, of what was important to the community itself.[28] To the no-longer-Muslim Guos of Lukang, it was the genealogical element of the origin story, with its potential for the strengthening of a transnational lineage group, that was more compelling. The donations from Taiwan Guos went to economic development, travel infrastructure, and an ancestral hall in the hometown of Baiqi. According to interviews conducted by Guo Zhichao in Baiqi, a hundred Guos traveled to the hometown for ceremonies commemorating the renovation of the Guo ancestral temple in Baiqi in 1993.[29] In the Guos' own writings, Islam explains something about their ancestors, but that chapter of the clan's history is no more important than the subsequent abandonment of Islamic belief.[30] Both are secondary to the more important goals of tracing genealogical connections, strengthening clan links, and maintaining (non-Islamic) ritual obligations to the ancestors, which are better understood in the context of wider patterns of Chinese lineage practices.

The two groups, insiders and outsiders, with their attention to different aspects of the Guo origin story, have benefited from each other's efforts and often worked together. For Taiwan's Muslims, the Guo story and the claim to an early or even pre-Qing mosque adds depth to the history of Islam in Taiwan. Academics have found the Guo community revealing as a point of articulation between Chinese, Muslim, and "Hui" identities. For the Guos of Lukang, the outside attention has brought additional research resources to the search for their origins and attention that has often been welcome. The Facebook page of the Bao'an temple proudly announces the visits of outsider researchers, Muslim community leaders, and media coverage such as the television documentary. Most emblematic of the symbiotic dynamic between insiders and outsiders is a written genealogy of the Guos published in 1987. After the discovery of the text in Hong Kong, lineage-tracing Guos worked with the China Muslim Association in Taipei to bring it to print.[31]

In Penang, Malaysia, the Guos faced an entirely different terrain of ethnic and religious identities, and they responded with very different deployments of their origin stories. Unlike in Lukang, where the Guos live exclusively among non-Muslims, the Guos of Penang have both non-Muslim and Muslim neighbors. The line between these two groups falls neatly along ethnic borders, such that it is widely, indeed normatively, expected that Malays are Muslims and Chinese are not. Based on fieldwork among the Guos of Koay (= Guo) Jetty in Penang, Rosey Wang Ma has shown that Guos have often felt that adherence to Islam brought them social disadvantages among ethnic Chinese neighbors, while Chineseness appeared to them as a barrier to full participation in Malay Muslim communities. The result, Ma argues, has been two diverging paths for Guos over the past century. Some have cultivated their Chinese origin stories, while abandoning most practices identified with Islam and losing, in the course of generations, knowledge of their Muslim origins. These families maintain their Guo surname and identity simply as ethnic Chinese. Meanwhile, others abandoned and even concealed their Chinese origins, often dropping their Chinese surname and intermarrying with Malays. These families now identify as Malays, and very much as Muslims.[32]

Of course, even the most powerful social structures do not entirely obliterate individual agency. Rosey Wang Ma documented the experiences of a non-Muslim Guo man who, upon learning of his lineage's origins, decided to convert to the religion of his ancestors. In 1997, Ma records, the man went to China to visit his ancestors' graves. There he acquired a copy of a Guo genealogy, likely the 1987 publication from Taiwan, which he brought back to Malaysia. He told Ma that he hoped to persuade other Guo members to convert to Islam.

In the most basic sense, an origin story has to be *valued* before it can have power. Descendents of Chinese Muslims in Penang found themselves living amid a dichotomous ethnic landscape. In neither of the predominant neighboring communities were *both* Chinese and Muslim origin stories valued. For some Guos of Penang, Chinese origins were devalued and even hidden. For others from the same community, it was the Muslim origin that was devalued, and it was the Chinese one that they acted upon. In the Taiwanese context, valuation divided instead along insider / outsider lines, in a dynamic that ultimately revived both Chinese and Muslim elements of the origin stories for the Guos of Lukang. In both cases, the power of origin stories as scripts for action was crucially dependent on wider social contexts.

Local Origin Journeys

In my exploration of Jahriyya history writing (Chapter 5), I spared the reader discussion of one important Jahriyya text, which usefully illustrates the final aspect of origin-driven action that I want to point out: Origins can multiply and, in the process, become local. The text in question is a short Arabic work of 1920–1921, entitled *al-Rashf* (The sip), a play on the title of the foundational Jahriyya history *al-Rashḥat al-sharīfat* (The dewdrop). It narrates a single important episode in the life of the seventh Jahriyya *murshid,* Siddiqallah Ma Yuanzhang 馬元章. It describes itself as follows:

> This text is named "The Sip" from the steady rain of secrets and states and miracles of our current Mawlana, shaykh of shaykhs, axis of axes, Muhammad Riyaḍ al-Dīn [Siddiqallah Ma Yuanzhang], may God sanctify his secret, which he manifested in his pilgrimage to the shrine of the greatest Mawlana, Wiqāyatallah QSA [Ma Mingxin], may God sanctify his secret, the famous noble tomb in . . . Lanzhou.[33]

According to *al-Rashf,* Siddiqallah Ma Yuanzhang left his headquarters in Zhangjiachuan, on the eastern edge of Gansu, with a retinue of scholars and disciples on May 7, 1919, heading for the provincial capital, Lanzhou. There they renovated the tomb of Wiqāyatallah Ma Mingxin before returning to Zhangjiachuan almost a year later, on April 25, 1920. The renovation of the tomb; the relationship between the journey's dates and the recitational cycle of the *Mukhammas;* the production of a written account; and the miracles it described combined to bolster Siddiqallah Ma Yuanzhang's claim to the status of seventh *murshid.* All of this depended on the significance of the tomb at Lanzhou.

In Jahriyya histories, as in many other Sufi traditions of China, travel to a place of originary authenticity has a strong authorizing function.

According to this historical tradition, the Jahriyya order came into existence as a distinct Muslim community in China because Wiqāyatallah Ma Mingxin embarked on a pilgrimage to Mecca. It was on that pilgrimage, in Arabia—Yemen, to be specific—that he received the central recitational texts of the order, *Mukhammas* and *Mada'ih,* which would set the sacred rhythm for community life for the next three centuries.

Siddiqallah Ma Yuanzhang was unable or unwilling to make such a grand odyssey. But by 1919, Wiqāyatallah Ma Mingxin's own tomb had become a symbol of the roots of the Jahriyya. A pilgrimage of a mere 240 kilometers, along with a substantial investment of resources to renovate the structure, provided sufficient connection to community origins. Today the Lanzhou tomb remains an object of pilgrimage. Siddiqallah Ma Yuanzhang died in December 1920, and in the intervening decades his own tomb has drawn pilgrims from across China. Origins beget origins. They move people not only across continents but along tighter circuits, closer to home.

The preface to Ma Dexin's 1861 account of his Hajj describes this proliferation of origins and the tombs that mark them thus:

> Facing East, unable to see the waters' end, gazing toward the ocean, one might sigh at his insignificance. His land, people, and political affairs face raging seas and terrifying waves. How can one dare to float on the sea in a raft for a grand tour? It is like tracing the origin of our ancestors from thousands of years ago. Dividing into branches, spreading out into sects, they display their graves as a detailed genealogy. This allows the clan of Muhammad in Yunnan to continuously know their origin, from the early sages to the late sages.[34]

Circulation

Origin-fueled travels, trade flows, and shifts in political terrain have combined to create circulation. And the effects of circulation reach well beyond the travelers themselves, building across generations. Such effects are visible in the following story of another well-traveled text: Liu Zhi's *Nature and Principle in Islam.* In the course of my research on Islamic China, I developed a want list of promising-looking sources that I had seen cited in other works but had eluded my searches for years. At the Ban Haw library in Thailand I crossed one last book off of this list: a 1983 Chinese translation of one of Ma Lianyuan's Arabic works, which I had seen mentioned in the work of Sachiko Murata.[35] The text's arrival in Thailand capped the work of multiple authors across five centuries, writing in Persia, India, and China.

The earliest seeds of the book are to be found in the writings of Sufi thinkers scattered across Persia and Central Asia. Their works were popular among Muslim scholars in the Yangzi delta, where in the early eighteenth century, Liu Zhi selected various passages as the core of the "root classic" for his *Nature and Principle in Islam*. Adapting these Persian and Arabic selections to Classical Chinese verse, he spliced several texts together to create a synthetic manifesto of Sufi metaphysics.

In the eyes of Ma Lianyuan (Chapter 1), Liu Zhi's Chinese-language works fit perfectly into an otherwise Persian and Arabic curriculum. In 1898–1899 Ma translated Liu's work (back) to Arabic as *Laṭa'if* (Subtleties).[36] In the same year he published another edition with explanatory commentary in Arabic.[37] Four years later, in Kanpur, India, Ma published a super-commentary of the text with the same publisher who brought his *Explication* to print.[38] The Kanpur edition made its way back to China, where it was copied into at least one manuscript in the "Sini" calligraphic form.[39]

The book I finally located in Chiang Mai is a translation of Ma's Arabic translation and commentary of the Kanpur edition into Chinese (the translator reverts to Liu Zhi's original text for the "root classic" portion). It was published in 1983 by the China Democratic League, one of the eight minor parties of the People's Republic of China that persist at the pleasure of the Communist Party of China.[40]

A summary of this text's history illustrates the scope of textual circulation from the Ming through the late twentieth century. It is a Chinese translation of an Arabic commentary on an Arabic translation of a Chinese adaptation / translation of selected Arabic and Persian texts. Those earliest texts were written in Persia and Central Asia; collated and translated into Chinese in Nanjing; translated again into Arabic in Yunnan; commented on and published in Kanpur, India; and translated again into Chinese for publication in Beijing, before the book arrived finally in Thailand.

Conclusion

The circulations, pilgrimages, and exiles described above are a small sample of inter-Asian mobilities shaped in part by investments that the Muslims of China have made in the question of origins. Attention to this kind of mobility sheds light on an aspect of Islamic China that has too rarely been remarked upon: the existence of multiple, often interconnected, Muslim Chinese diaspora communities, spread across Asia (the work of Janice Hyeju Jeong and Oded Abt are stand-out exceptions). Communities that understand themselves as both Chinese and Muslim can be found in Indonesia, Malaysia, Myanmar, Thailand, Kyrgyzstan, Uzbekistan, and Saudi Arabia. Other diaspora communities recognize that their ancestors lived under Chinese rule but do not consider themselves Chinese. These include the Turkistanis of Saudi Arabia and the Uyghurs of Turkey, Pakistan, Central Asia, Western Europe, and North America, as well as many descendants of Chinese Muslims in Malaysia. In Malaysia and Taiwan we also find communities that consider themselves Chinese but no longer Muslim, despite embracing their origins in Muslim communities of China. A sense of distant origins defines diaspora communities. The diaspora of Islamic China see themselves as having two distant origins, in China and Arabia.

I have focused on more recently established diaspora communities, because they survive today and maintain records of their distinctive histories. Many others have ceased to define themselves in relation to China or to Islam, blending into the societies where they settled. Already in the Ming period, Chinese Muslim trading communities were scattered around the Indian Ocean and Southeast Asia. In earlier chapters we encountered other, more ephemeral mobilities directed by originary geographic imaginations: Wang Mingyu, who settled in Mughal India; Ma Lianyuan, who died in Kanpur; Wiqāyatallah Ma Mingxin, who brought texts from Arabia; and Ibrāhīm Sunnī Qi Xinyi, who traveled to meet a descendant of the prophet (Afaq Khoja).

Many histories of pre-twentieth-century Chinese Islams highlight isolation and localization. But the distinguishing feature of most Chinese Muslim self-imaginations, at least those recorded in writing, has been connection. The connecting thread between the various historical imaginations of Muslim communities is a fixation on origins and transmissions, which inevitably lead not only to Mecca but also to a wide range of nodes in inter-Asian Muslim networks. Self-identification as Muslim helps to create networks because self-identification creates responsibilities, including to others who self-identify as members. Historical imagination, including the list of places with fellow "Muslims"—India, Bukhara, Badakhshan, Mecca—can become activated and instantiate networks when people need or want to move, whether to escape war, do business, or pursue authentic knowledge.

The Guo clan of Taiwan and the Turkistanis of Mecca show that origins alone are not sufficient to sustain ethnic or religious identities, though origin stories play a crucial role in maintaining those imaginations and allegiances in so many other cases. At the same time, they demonstrate that a lack of ethnic or religious identification does not sap the power of origins to move. Turkistanis "return" to Chinese-controlled Eastern Turkistan and Guo clan members "return" from Taiwan to mainland China.

The Guos remind us that an origin story is a choice, not a destiny. What one Guo community treasures, another discards. Their devaluation of some origin stories casts the other origin scripts in this chapter in a different light. Outsider discourses about communities that happen to be Muslim often regard them as uniquely defined by their religious inheritance. In the case of the Hui ethnicity in today's China, it is Islam that primarily distinguishes the Hui from the Han, making them the only ethnic group in China defined above all by religious affiliation. For many residents of Europe and the Americas, communities made up of Muslims are defined by a presumed religious devotion—one that diverges from shared norms. In this context it would be easy to presume an emphasis on Meccan origins for China's Muslims. The wider context of Islamic China's diverse origin accounts suggests that the valuing of Meccan or any other origin is a significant community choice, an inheritance whose reproduction across centuries carries its own shifting meanings.

The interplay of origin story and self-identification is crucial to the formation of categories such as Chinese, Muslim, Hui, Uyghur, Turkistani, and others. The anthropologist Fredrick Barth, whose understanding of ethnic group construction has come to dominate the social sciences, privileges self-ascription as the foundation of ethnic groups, describing cultural "content" and symbolic markers—to include origin stories—as important for their role in advertising and maintaining boundaries.[41] But that content, especially origin stories, by virtue of being singled out as supposedly constitutive of the group (by members of the group), gains power that can in turn move identity boundaries, ethnic or religious.

8

Origins Distort

Myths of the Han Kitab

ROUGHLY SIXTY YEARS after Wang Daiyu published his extraordinary text—the earliest surviving Islamic book in Chinese and the world's oldest surviving printed book to be published by a Muslim (see Chapter 2)—a work destined for greater fame appeared: Liu Zhi's *Nature and Principle in Islam* (*Tianfang xingli* 天方性理). Liu has been called "the most profound and subtle" of the Muslim authors writing in Chinese, and he has been venerated widely across sects and schools.[1] Like Wang Daiyu, Liu resided in Nanjing and was deeply educated in Chinese-, Persian-, and Arabic-language scholarship, though Liu was different in that he studied Chinese texts first. But conditions for Islamic scholars had shifted by the time Liu published his first major text around 1704. As Wang Daiyu had predicted of himself, he had become an "opener of the field" of Islamic writing in Chinese, succeeded most notably by Ma Zhu (c. 1640–after 1710). Composing new Chinese-language texts about Islam was no longer such a lonely affair. And no longer were the "classics" of Islam entirely unavailable to readers in Chinese, as Wang had complained. At least four Persian or Arabic books had been published in Chinese translations. Even elements of the Qing central bureaucracy had encountered Chinese-language Islamic scholarship, thanks to Ma Zhu's trip to Beijing to get the emperor to recognize his work.

It makes sense, then, that Liu Zhi expressed a somewhat different purpose for his first major composition. Wang Daiyu wrote only of non-Muslims when describing his interlocutors and intended readership. Liu Zhi describes a more mixed audience. Here I quote the authoritative translation by Murata, Chittick, and Tu:

> Although I am indeed a scholar of Islamic Learning [天方之學], I privately venture to say that unless there is an exhaustive prying into the [Chinese] Classics and Histories and a wide inquiry into the hundred families of books, Islamic Learning will stay in a corner and not become public learning under heaven [天下之公學; James Frankel translates as "not be the common learning of the world"[2]] . . .
>
> My deceased father went deep into the purport of the nature and mandate of Heaven and humans. He used to exhibit to his colleagues what he had silently become acquainted with. He would often beat his breast in lamentation and say "The Islamic classics elucidate the principles in their furthest essence, but unfortunately I am unable to translate them into Chinese so that they might be shown widely in this land." That is why I was inspired by my deceased father to engage in [writing this book].[3]

Liu's metric of success, making Islamic thought "public learning under heaven" or "the common learning of the world," refers to an audience rather wider than just the existing Muslims of China. For Liu, such publicness could be achieved only by articulating Islamic learning with the Chinese classics and histories. And the Islamic classics cannot be "shown widely in this land" unless they are translated into Chinese. (If we were to assume—wrongly in my view—that spreading the classics widely among China's Muslims required writing in Classical Chinese, despite the China-wide Islamic education system in Persian and Arabic, we would still not be able to account for Liu's call to engage the Chinese classics and histories.)

Liu is clearly attending to non-Muslims with a Classical Chinese education. Liu has not, however, excluded Muslims from his audience, and he will come back to them later in his introduction.

After a decade of study and contemplation, sequestered in a mountain forest, Liu says,

> I suddenly came to understand that the Islamic classics have by and large the same purport as Confucius and Mencius. . . . Then I sighed deeply and said: The [true] classics are the Islamic classics, but the principle is the principle under heaven.[4] If the people under heaven do not come to have a share in hearing and clarifying the principle under heaven, that is by no means the intention of the sages who authored the classics. If I make them public under heaven, then the

> intentions of those who authored the classics will be satisfied and the will of my deceased father will also be satisfied.[5]

Here he has described an investigation of the Confucian classics much like what Wang Daiyu had undertaken with the three main Chinese schools of thought, but Liu comes to a different conclusion. Wang thought "that their arguments are strange and their ways different and mutually contradictory. If I measure them in terms of Islam, the differences and distinctions are like those between heaven and earth."[6] Liu, by contrast, found their meaning "by and large the same."

Further on, Liu writes,

> Humbly, I hope that students of Islamic Learning will understand the meaning by looking at the diagrams [in this book] and that they will be opened up to the classics by looking at the text. May they not become stagnant in the opinions of one corner, but rather awaken to the sameness of heart and principle. May they not wade in the flow of heresy, but rather rely on the teaching of the great public [大公].[7]

It appears that Liu not only wants to bring the Islamic classics to a broader public, but to open the classics of "Confucius and Mencius" to "students of Islamic Learning," to bring the students of Islamic learning into line with that "great public." His effort is one of both revealing to the two communities the fundamental sameness of their worldviews and bringing together two systems of conceptualizing this shared reality (as communicated in the two separate canons of "classics"). In doing so, he aspires to bring communities, until now learning the same reality from different books in different languages, into a single, shared "great public" that is Islamic.

The book that Liu produced is true to the values he set out in the introduction. It engages with the Neo-Confucian canon in a far deeper and more thorough way than Wang Daiyu did. Liu also had formal and stylistic tactics for spreading his unifying message. In his plan of the book, he describes the core of the work as a translation, cobbling together sentences from various, mostly Persian but also some Arabic, Islamic texts to convey what he sees as a shared meaning across all of them. This core "translation" he calls the "original classic" [本經], while the rest of the text is a series of explanations of this original classic. This approach is remarkably similar (minus translation) to one of the "Four Books" of the standard Neo-Confucian educational curriculum that was used in the Qing: *The Great*

Learning, in which Zhu Xi assembled passages from the ancient *Classic of Rites* and expounded on them with longer explanations.

Formal similarity is only the beginning of Liu's engagement with Neo-Confucian thought. The "Nature and Principle" of Liu's title nods to a common Chinese term for the discipline we today call "Neo-Confucianism": *xingli xue* (性理學), the study of nature and principle. The texts from which Liu assembled his "original classic" are dominated by Sufi philosophy from the authors Jamī, Rāzī, and Nasāfī, who each offered highly abstract and subtle theories on the nature of existence, God, and the universe. Liu finds parallels in Neo-Confucian discussions of "principle" as the blueprint of existence and the "Great Ultimate" as the simultaneous ultimate principle and ultimate good. He cites or quotes numerous leading (non-Muslim) Confucian thinkers. I could go on at length, but Murata and colleagues have already explored with great erudition and nuance the philosophical moves that Liu uses to unify the thought of his Perso-Arabic classics with the concepts of Zhu Xi and others that we call Neo-Confucian today. Short of inventing new terminology, it was impossible to translate metaphysical works into Classical Chinese without employing terms with deep Confucian resonance. Whereas Wang Daiyu did so out of necessity, Liu Zhi did so with enthusiasm. For him the equation of the two bodies of texts was the point.

The reception of Liu's work was ultimately mixed among non-Muslims and enthusiastic among Muslims, as Frankel has described in detail.[8] Liu managed to gather multiple laudatory prefaces for his publications from non-Muslim literati, some of which included exhortations to respect the teachings of Islam. This attitude was, however, not universally shared; in 1782 an itinerant scholar carrying some of Liu's texts was arrested, and the responsible official declared his books heterodox, ludicrous, and dishonest. The scholar was eventually released upon orders from the capital, but not before his books were destroyed, along with printing plates kept elsewhere. One of Liu's works was reviewed in the Qianlong emperor's great effort to collect, catalogue, or purge the books of the empire, the *Si ku quanshu.* Liu's work earned official approval as a nonheterodox text, but it was judged to have excellent literary style combined with fundamentally flawed arguments. Ultimately, Liu's project succeeded in protecting Muslims from the dangerous charge of heresy but failed in gaining widespread respect from non-Muslims.

Among Muslim readers of Classical Chinese, on the other hand, Liu's publications eventually established him as China's greatest scholar of Islam, earning him the title of *Xianxian,* or ancient sage. Later writers, including Lan Xu, whose 1852 history of saints was discussed in Chapter 5, repeated and rephrased Liu's ideas over the ensuing centuries. His almost saintly reputation among Muslims would eventually spread even beyond those who could comprehend his writing, and in the early twentieth century, his ideas would reach a humbler audience through pamphlets and magazines published in language that was increasingly close to the spoken (Chinese) form. In 1898–1899 Ma Lianyuan translated Liu's "root classic" into Arabic.[9] The sayings of Confucius and the metaphysical concepts of Zhu Xi had become an inextricable part of Islamic learning for a wide range of Muslims in China.

Essence and Origin

"Are they really Muslims?" So begins the cover blurb of a 2002 collection of essays on Islam in China by Raphael Israeli.[10] While it is unclear what role, if any, the author played in composing this cover text, it neatly reflects the feelings of surprise that figures like Liu Zhi have so often elicited in the West, surprise of at least two kinds: (1) surprise that Islam has been expressed using ideas from China's most famous philosophers and (2) surprise that Chinese Muslims could even exist, because China and Islam are presumed to be so thoroughly and essentially different. In this sense it also resonates with Israeli's essentialist understandings of both Islam and China, which he expounds upon in the opening essay, revealingly titled "Muslims in China: The Incompatibility Between Islam and the Chinese Order." Such "incompatibility" can only occur if Islam and "the Chinese Order" are defined by immutable essences, essences that are inherently at odds, deep gorges in the cultural landscape that never intersect. In the view from within these gorges, Liu Zhi presents a challenge and a curiosity. If Islam and China have irreconcilable essences, Liu Zhi's portrait of a deeply *Chinese* Islam (in the essentialist view) calls both essences into question, demanding an explanation quite different from what Liu Zhi said his project was all about. If, for example, the Qur'an is inherently un-Chinese (despite being venerated by parts of Chinese society for more than a millennium), then Liu Zhi's Qur'anic explications in Confucian terms become an exquisite oddity.

Israeli's essay title is a robust expression of essentialism, and as such it is one that most Anglophone scholars of Islams or Muslims in China would reject. Its contemporary political salience is immediately apparent, both in terms of the global politics of Islam and Islamophobia, and in the context of the People's Republic of China today. The phrase "incompatibility of Islam with the Chinese Order" is not far at all from the language we see in recent pronouncements of the Chinese Communist Party demanding the assimilation of Muslims to an authentic, Han-dominated, "Chinese" culture.[11] Israeli's stark essentialism is an outlier in Anglophone academia, but less direct expressions of essentialist thinking still pervade the study of Islams in China, often surfacing even in writing that explicitly rejects essentialism and its partner concepts, such as syncretism.

Perhaps no one is immune to essentialist intuitions. If you felt a sense of surprise in Chapter 1 when Ma Lianyuan and Nūr al-Ḥaqq were revealed to be the same author, I would argue that essentialist assumptions played an important role (as, admittedly, did my narrative framing). Humans are pattern seekers and generalizers. Numerically smaller communities of Muslims that defy popular expectations—Muslims in India who believe in reincarnation, Qur'anists who reject the *hadith,* Chinese Muslims who quote Confucius—get framed as exceptions, quarantined from our generalizations about Islam. But generalization (e.g., "most forms of Islam do not accept reincarnation" or "Islams, in general, tend to reject reincarnation") is different from definitional statements (e.g., "Islam rejects reincarnation"). When the useful tool of generalization is conflated with definition, essentialism results, with all of its distorting properties. It doesn't help that the essentialist impulse is amplified by a deluge of media depictions of Islam that represent only a narrow range of Islams, usually drawn from the Arabic-speaking and Persianate parts of the world. Surely these images have some effect even on the most perspicacious of readers.

Complicating the matter, the historical actors we study were essentialists. Recall the poem in *The Origins of the Huihui,* circa 1710: "The *Huihui* were originally all in the Western Regions, who would know that they would reside in China forever?" Even the Muslims of China seem to be surprised that there are Muslims in China.

Liu Zhi's own essentialism was strict and deeply rooted. For him there was one true and immutable Islamic teaching, defined by its origin and its essence. The "Islamic classics have by and large the same purport as Confucius and Mencius," he argued. Nonetheless, the texts of Confucius and Mencius were not fully *Islamic* classics, and he never labeled them as such. Liu was aware that he was dealing with texts that were divided by his contemporaries into two socially boundaried sets, or what we would call canons. He participated in this boundary-making, refusing to admit Confucius and Mencius into the canon of Islamic classics. The canons were passionately contested and carefully policed. Participants in these debates, including Liu Zhi, saw their preferred boundaries not as constructions or products of community contestation but as neat delineations of where essential, immutable truth and untruth lay. The contestation thus produced powerful social realities. For the Confucian side, the state often stepped in to distinguish between canonical and heterodox, sometimes with life-terminating consequences; for the Muslims the task fell to individual intellectuals in their intra-Muslim discussions, but even alternative curricula for grammar could elicit venomous condemnation.[12] Liu Zhi was ultimately arguing that behind these mutually exclusive, boundaried canons lay two essences that mostly overlapped. If he successfully argued his case, the socially constructed boundaries might shift to match the essences, overlapping to create a shared set of texts and concepts. For Liu, the social boundaries were out of alignment with the shared reality of the canons.

Showing *how* these texts had the "same purport" occupied most of Liu's writing. But he also needed to explain *why* they had the "same purport." In another of his works, *The True Record of the Islamic Ultimate Sage* (*Tianfang Zhisheng Shilu* 天方至聖實錄), Liu Zhi addressed the problem using an origin story. According to Liu, the legendary first Chinese emperor Fuxi was in fact a son of Noah, and he brought Islam to China. Over time the message of Islam progressively deteriorated in China, but it was still largely intact in the days of Confucius and Mencius. Their texts thus capture substantially correct views of Islam.[13]

Here Liu makes use of a double origin ascribed to Islam by numerous Muslims across the world. There is, first, the prehuman truth of Islam, transmitted to Adam at the creation and encapsulated in the uncreated Qur'an. The origin of human Muslims is thus Adam. Then there is a second origin: After millennia in which human understanding of Islam deteriorated, God delivered the Qur'an to Muhammad so that he could reestablish human awareness of the true Islam. Liu Zhi uses the first origin to explain how a mostly correct approximation of Islam came to Confucius and Mencius through Fuxi. The second origin explains for Liu how certain humans, scholars of *Tianfang* teachings (i.e., Muslims), came to possess a more accurate understanding of metaphysics and morality, and why those humans (at a distant point in the past) first arrived from outside of China. It is through this origin story that Liu Zhi explained both the overlap of canons and the ultimate superiority of *Tianfang* teachings. By giving the philosophy of Confucius and Mencius a new origin story, he opened the door to a shifting of canonical boundaries that would place the two sages in a zone of overlap with Islam, creating a Confucian-Islamic zone for Liu Zhi to inhabit. As we have seen, many of China's Muslims eventually walked through that door, while few of China's non-Muslims did.

It is not a coincidence that origin stories play such a prominent role in the essentialist maneuvering of Liu Zhi; the anonymous author of *Huihui yuanlai;* Lan Xu; and countless other writers in Islamic China. Essentialism is a common approach (though one among many) to understanding identity categories, such as Muslim, Jahriyya, *Huiru,* and Chinese. And, as we saw in Chapter 5, identity categories create origin stories. When an origin story, deployed to explain and buttress a category, is taken at its word and accepted as a central part of the category's definition, we are no longer just constructing categories but imparting to them an essence. Why should we be surprised that the *Huihui* would reside in China forever? The essentialist answer is an origin story: "the *Huihui* were originally all in the Western Regions." Although the presence of the *Huihui* in China began, according to the story, during the lifetime of the prophet himself, the *Huihui* people's character, their essence, is defined by that brief period between the Prophet Muhammad's first revelation and the arrival of his uncle in China a few years later. That ancient but brief decade of separateness defines the true *Huihui,* not the ensuing nine centuries of supposed *Huihui* residence in China. This essential and, importantly, *original,* alienness can never be shaken off. It engenders the surprise.

But at some point, the analyses of the historian and the historical actor must part ways. We have seen that embracing the origin drive of our late-imperial Chinese Muslim predecessors can lead to new historical understandings. This chapter turns to a different side of origin-seeking, tracing the means by which origin stories can cloud our historical vision. It argues that a focus on origins continues to smuggle essentialist distortions back into humanistic scholarship even when researchers reject essentialism explicitly, and that this origin focus has done so extensively in the study of Islamic China.

Syncretism, Essentialism, Origins

Liu Zhi's work was in one way utterly unextraordinary among Chinese-language philosophical texts of the Ming and Qing. Liu's interest in the boundaries between various "teachings" (教) was shared by countless authors of the period, including those who wanted to keep the teachings separate, those who wanted to bring them into closer interaction, and those who, like Liu, wanted to prove that they reflected the same underlying truths. This enormous literature normally ignored Islam, counting instead three teachings: Buddhism, Daoism, and Confucianism. Nonetheless, Liu Zhi's view that two clearly distinguishable sets of texts had "by and large the same purport" was a common argument by his day, even if normally applied to the "Three Teachings," not Islam.[14] The resolution of these boundaried bodies of ideas became known as "the unity of the Three Teachings" (*sanjiao heyi* 三教合一), or, in earlier formulations, "the Three Teachings have one origin" (*sanjiao yiyuan* 三教一源). The combination of a lively, continuous construction of boundaries between teachings with efforts to cross those boundaries has led many intellectual historians of the Three Teachings to employ the concept of "syncretism."[15] The same can be said about scholars studying Liu Zhi and associated Muslim thinkers.

In a 1969 essay lamenting that the term "syncretism" "is often used without a clear and unambiguous definition," Helmer Ringgren offered a descriptive definition: "any mixture of two or more religions."[16] This remains probably the most common usage of the term and the dominant, perhaps sole, usage in the study of Islamic China. Outside of this narrow field, however, scholars have produced an enormous literature defining, redefining, and debating the concept of syncretism, a literature that scholars of Islamic China have not yet engaged in any extended way, despite the frequency with which the term is used.

Syncretism has carried a host of connotations during its five centuries of use in the English language. In a recent history of the term, Ross

Kane sums up what the various usages share: "The one consistent aspect of syncretism—whether in irenics, invective, or something in between—has been a surprising or unexpected mingling of seemingly unlike elements of human culture, whether religious, political, philosophical, or otherwise. The notion indicates that, through cultural mixture, people are stretching categories and classifications beyond their perceived capacity."[17] More often than not, this evocation of surprise posits some cultural expressions as ordinary or normal, and others as extraordinary or exceptional.

Restricting our view to usage of the last two centuries, it is important to note that "syncretism" long held a derogatory meaning, particularly among Christian missionaries. Nonetheless, by the middle of the twentieth century it was widely embraced within the academic study of religion. There is no space here for an extended historiography of the term, but a few important trends should be noted. The term has been controversial since at least the early 1970s, when Robert Baird questioned its underlying assumptions, calling it an "inadequate category." A wide variety of arguments against the term have been offered, but Baird brought together some of the most durable concerns. One is that syncretism concepts usually imply an immutable "essence" to the religious traditions that are supposed to be meeting and blending, and that "the attempt to arrive at the 'essence' of a religion by examining its numerous historical manifestations has been shown to be unsuccessful." Another is that the idea of syncretism as a historical phenomenon involves a "quest for origins," which runs counter to proper historical method, in which there is "no room for a beginning, a first cause." And if we do seek the "origins" of religions we find that "syncretism is universal and inevitable and is merely a term used to describe a dictum of historical knowledge—any subject fitting for historical research has historical antecedents. If all religions are syncretic, then categorizing any one religion as syncretic is meaningless."[18] Put in essentialist terminology, at the purported origin of any religion, we find a mixing of prior religions.

From the 1990s onward there have been efforts to find new uses for the concept. One of the most successful conceptual moves has been to re-appropriate "syncretism" as a form of anticolonial resistance. Rosalind Shaw and Charles Stewart coined the term "anti-syncretism" to describe normative and essentialist understandings of syncretism, including pejorative uses that presume the possibility of authenticity and supposedly "pure" religious forms. By contrast Shaw and Stewart highlight the agency of colonized people involved in a neutral or positively defined "syncretism" that consists of making meaning from material drawn across constructed cultural boundaries.[19] Citing this and other efforts to recover a useful technical term from the variegated history of syncretism's uses, Kane concludes in his 2020 survey that "the notion of syncretism, then, need not inherently assume cultural essentialism." Kane then outlines steps required to avoid essentialism while maintaining the term "syncretism."[20]

But these are novel, prescriptive definitions that rely on deep familiarity with complex debates in religious studies. They require a scholar to go well beyond the most common usage—"any mixture of two or more religions"—and to engage with specialized rehabilitating arguments, such as Shaw and Stewart's segregation of problematic, essentializing ideas into the neologism of "anti-syncretism." I share Luther Martin's view that "such transcriptive efforts necessarily retain some normative point of reference to non-syncretistic origins characteristic of earlier usages."[21] But even if we accept that carefully laid out (re)definitions of syncretism can avoid such problems, that careful work needs to be undertaken whenever the term is used. I am not aware of any examples from the study of Islam in China that apply "syncretism" in this careful way and manage to avoid its more common, essentialist, origin-focused implications.

Multiple specialists in the history of Islamic China have eschewed or criticized the concept, including Élisabeth Allès, Zvi Ben-Dor Benite, and Kristian Petersen, as well as the present author.[22] But uncritical or undefined use of the syncretism concept has been even more common, from the 1970s to the current decade.[23] And that is just to look at the Anglophone specialist literature. If we turn to synthetic studies for more general audiences, syncretist appraisals of Islam in China seem to get taken up most readily. In the Chinese-language scholarship, particularly in the People's Republic of China, syncretism, represented in a variety of terms, including "sinicization," has been the dominant conceptual lens for the last few decades, and it has only been boosted by the communist party's recent commitment to "sinicization" of religions.

The most fully elaborated application of the syncretism notion to Islamic China is James Frankel's 2011 study of Liu Zhi, a work whose contributions are otherwise quite substantial and function independently of its syncretist framing. Indeed, I am indebted to Frankel's work on Liu Zhi's audience, historical context, and reception in the opening section of this chapter. Nonetheless, his conceptual framing provides a clear entry point into the problems that the "syncretism" concept has introduced into the study of Muslims in China. For Frankel, Liu Zhi's writings represent "an instance of syncretism of Chinese and Islamic thought." Liu's texts are part of a larger body of writing he calls "Han Kitāb," using a term first found a century after Liu's death and now common among Anglophone scholars of Chinese Islams. Frankel writes that Liu Zhi's "heritage of accommodation and assimilation produced a simultaneity that resulted in the sophisticated syncretic thought found in the Han Kitāb literature." Such assimilation, Frankel argues, "produces communities that straddle, or blur, civilizational boundaries and participate simultaneously in two or more cultures, often creating a new, hybrid culture of their own." Liu Zhi had exactly this kind of "unique hybrid identity."[24]

The essentialist assumptions behind this framing, and the dynamic between categories and origins, are neatly summed up in Frankel's statement that "the Han Kitāb is a tangible representation of the meeting of two civilizations." This idea requires two chronological displacements, which bring category, origin, and Liu into alignment. It begins with a move forward in time from Liu's era, to find the "new, hybrid culture of their own," fully formed into something different and canonized: the Han Kitab. In the earliest known use of the term (1852), Lan Xu explains it thus: "The classic, Qur'an [古爾阿儀], is called Kitab. Now, translated into Chinese writing [*Hanzi* 漢字], it is called Han Kitab [*Han Qitapu* 漢啓佗補]." A preface in the same 1852 work says of Liu's oeuvre that Liu "explicated the Chinese *Kitab.*" Frankel, however, is deploying "Han Kitab" in a much more recent usage, wherein it indicates an entire "canon" of Islamic texts written in Chinese, usually conceived as a discourse separate from the Perso-Arabic tradition. But there was no Han Kitab in Liu's time. Only a handful of Islamic works in Chinese existed when he was writing. These were dwarfed by the vast quantity of works in Persian and Arabic that Liu not only read but cited and summarized in his books. Indeed, even the Chinese-language Islamic texts down through Liu's time and into the era of Lan Xu were, without exception, based on their authors' readings in Persian and Arabic texts. And when the word "Han Kitab" did appear in 1852, it referred to something narrower, not the entirety of a large body of Chinese-language Islamic texts. Framing Liu as a part of the Han Kitab tradition projects a late nineteenth-century, or, more likely, twentieth-century category, where we can locate a "new, hybrid culture of their own," back to the early eighteenth century.

Through a displacement backward in time, the origins of this retrospective category are then presented as "the meeting of two civilizations," presumably Chinese / Confucian and Islamic. By Liu's day, Muslims had been living in China for at least eight centuries, following the "meeting of two civilizations" no later than the ninth century. Frankel is fully aware of Liu's chronological distance from this meeting, stating, for example that Chinese Muslims "had built up, through centuries of assimilation, a critical mass of literacy in the local scholarly idiom." Liu, Frankel writes, is able to contribute to the transformation of this meeting into a new, syncretic culture because he accepts "the essential ethical and metaphysical harmony of Islam and Confucianism."[25] Here the category, framed as a hybrid of two essentially different if harmonious cultures, has created the origin: the Tang-dynasty meeting of Islam and China. Alternative origin stories might otherwise be possible, for example, the Neo-Confucian adoption of Buddhist ideas, or the Persianate Sufi writers' debt to Greek philosophy. Both shape the philosophy of Liu Zhi.[26] But once the category has been framed as a Confucian-Islamic mixing, these inheritances are pruned from the family tree of Liu's thought, leaving a single origin cleanly situated in the meeting of Chinese and Islamic civilizations.

I have taken Frankel's work as an example here because among the many scholars who have applied the syncretism framing to Chinese Islams, he is admirable as one of the few to offer a sustained and explicit reflection on his conceptual scheme. But the approach was already deeply embedded in the field, even if in less considered ways. As we saw from Israeli's work, Frankel was not the first to interpret Chinese Islams by means of essentialist syncretism. The term has more often been deployed briefly and without definition, which has allowed the notion to reappear continuously in descriptions of Chinese Islams. And beyond explicit evocations of the term, the notion of two essentialized cultures of different origins mixing, interpenetrating, or blending, is even more widespread.

Meanings of "Han Kitab"

The use of the phrase "Han Kitab" is a surprisingly recent phenomenon in Chinese-language secondary scholarship. In Chinese it remains uncommon even today, though the works of Anglophone scholars on the Han Kitab have begun to feed back into the Chinese-language academic conversation. Before the boom in Han Kitab studies in the Anglophone world (1997 to the present), the term was all but absent. The earliest instance I have so far been able to trace in secondary literature appears in Ma Tong's 1981 survey of *menhuans*. Ma Tong does not use the term in his section on "Chinese translations of classics and Chinese-language compositions," but he does use it in his description of the early twentieth-century Xidaotang movement, which advocated the integration of Chinese-language texts into the Perso-Arabic curriculum. The term was used again in connection with Xidaotang in a 1982 essay by Zhu Gang.[27]

But the publication that appears to have been pivotal in bringing "Han kitab" to English-language scholarship is a 1982 essay by Feng Jinyuan [冯今源], about what he calls the "penetration" (or permeation) of Islam by Confucianism. Feng uses "Han Kitab" only once, in the concluding paragraphs of his article, elsewhere preferring "Chinese Islamic translations and compositions." He writes that the Muslim authors under consideration "constructed a complete Chinese Islamic intellectual system, writing a set of Chinese-language Islamic works with a uniquely Chinese style. These works are called by the Muslims in China the 'Han Kitab'—that is, the Chinese canon—and they have had a definite influence in Sino-Muslim society."[28] Feng provides no citation for the phrase "Han Kitab." It is unclear what period or what specific groups he is referring to, or whether he is claiming a written or oral usage.

"Han Kitab" does not seem to have reached print in English until 1996. In that year Jonathan Lipman published his influential essay "Hyphenated Chinese: Sino-Muslim Identity in Modern China," in which he glossed the term as the "Sino-Muslim canon" of Islamic texts written in Chinese, devoting several paragraphs to the topic.[29] In the same year Michael Dillon used the phrase in a shorter summary for his brief survey, *China's Muslims*.[30] Lipman's essay was in many ways a preview of the book he published the following year, where we find a more detailed exploration of the Han Kitab notion. There he quotes Feng's 1982 paper to open a substantial section on the Chinese-language texts of the seventeenth and eighteenth centuries, following Feng in treating them as a "canon" called Han Kitab.[31]

In 2005 we find what appears to be the first effort to root the idea of a Han Kitab tradition in primary sources. In his groundbreaking *The Dao of Muhammad*, Zvi Ben-Dor Benite brought Lan Xu's use of the term to notice, perhaps for the first time.[32] Ben-Dor Benite argues that Lan Xu presented the Islamic "scholarly tradition" in China as the "Han Qitabu"; that Lan referred to the Han Kitab as "the canon"; and that Lan Xu regarded Wang Daiyu as "the first scholar of the Han Kitab." Much of his argument seems to rest on the claim that Lan Xu equated *jingdian* (經典; classics or canon), which occurs frequently in the text, with Han Kitab, of which I can find only two occurrences in Lan's writing and one in the laudatory preface by another scholar, Wang Shouqian 王守謙. Below are the full passages containing the phrase. One is Lan Xu's authorial preface:

> I wrote this *Tianfang zhengxue* as a Chinese *Kitab* [*wei Han Qituobu* 為漢启佗補]. Though I live abroad in the eastern lands, all of my comments on the classics and discussion of the Dao respectfully rely on the Western classic, the Qur'an. This classic, the Qur'an, is called the *Kitab*. Now, translated into Chinese characters [*hanzi*], it is called the Chinese *Kitab* [*Han Qituobu*].[33]

The other is Wang's laudatory preface, presumably written after reading Lan Xu's manuscript:

> There is no lack of people crowding to transmit [the true teaching] in each period. Formerly, in the Ming dynasty, Wang [Daiyu] promulgated it. In the current dynasty Liu Jielian [i.e., Liu Zhi] explained the meaning of the classics one after another. Each explicated (著有) the Chinese *Kitab* [*ge zhuyou Han Qitabu* 各著有漢啓他補].[34] Now Lan Zixi contemplates the learning of the West and studies the Confucian books of the East.[35]

Lan Xu is clear that the phrase "Han Kitab" (or Chinese-language Kitab) refers to the Qur'an [古爾阿儀]. In fact, much of the *zhengxue* (correct learning) he is introducing consists of translations of selections from the Qur'an. In Muslim communities across Eurasia the Qur'an was widely known simply as *al-Kitab* (The book), much as Christian sacred texts are known as the Bible (from the Greek *biblos,* i.e., book). Wang Shouqian's comments are more ambiguous. Exactly what activity does 著有 indicate here? Is it composition or explication? One possibility, extrapolating from Lan's remark, is that he is referring to the fact that both authors quoted from the Qur'an and expressed its meaning more generally in their works. Or perhaps Wang Shouqian is saying that Liu and Wang Daiyu composed Chinese Kitabs in the same sense that Lan Xu says he wrote his book as a

Chinese Qur'an. It is difficult, however, to imagine a reading by which Wang is identifying Liu's and Wang Daiyu's texts as parts of a canon called Han Qitabu. Certainly, neither passage equates the phrase with *jingdian*. I would be more inclined to understand Han Kitab as a phrase that indicates either strictly the Qur'an or Chinese-language books that transmit the meaning of the Qur'an. In any case, these passages are a weak foundation on which to claim that a broad scholarly community regarded Wang, Liu, and Lan as authors in a distinctive canon, generally called the Han Kitab. Lan does not return to the phrase in the rest of his text, despite his book's discussion of the transmission of the Islamic Dao and the classics / canon. We could speculate that the popularity of Lan Xu's work subsequently helped engender in his readership a familiarity with the term "Han Kitab" through its brief appearance in the prefaces. However, that term does not seem to appear with any frequency in later works. Many texts remain unstudied, but no scholar to date has pointed out another instance of the phrase in any Qing-period primary source. In my own survey of sources, I have failed to locate any further example.

Lan Xu's work was republished in 1925. "Han Kitab" then appeared in an anonymous article in *Islam Youth Monthly* (*回教青年月刊*), which was published from 1936 to 1946. In this case, the author also felt the need to explain the term. He used it once, when listing Liu Zhi's works, writing that Liu "authored *Tianfang xingli, Tianfang dianli,* and other Han Kitab (meaning both Chinese and Hui languages) classics."[36] Here the idea of Han Kitab as a subset of canonical "classics" (经典) has finally reached print, two centuries after Liu Zhi's death. The term remained rare, and I have located no other appearances in the Republican period.

Feng Jinyuan's use of the term in 1982 may have come from his reading of Lan Xu, whose work he quotes elsewhere in the essay for its Confucian concepts. But Feng uses different characters with a different pronunciation: *Han Ketabu* [汉克塔卜]. He may be drawing from modern oral usage, perhaps from the Xidaotang community. Lipman, in a footnote, says that in China's Northwest, people use the term to refer to Chinese-language Islamic texts. Elsewhere in China people use "Chinese-language Islamic translations and commentaries"—roughly the terminology Feng used in his title. The brief uses of the term in 1981 and 1982 do not appear to have been taken up widely by other scholars writing in Chinese. "Han Kitab" has no entry, for example, in the 1994 *Chinese Encyclopedia of Islam.*[37]

In sum, we have, to date at least, only one primary source that uses "Han Kitab" before the mid-twentieth century, and its clearest use of the term defines it as the Qur'an in Chinese translation. That source comes 150 years after the supposed golden age of Han Kitab authorship. More evidence will be needed to know with any certainty when and for whom the Han Kitab eventually came to designate a canon of Chinese-language Islamic literature, but whatever details emerge, we can say with confidence that the written footprint of this hypothetical usage is extremely small, too small to establish any substantial presence in the secondary literature in Chinese until the 2000s, when some Chinese researchers adopted ideas from Anglophone scholarship. Nonetheless, the idea of a Han Kitab canon has dominated recent Anglophone scholarship on Chinese Muslims of the seventeenth to mid-nineteenth centuries. From there it has moved to synthetic works and high-quality journalism.[38]

Why has this framing become so popular in English? The trail of publications and citations I have presented here suggests that the idea of the Han Kitab entered English scholarship from the 1982 essay in Chinese by Feng Jinyuan. This essay, while not espousing syncretism under that name, offers a narrative of two cultural essences meeting, with one receiving an influence and permeation from the other, creating a new and distinct "Chinese Islam." In Feng's analysis, the Islam of Muslims in China becomes Chinese by adopting Confucian ideas and literary styles. The implication is that for the preceding centuries China's Muslims had preserved their foreign essence, brought to China from their point of origin. By adopting a characteristic supposedly essential to Chineseness—Confucianism—they finally became Chinese. This is a syncretistic framing, despite the absence of the word.

Some later authors who adopted the Han Kitab framing have endeavored to rescue it from its essentialist roots. Ben-Dor Benite explicitly rejected syncretism, arguing that Han Kitab authors evinced a "simultaneity" of Muslimness and Chineseness. This approach elegantly grants Chinese Muslims full membership in both identities, rather than assigning them to a new and unique category that marks them as exceptions to both normal Chineseness and normal Muslimness. By contrast, syncretism as a descriptor has a long history of indicating traditions that are compromised, impure, and thus no longer fully representative of the religions from which they are patched together. If we apply Ben-Dor Benite's "simultaneity" to the life and works of Ma Lianyuan, which we explored in Chapter 1, we find a satisfying fit, in which Ma Lianyuan and Nūr al-Ḥaqq can be one person without causing surprise. More recently, Kristian Petersen rejected syncretism in his study of Han Kitab works, preferring instead the notion of vernacularization, to which we will return further below.

Nonetheless, distortions persist, and in some cases have even grown, among the many studies that have taken up Chinese-language Islams under the Han Kitab concept. We have already seen that the anachronistic projection of "Han Kitab" onto a selection of texts written much earlier produces an ahistorical category that supports origin-based, essentializing explanations. In neatly representing the "mixture" of what were, at their purported origins, for a brief moment, distinct and separate communities, the Han Kitab literature has often been presented as the quintessential or representative form of simultaneous Chineseness / Muslimness. The seductive, origin-focused approach to Islamic China has helped an ahistorical category to proliferate, leading to the widespread decontextualization of the works of Wang Daiyu, Ma Zhu, and Liu Zhi, separating them out from the vast Perso-Arabic literature that those authors engaged.

Canon? Genre?

When scholars present "Han Kitab" as an emic term (one purportedly employed by the community being studied), they impute to it an emic referent (a phenomenon present among and recognized by the community). They claim or imply that historical actors used the term to describe an emic category, specifically a canon or a genre of texts. Among today's scholars using the Han Kitab framing, there is some disagreement about what this canon looked like. Most commonly, "Han Kitab" is taken to refer to Islamic texts written in Chinese.[39] So it was in Feng's original interpretation, as well as Lipman's popularization of the concept in Anglophone scholarship. On the other hand, the first extensive study of the Han Kitab, Ben-Dor Benite's seminal *Dao of Muhammad* (2005), described the Han Kitab as a canon of works not only in Chinese but also in Persian and Arabic, though specific Persian or Arabic titles are not given, nor are any discussed in detail. Frankel and Petersen revert to the all-Chinese model. All, however, agree that Wang Daiyu's, Ma Zhu's, and Liu Zhi's works are quintessential Han Kitab texts. In contrast to our lone, ninetheenth-century primary source, none of these secondary works include the Qur'an in any form as an example of the Han Kitab.

Given that all Han Kitab framings focus on texts from the mid-seventeenth century to the mid-eighteenth century, it is worth asking what textual groupings Chinese Muslims in that period made for themselves. Here we have three strong source types: citations of works in Islamic texts; mosque steles that mention texts; and Muslims' publishing projects. The groupings in these sources vary greatly. The main writers who are usually purported to be Han Kitab representatives (Liu Zhi, Ma Zhu, and Wang Daiyu) were very stingy with citations of other Chinese-language Islamic works. Wang criticizes two earlier works and Ma briefly mentions one of Wang's works. But both scholars are generous with citations of Confucian classics and the Qur'an, with Ma also citing the old and new testaments of the bible, Buddhist books, and the Daoist Laozi. Liu Zhi is much more systematic about citing his sources. At the beginning of two of his works he provides lists of "classics" (經書) consulted. Together they add up to at least sixty-six distinct titles, most of them Persian texts, with a smaller number in Arabic and none in Chinese.[40] The eighteenth-century mosque inscriptions also list Persian and Arabic works exclusively.[41] For the main authors of the Chinese-language compositions, the conversations they sought to join, both Confucian and Islamic, were not characterized by Chinese-language Islamic texts.

There is one other source of particular value for understanding the role of Chinese-language texts toward the final years of the supposed golden age of the Han Kitab. It is a manuscript completed in 1714, which documents an educational network over the course of seven generations, including Wang Daiyu, a member of the fifth generation. The author, Zhao Can 趙燦, describes the curriculum and methods of his teacher, She Yunshan 舍蘊善, beginning with his approach to selecting students. Before laying out the standard curriculum, he explains how to handle students of various special types. One is of particular interest to us: "Those who understand Chinese-language texts but cannot go deep into the classics of Islam [吾教] are taught with translated classics such as *The Necessity of Returning to the Real,* and eventually they will also understand the [Persian and Arabic] textbooks, their spirit attaining the innate principle."[42] Zhao goes on to explain the progression through a curriculum of twenty-seven works, all in Persian or Arabic, beginning with the three Persian works on basic

Islamic practice and belief that we encountered among Ma Lianyuan's publications (Chapter 2). Interestingly, Zhao himself was once in this category of Chinese readers who could not understand the Perso-Arabic scholarship. He writes, "Although I knew that my family tradition had its own teaching, and I knew that in our teaching was the true God, as for the rewards and penalties of charity, prayer, fasting, and pilgrimage, I self-assuredly did not know and did not ask. . . . Later I examined Wang Daiyu's *Real Commentary*. I then first knew that my teaching was called 'Pure and True' [*Qingzhen*, i.e., Islam]."[43] Zhao then went on to pursue an Islamic education under She Yunshan.

Elsewhere in the text there is one other reference to a scholar translating a text into Chinese to fight against incorrect ideas among those uneducated in the Perso-Arabic classics. However, the rest of the text is devoted to the interactions of scholars with texts from the twenty-seven Perso-Arabic "classics." The rare appearances of Chinese-language texts present them as translations that serve as initial gateways to the study of Islam for certain students and redound to the credit of the translator. The Chinese-language texts were, as Dror Weil has argued, "an auxiliary teaching device."[44]

It is not until the middle of the eighteenth century that we see citations that begin to link Chinese-language Islamic texts together. The first of these appears in *Clearing Up Doubts About Islam* (*Qingzhen shiyi* 清真釋疑) by Jin Tianzhu 金天柱. This work was explicitly aimed at explaining Islam to people of other religions (*gejiao* 各教, literally "the various teachings"). In his 1738 preface to the work, Jin lists the works of Wang, Ma, and Liu, but this is only to argue that these authors (who wrote in a language that non-Muslims in China could understand) did not explain the faith in a way that addressed outsiders' misunderstandings.[45] His listing is thus an insufficient basis for considering these texts as a genre or canon, rather than simply a list of widely known books about Islam accessible through the Chinese language.

The 1782 incident in which an itinerant scholar's books were confiscated gives us perhaps the earliest documentation of a physical collection of Islamic books. The governor who reported the scholar's arrest described twenty-six books that he carried. Five were printed works by Liu Zhi, while the remaining twenty-one were manuscripts written in "Hui characters" (i.e., Persian and / or Arabic), which the governor could not read.[46]

For publishing projects we have a preface by the publisher Ma Da'en in 1828, in which he lists the titles of books he has brought to print. The three famous authors appear, along with the lesser-known Ma Junshi. Here, however, it is important to remember that Arabic-script works required an as-yet nonexistent printing infrastructure (see Chapter 2). No such works reached print until a Muslim publisher found himself with access to the resources and will of the state, that is, when Ma Dexin was elevated to an official position in a breakaway Muslim state amid the Panthay Rebellion (1856–1873). Both Ma Dexin and, later, Ma Lianyuan published a mix of Chinese-language texts by Liu Zhi and Arabic and / or Persian texts, many written outside of China but with long histories of circulation within China. Ma Da'en's list therefore represents an accounting of works in print, not necessarily a genre or canon.

Finally, we should consider the reading habits of the men who authored the texts that are purported to make up the Han Kitab. Where such information can be discerned, it invariably shows that the authors were basing their work on readings of Persian and Arabic texts. This goes for the three big names, as well as numerous less-famous authors, down through the mid-nineteenth century, including Lan Xu, who wrote a dictionary of Persian terms. For the works before the mid-eighteenth century, liberal translations of Persian texts make up roughly half of the Chinese works.

In sum, it is clear that the authors of Chinese-language Islamic works were reading the Chinese texts and the Perso-Arabic Islamic texts together. At the same time, they sometimes listed texts separately by language. They did this in two cases: when providing a history of authors composing new texts in Chinese (the act of writing Islamic texts in Chinese continued to be the subject of explanation and justification for two centuries) and when enumerating printed works. When Arabic-script printing became feasible, the continuous crossing of language lines became more visible in the historical record. As we have seen, Ma Lianyuan even translated Liu Zhi's work into Arabic and glossed Liu's *Three-Character Classic* in Persian. More research will be necessary to conclusively rule out the possibility that Chinese-language works were seen as a distinct canon or genre. They were not called Han Kitab, and I can find no alternative name for such a canon or genre. At the same time, it would be premature to dismiss the possibility entirely, as by the nineteenth century there was a widely used term for *authors* who applied Confucian scholarship to Islam, if not for their texts. These were the men known as *Huiru*.[47]

But until we have more analysis of how Chinese Muslims discussed these texts as groups, the existence of a separate tradition or canon or genre cannot be assumed and indeed looks doubtful. Canons and genres are socially constructed. And yet we have no studies of how the Chinese-language works of the *Huiru* were consumed or by whom before the turn of the twentieth century.[48] To separate these texts from the Persian and Arabic works that they endeavored to transmit, the very texts that the authors argued conveyed the same core meaning as the Confucian classics, is to create what the syncretism model seeks—"a new, hybrid culture of their own"—and to distort the role of these texts in Islamic learning among China's Muslims down through the nineteenth century.

"Vernacularization"

As the Chinese-language texts have come to represent what is distinctive or even characteristic of Islam in China, the Persian and Arabic texts that accounted for so much knowledge transmission among Chinese Muslims have faded into the background. Murata and Chittick's study of Liu Zhi's work in its full Persianate context has been the exception in secondary scholarship.[49] The best studies within the Han Kitab framing are careful to emphasize that Liu Zhi and others were very much in conversation with works in Persian and Arabic, but the close readings they provide are almost without exception analyses of the Chinese texts.[50] The near-exclusive focus on Chinese-language texts perpetuates syncretistic analysis, whether explicit or implicit, because the Persian and Arabic corpus simply does not look much different from what was circulating in the Mughal Empire and Muslim Central Asia. The Chinese texts, with their engagement of Confucian thinkers, do look distinctive and thus, particularly when studied in isolation, lend themselves to syncretism narratives.

The elision of Persian and Arabic texts results partly from the connections that scholars have drawn between the *Huiru* authors and "scripture hall education" (*jingtang jiaoyu* 经堂教育). As we have seen in Chapter 2, this educational system was based in a curriculum that was remarkably consistent across centuries, a curriculum primarily written in Persian and Arabic. Several authors writing in Chinese were educated in this system, but their writings never became a part of the main curriculum.

Chinese-language texts could play a role, attracting people to the Perso-Arabic education that dominated Islamic learning. In an appendix to the *Genealogy,* its author Zhao Can credits Wang Daiyu's writing with first teaching him about his ancestral faith. After failing to enter the Confucian literati class through the exam system, he read Wang's *Real Commentary* and then began to pursue learning in Perso-Arabic texts. The Persian books, he wrote, were "a hundred times more difficult than the Confucian classics." In the same work, Zhao says that Ma Junshi wrote a Chinese-language translation because many of his fellow Muslims had fallen into strange and evil beliefs. But these appearances of Chinese-language compositions in the *Genealogy* are exceptional. A total of four such works appear in the text, plus six Chinese translations of Persian works. Where these titles appear they are mainly recorded as works produced by the scholars whose biographies are outlined, not as works that are part of the educational system. The curricular texts are drawn from a larger range of Persian and Arabic works, twenty-nine of which are mentioned favorably (another twenty-seven are listed as a heretical curriculum).[51]

One strategy to avoid the essentialist distortions of syncretism theory has been to regard the rise of Chinese-language texts as a "vernacularization." This is a far less problematic approach, though it once again separates these texts from the Perso-Arabic context in which they functioned. And the Classical Chinese of authors like Liu Zhi was of course not a vernacular.[52] It was distant from spoken Chinese and required intense specialized education to achieve even a modest level of literacy. Most of the purported Han Kitab texts were written with an eye toward a readership of highly educated non-Muslim literati. Ma Zhu's *Compass of Islam* may be an exception, as it was likely targeted primarily at Muslim literati, but this narrow audience can hardly justify the notion of vernacularization. Even if we take the term "vernacular" loosely and accept Classical Chinese as a vernacular, the fact remains that all documented Islamic education in China relied primarily on Persian and Arabic texts through at least the late nineteenth century.

The Myth of Isolation

The overwhelming focus on Chinese-language texts among academic historians working on the seventeenth and eighteenth centuries has also led some scholars to conclude that the Chinese texts were a product of "relatively isolated Sino-Muslim intellectual evolution."[53] This, the argument goes, resulted in China's Muslims "evolving into a self-generating Muslim community largely independent of developments in the rest of the Islamic world."[54] The trans-Asian connections explored in Chapter 4, all of which occurred in the 1640s through the 1680s (the same period in which the early Chinese-language texts were published), suggest that these isolation claims are overstated. To the examples in Chapter 4, further cases can be added. Notably, Hu Dengzhou, credited with founding the "scripture hall education system" so often linked to the Han Kitab, was reported to have made the pilgrimage to Mecca. The vast majority of Persian and Arabic texts read by Liu, Ma, and Wang were authored abroad. Jamī's work, which had a central place in Liu Zhi's philosophy, was authored in Central Asia in the late fifteenth century, after China's period of isolation is said to have begun. The translations that accounted for over half of the Chinese works were foreign-authored texts; one of them, Zhang's translation of Ashige's teachings, was delivered in person by an Indian Sufi. Important connections continued to be formed in the eighteenth century, when, as we have seen, the Mujaddidiyya first entered China, eventually touching almost every sectarian grouping. Connections to other Muslim-majority lands do seem to have increased substantially in the late nineteenth century, with more confirmed cases of *Hajj,* but the evidence on the whole suggests that the claims of seventeenth- to eighteenth-century isolation are greatly overstated.

The idea of isolation is doubtless encouraged by the famous bans on seaborne connection that were frequently imposed in the late Ming, which receive prominent treatment in many histories of China. However, the isolation argument also encourages, and is perhaps encouraged by, origin-focused and syncretistic history. From whom are China's Muslims said to be isolated? The answer is other Muslims, and especially Muslims in the heartland, the Middle East, the people at the *origin.* Isolation looms large because Chinese Islams are framed as peripheral (as they often, admittedly, frame themselves) and because it explains the emergence of a "new, hybrid culture of their own." By contrast, historians show little concern as to whether Ming isolationist policies caused the Confucians of China to become isolated from the Confucians of Japan.

Conclusion

It is telling that Confucian-tinged Islamic texts written in the early twentieth century, the period when Confucian-Islamic writing can most plausibly be said to constitute an influential and independent canon, remain almost entirely unstudied. It was in the early twentieth century that hundreds of Chinese-language Islamic books and pamphlets appeared, most of them highly derivative of the works of Liu, Ma, and Wang, many of them simplified into more widely consumable forms.[55] The publishers and authors seem to have been responding to a large reading public prepared to engage Islam exclusively through the Chinese language. It appears to be a Confucian-tinged genre or canon, operating largely independently of the Perso-Arabic literature, aimed mainly at Muslim readers—something very close to what the Han Kitab narrative projects onto seventeenth- to eighteenth-century authors. It would seem to be fertile territory for Han Kitab studies, but it remains largely untouched.

But the Han Kitab narrative as it currently stands is operating differently. It is presented as an explanation for "syncretic" Chinese Islam, a surprising Islam that appears as an inherent challenge to the concepts of both China and Islam. As a "new, hybrid" form it calls for an origin story. And as origin stories so often do, the Han Kitab narrative skips intervening and subsequent centuries, including the period in which a Han Kitab–like social construction is most plausible: the early twentieth century. The problem I have outlined here—the distortions to the histories of authors such as Liu Zhi and the erasure of the more widespread Perso-Arabic discourse—is just one kind of casualty. We tend to overlook the as-yet-untold story of *becoming,* the transmission of Liu Zhi's works across three centuries and the constant transformations his writing both wrought and underwent. Roberta Tontini has made an invaluable first step in this direction through her study of three-character primers—a model for much-needed future work—but the larger history of continued transformation still awaits investigation.[56]

The embrace of Confucian thinkers by some of China's Muslim philosophers was indeed unprecedented in the history of Islamic thought. The conversations they initiated between Jamī and Mencius, Razī and Confucius, the Qur'an and *The Doctrine of the Mean,* comprise an important and fascinating chapter in the development of Islam, one worthy of continued study. But the framing matters. The overlay of anachronistic category (Han Kitab) and origin story (eighth-century meeting of civilizations) has led us to ignore crucial questions about the development of these conversations. What forces shaped the selection of Persian and Arabic texts that the Chinese-language authors used as a basis for their understandings of Islam?[57] When did Chinese-language and Confucian-engaged Islamic texts begin to operate semi-independently of the Perso-Arabic texts and why? Who, for example, was the first author to write a Chinese-language Islamic text without any knowledge of Persian or Arabic? What did Islam look like to the much larger number of Chinese Muslim scholars of Liu Zhi's time who only studied the Persian and Arabic texts? Which of those were authored in China and what do they say? What innovations did they offer, and for what purposes? And is it not possible that Liu Zhi's ambition was to make a lasting contribution to Confucian thought, not just to Islamic learning? We remain mostly blind to the shape of Islamic China in the age of Wang Daiyu and Liu Zhi.

9

Origin Without Essence

Ascription and Transmission in Islamic China

We have seen in the last four chapters that origin stories can provide useful data for historians, revealing connections across ethnic groups and sectarian affinities that have been obscured over time. We have also seen that origin stories, important as they are in all human societies, have a particular centrality in Chinese Muslim efforts to engage with the past, appearing as something more than just a habit of history-writing or a genre convention; to tell an origin story has been for many a moral imperative, even merged with the five pillars of Islam. And origin stories have become charts of the future, whether through the recursive time of the Jahriyya or the travel plans of soon-to-be exiles. Across the stunning diversity of Chinese Muslim communities, the compulsion to narrate origins is one of the most recognizable shared phenomena. At the same time, we have seen that the adoption of origin focus in the writing of professional, academic history, not just as a data source but as an epistemological pillar, can lead to fundamental distortions, distortions that are ripe for exploitation by repressive powers, as the Conclusion of this book discusses. How do we approach these competing opportunities, dangers, and commitments? And how do we deal with the divergence between our own historical practices and those of our source authors?

On one extreme we could eschew origin focus entirely, confining our engagement with origins to harvesting the data that origin stories preserve across time, or to the ethnographic or literary analysis of origin stories as cultural phenomena, without any embrace of the epistemological and moral drive behind them. Another extreme would be to adopt the origin focus wholesale, embracing essentialism in an effort to incorporate the views of the communities we study. This chapter argues that we can learn from the origin obsession in ways that go deeper than description or data harvesting—and we can do so without opening the door to essentialism. Origin stories are not just an accounting of the emergence of groups; they continually produce those groups and their senses of the ordinary. They are not just a peculiar form of historical production; they are the shifting boundary markers for groups. If this is the case, we might learn from our Chinese Muslim authors in more deeply embracing history, a diachronic phenomenon, in our understanding of what these groups are.

Any effort to assess China's Islamic past ultimately rests on some delineation of the phenomena we are assessing—what to include and what to exclude from our narratives and arguments. This book has focused on individuals who regard themselves as both Muslim and Chinese. In following historical actors' own understandings of their identities (self-ascription), it has so far avoided committing to any definition of Islam or China. However, it is my hope that the book will be read by those interested in "China" and / or "Islam" as supposedly stable historical phenomena, and especially by those interested in how such categories are best understood. This chapter explores how the self-ascriptive approach can be enriched by elements of the origin- or history-focused approach to making group boundaries that we have observed in the writings of Chinese Muslims. To do so, it focuses on one of the two categories just mentioned (Islam and China): Islam. The argument could be applied equally to the category of China, but I will focus on Islam in the interest of space.

Incorporating Islamic China's practices of history into our understanding of Islam implicates us in a rich debate over the nature and definition of Islam, but by no means does it require that we construct a new definition. The body of writing on the question "what is Islam?" is so large that most plausible answers to the question can be conveyed in a few citations. The menu of definitions of "history" and "the past" is even longer. It is thus easy enough to pair a preferred definition of Islam with a well-chosen theory of history and move on to the particulars of one's expertise. In this chapter, however, I want to explore some questions that engage the interaction of the two problems, that is, the problems of delimiting "Islam" and delimiting "history," not least because the case of China's Muslims offers its own insights. In particular, I want to reexamine one approach to defining Islam in light of both historical processes and the writing of history. That definitional approach is one I will sum up under the term "self-ascription," which has also been called the "whatever-Muslims-say-it-is" argument.[1]

My primary concern here is not the related question of what kind of category Islam is, for example, discourse versus social system versus religion and so on, but rather how we determine which discourses, social systems, and so on are appropriately designated Islamic. If, for example, we accept Talal Asad's influential argument that Islam is a "discursive tradition," we are still left with the questions of which discursive phenomena are part of Islam and which belong to other discursive traditions.[2] Any approach to such delimitation unavoidably emphasizes some kinds of phenomena over others, all but engendering its own answer to the question of what kind of category Islam is. These ramifications are addressed in the second half of the chapter.

In delimiting which phenomena can be called "Islamic," the self-ascription or "whatever-Muslims-say-it-is" argument avoids endorsing one of the countless contradictory claims to the true understanding of Islam by accepting them all. In the words of Albert Hourani, a proponent of the approach, "whatever people have believed to be Islam is Islam."[3] It follows, then, that since each individual conception of Islam is Islam, and since many of these conceptions rule one another out, there are many Islams. Indeed, proponents of the self-ascription approach often write about "Islams" rather than "Islam," as I have done in this book.

This position has some obvious scientific and ethical advantages. Scientifically, it is precise and yet flexible, productive rather than reductive, bringing a wide range of apparently mutually exclusive (yet connected) phenomena into view without relying on subjective measures, all while allowing for infinite new formulations of its object. Ethically, it avoids the epistemic violence of telling people who regard themselves as Muslims that their faith is not Islam. And it very effectively gives the lie to essentialism, the flawed epistemology at the root of most anti-Muslim repression.

Nonetheless, the self-ascription approach has also raised strong objections, counting among its detractors Talal Asad and Shahab Ahmed. One prominent concern is that such a definition is empty, nominal, or meaningless. Of course, the linkage of nominalness and meaninglessness is not as obvious or unproblematic as it might appear at first sight, and the conceptual baggage of such a move, particularly in the Islamic context, will be examined later in this chapter. Nonetheless, critics worry that by accepting everything, Islam becomes nothing. The door to an Islam without Muhammad, or without the Qur'an, is seemingly left wide open. A secondary complaint (and the root of Asad's very brief critique) is that the self-ascription approach in fact dismisses certain Muslim claims about Islam. Many, perhaps most, Muslims define Islam in ways that exclude some other self-identified Muslims' beliefs from the category of Islam. These particular claims about the boundaries of Islam are openly rejected by the self-ascription approach as analytical definitions of Islam (though they are not rejected as forms of Islam). Thus the self-ascription argument has been said to contradict Muslims' beliefs even as it claims to emerge from them.

This chapter addresses questions about self-ascription that have received little attention from either side. Most important, why do people self-identify as Muslims in the first place? And what exactly does self-ascription comprise? What effects follow from the act of self-ascription? Finally, if we survey scholarship on Islam, how does the term "Islam" actually get used? In addressing these questions, I aim not only to mount a defense of the self-ascription approach, but to understand more fully the implications of self-ascription in Islamic contexts across time: the inducements to self-ascribe, the ramifications, and the consequent entanglements with historical representation and origin stories. I argue that self-ascription is not merely an act of naming, but rather an engagement with a long, many-tendriled historical process, and that this process, the reproduction and spread of ascription, is also a uniting focus of diverse Islamic historiographical traditions. The self-ascription approach leads to an expansive, flexible definition of Islamic history, embracing a wide variety of traditions. And when we generalize about these traditions, that is to say, when we describe the features most widely shared among them, we find an Islamic history that reflects and substantiates the centrality of self-ascription in delineating the scope of Islam.

"Nominal" and "Underdetermined"

Explicit critiques of the self-ascriptive approach are prominent but not all that numerous. Of the two main critics already mentioned, Asad devotes only a few sentences in his influential article "The Idea of an Anthropology of Islam." For a sustained and direct critique, we must turn to Ahmed, who detailed a long series of objections over the course of twenty-eight pages of his *What Is Islam?*[4] Ahmed's objections are too numerous to address individually here, but there is a connecting thread that makes his work an effective starting point for my argument. That thread is the notion that what he called the "islams-not-Islam" argument and particularly its "whatever-Muslims-say-it-is" subset are "underdetermined" and "nominal."

For Ahmed, mistaken conceptions of Islam are placed along a spectrum of overdetermined to underdetermined (in his metaphor, they turn in opposite directions along an axis of determinedness). This is one of two main problems he finds in all such failed conceptions of Islam. The implication is that this is a matter of proper calibration, that the proper understanding of Islam is not over- or underdetermined but rather just-right-determined, a Goldilocks Islam that turns neither clockwise nor counterclockwise around the axis of determinedness. Ahmed objects to definitions that have given Islam too strong an essence, but he does not want Islam to have no essence. He appears to advocate for a kind of light-touch essentialism. In this view, islams-not-Islam falls on the underdetermined side or, rather, spins in the underdetermined direction.

Ahmed argues it is not enough to say that there are Islams, in the plural, without defining what Islam, the singular, would then represent. Thus, Ahmed asks, "Is there a single Islam of which these plurals are somehow expressions?" Those in the islams-not-Islam camp would simply answer that there is not. But this hints at a practical question: Of all the varied local cultural and religious phenomena, Islamic and not Islamic, how do we determine which are Islams and which are not? It is much later in the book that Ahmed confronts the simplest solution to this problem, one that has been employed not just in the study of religion, but also, and more notably, in the study of ethnicity: self-ascription.[5] Under this view, an Islam is any phenomenon that is claimed to be Islam by someone who considers her- or himself a devotee of Islam, that is, a Muslim. To return to Ahmed's question, although any individual Muslim's Islam can exist in the singular, it is no more an expression of a single, overarching Islam than individual birds are expressions of a single ur-bird.

Ahmed's central criticism of self-identification is that it is "nominal":

> [Hourani's] analogy suggests that, merely because Muslims identify with Islam . . . , we should not assume that there is in fact a relation-

ship between the act of identification and the putative object of identity. Rather, the relationship is with a "symbol" that can be invoked in diverse circumstances with no necessary continuity—that is to say, no necessary coherence—between the various instances of invocation. This would imply that symbol is only *nominally* the same in each instance, but is *substantively* different.[6]

If Muslims are not doing what they are supposed to be doing in order to be Muslims—if they are doing "much that would be non-Islamic or even anti-Islamic" according to "Islamic revelation vouchsafed by God to the Prophet Muhammad and embodied in the Holy Book of the Qur'ān" and according to "the whole imposing corpus of Islamic law, theology, tradition, and practice"—then what is the *connection* between what they were supposed or required to think and do and what they actually thought and did? If there is no connection, then how is it in any way *meaningful* to name what they are doing "Islam"? In the absence of a meaningful connection, Braude and Lewis' use of the word "Islam" is entirely *nominal*—they have *named* the civilization Islamic, but without telling us what makes it so.[7]

This idea that the "whatever-Muslims-say-it-is" approach is nominal, meaningless, and unsubstantive shares much with Ahmed's essentializing (though he objects to this description) critique of the islams-not-Islam approach as "underdetermined." Ahmed worries that we have opened the door so wide that it is no longer a door at all, or that we have reduced Islam to nothing more than a name. Is this not an abandonment of the entire Islamic tradition? Where is the Prophet Muhammad? Where is the Qur'an?

Extremes

Rather than seeking a moderate approach that softens such objections, let us explore the extremes. Let us see how the self-ascription model operates in its most uncompromising form and on the most troublesome cases, where the objections outlined above are most attractive. A particularly pure reliance on self-ascription for the formation of subjective categories can be found in Fredrik Barth's revolutionary essay on ethnicity in the 1969 volume *Ethnic Groups and Boundaries: The Social Organization of Culture Difference*. To this day Barth's work is perhaps the most influential formulation of ethnicity for anthropologists, and it certainly lies at the root of the "whatever-Muslims-say-it-is" position, if not also the "islams-not-Islam" argument. Indeed, anthropologists have been central to the formulation of these positions.[8] And Barth's theory leads directly to an extreme real-world example in Islamic China. Following Barth's lead, anthropologist Dru Gladney described as Muslims a group of people who would seem to confirm Ahmed's fears about the "nominal": the Chendai Hui of Fujian, China, who called themselves *Huijiao ren* (回教人) and "do not follow Islamic practices."[9]

Barth's concerns about ethnic categorization share much with Ahmed's goals in delineating Islam, even if his solutions were different. Just as Ahmed repeatedly frames his study as a search for "coherence" in the face of diverse and contradictory understandings of Islam, Barth asks what coherence it is that makes us regard an ethnic group as identical across long stretches of time, even when the cultural traits of that group change diachronically. Barth was reacting to the then widely accepted claim that an ethnic group:

1. is largely biologically self-perpetuating;
2. shares fundamental cultural values, realized in overt unity in cultural forms;
3. makes up a field of communication and interaction; and
4. has a membership which identifies itself, and is identified by others, as constituting a category distinguishable from other categories of the same order.[10]

His answer was to discard all but the fourth element of the definition, to regard "ethnic groups . . . as a form of social organization" expressed in ascription, rather than an assemblage of particular biological, cultural, or social traits.[11] Barth would later be accused of disregarding cultural content entirely, and he would rebut that charge in useful ways I will return to below.[12] Nonetheless, Barth's understanding of ethnicity gained a wide following among anthropologists, including those who applied it to the case of Islam and Muslims.

So it was that Gladney surveyed "Muslim Chinese" across the People's Republic of China by studying any groups that called themselves "Hui." Groups identifying with this term included the Ding lineage of Chendai, Fujian, who, as of 1940, referred to themselves as people of the Hui teaching

(*Huijiao ren*), a term used by many of the authors we have examined in this book when writing in Chinese. When Gladney met them in the 1980s, the Dings were fighting to be recognized officially by the state as Hui, a designation that had come to indicate not just membership in a religious community but an ethnic group.[13] According to Gladney, the Dings openly professed not to participate in Islamic practices, so we might say, for example, that their consumption of pork is not regarded by them as violating a tenet of Islam.[14] In a strict understanding of self-ascription, the practices and beliefs of the Dings would not be considered Islam, because the Dings count themselves as nonbelievers and nonpractitioners of Islam, even though they are "of" Islam (this by virtue of their descent from Muslims). Without the original Chinese-language transcripts of Gladney's Ding interviews, it is difficult to analyze the Ding case in much more detail, but their example raises more general questions about self-ascription and the relationship of Chinese Muslims to the category of Islam.

When confronted with purported Muslims calling themselves *Huijiao ren,* we are immediately forced to ask what it means to self-identify as a Muslim. An extraordinary historical phenomenon, almost entirely unremarked upon in the scholarly literature, becomes suddenly apparent: With only a few exceptions, every group that has been considered Muslim, and every tradition (or religion or civilization or discourse) that has been considered a manifestation of Islam, has employed words whose etymological linkage to "Islam" and "Muslim" is not only close but conspicuous. Thus we have people, for example the exiles from Eastern Turkistan, who call themselves musulmān rather than muslimūn, but only rare cases of etymologically divorced terms like *Huijiao ren* for Muslim and *Qingzhen* for Islam.

The case of Chinese Muslims who call themselves by some form of the word "Hui" may be one of very few exceptions to the rule, but it is a significant one. In the People's Republic of China, "Hui" is entangled with ethnicity, as the Hui are one of fifty-six official *minzu* (nationalities). Before this codification, however, Hui and Huihui usually denoted either adherents of Islam in general or, later, Chinese-speaking Muslims. The etymological roots of the term are not fully traceable, but it is widely understood to be a derivation of *Huihu*. Huihu, in turn, was the Sinicized form of Uighur, the name of a kingdom and tribal confederation to the west of China. Today, roughly eleven million people in China (about half of the country's Muslims), call themselves Hui. Among them, the most common term for Islam is *Qingzhen,* a combination of Chinese words for pure and true.

A key moment in the rise of these etymologically distant Islamic terms was the first publication of Islamic religious texts in the Chinese language, more than eight centuries after the first Muslims arrived in China. As we have seen, the earliest work to have lasting influence was Wang Daiyu's *Great Learning of the Pure and Real* (清真大學) of 1642, in which Wang attempted to explain his belief system, one derived from Sufism in the vein of Ibn 'Arabi,[15] to Confucian, Buddhist, and Daoist literati, expressing concern that "the books of Islam are seldom seen by Confucians."[16] Six decades later, Liu Zhi attempted through his writings to gain respect for Islam (and himself) in the Confucian-dominated world of Qing scholar-officials. Both authors based their writings on sources in Persian and Arabic, such as the works of Rāzi, Nasafī, and Jāmī, which Liu Zhi named in his text. Both authors wrote at a time when they would have been called Hui or Huihui by non-Muslims, and Wang Daiyu referred to himself as the "old man of the real Hui." When they labeled their thought system, they used the phrases "pure and true," "the Ultimate Way," and "our teaching."

Recall that Wang Daiyu addressed the problem of terminology explicitly in the introduction to his work. His attitude toward language and translation is clearest in his discussion of Buddhist and Daoist resonances in the text, which we examined briefly in Chapter 2:

> There is nothing lacking in the classical canon of Islam [清真], but there is no one outside the teaching [i.e., outside of Islam] who knows this. This is because our languages [文字] are different. I wrote and discussed using these expressions precisely to make our teachings comprehensive. All the borrowed expressions I used were because of my concern to show how the principles work. The expressions do not carry the same meaning, but if I had not borrowed them, how could I make clear that these two doctrines [Buddhism and Daoism] are different from ours?[17]

This passage is important for its explicitly practical approach to terminological borrowing. It shows that Wang regarded his work as an effort at translation for non-Muslims, rather than the syncretic project that scholars would later see in early Chinese-language Muslim authors.

As active readers of Persian and Arabic, Wang and Liu were familiar with the terms "Islam" and "Muslim," as well as many of their derivative forms. So too were the Muslims across the breadth of China educated in the Perso-Arabic canon described in Zhao Can's *Genealogy,* as well as those who emerged from Ma Lianyuan's late nineteenth-century educational project, with its textbooks in Arabic and Persian. However, in the early twentieth century, Chinese began to overtake these languages as a medium through which Muslims learned about Islam in China proper (that is, excluding the Qing colonial territories of Xinjiang and Tibet). It was then that Muslims began relying on the Chinese-language texts of Liu Zhi, Wang Daiyu, and others—texts originally aimed, at least in part, at explaining Islam to non-Muslims using Confucian, Buddhist, and Daoist terminology—for their understanding of Islam. *Qingzhen* emerged as the common designation for Islam, *Qingzhensi* (temple of the pure and real) for mosque, and *Huihui* for Muslim.

An Arabic revival over the course of the twentieth century eventually brought Sinicized Arabic terms like *Yisilan* (Islam) and *Musilin* to prominence, but it is probably safe to say that at times there have been Huihui in China who professed allegiance to Huijiao or Qingzhen, with no awareness that those terms were translations of the terms "Islam" and "Muslim." By the self-ascription approach, do they count as Muslims? Does their "Hui teaching" count as Islam?

Two possible responses are obvious. One option is to take the words of Hourani and other "whatever-Muslims-say-it-is" supporters in a literal sense, rejecting such claims for these Huihui on the basis that they do not literally call their teachings "Islam." This would confirm Ahmed's argument that the self-ascription approach is merely nominal. It is also a position that no self-ascription supporter has ever described or employed. Certainly Gladney, for example, when faced with the variation among the Hui, did not adopt this kind of extreme phonemic literalism. There is something that feels instinctively absurd about such literal nominalism. One might argue that this is the exposure of a fatal flaw in the self-ascription position. I argue that it exposes something else: Self-ascription is something more than simply attaching oneself to a name devoid of meaning. What makes Huihui and Muslims (and Qingzhen and Islam) equivalent is the very history of Islam in China that Liu Zhi, Lan Xu, Manṣūr Ma Xuezhi, and others recounted in their histories. Theirs are histories of origins and transmission and, in this particular case, efforts at translation that were regarded as crucial to transmission. Self-ascription is, among other things, an engagement with the whole of the Islamic past that brought the Huihui to call their "teaching" Qingzhen.

To understand self-ascription as the mere attachment to a particular combination of phonemes or a particular empty symbol is, I would argue, ahistorical. It fails to consider why people have devoted themselves to a phenomenon and called it Islam. Where did they get the idea to use this "mere name" and why did they find it beneficial to do so? The answer is the entire sweep of the history of Islams. Without the Qur'an and without Muhammad, no one would claim to be Muslim or to devote themselves to Islam (and no one would feel the need to translate these terms into Chinese). Without the Indian Ocean trade, perhaps no one in Indonesia would use these words. Without the beauty of Rumi's poetry, or the miracles of an itinerant Sufi preacher, some part of the population of Central Asia would have taken generations longer to embrace something they called "Islam." Everyone had to learn of the existence of the name "Islam" from someone else. The chain of transmission proceeded mostly through Muslims and in all cases can be traced ultimately to the Prophet Muhammad and his companions. The shapes of various Islams were determined by the Muslims from whom new Muslims learned the word "Islam" and from the original insights, transmitted texts, old habits, foreign influences, local wisdoms, origin stories, and so on of people who convinced (often fellow) Muslims of some part of their understanding of "Islam." The name "Islam" has been driven across the globe by the entire history of Islamic societies (societies in which Muslims were predominant) and brings with it that history, or, if we are interested in some particular slice of the human experience, that body of rituals, that discourse, that accumulation of laws, that literature, and on and on: all of the things we might fear losing with the self-ascription argument.

The act of self-ascription also goes beyond reflection of and engagement with the history of transmission, in ways that are particularly visible in religious conversion. Conversion itself is an extreme case, insofar as most Muslims over the last fourteen centuries have inherited rather than adopted their identification as Muslims. In his work on conversion among the Golden Horde of the Russian and Central Asian steppes, Devin DeWeese pointed out unrecognized significance in the adoption of the designation "Muslim." DeWeese was partly arguing against the commonplace that the Islam of Inner Asian Muslims has historically been "'nominal' and superficial," but his insights on the potential meaning of self-ascription are valuable in and of themselves: "To call oneself 'Muslim' or by a name whose mention evokes recollection of an islamizer, or of an entire 'sacred history' or genealogy linked to Islamization, is no trivial matter. To adopt a name is to change one's reality, and in this sense there is hardly a deeper 'conversion' than a nominal one." DeWeese goes on to emphasize the difficulty of abandoning old spoken rituals (such as acts of self-ascription), the correspondences between name / form and spiritual power in many Islamic traditions, "Islamic assumptions regarding the sacred power of the external to affect the internal," and the implications of "opening" inherent in communal adoptions of the name "Islam." Here I simplify a sophisticated argument, but the point is that DeWeese argues from within both Islamic and pre-Islamic Inner Asian discourses that self-ascription is something much richer than "nominal" would suggest.[18]

What does it take for individuals to present themselves as devoted to a phenomenon called Islam, especially when, in all known cases of such devotion, they believe that phenomenon to include a host of actions beyond a speech act, for example, the assumption of certain loyalties or duties? Beyond a history of transmission or a moment of conversion, there is a present and future of self-ascription's continuing effects. Presenting oneself as a Muslim has practical consequences. In a given context, a Muslim is expected to act in certain ways, to consume certain texts, to honor certain loyalties, or to hold certain beliefs. Rather than an empty, symbolic association, self-ascription is an embrace of a world of context-dependent expectations, requirements, responsibilities, privileges, and disadvantages—in short, a certain way of making meaning and relating to others understood as "Islam." We might say that self-ascription is what Ahmed calls, in his discussion of Islam as means and meaning, a "consequential truth."[19]

Islamic History

Because self-ascription as a Muslim involves identification with other (self-ascribed) Muslims, it implicates a Muslim in shared Islamic representations of the past. This is another of the continuing effects of self-ascription: A Muslim, by virtue of self-ascription, situates herself in some version of

Islamic history, laying claim to a particular origin story. Islamic historical traditions have obviously varied greatly across societies in which Muslims are / were predominant. Nonetheless, the great majority of Islamic historical traditions have in common an emphasis on origins and transmission (of the idea of being Muslim and of the willingness to personally embrace that idea), the phenomenon that drives self-ascription and ties all Muslims back to the earliest Islamic community. Thus, the use of transmission to understand the scope of Islam (via self-ascription) is therefore not entirely alien to Islamic historical traditions themselves.

Thus far I have used "history" in the lay sense of everything that happened in the past, but for the remainder of this chapter I will reserve that word for a narrower phenomenon. For this purpose, I borrow Greg Dening's definition of history as the past "transformed into texts—texts written down, texts spoken, texts caught in the forms of material things" and "the texted past for which we have a cultural poetic."[20] Even accepting this definition of history alongside the self-ascription definition of Islam, there are still numerous possible meanings of "Islamic history." The phrase could indicate the history of Muslims' pasts, the history of Islams past, histories that Muslims deem Islamic, histories created by Muslims, histories of Muslims' pasts created by Muslims, histories of societies in which Muslims have been predominant, and so on. The openness of the term is reflected in the multiplicity of ways it is used. And this is to ignore formulations based on other understandings of "history": Islamic history often denotes the professional academic study of the pasts of societies in which Muslims have been predominant. Without advocating for the superiority of any one of these framings, here I will use "Islamic history" to denote the vast collectivity of histories (texted pasts) created by Muslims, and I use "Islamic histories" to denote narrower bodies of texts or individual texts created by Muslims. This is roughly what has sometimes been covered under the study of "Islamic historiography" or "Islamicate historiography."[21]

If Muslims are people who identify as Muslims, and Islam is whatever they say it is, then Islamic history as I have framed it is an extraordinarily large, diverse, and geographically widespread phenomenon, including oral performances of the West African epic of Sundiata, the *Huihui yuanlai* (Origins of the Huihui), historical essays in the Nation of Islam's official US newspaper, oral accounts of Sunan Kalijaga from Indonesia,[22] the Alexander Romance, and perhaps Ahmad's *What Is Islam?,* not to mention more widely recognized Islamic histories such as Ṭabari's chronicle, dynastic histories such as the Saljuqnama, Persian local histories, and the Qur'an. This is a more expansive conception of Islamic history than what is found in most English-language scholarship. The current academic historiography of Muslim societies is overwhelmingly dominated by cultural products of the Middle East, as is the modern academic field of the history of Muslim societies. Marshall Hodgson's influential *Venture of Islam* presented Muslim societies beyond the Middle East as "Islamicate" rather than Islamic, a term that has gained wide currency despite its essentializing assumptions.[23] Much of Ahmed's energy was aimed at breaking the Middle Eastern monopoly on Islam, but his own conception is rooted in a "Balkans-to-Bengal complex" that de-emphasizes enormous populations of Muslims with rich historical traditions (the present book suggests adding at least one more alliterative place-name: Balkans-to-Bengal-to-Beijing). Outside of the realm of historiography, expansive understandings of Muslim and Islam are not rare.[24] However, to date there have been few efforts to survey the whole historiography of self-ascribed Muslims. The raw population figures for Muslims who are thereby excluded from most images of Islamic history are staggering: Approximately half a billion Muslims—one-third of the global Muslim population—live in Southeast Asia or Sub-Saharan Africa.

It is clear that there is no essential character to Islamic history in the broad formulation I apply here (nor, I would argue, in any other), but that does not mean it is impossible to generalize. We may not be able to identify traits shared universally among such histories, but we can find traits that appear with remarkable frequency in that vast corpus of Islamic histories. One of these is a common guiding question: How did Islam arrive here (wherever that may be)? The answers are different in every place, but they are all histories of origins and transmission, of the movement (and contestation) of self-ascription across space and time, with all of its attendant texts, beliefs, loyalties, practices, and so on. Islamic history is, most commonly, a history of arrival.

At the birth of Islam, the guiding question of arrival was answered by the Qur'an, the first Islamic history, but within a few generations Muslims found themselves chronologically and often spatially distant enough from the events of the Qur'an that they needed new answers. The *hadith* literature, accounts of the deeds and words of the Prophet Muhammad and his companions, answered this obliquely through the *isnads* (chains of transmission) that accompanied the *hadith*. Biographical compendia that helped establish the authority of *hadith* transmitters provided richer descriptions of the community's links back to the Prophet. As time passed and Islam spread, genealogies often did the heavy lifting, especially where Muslims have been eager to claim descent from the Prophet Muhammad or one of his prominent family members.[25] Where Islamic genealogies were rare or deemphasized, other historical literatures filled the gap. In Persia and urban Central Asia, local histories often claimed authority and legitimacy for cities or regions by connecting them to the birthplaces of Islam.[26] In places such as the Inner Asian steppe and Java, conversion narratives gained remarkable popularity, distilling the arrival of Islam into the story of one great man's act of self-ascription.[27] Among Chinese Muslims, conversion narratives are almost entirely absent. Instead, purportedly "first" arrivals have often been the focus, in the form of origin stories. In other places, such as nineteenth-century Hausaland or the Eastern Turkistan of the eighteenth century, tales of holy war proliferated, in which the readers' ancestors are figured as unbelievers, Islam's reluctant hosts rather than Muslim guests.[28] In all of these cases, Islamic histories trace the very paths expressed in self-ascriptive definitions of Islam, the multifarious, intertwined branches of transmission of the idea that something called Islam exists, and that people can align themselves with it.

Conclusion

At the most practical level, the self-ascriptive approach to delimiting Islamic history has already been implicitly adopted by the community of historians who see their business as "Islamic history," at least as far as one can judge from the aggregate of these historians' more narrowly focused, regionally specific works. The mass of books and articles that frame their subject as part of "Islamic history" represents a cultural geography that maps neatly onto the range of communities that consider themselves Muslim. Even if some historians may, for example, divide the world into a truly Islamic Middle East and a secondary "Islamicate" sphere, when we look at who among professional historians presents their work as Islamic history, we find representation for all self-ascribed Muslims, from Siberia to the Philippines to Detroit.

Is this category of "Islamic history" worth talking about, not just for the value of its contents (the creative output of Muslims over the centuries) but in terms of this category? What would be lost if we used other categories for Muslims' "texted pasts"? To begin with, there are good practical reasons to continue debating the nature of Islamic history, to map the contours of Islamic history, and to offer Islamic approaches to history as comparative examples. The salience of the notion of "Islam" in the world today makes an exploration of a category called "Islamic history" of inherent value. There are simply too many world-shaping decisions being made based on (mis)understandings of Islam and its histories to ignore framings of the past in terms of "Islamic history." Moreover, if we adopt the self-ascriptive understanding of Islam, then "Islamic history," when used as it is here, can be seen as an emic reflection of the process and importance of self-ascription. This process is the content of the community histories of Islamic China: the account of how people who ascribed to "our teaching" (various Islams) came to be "here" (China), and to continue passing on that self-ascription across generations. Islamic history is valuable as an Islamic explanation for the contradiction apparent in academic definitions, that is, the mutual exclusivity of so many Muslims' understandings of Islam. It is a script for the lives of communities, future-oriented as much as past-oriented. And if "Islamic history" is used in the more common sense of "all the things that happened in Muslim societies," it encompasses the very process of the spread and reproduction of self-ascription.

Islamic history is at once delimited by the diachronic unfolding of transmission from the origin and the account of that unfolding. Moreover, Muslims' attention to transmission emerges in any view of the aggregate of Islamic histories as a predominant trait. Those transmissions of Muslim identity occur most often *within* Islamic societies, across generations and among members of the same communities. They are facilitated and reshaped by mechanisms that include translation, contestation, and historical production by Muslims for Muslims. More rarely, those transmissions take place across great social distances, sometimes taking the form of conversions, and even involving arrivals of Muslims in non-Muslim contexts. Even efforts at cross-community transmission that are largely unsuccessful, such as Wang Daiyu and Liu Zhi's efforts to gain a foothold for Islam in among non-Muslim literati, can be folded into the histories of transmission within a community. In this sense Islamic history is a history characterized by an extraordinary emphasis on arrivals and transmissions; it is created by arrival and transmission; and its defining, self-ascribing feature, at least as proposed here, is generated by arrivals and transmissions. In Islamic contexts this is particularly important because the notion of transmission is itself a prominent part of that which is transmitted, that is to say an emphasis on traceability back to some vision of original Muslims is so often a part of Islamic histories, not least among those Muslims who identify as Chinese. It is only by setting aside this "contingent working-out"[29] of Muslim identities across time that essentialisms creep back into the study of Islamic history, and it is by highlighting them that we might begin to answer the question "what is Islam?" in ways that are more productive than reductive.

A similar approach could be taken to the questions of "what is China?" and "what is Chinese history?" These questions bring their own particular challenges. Notably, the English term "China" and the Chinese word *Zhongguo,* which are widely seen as equivalent today, have different origins and distinct histories of transmission, coming into contact with each other only in the sixteenth century. Chen Bo has argued that this separate development has effects that linger today, to the extent that, for Chen, "'China' never means 'Zhongguo.'"[30] This is something of a prescriptive claim, given that many people do understand the terms as neatly equivalent and use them that way,[31] but Chen's argument points to real disjunctures in the ways these terms have been used over time. Others point out that the English word "Chinese" can refer to a citizen of the People's Republic of China, a member of the "civilization" of China, or a member of the Han ethnic group.[32] Even if we restrict our view to Chinese-language terms, exactly what one is ascribing to when one calls oneself Chinese has varied greatly. Is it loyalty to a state? Is it an ethnic identity? Is it subjecthood?

As with the category of Islam, one reason to use "China" and "Chinese" as historical categories despite these complexities and contradictions is that so much of the world's population takes the category to be meaningful, not to mention politically relevant. It is useful to increase our historical understanding of the people who are widely understood to fall under this term, even if the category is incoherent or ahistorical, and especially if that history lays bare the incoherence.

However, attention to transmitted self-ascription may allow us to embrace these complexities and contradictions in the pursuit of coherence, rather than just practical or heuristic ends. As with the case of "Islām"and "Qingzhen," emic histories have much to say about the links between the myriad terms that have been equated to "China," including *Zhongguo, Han, Zhongyang, Song, Tang, China,* and *Sīn.* An imagined continuity of a community can be traced across these terms in genealogies, gazetteers, philosophical works, and the canonical twenty-four dynastic histories. It is imagined in different ways by different people, just as Islam looks different to every Muslim. "Chinese" people are those who identify themselves by one from among this group of historically interrelated terms with distinct but overlapping meanings, all of which refer to an imagined community[33] that is understood to be part of a transmission of political and cultural legitimacy constructed in historical works such as the twenty-four histories. The tracing of these transmissions may be far from complete, but it has begun in various subfields of Chinese history, appearing in debates about New Qing History, histories of Chinese nation formation, and historical studies of ethnicity in China. Many of these studies already take self-ascription as a fundamental form of evidence. And the special role of history in creating a subjective equation of the various kingdoms retrospectively deemed "Chinese" is already widely appreciated in Chinese studies, leading Haun Saussy to call China "the artwork whose medium is history."[34]

Some of China's Muslims eventually constructed for themselves another kind of identity, which fully intertwined Chineseness and Muslimness, to the extent that it *excluded* both non-Chinese Muslims and non-Muslim Chinese. The category of Hui under the People's Republic of China is the strongest example of this intertwining. By contrast, in the Ming, Qing, and Republican eras, this term and its cousin, Huihui, often referred to any Muslims, not just those associated with China. Most of the authors treated in this book considered their Chinese and Muslim identities to be distinct, two identities held at once. Manṣūr Ma Xuezhi described himself in Arabic as Muslim, Chinese, and Jahriyya. The origin story of the exclusive Muslim-*and*-Chinese identity unfolded in the course of the twentieth century.[35]

My goal is not to leave these categories too neat, to grasp them so tightly that they slip through our fingers. One community will not be ordered. Many communities much less so. There is a value in a plurality of orderings, in putting them side by side and demonstrating their limits.

Orderings are for purposes, and our purpose at any moment, in any particular matrix of ordinariness, may be better served by one ordering than another. Bruno Latour argued that "groups are not silent things, but rather the provisional product of a constant uproar made by the millions of contradictory voices about what is a group and who pertains to what."[36] Ascription is deeply meaningful. The uproar is not only reflected in historical sources but viewed as a question of history and transmission by the actors themselves. Recognizing this is indispensable if we are to reach an understanding of the Muslims of China, or any other community, that captures their ordinariness and renders them unsurprising.

Conclusion

On a cool evening in November 2018, a small group of men and women gathered around a party of *qawwali* musicians at the tomb of a Sufi saint in Kanpur, India. The pop of the tabla and the drone of the harmonium reverberated across the graveyard's eclectic monuments to the dead as the lead vocalist sang passionate verses about the beloved. Similar gatherings may have occasioned Ma Zhu's seventeenth-century complaint about foreign Muslims gathering at night and playing music in Yunnan. Ten meters away, a different Yunnanese Muslim's bones vibrated to the plaintive sounds of the *qawwali*'s verses.

At both ends of a rectangular brick structure with a pitched cornice, there are stone plaques identifying the building as the grave of Nūr al-Ḥaqq / Ma Lianyuan, the "Link to the Origin" (Figures C.1 and C.2). One is engraved in Chinese, giving Ma's year of death as the twenty-ninth year of the Guangxu emperor. The other, in Arabic, gives it as the 1,321st year of the Hijri calendar, which begins with the Prophet Muhammad's emigration from Mecca to Medina. The Chinese inscription records the names of Ma's three sons, who take credit for erecting the tomb, memorializing themselves as links to the future world without Ma Lianyuan.

Ma's year or two in Kanpur left few traces in the historical record or local memory. He left the Qing Empire in 1901. Preparation of *Explication* for its Kanpur publication began in the month of Safar, 1320 (May–June 1902), the book was printed in the spring of 1903, and Ma died in July of that year. This suggests that Ma spent one to two years in Kanpur. Why he spent so long there, rather than continuing on to his final goal, Mecca, remains a mystery. Some personal or scholarly connection must have brought Ma to Kanpur, as it is far from ports that were stops on the Hajj route, and it was overshadowed in both commercial and intellectual

FIGURE C.1 Nūr al-Ḥaqq / Ma Lianyuan's grave in Kanpur, 2018. *Credit:* © Rian Thum

FIGURE C.2 The Arabic and Chinese inscriptions on Nūr al-Ḥaqq / Ma Lianyuan's grave. *Credit:* © Rian Thum

importance by nearby Lucknow. During his time in Kanpur, Ma also published a *ḥāshiyah,* or marginal super-commentary, on his own commentary, *Sharḥ al-laṭā'if,* on the "original classic" of Liu Zhi's *Nature and Principle in Islam.* The major lithograph publishers of Kanpur were clustered around the Patkapur mosque, but I could not identify the location of the ʿAlī Maḥmūd operation, which produced Ma's books. Nor could I locate any copies of Ma's books during a two-week visit to Kanpur in 2018, including in the rich library of the Patkapur mosque, which preserves thousands of lithographs (I eventually located a copy of Ma's *Sharḥ al-laṭā'if* in nearby Lucknow). In my conversations with Islamic scholars around Kanpur, only one claimed to have heard of a scholar from China visiting the town. He gave me the name of a Sufi scholar who he thought may have acted as Ma's teacher, but I was unable to find any records of this person.

In the same year that I visited Ma's grave in Kanpur, he was memorialized very differently in his hometown of Yuxi, Yunnan. Three state-sponsored organizations cooperated to host an academic conference, entitled "Ma Lianyuan and the Chinafication [中国化] of Islam."[1] Scholars from prestigious institutions across China attended. Scholar-officials gave speeches, saying that Ma Lianyuan made "great contributions to the localization [本土化] of Islam," providing "a scriptural basis and practical example for today's Chinafication of Islam." This, they said, followed the urging of Chairman Xi Jinping to "Chinafy" religion.[2]

Chairman Xi has not provided a clear definition of "Chinafication," but bureaucratic proclamations and state-approved academic works associate certain traits consistently with Chinafication. In the realm of Islamic architecture, it usually involves the adoption of aesthetic forms that were shared with non-Muslim communities of premodern China: curving tiled roofs and an absence of domes. In the realms of Islamic philosophy and theology, it refers to the use of concepts or terminology shared by non-Muslim Chinese thinkers, especially concepts perceived as Confucian, Daoist, and Buddhist. The "China" it refers to is, in its essence, non-Islamic, and Islam is, in its essence, alien to China. So it was that in 2018 the central leadership instructed officials to "use the excellent culture of China to permeate Islam in China."[3]

The state's phrasing echoes the title of Feng Jinyuan's 1982 study, "The Influence and Penetration of Confucian Thought in Chinese Islam . . . ," which introduced the notion of the Han Kitab into Anglophone scholarship.[4]

Indeed, the state policy of Chinafication that has emerged under Xi Jinping's rule is heavily indebted to the prevailing syncretism-oriented scholarship on Chinese-language Islamic texts. The party-state urges that the "permeation" be based on "systematically summarizing the historical experience of the Chinafication of Islam." That historical experience is sketched out in a key planning document for the Chinafication policy: "During the Ming and Qing Dynasties, the 'use of Confucianism to interpret scripture' was implemented, thus gaining valuable experience for the Chinafication of Islam." The syncretism orientation is not only enshrined in the state's understanding of Islam. The state also glorifies texts seen as most syncretic, presenting them as exemplars of the desired Chinafication.

As his burial in India might hint, Ma Lianyuan is not an obvious choice for a model of "localization" or Chinafication. After all, his main activities were publishing South and Central Asian works in Arabic and Persian and revitalizing an educational system for teaching these works. The "Chinafication" idea posits that Islamic texts that do not use philosophical terms shared by non-Muslim Chinese thinkers are insufficiently "Chinafied." Although the woodblock technique, Ṣīnī calligraphy, and Chinese-language title pages of Ma's foreign-origin publications were certainly specific to their Chinese context, and Ma frequently described himself as Chinese, these are not the characteristics that the Chinafication policy seeks. Ma did, however, publish some of Liu Zhi's Confucian work, mostly in Arabic translation. And one scholar of public policy, Ma Jia, has argued that the Chinese version of Ma's anti-Christian polemic shows signs of Confucian values, qualifying the work as "Chinafication."[5]

But there are also practical reasons to present Ma Lianyuan as a practitioner of Chinafication. The state's designation of some manifestations of China's thousand-plus-year Islamic history as more "Chinese" than others, and the call to make all forms *more* "Chinese," is backed by its vast resources and monopoly on legitimized violence. It is also accompanied by efforts to reduce the footprint of Islam more generally. A few selected commands from the central leadership's 2018 directive suffice to convey the vision:

- "Construct an ideological system of Islamic scriptures with Chinese characteristics"
- "We must gradually reduce large-scale religious activities"

- In the western parts of China, construction of religious structures should follow "the principle of demolishing more and building less"
- In other areas, "in principle it is not suitable to build a new mosque"
- "Strictly control those who study abroad privately to study religion"
- "Arabic must never be allowed to be promoted and used as a minority language in our country. Arabic schools are not allowed to train teaching staff, are not allowed to offer religious courses."[6]

Ma would seem to be a symbol of what Islam is *not* supposed to be in Xi's China. Thus, framing Ma as a model syncretizer is probably wise if one wants to conduct research or organize a conference on his work in China today.

Xi's state has shown itself ready to enforce its Chinafying vision. Minarets and domes have been removed from thousands of mosques across China for being insufficiently "Chinese," sometimes sparking protests. In some cases, the destroyed elements are replaced with towers that match the state's idea of what is authentically "Chinese." In most cases they are simply removed, leaving bare, boxlike buildings. Minarets, despite a millennium-long history in China, are now seen as "Arab." In Gansu and Ningxia, officials have enforced a mosque closure program euphemistically called "consolidation," forcing congregations to combine and repurposing existing mosques as craft or community centers. Ablution stations have been removed from other mosques, making it difficult for congregants to perform daily prayers.[7]

In Xinjiang (Eastern Turkistan), where Uyghurs, Kazakhs, and other Turkic Muslims are judged to be the least Chinafied, policies have reached notorious extremes. Thousands of mosques have been closed or destroyed. Nearly a million children have been forced to move to residential schools, where they are taught in the Chinese language. A million or more people have been placed in various forms of internment or prison, based on their identity. The substantial population of Hui people in Xinjiang have not gone untouched by these policies, but they have, on the whole, fared better. The causes of this ethnic divide in policy are complex, but the sense that

Uyghurs and others are less Chinese than the Hui—more in need of Chinafication—plays a substantial role.

Empirical Assessment

By examining Persian-, Arabic-, Turkic-, and Chinese-language sources in their interaction, this book arrives at a number of empirical conclusions about the history of Islamic China in the era before the dominance of modernist reform and nationalism. The most fundamental of these relates to the source base itself: Non-Chinese-language texts, referred to in this book by the heuristic term "Perso-Arabic," played a far greater role, across a wider geography, and for a longer period, than is typically acknowledged. Until the beginning of the twentieth century, Persian and Arabic texts served as the primary Islamic educational curriculum across the breadth of Islamic China (including in specialized women's classes), shaped the views of all the authors who wrote Islamic texts in Chinese (so-called Han Kitab), and facilitated Chinese Muslims' communications with other parts of Asia. The roles of Persian and Arabic were not homogeneous across this terrain. For example, their use for recording community *histories* appears to be confined to the western parts of China, including Yunnan, though brief histories in these languages do appear on stele inscriptions well beyond the western provinces. But this unevenness does not make the Persian and Arabic texts any less integral to our understanding of communities on the coastal regions of China.

The examination of Persian and Arabic sources is not just crucial to understanding Islamic China as a whole, or Persian and Arabic discourses within China. It is also indispensable for understanding the Chinese-language texts that have drawn so much of historians' attention. Even if we were interested solely in understanding the Chinese-language contributions of Liu Zhi, Wang Daiyu, and Ma Zhu, all of whom read widely in Persian and Arabic texts, or of Lan Xu, Ma Dexin, Ma Anli, and Ma Lianyuan, all of whom also *wrote* texts in Persian or Arabic, we could not restrict our source base to the Chinese-language texts. And if we want to understand certain east-coast communities whose members were mostly monolingual, we must also consider that their religious leaders, many of whom were migrants from the northwest or the southwest, were educated in Persian and

Arabic literature and taught their students basic texts in those languages. In short, the Persian and Arabic discourses that threaded through China's Muslim communities cannot be disentangled and excised from their histories.

This linguistic entanglement facilitated and reflected a level of cross-sectarian, cross-ethnic, and geographic interconnection that has been under-researched, to the extent that it came as a surprise to me in the course of my research. The lives I selected to represent in this book were chosen, above all, to demonstrate the diversity of Islamic China, but they turned out to be interconnected in ways that I could not have predicted. For example, it was only during the final revisions to my manuscript that I discovered one of the key connections: Ma Lianyuan's *dhikr* instructor in Mecca appears to have been a Mujaddidī shaykh, one of the teachers mentioned in the Deaf Cleric's account of Qi Huantang's travels. Many of the specific, individual connections that I documented here emerged from the spread of the Mujaddidiyya or from the earlier activities of Afāq Khwāja. But a more general interconnection is visible in the textual heritage shared across China's Muslim communities. The *Maktūbāt* dispersal described in Chapter 6 is only one example. The texts of the basic Persian curriculum described in the *Jingxue xi chuan pu* (1714), republished by Ma Lianyuan (late nineteenth century), and described again by Pan Shiqian in 1945, are another example. But there are others that are only briefly mentioned in this book. *Tafsīr al-ḥusaynī* and *al-Wiqāya,* for example, are studied by Hui and Uyghurs, Salafis and *menhuan* members, and found in libraries and archives from Guangzhou to Beijing to Linxia to Urumqi. At the same time, versions of the Chinese-language *Huihui yuanlai* are read in the northwest as well as on the coast. These connections should caution against framings of Islamic China that overemphasize the distinction between the northwest, where the largest concentrations of Muslims live, and the rest of China proper. And they call for further study of the interethnic exchanges between Huihui and Turki peoples, as well as the Salars and Dongxiang.

Following Islamic China's connections beyond China itself, we find that South Asia has been a far more important partner in Muslim circulations than has been recognized. Even before the Mujaddidī expansion, seventeenth-century trade connections and pilgrimage routes brought

Chinese Muslims to India, and Indian Muslims to China and Eastern Turkistan. These led to the widespread adoption of a preferred South Asian statement of faith (*Īmān-i mujmal*) and the production of a classic Chinese-language text (*Gui zhen zong yi*), and they likely account for the inclusion of the Persian-language *Pillar of Islam* in the elementary curriculum. When Mujaddidī proselytizers arrived from South Asia in the eighteenth century, they were repeating a long-standing pattern, as was Ma Lianyuan when he settled in Kanpur for the final years of his life.

Islamic China's connections to the rest of the Muslim-majority world certainly accelerated from the late nineteenth century onward, with a larger number of individual journeys beyond the borders of the Qing Empire and then the Republic of China. But long before this acceleration, constant circulations across border regions drew Muslim scholars into inter-Asia relationships that were no less important than the rare Hajj journeys that have made it into the historical record. These earlier exchanges, if less frequent, had profound effects on the shape of Islamic China. The entirety of the basic educational curriculum recorded in 1714 is composed of books written outside of China, as is the list of books consulted by Liu Zhi, the great eighteenth-century author of Chinese-language Islamic texts. Islam did not just arrive in China in the seventh century, or in three or four tides, but continuously and repeatedly.

And Chinese Muslims did not just receive foreign visitors and make short trips abroad. They also settled in new places, bringing Islamic China and their own sense of ordinariness with them—and reframing China as a new point of origin. Many of these communities have adapted so fully to their host societies that they have disappeared from the historical record as distinctive populations. Other, more recent, diasporic communities have maintained their distinctiveness into the present, including communities in Southeast Asia, Central Asia, and Saudi Arabia. Most have been the subject of scattered, article-length studies or PhD dissertations. There is value in reintegrating them into synoptic accounts of Islamic China. Like the inter-Asian networks that shaped China's Islams in the Ming and Qing, their continued sense of connection to China engenders travel and the sharing of texts, such as the Thai republication of Ma Lianyuan's India-published *Tawḍīḥ* that made its way back to Yunnan, or the 2010s flow of brides from Xinjiang to Saudi Arabia. Islamic China is, in short, a trans-Asian phenomenon.

Abstractions

Some of the issues confronted in this book may seem arcane at first glance: debates about the construction of social categories, the role of origin-oriented thinking in history writing, and the problems of syncretism as a conceptual model. These are abstractions about the ways that people make abstractions. But they all have powerful effects on the lives of China's Muslims. As the 2018 conference on Ma Lianyuan demonstrates, these debates are conceptual contests in which the Chinese state is directly engaged. The state's answers to these abstract questions provide it with blueprints for its efforts to transform Chinese Islams into allies of the party, often with violence. Those blueprints quite explicitly credit history, as practiced by academic historians, with a guiding role.

Social categorizations of cultural difference—group names like "Muslim," "Huihui," and "Chinese"—are visible indications of an incomprehensibly vast tangle of connection. They are also the stories that persuade us not to look too closely at those interconnections. When category stories contradict each other, as they inevitably do, we are tempted to see those backed by greater political power as more believable, and those that define the disempowered as contradictory. The story of China as homogeneous is widely believed, as is the story of homogeneous Islam. The stories of Islamic China, on the other hand, tend to be valued for their apparent contradiction. "Are they really Muslims?" But the stories of Islamic China are not contradictory in and of themselves. Rather, they contradict the dominant "China" and "Islam" stories. Stories like those of Islamic China, rendered contradictory by their lack of political power, surprise us by revealing the tangled veins of human interconnection that masquerade as categories. Because they are superficially implausible, they compel us to look below the narrative surface, draped in a puzzle-piece cloth of identity categories, at the tangle of human intercourse. Such tangles are the subject of much scholarship, but too often they feature as exceptions—the routinized exceptions that buttress category narratives. This book has aimed to normalize the tangle itself (rather than a few exceptions) and, where possible, to do so without allowing categories to paper over interconnection.

The disentangling effects of origin stories make them powerful tools in identity claims and claims of distinction. They allow one to simultaneously claim identity with a larger group and claim distinction, often of higher authority or authenticity, within the group. Origin stories are attractive to both outsider observers and participants because of their perceived power to disentangle, but they are doing different work for the two constituencies. For the outsider or second-order observer,[8] they simplify the work of categorization by disentangling. Because origin stories cross time and pass through multiple categories, purportedly creating a new category, they both transform an abstraction (the category) into the digestible form that is narrative, and they link that abstraction to other abstractions with which the observer is comfortable.[9] For the insider, they disentangle the individual from the wider identity group. They are deployed based on audience, in a fashion similar to the nested identities they uphold. *The Origins of the Huihui* distinguishes Chinese Muslims from non-Muslim Chinese. *Al-Rashḥat al-sharīfat* distinguishes Jahriyya from other Chinese Muslims. *The Briefest Treatise* distinguishes Shagou Jahriyya from other Jahriyya branches. When we retell origin stories, we resubmit those claims of distinction. We disentangle for our own understanding, or to pursue our own vested interests, while unwittingly making the case for old (sometimes still relevant) identity claims to authority and power, such as Siddiqallah Ma Yuanzhang's claim to be the rightful seventh *murshid* of the Jahriyya.

One of the many interests I am pursuing with this book is the bridging of public and academic discourses. If it were not, I could shed all generalizing categories and speak only of individuals, local expectations, and systems of ordinariness, scaling up from time to time to broader discourses, but maintaining always the local, rather than the synoptic view, letting the reader assemble the entangled lives and texts into group categories if they wish. But if we are going to talk about any human groups beyond the most particular, we will ultimately rely on generalizing categories such as Chinese, Muslims, and Muslim Chinese. Nation-states and religious organizations are powerful actors, and publics rightly want information about the cultural inheritance of discrete nation-states or religions. The challenge is to deliver knowledge about such broad topics while minimizing the distortion created by filing particulars into topics (such as Islam in China), which bring their own, sometimes overwhelming, conceptual baggage.

The origin-fueled concept of syncretism is a way of confronting the contradictions of widely used social categories. It is a way of dealing with the fact that humans often, perhaps almost always, adopt cultural material from beyond the socially constructed borders of their ethnicities and religions. To reject the syncretism model is not to deny the existence of such sharing across constructed identity boundaries. But the term "syncretism" is ultimately a manifestation of power imbalances, of marginalization. What allows the syncretic form that is the "original" Islam to avoid the syncretic label? The power of an enormous, global population, with Islam-identified states. What allows Confucianism to appear as a sui generis form rather than a syncretic one? The power of the Confucian-identified states of China. It is only when a tradition is marginalized that it tends to be seen as syncretic, a conceptual move that is ultimately nothing more than a reference to moments and places of power. Chinese Muslims, lacking such power, have often explained themselves by reference to power centers (topographically and metaphorically): the Tang emperor in his capital, the Prophet Muhammad in Tianfang.

All of this makes the tangled, contradictory, slippery mechanisms of category construction deserving of close study. These mechanisms are at work simultaneously in the scholarship and in the communities that scholars study. They fold onto each other and influence each other. And they shape state policies and human interactions. We will never "solve" the problems of categorization, which is all the more reason to continuously subject them to scrutiny and debate. The power of the categories "Islam" and "China" conspire to make Nūr al-Ḥaqq / Ma Lianyuan, Manṣūr Ma Xuezhi, Yūsuf Ma Zhu, and other Chinese Muslims appear surprising to many observers. My effort to recapture the ordinariness of these individuals and the texts they wrote is an attempt to free them from the distorting power of the globally recognized social categories that they dually inhabit and to bring us closer to engaging them on their own terms.

Appendix

Books Published by Ma Lianyuan

Books Published by Ma Lianyuan
(asterisked works are known only from manuscripts)

#	Title in main language	Date	Main languages	Contents
1	*Tianfang san zi you yi*	none	Chinese	Faith primer
2	*Ḥurūf al-hijā'*	1891	Arabic, Chinese	Arabic alphabet
3	*Ḥawāṣil al-naḥw*	1893	Arabic	Arabic grammar
4	*Mukhtaṣar sharḥ al-ʿaqā'id*	1893	Arabic	Doctrine / creed
5a	*Tafṣīl al-īmān*	1894	Arabic	Pillars of faith
5b	*al-Faṣl*	1894	Persian	Catechism
6	*Khutab*	1894	Arabic, Persian	Sermons / hadith
7	*Muhimmāt*	1894	Persian	Religious duties
8	*Kīmīā' al-Fārsi*	1895	Arabic	Persian grammar
9	*Hawā-ye*	1895	Persian	Arabic grammar
10	*Miftāḥ mirāḥ*	1895	Arabic	Arabic morphology
11	*al-Qur'ān kalām Allah*	1895	Arabic	Edition of the Qur'an
12	*Tanwīr al-abṣār*	1895	Arabic	Islamic law (*furūʿ*)
13	*ʿUmdat al-Islām*	1897–1898	Persian	Religious duties
14	*Laṭā'if*	1898	Arabic, Chinese	Sufi philosophy
15	*Sharḥ al-laṭā'if*	1898	Arabic	Sufi philosophy
16	*Kayfiyāt al-istisqā'*	1898	Arabic	On praying for rain
17	*Tabṭīl al-thathlīth wa tathbīt al-tawḥīd*	1899	Arabic	Anti-Christian polemic
18	*Bian li ming zhen yu lu*	1899	Chinese	Anti-Christian polemic
19	*Haiting jie yi*	1900	Chinese	Qur'an translation
20	*Sharḥ al-Laṭā'if*	1902–1903	Persian, Arabic	Sufi philosophy
21	*Tawḍīḥ*	1903	Arabic	Islamic law (*furūʿ*)
22	*Muttasiq al-balāgha*	none	Arabic	Rhetoric
23*	*Khulāsat al-manṭiq*	1885–1886?	Arabic	Logic
24*	*Jawāmiʿ al-daʿawāt*	c. 1901	Arabic	Prayer handbook

Notes

Introduction

1. Bruno Latour, *Reassembling the Social: An Introduction to Actor-Network-Theory* (Oxford: Oxford University Press, 2007), 29.

2. Michael Sheringham, *Everyday Life: Theories and Practices from Surrealism to the Present* (Oxford: Oxford University Press, 2006).

3. Paolo Heywood, "Out of the Ordinary: Everyday Life and the 'Carnival of Mussolini,'" *American Anthropologist* 125, no. 3 (2023): 497.

4. Ulrich Brandenburg, "Bindeglied Asiens? Chinesischer Islam zwischen Orientalistik und imperialer Politik," paper presented at the "Islamic Pasts and Presents in East Asia's Worldmaking" conference, Göttingen, 2022; Ármin Vámbéry, *Der Islam im neunzehnten Jahrhundert* (Leipzig: F. A. Brockhaus, 1875), 10.

5. Samuel P. Huntington, "The Clash of Civilizations?," *Foreign Affairs* 72, no. 3 (1993): 22–49.

6. This book is less concerned with another kind of origin thinking: the effort to authorize or convince by origins, commonly described as "the fallacy of origins." While convincing by origins is very much present across the works of Chinese Muslims, this approach is generally not paralleled by the academic scholarship.

7. Jacques Derrida, "Structure, Sign, and Play in the Discourse of the Human Sciences," in *Writing and Difference,* trans. Alan Bass (London: Routledge, 2001), 369–370.

8. Stuart Hall, "Cultural Identity and Diaspora," in *Colonial Discourse and Post-Colonial Theory,* ed. Patrick Williams and Laura Chrisman (London: Routledge, 1994), 395. Interestingly, the original publication of this article had "law of history." Stuart Hall, "Cultural Identity and Cinematic Representation," *Framework: The Journal of Cinema and Media,* no. 36 (1989): 68–81.

9. Anne Phillips, "What's Wrong with Essentialism?," *Distinktion: Journal of Social Theory* 11, no. 1 (January 2010): 47–60. Some psychologists take the ubiquity of essentialism further, suggesting that it is a universal human approach to category-making. George E. Newman and Joshua Knobe, "The Essence of Essentialism," *Mind and Language* 34, no. 5 (November 2019): 585–605.

10. Marshall Sahlins, "In Anthropology, It's Emic All the Way Down," *HAU: Journal of Ethnographic Theory* 7, no. 2 (2017): 157–163.

11. Noriko Unno, "Mirror of Desire or Fear? Chinese Emperors in Muslim Folklore and Modern Historiography," in *Fear, Heterodoxy, and Crime in Traditional China,* ed. Tommaso Previato (Leiden: Brill, 2024), 163–192.

12. Jin Jitang 金吉堂, *Zhongguo Huijiao shi yanjiu* 中國回教史研究 [Research on the history of Islam in China] (Beiping: Chengda Normal School, 1935–1936).

13. Donald Leslie, *Islam in Traditional China: A Short History to 1800* (Belconnen, Australia: Canberra College of Advanced Education, 1986). Raphael Israeli's 1978 polemic, while speculative and full of factual errors, is important for marking the reemergence of "Muslims in China" as a historical category in European-language scholarship. Raphael Israeli, *Muslims in China: A Study in Cultural Confrontation* (London: Curzon Press, 1978).

14. Fredrik Barth, *Ethnic Groups and Boundaries: The Social Organization of Culture Difference* (Prospect Heights, IL: Waveland Press, 1998); Rogers Brubaker, Mara Loveman, and Peter Stamatov, "Ethnicity as Cognition," *Theory and Society* 33, no. 1 (February 2004): 31–64.

15. Isaac Mason, "Notes on Chinese Mohammedan Literature," *Journal of the North-China Branch of the Royal Asiatic Society* 56 (1925): 174.

16. Sachiko Murata, *Chinese Gleams of Sufi Light: Wang Tai-Yu's Great Learning of the Pure and Real and Liu Chih's Displaying the Concealment of the Real Realm. With a New Translation of Jami's Lawa'ih from the Persian by William C. Chittick* (Albany: State University of New York Press, 2000); Nakanishi Tatsuya [中西竜也], *Chūka to taiwa suru Isurāmu: 17–19 seiki Chūgoku Musurimu no sisōteki eii* [Islam in dialogue with Chinese civilization: Intellectual activities of Chinese Muslims during the seventeenth to nineteenth centuries] (Kyoto: Kyoto University Press, 2013); Florian Sobieroj, "The Chinese Sufi Wiqāyatullāh Ma Mingxin and the Construction of His Sanctity in Kitāb Al-Jahrī," *Asiatische Studien-Études Asiatiques* 70, no. 1 (2016): 133–169; Dror Weil, "The Vicissitudes of Late Imperial China's Accommodation of Arabo-Persian Knowledge of the Natural World, 16th–18th Centuries" (PhD diss., Princeton University, 2016); Masumi Matsumoto, "Secularisation and Modernisation of Islam in China: Educational Reform, Japanese Occupation and the Disappearance of Persian Learning," in *Islamic Thought in China: Sino-Muslim Intellectual Evolution from the 17th to the 21st Century,* ed. Jonathan Lipman (Edinburgh: Edinburgh University Press, 2017), 171–196.

17. For a survey of Qing state discourse on Chinese Muslims, see Jonathan N. Lipman, "'A Fierce and Brutal People': On Islam and Muslims in Qing Law," in *Empire at the Margins: Culture, Ethnicity, and Frontier in Early Modern China,* ed. Pamela Kyle Crossley, Helen Siu, and Donald Sutton (Berkeley: University of California Press, 2006), 83–110.

18. Each of these five texts was also part of a broader curriculum pursued by men. On the role of "women's classics," see Maria Jaschok and Jingjun Shui, *The History of Women's Mosques in Chinese Islam* (London: Routledge, 2001).

19. Engseng Ho, "Inter-Asian Concepts for Mobile Societies," *Journal of Asian Studies* 76, no. 4 (2017): 907–928.

20. I concentrate on widely taught books, but the same holds for the wider range of extant and lost-but-documented texts meticulously catalogued and analyzed in Weil, "Vicissitudes of Late Imperial China's Accommodation."

1. Two Ordinary Books

1. The original title of the work seems to have been *Jawāmiʿ al-daʿawāt* [Compendium of prayers], but it is better known today under the Chinese title, *Da Zaxue*. The preface has come down to us in two versions. The Arabic version is probably the original, although some have speculated that it is a translation of a Persian original. This manuscript was not published until 2017. Ma's grandson, Ma Yulong / Ruitu (馬玉龍 / 馬瑞圖), published a Chinese translation in 1932, which is true to the basic meaning of the Arabic text but includes some embellishments. Ma Lianyuan 馬聯元, "Fu: 'Bianshu Da Zaxue' Ma Zhiben zi xu Alabowen (yuan wen) 附:《编述大杂学》马致本自序 阿拉伯文 (原文)" [Appendix: "Compilation of the Great Miscellany," Ma Zhiben's self-preface in the original Arabic], in *Weishan Huizu wenshi ziliao 巍山回族文史资料* [Weishan Hui ethnicity historical materials], vol. 12, *Ma Lianyuan jingxue shijia 马联元经学世家* [The religious scholar family of Ma Lianyuan], ed. Ma Yunliang 马云良 (Kunming: Yunnan Ethnicities Publishing House, 2011), 7–18; Ma Lianyuan, "編述大雜學序" [Bianshu Da Zaxue Xu], trans. Ma Yulong [Ma Ruitu], *Tianfang xueli yuekan 天方學理月刊* 9, no. 4 (1932): 12–14.

2. Maung Maung Lay, "The Emergence of the Panthay Community at Mandalay" (Mandalay, 1998).

3. In fact it was not fully published until 2017, more than a century after Ma's death.

4. There are of course exceptions to Ma's near absence from Anglophone scholarship. The two most substantial are the works of Sachiko Murata, which first sparked my interest in Ma Lianyuan, and Chang-kuan Lin. Murata, *Chinese Gleams of Sufi Light: Wang Tai-Yu's Great Learning of the Pure and Real and Liu Chih's Displaying the Concealment of the Real Realm. With a New Translation of Jami's Lawa'ih from the Persian by William C. Chittick* (Albany: State University of New York Press, 2000); Sachiko Murata et al., *The Sage Learning of Liu Zhi: Islamic Thought in Confucian Terms* (Cambridge, MA: Harvard University Asia Center, 2009); Chang-Kuan Lin, "Three Eminent Chinese 'Ulama' of Yunnan," *Institute of Muslim Minority Affairs Journal* 11, no. 1 (1990): 100–117. Remarkably, Ma Lianyuan does not appear in the otherwise comprehensive bibliography by Donald Daniel Leslie, Yang Daye, and Ahmed Youssef, *Islam in Traditional China: A Bibliographical Guide* (London: Routledge, 2006). More recently, Ma received prominent treatment in Guangtian Ha, "Translingual Islam: The Perso-Arabic Cosmopolis in China," *International Journal of Islam in Asia* 4, no. 1–2 (2024): 20–47.

5. Lin Song 林松, "Xu Er 序二" [Second preface], in *Weishan Huizu Wenshi Ziliao 巍山回族文史资料* [Weishan Hui ethnicity historical materials], vol. 12, *Ma Lianyuan jingxue shijia 马联元经学世家* [The religious scholar family of Ma Lianyuan], ed. Ma Yunliang 马云良 (Kunming: Yunnan Ethnicities Publishing House, 2011), 7–15.

6. Luo Yunxi 罗韵希 and Shi Chuyang 师初阳, eds., *Zhongguo Yisilan baike quanshu 中国伊斯兰百科全书* [Chinese encyclopedia of Islam] (Chengdu: Sichuan Lexicographical Publishing House, 1994).

7. Hu Long 虎隆, "Ma Lianyuan de zhushu yanjiu zhong 马联元的著述研究中," *Zhongguo Musilin 中国穆斯林*, no. 11 (2018): 33–40.

8. See Chapter 2.

9. Ma Lianyuan, *Tianfang fen xin pian ji si pian yao dao 天方分信篇暨四篇要道* [Essay on the divisions of faith and four essential principles] (Yuxi, Yunnan: 哦山白吧清真寺 [Eshan Bai Ba Qinzhensi], 2018); Ma Lianyuan, "編述大雜學序" [Bianshu Da Zaxue Xu]; Ma Lianyuan, *Jawāmiʿ al-daʿawāt / Da Zaxue 大杂学* [Gatherings of prayers / Grand miscellany] (Beijing: 宗教文化出版社 [Zongjiao wenhua chubanshe], 2017); Ma Lianyuan 馬聯元, *Tianfang xingli Awen zhujie 天方性理阿文注解* [Arabic commentary on the precis] (Shanghai: 寫真製版印刷 [Xie zhen zhiban yinshua], [c. 1930s]); Hu Long, "Ma Lianyuan de zhushu yanjiu zhong," 40. These are just a few examples among many. Others include reprints from the original plates in the early twentieth century, along with spirit duplicated and photocopied editions of translations in the 1980s and 1990s, such as Ma Lianyuan 马联元, *Qingzhen yuzhu A Han duizhao 请真玉柱阿汉对照* [Jade pillar of Islam: Arabic Chinese comparison], trans. Muhammad Ramadan 穆罕默德来迈丹 ([Northwest China?]: n.p., 1981).

10. Ma Lianyuan, "Fu: 'Bianshu Da Zaxue,'" 7.

11. For example Ma Zhu 馬注 and anonymous, "Saidianchi jiapu 賽典赤家譜" [Genealogy of Saidianchi] (n.d.), in *Yunnan Huizu guji diancang 云南回族古籍典藏* [Collection of ancient texts of the Hui nationality of Yunnan], vol. 11, ed. Yao Jide 姚继德 (Kunming: Yunnan Chuban Jituan 云南出版集团, 2019). For an analysis of this type of genealogy, see J. Lilu Chen, *Chinese Heirs to Muhammad: Writing Islamic History in Early Modern China* (Piscataway, NJ: Gorgias Press, 2020).

12. Ma Lianyuan, "Fu: 'Bianshu Da Zaxue.'"

13. Jacqueline Misty Armijo-Hussein, "Sayyid'Ajall Shams al-Din: A Muslim from Central Asia, Serving the Mongols in China, and Bringing 'Civilization' to Yunnan" (Cambridge, MA: Harvard University, 1996).

14. David G. Atwill, *The Chinese Sultanate: Islam, Ethnicity, and the Panthay Rebellion in Southwest China, 1856–1873* (Stanford, CA: Stanford University Press, 2005).

15. Ma's grandson, Ma Ruitu, gives this sentence as "war of the Hui and the Han" in his 1932 Chinese translation. Ma Lianyuan, "編述大雜學序" [Bianshu Da Zaxue Xu].

16. Ma Lianyuan, "Fu: 'Bianshu Da Zaxue,'" 11.

17. Jin Hanqing 金漢青, *Zhiben Ma laofuzi liu xun shou xu 至本馬老子六旬壽序* [Preface for teacher Ma Zhiben's sixtieth birthday] [Yunnan]: n.p., 1900.

18. Liu Zhi 劉智 and Ma Lianyuan 馬聯元, *Tianfang san zi you yi 天方三字幼義* [Islamic three-character primer] (Kunming, c. 1890s).

19. Muḥammad Nūr al-Ḥaqq ibn Sayyid Luqmān, *Min sharḥ al-Wiqāyah al-masmi bi-al-tawḍīḥ* [Commentary on the Wiqāyah called the Explication] (Kanpur: Maḥmūd al-Maṭābi', 1903).

20. In order to improve readability, I omitted Ma's numerous annotations, most of which aim to explain the meaning of individual words with Chinese synonyms or to provide the Persian-language equivalents. Translation adapted from

Roberta Tontini, *Muslim Sanzijing: Shifts and Continuities in the Definition of Islam in China* (Leiden: Brill, 2016), 59.

21. *Dao de jing* 42, as translated by Roel Sterckx, *Ways of Heaven: An Introduction to Chinese Thought* (New York: Basic Books, 2019), 75.

22. Here I adopt the translation of the term from Murata et al., *Sage Learning of Liu Zhi.*

23. I have used James Frankel's translation of this passage from the *Siku quanshu zongmu tiyao 四庫全書總目提要* (1773) in James D. Frankel, *Rectifying God's Name: Liu Zhi's Confucian Translation of Monotheism and Islamic Law* (Honolulu: University of Hawai'i Press, 2011), 53.

24. Ulrike Stark, *An Empire of Books: The Naval Kishore Press and the Diffusion of the Printed Word in Colonial India* (Ranikhet: Permanent Black, 2007).

25. William Milne, "Extracts from Dr. Milne's Journal, Illustrative of His Mind and Character," in *Memoirs of the Rev. William Milne, D.D. Late Missionary to China, and Principal of the Anglo-Chinese College,* ed. Robert Morrison (Malacca: Mission Press, 1824), 97–98.

26. Muḥammad Nūr al-Ḥaqq ibn Sayyid Luqmān, *Al-tawḍīḥ.*

27. *Wiqayat ar-riwāya fi masă'il al-hidaya* by Maḥbūb ibn Ṣadr al-Shariʿa al-Awwal, a compendium of Marghīnānī's *al-Hidāyah fī sharḥ bidāyat al-mubtadī,* a commentary on Marghīnānī's own *al-Bidāyat al-mubtadī.*

28. For example, the variety and absolute number of these works is apparent in the library of the Patkapur Mosque library in Kanpur. They can also be found at any northern India bookstore that stocks old lithographs in Arabic scripts.

29. For a detailed analysis of the industry, see Stark, *Empire of Books.*

30. There is a listing for the three-character classic in the Chinese national library, but without any call number or location.

31. Ma Lianyuan's full name in Arabic, with titles, was ʿAbd al-Hakīm al-Ḥajj al-Sayyid Muḥammad Nūr al-Ḥaqq ibn Sayyid Luqmān al-Sīnī.

32. The image here is an accurate woodcut image of Ma's Arabic-language seal, which appeared in Ma Lianyuan, *Tafṣīl al-īmān: al-Faṣl / Tianfang fen xin pian ji si pian yao dao 天方分信篇暨四篇要道* [Elements of faith: The chapter / Essay on the divisions of faith and four essential principles] (Kunming: Xing Shun He, 1894). Original impressions of the seal can be found on at least three books in the library of the mosque described in Chapter 2. The date, 1288 (1871–1872) AH, presents some questions about the timing of Ma's return to China. His autobiographical introduction to *Da zaxue* says he returned in 1289 (1872–1873), after the fall of Dali (early 1873). The calligraphy on the seal is in the *ṣinī,* or Chinese style, which makes it most likely to have been carved in China. Al-Ḥājj is a title Ma earned by making the pilgrimage to Mecca. Ultimately, the two pieces of evidence (seal and autobiography) seem to have a one-year discrepancy in regard to the date of Ma's return.

33. An alternate term for the phenomenon is *daohao* 道號. See Lan Xu 藍煦, *Tianfang zhengxue 天方正學* [Correct learning of Islam] (Beijing: Qingzhen Shu Bao Shi 清真書報社, 1925 [1852]), 41 juan 7.

34. This route is described in Chapter 4.

35. Ma Lianyuan 馬聯元, *Haiting jie yi 赫聽解譯* [Explanatory translation of the khatm] ([Kunming]: Guang Ji Tang 廣濟堂, 1900).

36. Muḥammad Nūr al-Ḥaqq ibn Sayyid Luqmān, *Al- tawḍīḥ,* 406.

37. E. E. Salisbury, "Arabs in Peking: From a Letter of Rev. Henry Blodget to Prof. H. A. Newton of New Haven, Dated Peking, Feb. 19, 1863; Communicated, with Remarks and Explanations, by the President," *Journal of the American Oriental Society* 8 (1863): xvii–xxiv.

38. Untitled Handwritten Catalog of the Lithographed Books in the Library of the Patkapur Mosque (Kanpur: Patkapur Mosque, n.d.).

39. Ma Zhiben 马致本 [Ma Lianyuan], *Sharḥ al-tawḍīḥ 教法简注* [Simple annotation of religious law], trans. Ma Xinsan 马新三, vol. 1 (Wenshan, Yunnan: Yunnan Sheng Wenshan Zhou Yisilanjiao Xiehui 云南省文山州伊斯兰教协会, 1991).

40. Ma's grandson, Ma Ruitu, calls the teacher *Lahemaitula* the author of *Hui ye bian zhen.* Ma Lianyuan, "編述大雜學序" [Bianshu Da Zaxue Xu]. This is Rahmatallah Kairawānī, author of *Izhar al-Haqq,* which became known in Chinese as *Hui ye bian zhen,* under which title it was translated into Chinese in 1922: Rahmatallah Kairawani, *Huiye bian zhen 回耶辨真,* trans. Wang Jingzhai 王静斋 (Peking: Qingzhen Shu Bao Shi 清真書報社, 1922). The work is an extremely influential polemic against Christian arguments attacking Islam. Christine Schirrmacher, "The Influence of German Biblical Criticism on Muslim Apologetics in the 19th Century," in *A Comprehensive Faith: An International Festschrift for Rousas John Rushdoony,* ed. Andrew Sandlin (San Jose, CA: Friends of Chalcedon, 1996).

41. The scholar was Abdullah ibn Rasuli.

42. Ma Lianyuan, "編述大雜學序" [Bianshu Da Zaxue Xu], 13. In some scholarship, a misreading of the Chinese translation of *Da zaxue* has led to the incorrect conclusion that Ma had traveled to India, Egypt, and Istanbul, rather than studying in Mecca with scholars who originally came from India, Egypt, and a Turkic-speaking region of the Caucasus. Lin, "Three Eminent Chinese 'Ulama' of Yunnan," 110.

43. Salisbury, "Arabs in Peking." Another foreign visitor similarly observed in 1842 that an *ahong* in Ningbo "can read the Arabic scriptures most readily, and talks that language fluently; but of Chinese writing and reading, he is as ignorant as an Englishman in England. This is very surprizing, considering that he can talk it so well, was born and educated in China, and is a minister of religion among the Chinese." W. C. Milne, "Notes of a Seven Months' Residence in the City of Ningpo, from Dec. 7th, 1842, to July 7th, 1843," *The Chinese Repository* 13, no. 1 (January 1844): 31.

44. Ma Jianzhi 馬健之, *Huijiao gangyao 回教綱要* [Essentials of Islam] (Kunming: Mu Guang Shu Dian 穆光書店, 1948), 1.

45. Ma Lianyuan 馬聯元, *Bian li ming zheng yulu 辨理明正語録* [Quotations discriminating the truth with clear proof] (Kunming: Nancheng Mosque, 1899); Ma Lianyuan, *Haiting jie yi.*

46. Kristian Petersen, *Interpreting Islam in China: Pilgrimage, Scripture, and Language in the Han Kitab* (Oxford: Oxford University Press, 2017), 47.

47. Ma Lianyuan, "Fu: 'Bianshu Da Zaxue,'" 10.

48. For a full list of Ma's works, see the Appendix in this book. As this work goes to press, I am revising a journal article that provides the full details of these texts.

49. Muḥammad b. ʿAbdallah Tumurtāshi, *Tanwīr al-abṣār* [The enlightenment of perception], ed. Ma Lianyuan 馬聯元 (Kunming: Nan Guo'an 男國安, 1895). *Tanwīr al-abṣār* is a sixteenth-century work of Islamic substantive jurisprudence (*furūʿ*).

50. Surviving editions are from 1817, 1867, and 1871. Li Xinghua 李兴华 and Feng Jinyuan 冯今源, "Beijing youguan danwei Yisilanjiao Hanwen cang shu 北京有关单位伊斯兰教藏书" [Chinese Islamic books collected by relevant units in Beijing], *Ningxia Daxue Xuebao 宁夏大学学报*, no. 3 (1984): 103.

51. Zhang Shizhong 張時中, trans., *Si pian yao dao 四篇要道譯解* [Four essential principles in translation] ([1653] Chengdu: 王占超, 1872).

52. Zhao Can 趙燦 and She Yunshan 舍蘊善, "Jingxue xichuan pu 經學系傳普" [Genealogy of the transmission and lineage of classical learning] (1714), 20:19. A manuscript facsimile is in Zhou Xiefan 周燮藩, ed., *Qingzhen dadian 清真大典* [The Islamic canon], vol. 20 (Hefei: Huangshan Shushe, 2005).

53. Zhao Can and She Yunshan, "Jingxue xichuan pu," 1714.

54. Fan Bao 范宝, *Fude tushuguan guancang guji mulu 福德图书馆馆藏古籍目录* [Catalog of the holdings of old books in the Fude library] (Beijing: Minzu Chubanshe, 2016), 197.

55. Ma Lianyuan 馬聯元, *'Umdat al-Islām / Qingzhen yuzhu 请真玉柱* [Pillar of Islam / Jade pillar of Islam], trans. Li Xiurong 李秀荣 and Liu Hongkuan 刘宏宽 (n.p., 2003). The publication is undated, but a preface by the two translators says they completed the manuscript in Inner Mongolia in 2002. The translation also bears a preface by the leader of the Huasi branch of the Khufiyyah order, in Linxia, composed in 2003.

56. Aḥmad Sirhindī, *Maktūbāt-i Imām Rabbānī* (Istanbul: Hakikat Kitabevi, 1977), 308.

57. See the Conclusion of this book for more details on this conference.

58. This teacher is discussed in more detail in Chapter 3.

59. Butrus Abu-Manneh, "The Naqshbandiyya-Mujaddidiyya in the Ottoman Lands in the Early 19th Century," *Die Welt des Islams* 22, no. 1–4 (1982): 9.

2. The Matrix of the Ordinary

1. Ma Lianyuan 馬聯元, *Haiting jie yi 赫聽解譯* [Explanatory translation of the khatm] (Kunming: Guang Ji Tang 廣濟堂, 1900).

2. Brian Street, *Literacy in Theory and Practice* (Cambridge: Cambridge University Press, 1985). Elman's concept of "primer literacy" is also useful in the Chinese Imperial context. Benjamin A. Elman, *A Cultural History of Civil Examinations in Late Imperial China* (Berkeley: University of California Press, 2000), 246, 266, 374–377.

3. Muḥammad ʿAbduh, *Huijiao renyi lun 回教認一論* [Treatise on tawhid in Islam], trans. Ma Ruitu 馬瑞圖 (Shanghai: Zhonghua Shuju, 1937); Muḥammad Rashīd Riḍā, *Muhanmode de moshi 穆罕默德的默示* [The revelation of Muhammad], trans. Ma Ruitu 馬瑞圖 (Shanghai: Zhonghua Shuju, 1946).

4. Books published in Egypt bear acquisition / donation dates of 1892 (published 1882 / 1883), 1907 / 1908 (publication date unknown), 1919 / 1920 (published 1877), and 1945 / 1946 (published 1900 / 1901), and two Egyptian publications bear Ma Lianyuan's seal, placing their acquisition no later than his death in 1902 / 1903.

5. Some of Arabic's prominence is due to the ritual use of the language. Duʿā', a common category of devotional prayer outside of the five daily prayers, is virtually always performed in Arabic, as are, of course, readings from the Qur'an. Duʿā' com-

pilations were mainly aimed at "readers" who would recite the texts for devotional or thaumaturgic purposes, without necessarily understanding the meaning of the text. These and other texts that were frequently recited without literal comprehension make up just over a third of the dealers' Arabic books. Five of the twenty-two Arabic texts in the dealers' accumulations are prayer compilations of this type. Another is a praise poem for the prophet, which would have been recited in celebration of the prophet's birthday. A further two of the Arabic texts in the dealers' corpus are the Qur'an, bringing the total number of Arabic recitational texts to eight.

6. The precise percentages are 51 percent and 63 percent.

7. M. J. Shari'ati, "The Library of the Tung-Hsi Mosque at Peking," *Asian Affairs* (1980): 68–70.

8. This is in stark contrast to the manuscript culture of Eastern Turkistan in the same era, where the dominant written language was also the vernacular, literacy was relatively widespread, and amateur manuscript copying was common.

9. The total may be higher, as one donor's contribution was left blank on the printed donor list. On the copy I examined, someone has written "five thousand yuan" in this space, using a different system of money counting from the other donations.

10. *Tawbah al-aghyār, Tawbah al-ʿajā'ib, Khwājah khatm, Barāt shaʿbān* (Dabai, Yunnan: Muslims of Dabai Village, 1894).

11. *Hawā-ye / Zifa chu cheng 字法初程* [The air of / Beginning rules of grammar], ed. Ma Lianyuan 馬聯元 (Xinping, Yunnan: The families in and around the Xinping county center, 1895); *Miftāḥ mirāḥ / Zi fa cuoyao 字法撮要* [The key of happiness / Synopsis of morphology], ed. Ma Lianyuan 馬聯元 (Taoguoyuan, Yunnan: The co-religionists of Taoguoyuan, 1895); ʿAbd al-ʿAzīz b. Ḥamīdullah Dihlawī, *ʿUmdat al-Islām / Qingzhen yu zhu 清真玉柱* [The pillar of Islam / The jade pillar of Islam], ed. Ma Lianyuan 馬聯元 (Heyang, Yunnan: Teacher Li Guozhu and the Muslims of Heyang County, 1897).

12. Ma Boliang 马伯良, "Huizu shanghao Xing Shun He 回族商号兴顺和" [The ethnic Hui company Xing Shun He], in *Yunnan lao zihao 云南老字号* [Yunnan's historic businesses], vol. 49, *Yunnan Wenshi Ziliao Xuanji 云南文史资料选辑* [Selected works from Yunnan historical materials], ed. Zhongguo Renmin Zhengzhi Xieshang Huiyi Yunnan Sheng Weiyuanhui Wenshi Ziliao Weiyuanhui 中国人民政治协商会议云南省委员会文史资料委员会 (Yunnan: Yunnan People's Press, 1996), 206–211.

13. Ma Da'en 馬大恩, "Chongke Qingzhen zhinan xu 重刻清真指南叙" [Preface to the reprinting of *Compass of Islam*], in Ma Zhu 馬注, *Qingzhen zhinan 清真指南* [Compass of Islam] (Guangzhou: Hao Pan Street Mosque, 1870–1871), 2r.

14. Shao Min 邵敏 and Hu Yubing 胡玉冰, "Qingdai Hanwen Yisilanjiao dianji keyin shulue 清代汉文伊斯兰教典籍刻印述略" [A brief introduction to the engraving of Chinese Islamic classics in Qing dynasty], *Beifang Minzu Daxue Xuebao: Zhexue Shehui Kexue Ban 北方民族大学学报:哲学社会科学版* [Journal of Northern Minzu University: Philosophy and social sciences edition], no. 2 (2021); Shaodan Zhang, "Muslim Printing in Late Imperial China: Woodblocks, Networks, and Creation of Chinese Islamic Knowledge," *Journal of Muslim Minority Affairs* 41, no. 3 (2021): 473–490.

15. The books collected during the D'Ollone mission included a *Tianfang liyuan* 天方歷源, 1876, with plates stored at Chengdu's Number Seven Mosque 清真七寺. A. Vissière, *Études sino-mahométanes* (Paris: Ernest Leroux, 1911), 128.

16. Ma Zhu, *Qingzhen zhinan.*

17. Shao Min and Hu Yubing, "Qingdai Hanwen Yisilanjiao dianji keyin shulue."

18. *Aṣl al-īmān* (Yongchang, 1907).

19. Vissière, *Études sino-mahométanes,* 133; Shao Min and Hu Yubing, "Qingdai Hanwen Yisilanjiao dianji keyin shulue."

20. Shao Min and Hu Yubing, "Qingdai Hanwen Yisilanjiao dianji keyin shulue"; Vissière, *Études sino-mahométanes.*

21. *Zaxue 雜學* [Miscellany] (Chengdu: Ma Shanqing 馬善慶, 1870). Like Zhou Mingde, the publisher Ma Shanqing writes that his publication is aimed at improving Muslims' religious knowledge, in part as a reaction to seeing worshippers at the mosque who don't know the words to various prayers.

22. Cynthia J. Brokaw, *Commerce in Culture: The Sibao Book Trade in the Qing and Republican Periods* (Cambridge, MA: Harvard University Asia Center, 2007).

23. [Ma Dexin 馬德新], *Taḥqīq al-salawat* ([Yunnan]: n.p., 1863). I have not been able to find any of Ma Dexin's names (in Arabic, Yūsuf) in the copy I photographed, but it seems he is generally regarded as the author. This makes sense, given the context, with many similar works bearing his name at this time. See Chang-Kuan Lin, "Three Eminent Chinese 'Ulama' of Yunnan," *Institute of Muslim Minority Affairs Journal* 11, no. 1 (1990): 100–117.

24. Ma Lianyuan, *Tafṣīl al-īmān: al-Faṣl / Tianfang fen xin pian ji si pian yao dao 天方分信篇暨四篇要道* [Elements of faith: The chapter / Essay on the divisions of faith and four essential principles] (Kunming: Xing Shun He, 1894).

25. These were Du Wenxiu, Ma Rulong, and Ma Dexin. Ma Rulong published an edition of Liu Zhi's *Tianfang xingli 天方性理* in 1863. Vissière, *Études sino-mahométanes,* 112.

26. *Baoming zhenjing 寶命真經* [The Qur'an] ([Dali, Yunnan]: Du Wenxiu, 1862).

27. Lin, "Three Eminent Chinese 'Ulama' of Yunnan," 105–107.

28. This may even be reflected in the terminology that one eighteenth-century book uses to distinguish Chinese script from Persian and Arabic, calling Chinese writing "book characters" 書字. Zhao Can 趙燦 and She Yunshan 舍蘊善, "Jingxue xichuan pu 經學系傳普" [Genealogy of the transmission and lineage of classical learning] (1714).

29. Prominent examples can be found in Ding Shiren 丁士仁, ed., *Zhongguo Yisilan jingtang jiaoyu 中国伊斯兰经堂教育* [Chinese Islamic scripture hall education] (Lanzhou: Gansu renmin chubanshe, 2013).

30. Ma Jianxiong, "Re-Creating Hui Identity and the Charity Network in the Imperial Extension from Ming to Qing in the Southwest Chinese Frontier," in *Charities in the Non-Western World: The Development and Regulation of Indigenous and Islamic Charities,* ed. Rajeswary Brown Ampalavanar and Justin Pierce (New York: Routledge, 2013), 163–186.

31. Aaron Nathan Glasserman, "Hui Corporate Strategies and Islamic Cultural Capital and in Qing Guangzhou," *Journal of the Economic and Social History of the Orient* 66, no. 1–2 (2023): 1–42; Shaodan Zhang, *Sino-Muslims, Networking, and Identity in Late Imperial China: Longstanding Natives and Dispersed Minorities* (London: Routledge, 2025).

32. Zhao Can and She Yunshan, "Jingxue xichuan pu," 1714, manuscript facsimile in Zhou Xiefan 周燮藩, *Qingzhen dadian 清真大典* [The Islamic canon] 20 (2005): 20–19.

33. Muḥammad Tawāḍu' (Pang Shiqian 龐士謙), *al-Ṣīn wa al-Islām* [China and Islam] (Cairo: Society of the Muslim Brothers Press, 1945).

34. Changde Huijiao jiaoyu fuzhu hui 常德回教教育輔助會, *Huiwen duben 回文讀本* [Arabic reader], vol. 8 (Changde Daqing Qingzhensi 常德大慶街清真寺, 1925), 47. Facsimile in Wang Jianping 王建平 and Bai Runsheng 白潤生, eds., *Zhongguo Yisilanjiao dianji xuan 中國伊斯蘭教典籍選* [Selection of Chinese Islam classical texts], vol. 4 (Shanghai: Shanghai Guji Chubanshe, 2007).

35. The three that are most widely documented are the same initial texts of the classics hall education for all genders (al-Faṣl, Muhimmāt, and 'Umdat al-Islām). The other two are 否足·耐贾提 and 哈噶伊格, according to Ma Qiang 马强, "Dushihua jincheng zhong de Qingzhen nüsi he nüxue 都市化进程中的清真女寺和女学" [Urbanization and the development of women's masjid and women's school in China], *回族研究* [Journal of Hui Muslim Minority Studies], no. 2 (2011): 114. In his table of texts, Dror Weil identifies both titles as Persian works mentioned in Zhao's *Jingxue xichuan pu.* Dror Weil, "The Vicissitudes of Late Imperial China's Accommodation of Arabo-Persian Knowledge of the Natural World, 16th–18th Centuries" (PhD diss., Princeton University, 2016).

36. Yang Daye 杨大业, *Ming Qing Huizu jinshi kaolüe 明清回族进士考略* [Outline study of the Hui jinshi degree holders of the Ming and Qing dynasties] (Yinchuan: Ningxia People's Press 宁夏人民出版社, 2011).

37. On "primer literacy," see Elman, *Cultural History.*

38. Ma Zhu 馬注, "Qingzhen zhinan 清真指南" [Compass of Islam], in *Huizu he Zhongguo Yisilanjiao guji ziliao hui bian 回族和中国伊斯兰教古籍资料汇编,* ed. Ningxia shaoshu minzu guji zhengli chuban guihua xiaozu bangongshi 宁夏少数民族古籍整理出版规划小组办公室编, vol. 1 辑 7 函 (Tianjin: Tianjin guji chubanshe 天津古籍出版社, 1987), juan 10, fols. 17r–18b, 26r–26v.

39. Roberta Tontini, *Muslim Sanzijing: Shifts and Continuities in the Definition of Islam in China* (Boston: Brill, 2016).

40. Marshall Broomhall, *Islam in China: A Neglected Problem* (London: Morgan and Scott, 1910), 240.

41. Ma Lianyuan 馬聯元, "Fu: 'Bianshu Da Zaxue' Ma Zhiben zi xu Alabowen (yuan wen) 附:《编述大杂学》马致本自序 阿拉伯文(原文)" [Appendix: "Compilation of the great miscellany," Ma Zhiben's self-preface in the original Arabic], in *Weishan Huizu wenshi ziliao 巍山回族文史资料* [Weishan Hui ethnicity historical materials], vol. 12, *Ma Lianyuan jingxue shijia 马联元经学世家* [The religious scholar family of Ma Lianyuan], ed. Ma Yunliang 马云良 (Kunming: Yunnan Ethnicities Publishing House, 2011).

42. Ma Jianzhi 馬健之, *Huijiao gangyao 回教綱要* [Essentials of Islam] (Kunming: Mu Guang Shu Dian 穆光書店, 1948), 1.

43. Jin Hanqing 金漢青, *Zhiben Ma laofuzi liu xun shou xu 至本馬老子六旬壽序* [Preface for teacher Ma Zhiben's sixtieth birthday] (n.p., 1900), fols. 5–10. For a study of this source, see Ma Zhihong 马志宏, "Guben 'Zhiben Ma laofuzi liu xun shou xu' 孤本《致本马老夫子六旬寿序》考释" [A philological study of the unique

text "Preface for Ma Zhiben's sixtieth birthday"], *Journal of Hui Muslim Minority Studies 回族研究,* no. 1 (2018): 69–73.

44. Ma Lianyuan 馬聯元, *Ḥurūf al-hijā'* [Letters of the alphabet] ([Yunnan], 1891).

45. See the Appendix in this volume.

46. Ma Lianyuan 馬聯元 and Abū Naṣr Muḥammad ibn Wadʿān, *Khutab: Zhisheng baolun 至聖寶論* [Sermons: Precious discourses of the prophet] (Kunming: Xifa Company 喜發號, 1894).

47. Muḥammad Nūr al-Ḥaqq ibn Sayyid Luqmān [Ma Lianyuan 馬聯元], *Sharḥ al-Laṭā'if* [Commentary on *Laṭā'if*] (Kanpur: ʿAlī Maḥmūd, 1902), 3. For a study of this text as it was later reprinted in Shanghai, see Matsumoto Akirō, "Ba rengen cho 'Tianfang xingli awen zhujie' no kenkyū" [A study of Ma Lianyuan's Arabic commentary on tianfang xingli], *Tōyōshi Kenkyū* 58, no. 1 (1999): 176–211.

48. Ma Lianyuan 馬聯元, *Bian li ming zheng yulu 辨理明正語録* [Quotations discriminating the truth with clear proof] (Kunming: Nancheng Mosque, 1899); Ma Lianyuan 馬聯元, *Tabṭīl al-thathlīth wa tathbīt al-tawḥīd* [Invalidation of the trinity and proof of the oneness of God] ([Kunming]: Guang Ji Tang 廣濟堂, 1899).

49. Ma Lianyuan, *Tafṣīl al-īmān / al-Faṣl.*

50. Ma Lianyuan, *Tafṣīl al-īmān / al-Faṣl.*

51. Ma Lianyuan, ""Fu: 'Bianshu Da Zaxue.'"

52. Donald Daniel Leslie and Mohamed Wassel, "Arabic and Persian Sources Used by Liu Chih," *Central Asiatic Journal* 26, no. 1 / 2 (1982): 78–104.

53. Donald Daniel Leslie, Yang Daye, and Ahmed Youssef, *Islam in Traditional China: A Bibliographical Guide* (London: Routledge, 2006), 72.

54. Samuel M. Zwemer, *A Primer on Islam and the Spiritual Needs of the Mohammedans of China* (Shanghai: Special Committee on Work for Muslims, 1919).

55. Shari'at, "Library of the Tung-Hsi Mosque at Peking."

56. Weil, "Vicissitudes of Late Imperial China's Accommodation."

57. Leslie and Wassel, "Arabic and Persian Sources Used by Liu Chih."

58. Leslie, Daye, and Youssef, *Islam in Traditional China,* 73–74.

59. C. Patterson Giersch, *Asian Borderlands: The Transformation of Qing China's Yunnan Frontier* (Cambridge, MA: Harvard University Press, 2006).

3. Extraordinary Books

1. *Rāhnamā-ye muwāfiq-i imām Ja'far Ṣādiq* (early nineteenth century).

2. Despite much interest from scholars over three decades, a facsimile publication of a manuscript of Rashaha was only published in 2021. Guanli Ye 關裡爺, *Reshiha'er: Zhengui de lushu (wanzheng diancang Gansu ban—yuanshi shougao kanbu. Xin yi. Zhushi. Jiaokan) 熱什哈爾: 珍貴的露珠 (完整典藏甘肅版——原始手稿刊布. 新譯. 註釋. 校勘)* [Rashaha: Precious dewdrop (Complete classic, Gansu recension—Publication of the original manuscript. New translation. Annotation. Collation)], trans. Ma Xuehua 馬學華 and Zhang Chengzhi 張承志 (Taipei: Net and Books Co., 2021). I am grateful to Aisajiang Youshe for alerting me to this publication.

3. Mawlāna Shāh Ghiyāth al-Dīn.

4. Guangtian Ha, *The Sound of Salvation: Voice, Gender, and the Sufi Mediascape in China* (New York: Columbia University Press, 2022), 17. The passing of a *silsila* from shaykh to follower is also cited in the key Jahriyya hagiography, Guanli Ye, *Reshiha'er,* 22.

5. "فإني أعجم من العجميين." Ma Lianyuan, *Jawāmiʿ al-daʿawāt / Da zaxue 大杂学* [Gatherings of prayers / Grand miscellany] (Beijing: 宗教文化出版社 [Zongjiao wenhua chubanshe], 2017), 9.

6. Zhang Shizhong 張時中, "'Kelimu' jie qimeng qianshuo '克里默'解启蒙浅说" [Explanatory primer on the Kalima], *中国穆斯林,* no. 2 (1983): 4–8.

7. The preface survives in Liu Zhi 劉智, *Tianfang zhisheng shilu nianpu 天方至聖實錄年譜* [Chronological veritable record of the ultimate sage of Islam] (Chengdu: Bao Zhen Tang 寳真堂, 1872), 15r–18r. See Donald Daniel Leslie, *Islamic Literature in Chinese, Late Ming and Early Ch'ing: Books, Authors and Associates* (Canberra, Australia: Canberra College of Advanced Education, 1981), 21.

8. *Sheng mi zhenyuan 省迷眞原* [Avoiding perplexity about the real origin] (Beijing: Beijing Fu Hua Yinshuasuo, 1914). Facsimile of 1914 "reprint" (重印) of c. 1630 text in Zhou Xiefan 周燮藩, ed., *Qingzhen dadian 清真大典* [The Islamic canon], vol. 18 (Hefei: Huangshan Shushe, 2005), 169–188.

9. Karl R. Schaefer, *Enigmatic Charms: Medieval Arabic Block Printed Amulets in American and European Libraries and Museums* (Leiden: Brill, 2006).

10. Adri K. Offenberg, "The Printing History of the Constantinople Hebrew İncunable of 1493: A Mediterranean Voyage of Discovery," *British Library Journal* 22, no. 2 (1996): 221–235.

11. Sachiko Murata, ed., *The First Islamic Classic in Chinese: Wang Daiyu's Real Commentary on the True Teaching* (Albany: State University of New York Press, 2017), 84.

12. Copies can be found in the Harvard Yenching Library and the Library of Congress. A later edition, with a 1657 preface, can be found in the Toyo Bunka Kenkyusho of Tokyo University. Murata, *First Islamic Classic in Chinese,* 32.

13. Wang Daiyu 王岱輿, *Zhengjiao zhen lun 正教真詮* [Real commentary on the true teaching] ([China]: Qingzhen Tang, 1642), 2r–2v. Throughout this chapter I use the translation of Murata, *First Islamic Classic,* for quotations.

14. Sachiko Murata has an excellent overview of these lexical transformations in Murata, *Chinese Gleams of Sufi Light: Wang Tai-Yu's Great Learning of the Pure and Real and Liu Chih's Displaying the Concealment of the Real Realm. With a New Translation of Jami's Lawa'ih from the Persian by William C. Chittick* (Albany: State University of New York Press, 2000), 17–19.

15. Such dictionaries are commonly aimed at individual Arabic texts and are still sold in Islamic bookshops in China today. See, for example, Hu Songshan 虎嵩山, *Lughāt Tafsīr Ḥusaynī: Housaini dacidian 侯賽尼大辭典* [Dictionary of the Tafsīr Ḥusaynī] ([China]: n.p., 1951).

16. Murata, *First Islamic Classic in Chinese,* 36–37; Wang Daiyu, *Zhengjiao zhen lun,* 2r–2v.

17. Murata, *First Islamic Classic in Chinese,* 35; Wang Daiyu, *Zhengjiao zhen lun,* 1r.

18. Murata, *First Islamic Classic in Chinese,* 35–36; Wang Daiyu, *Zhengjiao zhen lun,* 1r–1v.

19. Murata, *First Islamic Classic in Chinese,* 7.

20. Murata, *Chinese Gleams of Sufi Light.*

21. Ma Zhu also presented his text to numerous scholars (Muslim and non-Muslim) for review, some of whom wrote prefaces for the work, but the Qing emperor is the only person to whom Ma attempted to deliver the text as a final product for a consumer rather than for collaborators.

22. Murata, *First Islamic Classic in Chinese,* 35; Wang Daiyu, *Zhengjiao zhen lun,* 1r.

23. Murata, *First Islamic Classic in Chinese,* 38; Wang Daiyu, *Zhengjiao zhen lun,* 2r.

24. Murata, *First Islamic Classic in Chinese,* 147; Wang Daiyu, *Zhengjiao zhen lun,* juan 2, 3v.

25. Murata, *First Islamic Classic in Chinese,* 94; Wang Daiyu, *Zhengjiao zhen lun,* juan 1, 56r–56v.

26. Murata, *First Islamic Classic in Chinese,* 146; Wang Daiyu, *Zhengjiao zhen lun,* juan 2, 2v.146.

27. Murata, *First Islamic Classic in Chinese,* 145; Wang Daiyu, *Zhengjiao zhen lun,* juan 2, 1v.

28. Heming Wang, *The General Theory of China's Genealogy* (Singapore: Springer Nature, 2023), 423.

29. Zhang Jianmeng, "Yuan xu," in *Huqiu Yishan Huangshi shipu,* cited in Michael Szonyi, *Practicing Kinship: Lineage and Descent in Late Imperial China* (Stanford, CA: Stanford University Press, 2002), 30.

30. Wang, *General Theory of China's Genealogy.*

31. Ahmet Kamil Cihan and Arsan Taher, "Muḥammad Amīn Al-Shirwanī's Treatise on Eschatology: An Analysis and Critical Edition of Risālah Fī Tahqīq al-Mabda'wa-al-Ma'ād," *Nazariyat* 2, no. 4 (2016): 62.

32. 'Abd Allāh ibn Muḥammad Najm al-Dīn Rāzī, *The Path of God's Bondsmen from Origin to Return,* trans. Hamid Algar (Delmar, NY: Caravan Books, 1982).

33. There have, of course, always been debates on some details, such as the controversy over whether the Qur'an is created or uncreated, a divide that eventually came to separate Twelver Shi'a from most Sunni Muslims.

34. Most high-status men used at least two names in addition to their surname: a given name (*ming* 名), bestowed at birth, and a courtesy name (*zi* 字), usually chosen themselves, upon coming of age. It was common to choose a courtesy name with a meaning that reflected the given name. Endymion Wilkinson, *Chinese History: A New Manual,* 5th ed. (Cambridge, MA: Endymion Wilkinson, 2018), 143.

35. "China's Geographical Center Marked," *People's Daily,* September 14, 2000, archived at https://web.archive.org/web/20230326031300/http://en.people.cn/english/200009/13/eng20000913_50419.html.

36. Luo Yunxi 罗韵希 and Shi Chuyang 师初阳, eds., *Zhongguo Yisilan baike quanshu 中国伊斯兰百科全书* [Chinese encyclopedia of Islam] (Chengdu: Sichuan Lexicographical Publishing House, 1994), 213. Hannah Theaker has shown that much of Linxia's importance was a result of late nineteenth-century upheavals. Hannah Theaker, "Moving Muslims: The Great Northwestern Rebellion and the Transformation of Chinese Islam, 1860–1896" (PhD diss., Oxford University, 2018).

37. [Qi Mingde 祁明德] and [Qi Jiequan 祁介泉], *Long Ahong 聋阿訇* [The Deaf Cleric] (Linxia: Gansu sheng Linxia shi Mingde Qingzhensi 甘肃省临夏市明德清真寺, 2004).

38. For a more detailed account of the publication of *Long Ahong* and its significance, along with a summary in French of the main parts of the text explored here, see Leila Chérif-Chebbi, "L'ahong Sourd," in *De l'Arabie à l'Himalaya: Chemins croisés en hommage à Marc Gaborieau,* ed. Véronique Bouillier and Catherine Servan-Schreiber (Paris: Maisonneuve and Larose, 2004), 407–421.

39. This mosque stands about 400 meters distant from Mingde Mosque.

40. The Bijiazhuang *menhuan* also reports that Qi learned from Afaq. Chen Guoguang 陈国光, "Apaike Hezhuo yu Xiyu Sufei pai de dong chuan 阿帕克和卓与西域苏菲派的东传" [Afaq Khoja and the eastward transmission of the Western Regions Sufi order], in *Zhongguo Weiwu'er lishi wenhua yanjiu luncong 中国维吾尔历史文化研究论丛* [Collected research on the culture and history of China's Uyghurs], ed. Liu Zhixiao 刘志霄 (Urumqi: Xinjiang Renmin Chubanshe, 1998), 87.

41. Khwāja Akhund Ibn ʿAli, "Siyar al-mukhliṣīn" [Lives of the loyal] (nineteenth c.), BP189.7.N35.A23 1700z (misidentified as Jāmiʿ al-Maqāmāt), Library of the University of California, Berkeley; "Tazkirah of Ḥaẓrat Āfāq Khojam" (n.d.), Manuscript # Prov. 369, Jarring Collection, Lund University Library.

42. Thierry Zarcone, "Le Mathnavî de Rûmî au Turkestan Oriental et au Xinjiang," in *De l'Arabie à l'Himalaya: Chemins croisés en hommage à Marc Gaborieau,* ed. Véronique Bouillier and Catherine Servan-Schreiber (Paris: Maisonneuve and Larose, 2004), 197–207.

43. In a 2024 article I suggested that Mulaji might be a transliteration of Mulla Hajji, but this was incorrect. Leila Chérif-Chebbi had earlier given the correct transliteration of Murad, in an article that had escaped my notice. Chérif-Chebbi, "L'ahong Sourd"; Rian Thum, "The Naqshbandiyya Mujaddidiyya in China," *Journal of the Royal Asiatic Society* 34, no. 2 (2024): 271–302.

44. For a more detailed analysis, see Thum, "Naqshbandiyya Mujaddidiyya in China."

45. Martin Van Bruinessen, "The Origins and Development of the Naqshbandi Order in Indonesia," *Der Islam* 67 (1990): 166. Shīrwānī died in 1884. It is likely that in *Long Ahong* the meeting with Shīrwānī is an embellishment, as both Zawāwī's exile and Manzilāwī's composition of his translation occurred after Shīrwānī's death. For the relationships between these scholars, see Abdulsait Aykut, "Muhammad Murād Ramzī (1855–1935) and His Works," Крымское Историческое Обозрение, no. 2 (2016): 8–26; Mariam Elashmawy, "Can the Qazani Speak? Nineteenth Century Naqshbandi Migrants and Translators in Mecca During the Age of Print," in *Narratives of Dislocation in the Arab World,* ed. Nadeen Daddak (London: Routledge, 2023), 138–160.

46. Democratic Committee of the Islamic Xianmen Shrine of Xining, Qinghai, "Qinghai sheng Xining Shi Yisilan jiao Xianmen Gongbei lishi 青海省西宁市伊斯兰教鲜门拱北历史" [History of the Islamic Xianmen Shrine of Xining, Qinghai] (Xining, 2010).

47. Jonathan N. Lipman, "Head-Wagging and the Sounds of Obscenity: Conflicts over Sound on the Qing-Muslim Frontiers," *Performing Islam* 3, no. 1–2 (2014): 45–59.

48. These are discussed in more detail in Chapter 5.

49. See Chapter 6 for the Ikhwani treatment of the *Maktūbāt.*

4. The Matrix of the Extraordinary

1. Zhao Can 趙燦 and She Yunshan 舍蘊善, *Jingxue xichuan pu 經學系傳普* [Genealogy of the transmission and lineage of classical learning] (1714), 100–103, facsimile in Zhou Xiefan 周燮藩, ed., *Qingzhen dadian 清真大典* [The Islamic canon], vol. 20 (Hefei: Huangshan Shushe, 2005), 72–73.

2. On dating and authorship, see Chen Hui's remarks in Zhao Can 赵灿 and She Yunshan 舍蕴善, *Jingxue xichuan pu 经学系传普* [Genealogy of the transmission and lineage of classical learning], ed. Chen Hui 陈晖 (Beijing: Zongjiao wenhua chubanshe, 2022).

3. M. Aurel Stein, *Serindia: Detailed Report of Explorations in Central Asia and Westernmost China* (Oxford: Clarendon Press, 1921).

4. Tansen Sen, *India, China, and the World: A Connected History* (Lanham, MD: Rowman and Littlefield, 2017).

5. For an overview of the growth of this field, see Tansen Sen, "China–India Studies: Emergence, Development, and State of the Field," *Journal of Asian Studies* 80, no. 2 (2021): 363–387.

6. Geoff Wade, "Southern Chinese Port Cities and the Islamization of Southeast Asia," in *Routledge Handbook of Islam in Southeast Asia,* ed. Syed Muhammad Khairudin Aljunied (London: Routledge, 2022), 68–87.

7. Yokkaichi Yasuhiro, "Chinese and Muslim Diasporas and the Indian Ocean Trade Network under Mongol Hegemony," in *The East Asian Mediterranean: Maritime Crossroads of Culture, Commerce, and Human Migration,* ed. Angela Schottenhammer (Wiesbaden: Harrassowitz, 2008), 92.

8. The teacher's name was Zhang Shaoshan, 張少山, who, like Zhang Shizhong, is recorded in the late seventeenth-century intellectual genealogy, Zhao Can and She Yunshan, *Jingxue xichuan pu* (1714), 63; Zhou Xiefan, *Qingzhen dadian,* 20:39.

9. Zhang Shizhong 張時中 and Ashige 阿世格, *Gui Zhen zong yi 歸真総義* [General meaning of the return to the True One] ([Sichuan]: [Baozhentang], 1878).

10. *Yimani muzhimole qimeng qianshuo* 以麻呢穆直默勒啓蒙淺說.

11. For an example of this formula in South Asia, see Mawlawi Amānatallah, *Hidayut Ool Islam in Arabic and Hindoostanee,* ed. John Borthwick Gilchrist (Calcutta: Hindoostanee Press, 1804). For a rare appearance in a Central Asia context, see Ḥāfiẓ Baṣīr, *Manifestations of a Sufi Woman in Central Asia: A Critical Edition of Ḥāfiẓ-i Baṣīr's Maẓhar al-ʿAjāʾib,* ed. Aziza Shanazarova (Leiden: Brill, 2020). Examples from China are given below.

12. Li Xinghua 李兴华 and Feng Jinyuan 冯今源, "Beijing youguan danwei Yisilanjiao hanwen cang shu 北京有关单位伊斯兰教汉文藏书" [Chinese-language Islamic books collected by relevant units in Beijing], *Ningxia Daxue xuebao 宁夏大学学报,* no. 3 (1984): 100; Ma Zaiyuan 马在渊, *Sufei you men: Gui Zhen zong yi li de mimi 苏菲有门: 归真总义里的秘密* [Sufi's gateway: The secret in general meaning of the return to the true one] (Hong Kong: Huai feng shushe, 2016).

13. Ma Anyi 馬安義, *Taḥqīq al-īman* [The realization of faith] ([Yunnan]: Guang ji tang 廣濟堂, 1905).

14. Abudunla Alei 阿布顿拉 阿雷, *Musilin bidu 穆斯林必读* [Required readings for Muslims] (n.p., 2010), 4; Ma Jun 马军, *Yisilan xinyang wenda 伊斯兰信仰问答* [Questions and answers on Islamic faith] (Gansu: Gansu minzu chubanshe, 2011), 66.

15. M. Nazif Shahrani, "Local Knowledge of Islam and Social Discourse in Afghanistan and Turkistan in the Modern Period," in *Turko-Persia in Historical Perspective,* ed. Robert L. Canfield (Cambridge: Cambridge University Press, 2002).

16. Li Xinghua and Feng Jinyuan, "Beijing youguan danwei Yisilanjiao hanwen cang shu," 100; Ma Lianyuan, *Tafṣīl al-īmān: al-Faṣl / Tianfang fen xin pian ji si pian yao dao 天方分信篇暨四篇要道* [Elements of faith: The chapter / Essay on the divisions of faith and four essential principles] (Kunming: Xing Shun He, 1894).

17. Lynn A. Struve, "The Southern Ming, 1644–1662," in *The Cambridge History of China,* vol. 7, *The Ming Dynasty, 1368–1644,* part 1, ed. Frederick W. Mote and Denis Twitchett (Cambridge: Cambridge University Press, 1998), 641–725.

18. Hu Yubing 胡玉冰, "Qingdai Yunnan ji Huizu xuezhe Ma Zhu shengping xin kao 清代云南籍回族学者马注生平新考" [The new textual research on the life and career of Ma Zhu in Yunnan of Qing dynasty], *Minzuxue Lun Cong 民族学论丛* [Journal of Hui Muslim Minority Studies] 1 (2013): 56–61; Ma Jianxiong, "Re-Creating Hui Identity and the Charity Network in the Imperial Extension from Ming to Qing in the Southwest Chinese Frontier," in *Charities in the Non-Western World: The Development and Regulation of Indigenous and Islamic Charities,* ed. Rajeswary Brown Ampalavanar and Justin Pierce (New York: Routledge, 2013), 163–186.

19. Our knowledge of Ma Zhu's life comes from the short (auto)biography written by Ma or one of his followers and included in his *Compass of Islam.* Ma Zhu, *Qingzhen zhinan 清真指南* [Compass of Islam] (Guangzhou: Haopan Street Mosque, 1870–1871).

20. C. Patterson Giersch, *Asian Borderlands: The Transformation of Qing China's Yunnan Frontier* (Cambridge, MA: Harvard University Press, 2006), 169.

21. Victor Lieberman, "Secular Trends in Burmese Economic History, c. 1350–1830, and Their Implications for State Formation," *Modern Asian Studies* 25, no. 1 (1991): 14.

22. Jonathan N. Lipman, "Head-Wagging and the Sounds of Obscenity: Conflicts over Sound on the Qing-Muslim Frontiers," *Performing Islam* 3, no. 1–2 (2014): 48.

23. Wang Jianping 王建平, "Lun shiba shiji chu de Yunnan gelandai jiaoan 论十八世纪初的云南格兰岱教案" [On the case of the early eighteenth-century kalandars in Yunnan], *世界宗教研究,* no. 3 (1998): 93–103.

24. Ma Dexin 馬德新, *Chaojin tuji 朝覲途記* [Account of the Hajj route], trans. Ma Anli 馬安禮 (Yunnan: n.p., 1861). Originally written in Arabic or Persian and translated into Chinese by his most prominent student.

25. Kristian Petersen, *Interpreting Islam in China: Pilgrimage, Scripture, and Language in the Han Kitab* (Oxford: Oxford University Press, 2017), 47.

26. Ma Dexin, *Chaojin tuji.*

27. For analyses of these sources, see Alexandre Papas, *Soufisme et politique entre Chine, Tibet et Turkestan: Étude sur les Khwâjas Naqshbandîs du Turkestan*

Oriental (Paris: J. Maisonneuve, 2005); Rian Thum, "Beyond Resistance and Nationalism: Local History and the Case of Afaq Khoja," *Central Asian Survey* 31, no. 3 (2012): 293–310.

28. Joseph Fletcher, "The Naqshbandiyya in Northwest China," in *Studies on Chinese and Islamic Inner Asia*, vol. 9 (Aldershot, UK: Variorum, 1995), 3–46; Papas, *Soufisme et politique entre Chine, Tibet et Turkestan.*

29. Khwāja Akhund Ibn ʿAli, "Siyar al-mukhliṣīn [Lives of the loyal]" (nineteenth c.), BP189.7.N35.A23 1700z (misidentified as Jāmiʿ al-Maqāmāt), Library of the University of California, Berkeley.

30. Morris Rossabi, "Muslim and Central Asian Revolts," in *From Ming to Ch'ing: Conquest, Region, and Continuity in Seventeenth-Century China,* ed. Jonathan D. Spence and John Elliot Wills (New Haven, CT: Yale University Press, 1979), 188–189.

31. Rossabi, "Muslim and Central Asian Revolts," 191–192.

32. Mīr Khāl al-Dīn, "Hidāyatnāma" (1729–1730), 196v–198, OR 8162, British Library.

33. Thum, "Beyond Resistance and Nationalism."

34. Democratic Committee of the Islamic Xianmen Shrine of Xining, Qinghai, "Qinghai sheng Xining shi Yisilan jiao Xianmen Gongbei lishi 青海省西宁市伊斯兰教鲜门拱北历史" [History of the Islamic Xianmen Shrine of Xining, Qinghai] (Xining, 2010).

35. Traditions regarding Afaq from all but the Xianmen *menhuan* are collected in Chen Guoguang 陈国光, "Apaike Hezhuo yu Xiyu Sufei pai de dong chuan 阿帕克和卓与西域苏菲派的东传" [Afaq Khoja and the eastward transmission of the Western Regions' Sufi order], in *Zhongguo Weiwu'er lishi wenhua yanjiu luncong 中国维吾尔历史文化研究论丛* [Collected research on the culture and history of China's Uyghurs], ed. Liu Zhixiao 刘志霄 (Urumqi: Xinjiang Renmin Chubanshe, 1998).

36. Khāl al-Dīn, "Hidāyatnāma," 196r.

37. Janet Rizvi, *Trans-Himalayan Caravans: Merchant Princes and Peasant Traders in Ladakh* (Delhi: Oxford University Press, 2004).

38. Rian Thum, "Moghul Relations with the Mughals—Economic, Political, and Cultural," in *Xinjiang in the Context of Central Eurasian Transformations,* ed. Takehiro Onuma, David Brophy, and Yasushi Shinmen (Tokyo: Toyo Bunko, 2018), 3–25.

39. Muḥammad Aʿẓam Dīdāmarī, *Wāqiʿāt-i kashmīr* (Oriental Research Library, Srinagar, manuscript #1843), fol. 132r.

40. Muḥammad Ṣādiq Kāshgharī, *Zubdat al-masāʾil wa-l-ʿaqāʾid* (Istanbul: Ḥājjī ʿAbbās Āqā, 1897), 6.

41. Zhang Shizhong and Ashige, *Gui Zhen zong yi,* 1r, 2r.

42. Khāl al-Dīn, "Hidāyatnāma," 198r.

43. Zhao Can and She Yunshan, *Jingxue xichuan pu* (1714), 121–122.

44. Marshall David Sahlins, *Islands of History* (Chicago: University of Chicago Press, 1985); Marshall Sahlins, *Historical Metaphors and Mythical Realities: Structure in the Early History of the Sandwich Islands Kingdom* (Ann Arbor: University of Michigan Press, 1981).

5. Origins Identify

1. Guangtian Ha, *The Sound of Salvation: Voice, Gender, and the Sufi Mediascape in China* (New York: Columbia University Press, 2022), 177.

2. Ha, *Sound of Salvation,*125.

3. Ha, *Sound of Salvation.*

4. Zvi Ben-Dor Benite, *The Dao of Muhammad: A Cultural History of Muslims in Late Imperial China* (Cambridge, MA: Harvard University Asia Center, 2005); James D. Frankel, *Rectifying God's Name: Liu Zhi's Confucian Translation of Monotheism and Islamic Law* (Honolulu: University of Hawai'i Press, 2011); Sachiko Murata, ed., *The First Islamic Classic in Chinese: Wang Daiyu's Real Commentary on the True Teaching* (Albany: State University of New York Press, 2017); Florian Sobieroj, "The Chinese Sufi Wiqāyatullāh Ma Mingxin and the Construction of His Sanctity in Kitāb Al-Jahrī," *Asiatische Studien-Études Asiatiques* 70, no. 1 (2016): 133–169; Ha, *Sound of Salvation;* Anthony Hayden Garnaut, "The Shaykh of the Great Northwest: The Religious and Political Life of Ma Yuanzhang (1853–1920)" (PhD thesis, Australian National University, 2011).

5. Tiffany Cone, *Cultivating Charismatic Power: Islamic Leadership Practice in China* (Cham, Switzerland: Palgrave Macmillan, 2018); J. Lilu Chen, *Chinese Heirs to Muhammad: Writing Islamic History in Early Modern China* (Piscataway, NJ: Gorgias Press, 2020).

6. Ben-Dor Benite, *Dao of Muhammad,* 199.

7. Kristian Petersen, *Interpreting Islam in China: Pilgrimage, Scripture, and Language in the Han Kitab* (Oxford: Oxford University Press, 2017), 1–2; Jonathan N. Lipman, *Familiar Strangers: A History of Muslims in Northwest China* (Seattle: University of Washington Press, 1998), 24–25; Ben-Dor Benite, *Dao of Muhammad,* 204–209; Marshall Broomhall, *Islam in China: A Neglected Problem* (London: Morgan and Scott, 1910), 62.

8. Ben-Dor Benite, *Dao of Muhammad,* 208.

9. Chen, *Chinese Heirs to Muhammad.*

10. *Qing Veritable Records,* quoted in Luo Yanhui 罗彦慧, "Xingzou zai shuangchong zhi jian—Lan Xu shengping shiji kaoshu 行走在双重之间— 蓝煦生平事迹考述" [Walking between doubles—Research on Lan Xu's life and achievements], *Journal of Hui Muslim Minority Studies 回族研究,* no. 3 (2011): 84–87.

11. This history of Lan Xu's official career and Confucian writings is based on Luo Yanhui's 罗彦慧 study of Lan Xu's life as recorded in Qing official sources and Lan Xu's writings.

12. Lan Xu 藍煦, *Tianfang zhengxue 天方正學* [Correct learning of Islam] (Beijing: Qingzhen Shu Bao Shi 清真書報社, 1925). I am grateful to Lilu Chen for sharing her copy, which is the same edition as the New York Public Library copy.

13. The Jahriyya community has instead interpreted the text as simultaneously describing later Islamic leaders in cryptic verses.

14. Here I follow J. Lilu Chen's interpretations of these titles. Perfected Being (真人) has a long history in Chinese-language moral philosophy, stretching back to the first millennium BCE. It may simultaneously be functioning as a translation of

the Perso-Arabic Sufi term *insan al-kāmil,* the Perfect Man. Chen also points out Lan Xu's unusual application of the *qutb* title to prophets, rather than saints (*awliya Allah*) exclusively. Chen, *Chinese Heirs to Muhammad,* 88.

15. Walter Benjamin, *Illuminations,* trans. Harry Zohn (New York: Schocken Books, 1969), 261, 262; Benedict Anderson, *Imagined Communities: Reflections on the Origin and Spread of Nationalism* (London: Verso, 1991), 24.

16. *Al-Kawkab al-anwar ʿalā ʿiqd al-jawāhir fī mawlid al-nabī al-azhar* [The star of lights on the jeweled necklace of the resplendent prophet's birth], by Jaʿfar bin Ḥasan al-Barzanjī.

17. This work is also listed by Liu Zhi as one of the sources for his *Tianfang xingli 天方性理.* Donald Daniel Leslie and Mohamed Wassel, "Arabic and Persian Sources Used by Liu Chih," *Central Asiatic Journal* 26, no. 1 / 2 (1982): 94.

18. See Chapter 2.

19. Burhān al-Dīn Ma Xuezhi 马学智 Manṣūrallah, Ibrāhīm, and Muḥammad ʿAbd al-Ḥakīm, *Risālah aqṣarayyah li-bayān al-silsilah al-Jahriyya* [The briefest treatise on the Jahriyya chain of transmission] ([Jinjipu, Ningxia]: undated facsimile publication circa 2010 under the title *Zheherenye shi 哲合忍耶史,* 1983), 211. Manṣūr wrote his portion of this text no later than 1933. The teacher's *nisba,* al-Shansī, refers to the province of either Shaanxi or Shanxi, most likely the former.

20. Manṣūrallah, Ibrāhīm, and ʿAbd al-Ḥakīm, *Risālah aqṣarayyah li-bayān al-silsilah al-Jahriyya,* 2–3.

21. Manṣūrallah, Ibrāhīm, and ʿAbd al-Ḥakīm, *Risālah aqṣarayyah li-bayān al-silsilah al-Jahriyya,* 1.

22. Manṣūrallah, Ibrāhīm, and ʿAbd al-Ḥakīm, *Risālah aqṣarayyah li-bayān al-silsilah al-Jahriyya,* 423.

23. This name, literally "horse bridge," may be a calque of a Chinese name with the same or similar literal meaning, perhaps 馬橋. "Al-Farisī" appears in other texts as an Arabic translation of the Chinese surname "Ma." The phenomenon is particularly fascinating because the common Muslim surname Ma 馬 (horse) probably came about as an abbreviated transliteration of the Arabic names Muhammad and / or Mahmud. The name Al-Farisī (of the horse) is then a translation back into Arabic, now carrying the equine meaning. In any case, the only Chinese-language name I have found recorded for Manṣūr is Ma Xuezhi. Alternatively it could be read with a different voweling to yield "Jisr al-Farsī," or "Persian bridge."

24. Anglophone scholars cite this text as *Kitāb al-Jahrī* (Book of the Jahriyya), presumably based on the appearance of the phrase *hadhā Kitāb al-Jahrī* ("this is the book of the Jahriyya" or perhaps "this is a Jahrī book") on the title page and the covers of various facsimile editions. However, within the text itself, Manṣūr very clearly indicates the title, writing "and I named it *Risālah aqṣarayyah li-bayān al-silsilah al-Jahriyya*" (3). Ibrāhīm, who completed the work, refers to it in abbreviation as *Risālah aqṣarayyah.* It is likely that the phrase *Kitāb al-Jahrī* (or *hadhā Kitāb al-Jahrī*) is a general description applied to books that are read only by the Jahriyya. It appears on a book entitled *Rashḥa,* kept in the library of the Banqiao Daotang. Another text of Jahriyya history, *al-Rashf* (The sip), follows the title on the title page with a similar phrase, *min kitab al-Jahrī* ("from the book of the Jahriyya").

25. Various titles have been proposed for this work, but this is the oldest documented title, appearing in Manṣūr's book on page 3. The available original manuscript, recently published in facsimile, does not mention the title in the text but has the same *al-Rashḥat al-sharīfat* stamped on its cover at an unknown date. Three specimens in the Banqiao library have the title *Rashḥa* on their covers. The work is more widely known today by the Chinese transliteration, *Reshiha'er* 热什哈尔. Guanli Ye 關裡爺, *Reshiha'er: Zhengui de lushu (wanzheng diancang Gansu ban—yuanshi shougao kanbu. Xin yi. Zhushi. Jiaokan) 熱什哈爾：珍貴的露珠 (完整典藏甘肅版——原始手稿刊布. 新譯. 註釋. 校勘)* [Rashaha: Precious dewdrop (Complete classic, Gansu recension—Publication of the original manuscript. New translation. Annotation. Collation)], trans. Ma Xuehua 馬學華 and Zhang Chengzhi 張承志 (Taipei: Net and Books Co., 2021), 9.

26. Ha, *Sound of Salvation,* 61. Compare, for example, page 4 of *The Briefest Treatise* with page 2 of Farīd al-Dīn ʿAṭṭar and Reynold A. Nicholson, *Taẕkirat al-awliyā* (London: Luzac and Company, 1905).

27. Farīd al-Dīn ʿAṭṭār, *Muslim Saints and Mystics: Episodes from the Tadhkirat Al-Auliy'a' ("Memorial of the Saints"),* trans. J. A. Arberry (London: Routledge and Kegan Paul, 1973), 14.

28. For examples of borrowed anecdotes, see those on pages 5, 18 (last anecdote), and 19 (first complete anecdote), in Abū al-Imān ʿAbd al-Qādir Guanli Ye 关里爷, *Reshihaer 热什哈尔,* trans. Yang Wanbao 杨万宝, Ma Xuekai 马学凯, and Zhang Yongzhi 张永志 (Beijing: Shenghuo Dushu Xinzhi Sanlian Shudian, 1993).

29. Abū al-Imān ʿAbd al-Qādir Guanli Ye 關裡爺, *Al-Rashaḥat al-sharīfat* (1830), 29.

30. The other two are the aforementioned *Rashḥat al-sharīfat* and a text by ʿAbd al-Aḥad known as *Manāqib al awliya* or *al-Manāqib al-Aḥmadiyya,* which I accessed as a spirit-duplicated manuscript in a small mosque in Yinchuan. Another work with a narrower scope, *al-Rashfa,* describes only the actions of the seventh *murshid* on his trip to consecrate the founder's grave at Lanzhou. ʿAbd al-Shukūr ibn Ibrāhīm, *al-Rashfa* (n.p., 1920). For Tayyib al-Dīn, see Manṣūrallah, Ibrāhīm, and ʿAbd al-Ḥakīm, *Risālah aqṣarayyah,* 2.

31. Garnaut, "Shaykh of the Great Northwest," 383n4.

32. Abū al-Imān ʿAbd al-Qādir Guanli Ye, *Reshihaer;* Ma Xuezhi 马学智, *Daotong shi zhuan 道统史传* [History of the transmission of the Way], trans. Ma Yi 马义 (Xiji, Ningxia: Xiji xian Beidasi, 1997).

33. Ha, *Sound of Salvation,* 6, 107, 109.

34. Garnaut, "Shaykh of the Great Northwest."

35. Ha, *Sound of Salvation,* 159.

36. Garnaut, "Shaykh of the Great Northwest," 350.

37. Muḥammad Yūsuf says he was twenty-seven years old (p. 294) around the time Shāh Ḥamza died, which occurred in 1827. In the pairings of age and date for other individuals in the manuscript, the author seems to use the Chinese method of calculating age, which adds one year. Thus he was likely born in or around 1802. The year of death comes from Ma Tong's research among the Beizhuang followers. Ma Tong 马通, *Zhongguo Yisilan jiaopai yu menhuan zhidu shilüe 中国伊斯兰教派与门宦制度史略* [Brief history of Chinese Islamic denomination and menhuan

systems] (Yinchuan: Ningxia People's Press 宁夏人民出版社, 1984), 173. Ma Tong also reports that Shāh Ḥamza's oldest son, Ḥasan, is credited with writing another text, *Duhufandu liman'adumi 杜乎凡杜里曼阿杜米,* perhaps *Tuḥfat al-munaẓim.* This text does not seem to have come to light outside of the Beizhuang order.

38. Muḥammad Yūsuf, *Nuzhat al-qulūb,* 1856 AH (1856–1857). The copy I used for this is a photocopy of a manuscript copy; the colophon says it was first printed in 1994 in one hundred copies.

39. It is also interesting that the letters are in Arabic.

40. Yūsuf, *Nuzhat al-qulūb,* 289.

41. In Muḥammad Yūsuf's text it is called Naqshbandiyya Sirhindiyya.

42. Ma Tong, *Zhongguo Yisilan jiaopai yu menhuan.*

43. The manuscript is messy, with numerous illegible words and some idiosyncratic grammar, but I could discern no sign of possible Sarta influence. I say this with the caveat, however, that I have no knowledge whatsoever of Sarta.

44. For a survey of the reception of the text, see Noriko Unno, "Mirror of Desire or Fear? Chinese Emperors in Muslim Folklore and Modern Historiography," in *Fear, Heterodoxy, and Crime in Traditional China,* ed. Tommaso Previato (Leiden: Brill, 2024), 163–192.

45. Ma Qirong 馬啓榮, *Xi lai zongpu 西来宗谱* [Genealogy of the arrival from the west] (Guangzhou: Huaisheng Mosque, 1877), 4a.

46. Ma Qirong, *Xi lai zongpu,* 2b.

47. The biographical details here come exclusively from Ma Qirong's publications. I have found no other sources that mention him.

48. Ma Qirong, *Xi lai zongpu.* The date is an estimate based on the date of the first preface, Guangxu 2 (1876–1877).

49. *Renli qieyao 認禮切要* [Essentials of faith and ritual], cited and described in Isaac Mason, "Notes on Chinese Mohammedan Literature," *Journal of the North-China Branch of the Royal Asiatic Society* 56 (1925): 197. For the initial publication date I rely on the catalog of the Toyo Bunko, which describes the photographic reproduction of the Guangxu 1 woodblock edition in Wu Haiying 吴海鹰, ed., *Huizu diancang quanshu 回族典藏全书* [Comprensive collection of Hui classics] (Lanzhou: Gansu wenhua chubanshe, 2008).

50. The two prefaces are those of Zhao Baoneng 兆保熊 and Yang Dianying 楊殿英.

51. Aaron Nathan Glasserman, "Hui Corporate Strategies and Islamic Cultural Capital and in Qing Guangzhou," *Journal of the Economic and Social History of the Orient* 66, no. 1–2 (2023): 1–42.

52. Shaodan Zhang, *Sino-Muslims, Networking, and Identity in Late Imperial China: Longstanding Natives and Dispersed Minorities* (London: Routledge, 2025).

53. Janice Hyeju Jeong, "Little Mecca in Canton: Representations and Resurgences of the Graveyard of Sa'd Ibn Abī Waqqās," *History and Anthropology* 34, no. 5 (2023): 859–882.

54. Ma Qirong, *Xi lai zongpu,* 8a.

55. Ben-Dor Benite, *Dao of Muhammad,* 207.

56. *Huihui yuanlai 回回原來* [The origins of the Huihui] (Laizhou, Shandong: n.p., 1894).

6. Origins Reveal

1. This was the shrine of Imam Ja'far Sadiq. For more on this site and other shrines of Twelver Shi'i imams, see Minoru Sawada, "Pilgrimage to Sacred Places in the Taklamakan Desert: Shrines of Imams in Khotan Prefecture," in *Central Asian Pilgrims: Hajj Routes and Pious Visits between Central Asian and the Hijaz,* ed. Alexandre Papas et al. (Berlin: Klaus Schwarz Verlag, 2012); and Rian Thum, "'Sunni' Veneration of the Twelve Imams in Khotan," *Journal of the American Oriental Society* 142, no. 3 (2022): 621–642. In my 2022 study of the topic, Professor Sawada's valuable study somehow escaped my notice, leading me to omit his pioneering work. I wish to apologize for this error.

2. Waleed Ziad, *Hidden Caliphate: Sufi Saints Beyond the Oxus and Indus* (Cambridge, MA: Harvard University Press, 2021), cover.

3. Alexandre Papas and Ma Wei, "Sufi Lineages Among the Salar," *Muslims in Amdo Tibetan Society: Multidisciplinary Approaches* (2015): 109–134; Alexandre Papas, "Note sur la Naqshbandiyya-Mujaddidiyya en Asie Centrale Chinoise (XVIIIe–XIXe siècles)," *Journal of the History of Sufism* 5 (2007): 319–328; Thierry Zarcone, "The Sufi Networks in Southern Xinjiang During the Republican Regime (1911–1949): An Overview," in *Islam in Politics in Russia and Central Asia* (London: Routledge, 2002), 119–132; Waleed Ziad, "Traversing the Indus and the Oxus: Trans-Regional Islamic Revival in the Age of Political Fragmentation and the 'Great Game' 1747–1880" (PhD diss., Yale University, 2017).

4. For example, two prominent surveys of the Naqshbandiyya only note the presence of non-Mujaddidi branches of the order among Sino-Muslims. Hamid Algar, "The Naqshbandī Order: A Preliminary Survey of Its History and Significance," *Studia Islamica* (1976): 123–152; Itzchak Weismann, *The Naqshbandiyya: Orthodoxy and Activism in a Worldwide Sufi Tradition* (London: Routledge, 2007).

5. Among these exceptional works are Tan Wutie 潭吴铁 and Fu Yu 傅禹, *Xinjiang Huizu Yisilan jiao shilue 新疆回族伊斯兰教史略* [Outline history of Islam among the Hui of Xinjiang] (Urumqi: Xinjiang Renmin Chubanshe, 1993); Chen Guoguang 陈国光, "A Preliminary Discussion on Imam Rebani and His Sufi School 略论伊玛目热巴尼及其苏菲学派," *Studies on World Religions 世界宗教研究* 3 (1989): 77–84; Leila Chérif-Chebbi, "L'ahong sourd," in *De l'Arabie à l'Himalaya: Chemins croisés en hommage à Marc Gaborieau,* ed. Véronique Bouillier and Catherine Servan-Schreiber (Paris: Maisonneuve and Larose, 2004), 407–421; Matthew S. Erie, *China and Islam: The Prophet, the Party, and Law* (Cambridge: Cambridge University Press, 2016); Guangtian Ha, *The Sound of Salvation: Voice, Gender, and the Sufi Mediascape in China* (New York: Columbia University Press, 2022); Papas, "Note sur la Naqshbandiyya-Mujaddidiyya."

6. Arthur F. Buehler, *Revealed Grace: The Juristic Sufism of Ahmad Sirhindi (1564–1624)* (Louisville, KY: Fons Vitae, 2011), 23–32.

7. Ziad, "Traversing the Indus and the Oxus," 150–153.

8. For a study of the order's spread from Central Asia to Ottoman lands, see Dina Le Gall, *A Culture of Sufism: Naqshbandis in the Ottoman World, 1450–1700* (Albany: State University of New York Press, 2005).

9. Algar, "Naqshbandī Order," 143.

10. Thierry Zarcone, "Sufi Private Family Archives: Regarding Some Unknown Sources on the Intellectual History of Sufi Lineages in 20th Century Xinjiang," in *Studies on Xinjiang Historical Sources in 17–20th Centuries* (Tokyo: Toyo Bunko, 2010), 140–161; Zarcone, "Sufi Networks in Southern Xinjiang"; Papas and Wei, "Sufi Lineages Among the Salar"; Ziad, "Traversing the Indus and the Oxus."

11. Chérif-Chebbi, "L'ahong sourd"; Erie, *China and Islam.* Thierry Zarcone also noted that *Manba al-Asrār,* a Mujaddidi text from Yarkand, found a readership among some Hui in Xinjiang and Gansu. Zarcone, "Sufi Private Family Archives," 149.

12. The following description of the pilgrimage is based on Kentaro Takahashi 高橋健太郎, "Chūgoku Kai-zoku no seija byō sankei to chiiki shakai: Neikakaizoku-jichiku no jirei 中国・回族の聖者廟参詣と地域社会: 寧夏回族自治区の事例" [Visitation to sacred shrines and local communities of the Hui in China], *Geographical Review of Japan* 地理学評論 78, no. 14 (2005): 987–999.

13. Calculation based on Google Earth satellite imagery.

14. Tongxin aixin jiuzhu xiehui 同心爱心救助协会 [Tongxin Compassionate Aid Association], "Honggang Gangzi Gongbei longzhong juxing Hong Laotaiye guizhen zhounian ermaili! 红岗岗子拱北隆重举行洪老太爷归真周年尔买里!" [Hongang's Gangzi tomb-shrine solemnly holds the ritual feast for the passing day of Hong Laotaiye!], Sohu.com, August 24, 2016, https://www.sohu.com/a/111924555_243876.

15. Ma Fengyu (马峰玉), "Hufuye Hongmen *menhuan* 虎夫耶洪门门宦" [The Hongmen *menhuan* of the Khufiyya], in *Tongxin wenshi ziliao 同心文史资料* [Tongxin historical materials], ed. Shi Chengxi 石成玺, vol. 3 ([Tongxin], 1990), 21–45; Ma Tong 马通, *Zhongguo Yisilan jiaopai yu menhuan zhidu shilüe 中国伊斯兰教派与门宦制度史略* [Brief history of Chinese Islamic denomination and menhuan systems] (Yinchuan: Ningxia People's Press 宁夏人民出版社, 2000), 218.

16. Ma Fengyu, "Hufuye Hongmen *menhuan,*" 26, 34. Much of the text of this article is identical to passages from Mian Weilin 勉维霖, *Ningxia Yisilan jiaopai gaiyao 宁夏伊斯兰教派概要* [Outline history of the Islamic denominations of Ningxia] (Ningxia: Ningxia People's Press 宁夏人民出版社, 1981), 45–53, which is not cited. However, the more recent article is slightly more detailed.

17. Ma Fengyu, "Hufuye Hongmen *menhuan,*" 35.

18. For example, see the ethnographic description in Ken Lizzio, "Ritual and Charisma in Naqshbandi Sufi Mysticism," *Anpere* (2007): 17: "Mujaddidis employ two basic dhikr khafi formulae. The first, dhikr-i ism-i dhat, entails pronouncement of one of the names of God alone, 'Allah,' or 'Hu,' (He) considered the essence of the divine name. The second, nafi wa ithbat, is a more advanced practice."

19. Ma Fengyu, "Hufuye Hongmen *menhuan,*" 25–26. *Dao* and *jiao* are glossed in the same passage as *tuolegeti* and *shere'erdi,* respectively.

20. Rian Thum, "The Naqshbandiyya Mujaddidiyya in China," *Journal of the Royal Asiatic Society* 34, no. 2 (2024): 271–302.

21. Ziad, "Traversing the Indus and the Oxus."

22. Papas, "Note sur la Naqshbandiyya-Mujaddidiyya"; Zarcone, "Sufi Networks in Southern Xinjiang"; Zarcone, "Sufi Private Family Archives."

23. Tan Wutie 潭吴铁 and Fu Yu 傅禹, "Xinjiang huizu de Dafang 新疆回族的'大坊'" [The 'Dafang' of the Hui people of Xinjiang], *Xinjiang Zongjiao Yanjiu Ziliao 新疆宗教研究资料* [Xinjiang religion research materials], supplemental issue: "Xi

bei wu sheng (qu) Yisilan jiao xueshu taolun hui (Wulumuqi huiyi) lunwen ziliao ji," 西北五省(区)伊斯兰教学术讨论会(乌鲁木齐会议)论文资料集 [Five northwestern provinces (region) Islamic studies conference (Urumqi meeting) collected papers] (1986).

24. Muḥammad Yūsuf, *Nuzhat al-qulūb,* 1856 AH (1856–1857).

25. *Jiu pin chengchuan 九品乘传* [The ninth-ranked transmission] (Hong Kong: Lan Yue Chubanshe, 2013).

26. Ding Zhengwu 丁正武 and Ma Fuchun 马富春, "Lintan Ding Zhengwu koushu Dingmen lishi 临潭丁正武口述丁门历史" [Oral narration on the history of the Dingmen by Ding Zhengwu of Lintan], in *Zhongguo Sufei xuepai dianji 中国苏菲学派典籍* [Sources on Chinese Sufi denominations], ed. Ma Tong 马通 and Ma Haibin 马海滨 (n.p., 2010), 539–541.

27. Ma Fengyu, "Hufuye Hongmen *menhuan*."

28. Tan Wutie and Fu Yu, *Xinjiang huizu yisilan jiao shilue,* 398.

29. The Beizhuang order is particularly influential among the Salar ethnic group, but it has taken root in Hui communities as well (for example, at Taozhou). Yue Que, "Hui Lineages in Taozhou and the Acculturation of Islam During the Qing Dynasty," in *Islam and Chinese Society: Genealogies, Lineage and Local Communities,* ed. Jianxiong Ma, Oded Abt, and Jide Yao (New York: Routledge, 2020), 80.

30. ʿAbd al-Qādir Guanli Ye 關裡爺, *al-Rashaḥat al-sharīfat* [The sublime dewdrop], c. 1830, 29, facsimile of an 1887 manuscript in Guanli Ye 關裡爺, *Reshiha'er: Zhengui de lushu (wanzheng diancang Gansu ban—Yuanshi shougao kanbu. Xin yi. Zhushi. Jiaokan) 熱什哈爾: 珍貴的露珠（完整典藏甘肅版——原始手稿刊布. 新譯. 註釋. 校勘）* [Rashaha: Precious dewdrop (Complete classic, Gansu recension—Publication of the original manuscript. New translation. Annotation. Collation)], manuscript transcription and translation by Ma Xuehua 馬學華 and Zhang Chengzhi 張承志 (Taipei: Net and Books Co., 2021).

31. Ma Lianyuan 馬聯元, "Fu: 'Bianshu Da Zaxue' Ma Zhiben zi xu Alabowen (yuan wen) 附:《编述大杂学》马致本自序 阿拉伯文（原文）" [Appendix: "Compilation of the great miscellany," Ma Zhiben's self-preface in the original Arabic], in *Weishan Huizu Wenshi Ziliao 巍山回族文史资料* [Weishan Hui historical materials], vol. 12, *Ma Lianyuan jingxue shijia 马联元经学世家* [The religious scholar family of Ma Lianyuan], ed. Ma Yunliang 马云良 (Kunming: Yunnan Ethnicities Publishing House, 2011).

32. Di Liangchuan 狄良川, *Hu Songshan sixiang yanjiu 虎嵩山思想研究* [A study on the thought of Hu Songshan] (Yinchuan, 2015), 66, 177.

33. The title appears in the catalog at the beginning of Mehmet Emin, *Majālis irshādiyyah* (Shanghai: Shanghai Believer's Classics Company 上海穆民經書公司, n.d.).

34. Aḥmad Sirhindī, *Maktūbāt-e Imān Rabbānī /Maiketubate 麦克图巴特,* trans. Muhanmode Ma Shengzhi 穆罕默德 马生智 (Hong Kong: Hong Kong Tianma Chuban Gongsi, 2010).

35. Aḥmad Sirhindī, *Maktūbāt,* trans. Ma Tingyi 马廷义 (Hong Kong: Hong Kong Tianma Chuban Gongsi, 2005).

36. Ding Shijun 丁士俊, "Kangle Dingmen Ding Shijun jishu Dingmen lishi 康乐丁门丁士俊记述丁门历史" [Written account of the history of the Dingmen by Ding Shijun of Lintan], in *Zhongguo Sufei xuepai dianji 中国苏菲学派典籍* [Sources

on Chinese Sufi denominations], ed. Ma Tong 马通 and Ma Haibin 马海滨 (n.p., 2010), 542–544.

37. This shrine was active until at least the mid-2010s. For a description see Rahilă Davut, *Uyghur mazarliri* (Ürümchi: Shinjang Khălq Năshriyati, 2001).

38. *Taẕkirah'i ḥaẕrat haft Muḥammadān,* in an untitled compilation of tazkirahs: uncataloged, paginated manuscript in the Library of the Minzu Research Institute, Minzu University, Beijing, 158; *Taẕkirah'i ḥaẕrat Khwāja Muḥammad Sharīf Buzurgwār,* Jarring Collection, Lund University Library, manuscript number Prov. 327, 23a.

39. For a study of *Makhzan al-anwār,* see Ziad, *Hidden Caliphate,* 93.

40. *Taẕkirah'i ḥaẕrat haft Muḥammadān.*

41. *Jiu pin chengchuan,* 78.

42. *Taẕkirah'i ḥaẕrat haft Muḥammadān,* 160.

43. *Jiu pin chengchuan,* 277.

44. *Taẕkirah'i ḥaẕrat haft Muḥammadān,* 154.

45. Mīrzā Haydar Dūghlāt, *Mirza Haydar Dughlat's Tarikh-i Rashidi: A History of the Khans of Moghulistan,* trans. W. M. Thackston (Cambridge, MA: Harvard University, Department of Near Eastern Languages and Civilizations, 1996), 190.

46. Shahzad Bashir, *Sufi Bodies: Religion and Society in Medieval Islam* (New York: Columbia University Press, 2011), 165.

47. *Taẕkirah'i Sayyid Afāq Khvājam,* manuscript number Prov. 22, Jarring Collection, Lund University Library, 3.

48. David Brophy and Rian Thum, "Appendix: The Shrine of Muḥammad Sharīf and Its Qing-Era Patrons," in *The Life of Muhammad Sharif: A Central Asian Sufi Hagiography in Chaghatay,* ed. Jeff Eden (Vienna: Verlag der Österreichischen Akademie der Wissenschaften, 2015), 55–76.

49. Thum, "'Sunni' Veneration."

50. Ma Tong, *Zhongguo Yisilan jiaopai yu menhuan zhidu shilüe.*

51. Tan Wutie and Fu Yu, "Xinjiang huizu de dafang"; Tan Wutie and Fu Yu, *Xinjiang huizu yisilan jiao shilue.*

52. Chen Guoguang, "Preliminary Discussion."

53. Devin DeWeese, *Islamization and Native Religion in the Golden Horde: Baba Tükles and Conversion to Islam in Historical and Epic Tradition* (University Park: Pennsylvania State University Press, 1994), 55–57.

54. Luo Yunxi 罗韵希 and Shi Quyang 师初阳, eds., "Qi Mingde 祁明德," in *Zhonggua Yisilan baike quanshu 中国伊斯兰百科全书* [Chinese encyclopedia of Islam] (Chengdu: Sichuan Lexicographical Publishing House, 1994).

55. [Qi Mingde 祁明德] and [Qi Jiequan 祁介泉], *Long Ahong 聋阿訇* [The Deaf Cleric] (Linxia: Gansu sheng Linxia shi Mingde Qingzhensi 甘肃省临夏市明德清真寺, 2004), 1.

56. M. Erie, personal communication, based on his ethnographic fieldwork with the Qi lineage community in Linxia.

57. *Hadhā silsīlah al-sharīfah / Zungui de xilixilai 尊贵的西里西来* [This is the noble sislsila / The honorable silsila] (n.p., c. 2000); [Qi Jiequan 祁介泉], *Long Ahong 聋阿訇* [The Deaf Cleric], vol. 3 (Linxia: Gansu sheng Linxia shi Mingde Qingzhensi 甘肃省临夏市明德清真寺, 2000). Thank you to Nakanishi Tatsuya for sharing the former publication with me.

58. Dru Gladney, *Muslim Chinese: Ethnic Nationalism in the People's Republic*, 2nd ed. (Cambridge, MA: Harvard University Asia Center, 1996), 35–53.

59. Joseph Trippner, "Islamische Gruppen und Gräberkult in Nordwest-China," *Die Welt Des Islams* 7, no. 1 / 4 (1961): 142–171; Joseph Fletcher, "The Naqshbandiyya in Northwest China," in *Studies on Chinese and Islamic Inner Asia*, vol. 11 (Aldershot, UK: Variorum, 1995), 3–46.

60. Author's fieldwork in 2004–2005, 2007–2008, and 2015.

61. Ziad, *Hidden Caliphate.*

7. Origins Move

1. From the translation of Sachiko Murata, ed., *The First Islamic Classic in Chinese: Wang Daiyu's Real Commentary on the True Teaching* (Albany: State University of New York Press, 2017), 153.

2. Rian Thum, *The Sacred Routes of Uyghur History* (Cambridge, MA: Harvard University Press, 2014), 137.

3. Janice Hyeju Jeong, "Homeland, Magnet, and Refuge: Mecca in the Travels and Imaginaries of Chinese Muslims," *Modern Asian Studies* 57, no. 6 (2023): 1743–1771.

4. Documents 1 and 4 in the family archive of Hajar Khenim, Jeddah, Saudi Arabia.

5. Rian Thum and Huda Abdul Ghafour Amin Kashgary, "The Turkistanis of Mecca: Community Histories of Periphery and Center," *Asian Ethnicity* 22, no. 1 (2021): 188–207; Bayram Balci, "Central Asian Refugees in Saudi Arabia: Religious Evolution and Contributing to the Reislamization of Their Motherland," *Refugee Survey Quarterly* 26, no. 2 (2007): 12–21.

6. Justin J. Rudelson, *Oasis Identities* (New York: Columbia University Press, 1998).

7. Jeong, "Homeland, Magnet, and Refuge."

8. Mūsa Turkistānī, *Ūlūgh Turkistān Fājiʿasi* [The tragedy of great Turkistan] (Madina: Maṭābiʿ al-Rashīd, 1979).

9. Ana Paula De La O Campus, Nynne Warring, and Chiara Brunelli, "Gender and Land Statistics Recent Developments in FAO's Gender and Land Rights Database" (Rome: Food and Agriculture Organization of the United Nations, 2015), 23.

10. [Qi Mingde 祁明德] and [Qi Jiequan 祁介泉], *Long ahong 聋阿訇* [The Deaf Cleric] (Linxia: Gansu sheng Linxia shi Mingde Qingzhensi 甘肃省临夏市明德清真寺, 2004), 20–22. For more details see Jeong, "Homeland, Magnet, and Refuge," 1757.

11. I have not been able to locate documentation for this *waqf*, but it was mentioned by several Turkistanis in Saudi Arabia.

12. Muḥammad Nūr al-Ḥaqq ibn Sayyid Luqmān, *Min sharḥ al-Wiqāyah al-masmi bi-al-tawḍīḥ* [Commentary on the Wiqāyah called the Explication] (Kanpur: Maḥmūd al-Maṭābi', 1903).

13. Attaqwa Mosque, *Taiguo qingmai yisilan jingzhen qingzhensi ershier xuexiao shiwu zhounian jinian kan 泰国清 迈伊斯兰敬真清真寺二十二学校十五周年纪念刊* [Commemorative publication for the twenty-second anniversary of the Islamic

"Venerating the Real" Mosque of Chiang Mai, Thailand, and the fifteenth anniversary of its school] (Chiang Mai, 1988).

14. This history of Xing Shun He is based on two secondary sources, neither of which cites any primary sources. Contradictions between the two suggest that at least one, or probably both, is not entirely reliable. I have related the most basic elements, preferring the earlier, more detailed study. I have not been able to identify any primary sources beyond the publications of Ma Lianyuan. Ma Boliang 马伯良, "Huizu shanghao Xing Shun He 回族商号兴顺和" [The ethnic Hui company Xing Shun He], in *Yunnan wenshi ziliao xuanji 云南文史资料选辑* [Selected works from Yunnan historical materials], vol. 49, *Yunnan lao zihao 云南老字号* [Yunnan's historic businesses], ed. Zhongguo Renmin Zhengzhi Xieshang Huiyi Yunnan Sheng Weiyuanhui Wenshi Ziliao Weiyuanhui 中国人民政治协商会议云南省委员会文史资料委员会 (Yunnan: Yunnan People's Press, 1996); Ma Yan 马燕 and Tian Xiaojuan` 田晓娟, *Sihai tongda Huizu shangmao 四海通达的回族商贸* [The globally connected Hui commerce] (Yinchuan: Ningxia People's Press 宁夏人民出版社, 2008), 102–103.

15. Ma Lianyuan 馬聯元, *Mukhtaṣar sharḥ al-ʿaqā'id / 天方释难要言* [Abridged commentary on the creed / Essentials of the explanation of the difficulties of Islam] (Kunming: Xing Shun He Company 興順和號, 1893); Ma Lianyuan 馬聯元, *Tafṣīl al-Īmān / Tianfang Fenxin Pian 天方分信篇* [Elements of faith / Essay on the divisions of faith] (Kunming: Xing Shun He Company 興順和號, 1894); Ma Lianyuan 馬聯元, ed., *Al-Qur'ān kalām Allah / Baoming zhenjing 寳命真經* [The Qur'an, the Word of God / The true classic of the precious command] (Kunming: Xing Shun He Company 興順和號, 1895).

16. Pilgrimage overland through Southeast Asia has even earlier documentation. The route from Yunnan to Mecca was already recorded in 1349 by the Yuan dynasty traveler Wang Dayuan. Wang Dayuan 汪大淵, *Daoyi zhilüe 島夷誌略* [Record of the island barbarians], ed. Su Jiqing 苏继庼 (Beijing: Zhonghua Shuju, 1981).

17. Holt Samuel Hallett, *A Thousand Miles on an Elephant in the Shan States* (Edinburgh: W. Blackwood and Sons, 1890), 210.

18. Frederick W. Mote, in 1967, says the mosque was founded "fifty years ago," which aligns with a more recent sign near the mosque naming early donors and recording the founding year as 1916. Mote, "The Rural 'Haw' (Yunnanese Chinese) of Northern Thailand," in *Southeast Asian Tribes, Minorities, and Nations,* vol. 2, ed. Peter Kunstadter (Princeton, NJ: Princeton University Press, 1967), 491.

19. Ma Lianyuan 马联元 and Liu Zhi 劉智, *Tianfang xingli benjing zhushi 天方性里本经注释* [Explanation of the original classic of nature and principle in Islam], trans. Ruan Bin 阮斌 ([Beijing]: Zhongguo Minzhu Tongmeng [China Democratic League], 1983).

20. Ḥasan Ẓiyāʾ al-Dīn Ma Anyi 馬安義, *Min sharḥ al-Wiqāyah al-masmi Bi-al-tawḍīḥ: Al-juz' al-thānī* [Commentary on the Wiqāyah called the explication: Part two] ([Yunnan]: Yunnan Hongwen Shiyin Ju 雲南宏文石印局, 1924).

21. Ma Zhiben 马致本 [Ma Lianyuan], *Sharḥ al-tawḍīḥ / 教法简注* [Commentary on the Explication / Simple annotation of religious law], trans. Ma Xinsan 马新三, 2 vols. (Wenshan, Yunnan: Yunnan Sheng Wenshan Zhou Yisilanjiao Xiehui 云南省文山州伊斯兰教协会, 1991, 1993).

22. Oded Abt, "Muslim Ancestor, Chinese Hero or Tutelary God: Changing Memories of Muslim Descendants in China, Taiwan and the Philippines," *Asian Journal of Social Science* 42, no. 6 (2014): 747–776.

23. Li Zhongtang 李忠堂, "Minguo sishiqi nian fang wen Lugang jishi 民國四十七年訪問鹿港紀實" [Record of a visit to Lukang in the year of the republic forty-seven], *Zhongguo Huijiao Xiehui Huibao 中國回教協會會報* 74 (1960). Barbara Pillsbury estimates that the last visit of an *ahong* from the mainland for funeral rites was in approximately 1922. Barbara Linne Kroll Pillsbury, "Cohesion and Cleavage in a Chinese Muslim Minority" (PhD diss., Columbia University, 1973), 147.

24. Guo Zhichao 郭志超, "Taiwan Baiqi Guo Huizu ji qi yu Dalu zujia de jiaowang 台湾白奇郭回族及其与大陆祖家的交往" [Contacts between the Taiwan Baiqi Guo Hui and their ancestral home on the Mainland], *Huizu Yanjiiu 回族研究,* no. 2 (1996): 20–22.

25. Li Zhongtang, "Minguo sishiqi nian fang wen Lugang jishi."

26. Ding Yushu 丁玉書, Ding Zhida 丁志達, and Ding Zhishen 丁志申, *Wuwangcao 勿忘草* [Forget-Me-Not] (Taipei: Ding Zhishen, 2017 [2006]), 35.

27. "Jianrong bing xu de gangkou—Lugang 兼容並蓄的港口—鹿港" [An eclectic port: Lugang], *Dagang ê Taiwan 大港ê台* [Taiwan of ports] (Taiwan Public Television Service 公共電視, October 18, 2022), https://www.ptsplus.tv/zh/programs/35eb2aa5-546a-4ce2-9e50-5fefe3d2c236.

28. Oded Abt, "Chinese Rituals for Muslim Ancestors: Southeast China's Lineages of Muslim Descent," *Review of Religion and Chinese Society* 2 (2015): 216–240.

29. Guo Zhichao, "Taiwan Baiqi Guo Huizu ji qi yu Dalu zujia de jiaowang."

30. *Baiqi Guo shi zupu 白奇郭氏族谱* [Genealogy of the Baiqi Guo clan] (n.p., 1987).

31. *Baiqi Guo shi zupu.*

32. Rosey Wang Ma, "Shifting Identities: Chinese Muslims in Malaysia," *Asian Ethnicity* 6, no. 2 (2005): 89–107.

33. ʿAbd al-Shukūr ibn Ibrahīm, *Al-rashfa* (n.p., 1920).

34. 徐之銘 Xu Zhiming, "Chaojin tuji 朝覲途記序" [Preface to account of the Hajj route], in *Chaojin tuji 朝覲途記* [Account of the Hajj route], ed. Ma Dexin 馬德新 (Yunnan: n.p., 1861), 1v–2r; Sachiko Murata, *Chinese Gleams of Sufi Light: Wang Tai-Yu's Great Learning of the Pure and Real and Liu Chih's Displaying the Concealment of the Real Realm. With a New Translation of Jami's Lawa'ih from the Persian by William C. Chittick* (Albany: State University of New York Press, 2000). "東面而視不見水端望洋向若以嘆如麼其土地民人政然涉驚濤駭浪乘桴海。豈以壯游觀哉譬溯始祖於千百年上分支衍派展厥墓以詳明宗譜焉使穆氏雲仍知淵源之有自先聖后聖."

35. Ma Lianyuan and Liu Zhi, *Tianfang xingli benjing zhushi;* Murata, *Chinese Gleams of Sufi Light.*

36. Liu Zhi 劉智, *Laṭāʾif/Xingli weiyan 性理微言* [Subtleties / Precis of metaphysics], trans. Ma Lianyuan 馬聯元 (Kunming: Ma Zilian 馬子廉, 1898). William Chittick has translated this into English in Sachiko Murata et al., *The Sage Learning of Liu Zhi: Islamic Thought in Confucian Terms* (Cambridge, MA: Harvard University Asia Center, 2009).

37. Ma Lianyuan 馬聯元, *Sharḥ al-laṭā'if/Weiyan Ji Zhu* 微言集註 [Commentary on *Laṭā'if*/ Collected commentary on the precis] (Kunming: Guang Ji Tang 廣濟堂, 1898).

38. Ma Lianyuan, *Sharḥ al-laṭā'if/Weiyan Ji Zhu.*

39. I am grateful to William Chittick for sharing a digitization of this manuscript.

40. Ma Lianyuan and Liu Zhi, *Tianfang xingli benjing zhushi.*

41. Fredrik Barth, *Ethnic Groups and Boundaries: The Social Organization of Culture Difference* (Prospect Heights, IL: Waveland Press, 1998); Fredrik Barth, "Enduring and Emerging Issues in the Analysis of Ethnicity," in *The Anthropology of Ethnicity: Beyond "Ethnic Groups and Boundaries,"* ed. Hans Vermeulen and Cora Govers (Amsterdam: Het Spinhuis, 1994).

8. Origins Distort

1. Sachiko Murata et al., *The Sage Learning of Liu Zhi: Islamic Thought in Confucian Terms* (Cambridge, MA: Harvard University Asia Center, 2009), 5.

2. James D. Frankel, *Rectifying God's Name: Liu Zhi's Confucian Translation of Monotheism and Islamic Law* (Honolulu: University of Hawai'i Press, 2011), 39.

3. Murata et al., *Sage Learning of Liu Zhi,* 93.

4. Ford understands this sentence differently, translating it as "the sacred book [i.e., the Qur'an] is the sacred book of Islam, but *li* [principle] is the same *li* which exists everywhere under Heaven." J. F. Ford, "Some Chinese Muslims of the Seventeenth and Eighteenth Centuries," *Asian Affairs* 5, no. 2 (1974): 150.

5. Murata et al., *Sage Learning of Liu Zhi,* 94.

6. Sachiko Murata, ed., *The First Islamic Classic in Chinese: Wang Daiyu's Real Commentary on the True Teaching* (Albany: State University of New York Press, 2017), 36.

7. Murata et al., *Sage Learning of Liu Zhi,* 95.

8. Frankel, *Rectifying God's Name.*

9. Liu Zhi 劉智, *Laṭā'if* [Subtleties], in *Xingli weiyan* 性理微言 [Precis of metaphysics], trans. Ma Lianyuan 馬聯元 (Kunming: Ma Zilian 馬子廉, 1898).

10. Raphael Israeli, *Islam in China: Religion, Ethnicity, Culture, and Politics* (Lanham, MD: Lexington Books, 2002).

11. "Yang Faming: Zhagen zhonghua wenhua wotu jianchi woguo Yisilanjiao zhongguohua fangxin 杨发明：扎根中华文化沃土　坚持我国伊斯兰教中国化方向" [Yang Faming: Taking root in the fertile soil of Chinese civilization: Persevere in the Chinafication of our country's Islam], *Xinhua.Net,* March 10, 2018, https://web.archive.org/web/20200808074958/http://www.xinhuanet.com/politics/2018lh/2018-03/10/c_1122516862.htm; Max Oidtmann, "The Xi Jinping Cohort and the Chinafication of Religion," Berkley Center for Religion, Peace, and World Affairs, *Berkley Forum* (blog), March 16, 2020, https://berkleycenter.georgetown.edu/responses/the-xi-jinping-cohort-and-the-chinafication-of-religion.

12. See the alternative curriculum of twenty-seven works in *Jingxue xichuan pu,* which includes grammar texts. The author says all of the works included are worthless. Zhao Can 赵灿 and She Yunshan 舍蕴善, *Jingxue xichuan pu* 经学系传普

[Genealogy of the transmission and lineage of classical learning], ed. Chen Hui 陈晖 (Beijing: Zongjiao wenhua chubanshe, 2022).

13. Liu Zhi 劉智, *Tianfang zhisheng shilu nianpu 天方至聖實錄年譜* [Chronological veritable record of the ultimate sage of Islam] (Chengdu: Bao Zhen Tang 寶真堂, 1872).

14. Sachiko Murata makes a similar point in *Chinese Gleams of Sufi Light: Wang Tai-Yu's Great Learning of the Pure and Real and Liu Chih's Displaying the Concealment of the Real Realm. With a New Translation of Jami's Lawa'ih from the Persian by William C. Chittick* (Albany: State University of New York Press, 2000), 7.

15. For an excellent overview of *sanjiao heyi,* along with an argument against the common use of "syncretism" to understand it, see Timothy Brook, "Rethinking Syncretism: The Unity of the Three Teachings and Their Joint Worship in Late-Imperial China," *Journal of Chinese Religions* 21, no. 1 (1993): 13–44.

16. Helmer Ringgren, "The Problems of Syncretism," *Scripta Instituti Donneriani Aboensis* 3 (1969): 7.

17. Ross Kane, *Syncretism and Christian Tradition: Race and Revelation in the Study of Religious Mixture* (Oxford: Oxford University Press, 2020), 19.

18. Robert D. Baird, *Category Formation and the History of Religions* (The Hague: Mouton, 1971); Bruce Lincoln, "Retiring Syncretism," *Historical Reflections / Réflexions Historiques* (2001): 453–459; Arthur J. Droge, "Retrofitting / Retiring 'Syncretism,'" *Historical Reflections / Réflexions Historiques* (2001): 375–387; Stephan Palmié, "Against Syncretism: 'Africanizing' and 'Cubanizing' Discourses in North American Òrìsà Worship," in *Counterworks* (New York: Routledge, 2003), 74–107.

19. Rosalind Shaw and Stewart Charles, "Introduction: Problematizing Syncretism," in *Syncretism / Anti-Syncretism,* ed. Rosalind Shaw and Stewart Charles (New York: Routledge, 1994), 6.

20. Kane, *Syncretism and Christian Tradition,* 128.

21. Luther H. Martin, "To Use 'Syncretism' or Not to Use 'Syncretism': That Is the Question," *Historical Reflections / Réflexions Historiques* (2001): 390.

22. Élisabeth Allès, *Musulmans de Chine: Une anthropologie des Hui du Henan* (Paris: Éditions de l'École des Hautes Études en Sciences Sociales [EHESS], 2000); Zvi Ben-Dor Benite, *The Dao of Muhammad: A Cultural History of Muslims in Late Imperial China* (Cambridge, MA: Harvard University Asia Center, 2005), 13; Kristian Petersen, *Interpreting Islam in China: Pilgrimage, Scripture, and Language in the Han Kitab* (Oxford: Oxford University Press, 2017); Rian Thum, "China in Islam: Turki Views from the Nineteenth and Twentieth Centuries," *Cross-Currents: East Asian History and Culture Review* 3, no. 2 (November 2014).

23. What follows is a small selection, chosen for coverage across time and with a preference for authors who either regularly publish on Islamic China or whose works are frequently cited. A search on Google Scholar yields many more: Raphael Israeli, "Established Islam and Marginal Islam in China from Eclecticism to Syncretism," *Journal of the Economic and Social History of the Orient* 21, no. 1 (1978): 99–109; Jonathan N. Lipman, "Ethnicity and Politics in Republican China: The Ma Family Warlords of Gansu," *Modern China* 10, no. 3 (1984): 297; Chang-Kuan Lin, "Three Eminent Chinese 'Ulama' of Yunnan," *Institute of Muslim Minority Affairs*

Journal 11, no. 1 (1990): 100–117; Frankel, *Rectifying God's Name;* David R. Stroup, "Boundaries of Belief: Religious Practices and the Construction of Ethnic Identity in Hui Muslim Communities," *Ethnic and Racial Studies* 40, no. 6 (2017): 988–1006; and Lloyd Ridgeon, "The Problems of Sinicizing Beijing's Mosques," *Journal of Muslim Minority Affairs* 40, no. 4 (2020): 576–596.

24. Frankel, *Rectifying God's Name,* xvi–xvii.

25. Frankel, xix.

26. More directly, Liu Zhi cites the work of the third-century philosopher Porphyry of Tyre, which was widely circulated in Arabic as Isāghūjī. Dror Weil identified this text from Liu Zhi's Chinese transliteration in Dror Weil, "The Vicissitudes of Late Imperial China's Accommodation of Arabo-Persian Knowledge of the Natural World, 16th–18th Centuries" (PhD diss., Princeton University, 2016), 110.

27. Zhu Gang, "Zhongguo Yisilanjiao Xidaotang xinyang shuping 中国伊斯兰教西道堂信仰述评" [Description of the beliefs of China's Islam's Xidaotang], *Qinghai Minzu Xueyuan Xuebao (shehui kexue ban)* 4 (1982): 66, cited in Marie-Paule Hille, "Les Han kitab et le Xidaotang: Réception et usage d'une littérature musulmane en chinois à la fin du XIXe siècle à Taozhou (Gansu)," *Etudes orientales* 27–28 (2016): 329.

28. Feng Jinyuan 冯今源, "Cong zhongguo Yisilanjiao hanwen Yizhu kan rujia sixiang dui Zhongguo Yisilanjiao de yingxiang he shentou 从中国伊斯兰教汉文译著看儒家思想对中国伊斯兰教的影响和渗透" [The influence and penetration of Confucian thought in Chinese Islam as seen in the Chinese Muslim Chinese-language translations and compositions], in *Yisilanjiao zai Zhongguo 伊斯兰教在中国,* ed. Gansu sheng minzu yanjiusuo 甘肃省民族研究所 (Yinchuan: Ningxia People's Press 宁夏人民出版社, 1982), 280. I have used Lipman's translation. In my own translations I use "classics" for *jingdian,* but the notion of canon will reappear in later scholarship, so I have kept his equally faithful alternative here. Jonathan N. Lipman, *Familiar Strangers: A History of Muslims in Northwest China* (Seattle: University of Washington Press, 1998), 72.

29. Jonathan N. Lipman, "Hyphenated Chinese: Sino-Muslim Identity in Modern China," in *Remapping China: Fissures in Historical Terrain,* ed. Gail Hershatter, Emily Honig, Jonathan N. Lipman, and Randall Stross (Stanford, CA: Stanford University Press, 1996), 97–112.

30. Michael Dillon, *China's Muslims* (New York: Oxford University Press, 1996).

31. Lipman, *Familiar Strangers,* 72.

32. Feng Jinyuan's 1982 article had also discussed Lan Xu's work, though without mentioning the appearance of Han Kitab. Feng Jinyuan, "Rujia sixiang dui Zhongguo Yisilanjiao de yingxiang he shentou."

33. Lan Xu 藍煦, *Tianfang zhengxue 天方正學* [Correct learning of Islam] (Beijing: Qingzhen Shu Bao Shi 清真書報社, 1925), 9r.

34. An alternative translation could be "In each work, the Chinese *Kitab* is present."

35. Wang Shouqian 王守謙, "Liyan 例言" [Preface], in Lan Xu, *Tianfang zhengxue,* 4v.

36. I am grateful to Nakanishi Tatsuya for finding this example and bringing it to my attention. "Huijiao 'Kubuleye' menhuan yalue biao 回教 '库布勒也' 门宦崖略 [Outline chart of the Islamic Kubriyya menhuan]," *Huijiao qingnian 回教青年月刊* [Islamic Youth Monthly] 5, no. 5–7 [n.d.], in *Zhongguo Yisilanjiao Shi Cankao Ziliao Xuanbian 中国伊斯兰教史参考资料选编* [Selected Research Materials on the History of Chinese Islam], ed. Li Xinghua 李兴华 and Feng Jinyuan 冯今源, vol. 1 (Yinchuan: Ningxia renmin chubanshe, 1985), 860.

37. Luo Yunxi 罗韵希 and Shi Quyang 师初阳, eds., *Zhonggua Yisilan baike quanshu 中国伊斯兰百科全书* [Chinese encyclopedia of Islam] (Chengdu: Sichuan Lexicographical Publishing House, 1994), 208–209.

38. Emily Feng, *Let Only Red Flowers Bloom: Identity and Belonging in Xi Jinping's China* (New York: Random House, 2025), 112.

39. Lipman, *Familiar Strangers;* Frankel, *Rectifying God's Name;* Petersen, *Interpreting Islam in China.*

40. For a study of these citations, see Donald Daniel Leslie and Mohamed Wassel, "Arabic and Persian Sources Used by Liu Chih," *Central Asiatic Journal* 26, no. 1 / 2 (1982).

41. Clément Huart, *Inscriptions arabes et persanes des mosquées chinoises de K'ai-fong-fou et de Si-ngan-fou* (Boston: Brill, 1905).

42. Zhao Can and She Yunshan, *Jingxue xichuan pu.*

43. Zhao Can and She Yunshan.

44. Weil, "Vicissitudes of Late Imperial China's Accommodation," 170.

45. Jin Tianzhu 金天柱, *Qingzhen shiyi 清真釋疑* [Clearing up doubts about Islam], ed. Hai Zhengzhong 海正忠 (Beijing: Zongjiao wenhua chubanshe 宗教文化出版社, 2020), 15.

46. Liu Zhi, *Tianfang zhisheng shilu nianpu,* juan 1, 5r–5v.

47. Lan Xu, *Tianfang zhengxue,* 7r.

48. Hille, "Les Han kitab et le Xidaotang."

49. Murata et al., *Sage Learning of Liu Zhi.*

50. Ben-Dor Benite, *Dao of Muhammad;* Petersen, *Interpreting Islam in China.*

51. Zhao Can and She Yunshan, *Jingxue xichuan pu.*

52. A better candidate for a written vernacular is *xiao'erjing,* the writing of colloquial Chinese in modified Arabic script.

53. Jonathan Lipman, ed., *Islamic Thought in China: Sino-Muslim Intellectual Evolution from the 17th to the 21st Century* (Edinburgh: Edinburgh University Press, 2016), 5.

54. Ford, "Some Chinese Muslims," 145.

55. Three hundred and eighteen of these works are listed, many with short summaries, in Isaac Mason, "Notes on Chinese Mohammedan Literature," *Journal of the North-China Branch of the Royal Asiatic Society* 56 (1925). Part of Mason's collection is available at the New York Public Library.

56. Roberta Tontini, *Muslim Sanzijing: Shifts and Continuities in the Definition of Islam in China* (Boston: Brill, 2016).

57. Dror Weil's groundbreaking dissertation has covered substantial distance toward answering this question. See Weil, "Vicissitudes of Late Imperial China's Accommodation."

9. Origin Without Essence

1. Shahab Ahmed, *What Is Islam? The Importance of Being Islamic* (Princeton, NJ: Princeton University Press, 2015), 246.

2. Talal Asad, "The Idea of an Anthropology of Islam," *Qui Parle* 17, no. 2 (2009): 1–30. However, in his further elaboration of that discursive tradition, Asad's focus on the Qur'an and *hadith* has an implicit delimiting and, one might argue, essentializing effect: see p. 20.

3. Albert Hourani, "Islamic History, Middle Eastern History, Modern History," in *Islamic Studies: A Tradition and Its Problems* (Malibu, CA: Undena Publications, 1979), 14.

4. Ahmed, *What Is Islam?,* 129–152, 266–270.

5. Ahmed, 266–270.

6. Ahmed, 267. Emphasis in the original.

7. Ahmed, 268. Emphasis in the original. Referring to Benjamin Braude and Bernard Lewis, *Christians and Jews in the Ottoman Empire: The Functioning of a Plural Society,* vol. 2 (New York: Holmes and Meier, 1982).

8. For a representative and fully developed expression of the "islams-not-Islam" position, both Talal Asad and Shahab Ahmed turned to anthropologist Abdul Hamid El-Zein, "Beyond Ideology and Theology: The Search for the Anthropology of Islam," *Annual Review of Anthropology* 6, no. 1 (1977): 227–254. Asad, "Idea of an Anthropology of Islam," 2. For self-ascription, Asad cites Michael Gilsenan, *Recognizing Islam: Religion and Society in the Modern Middle East,* rev. ed. (London: I. B. Tauris, 2000).

9. Dru Gladney, *Muslim Chinese: Ethnic Nationalism in the People's Republic,* 2nd ed. (Cambridge, MA: Harvard University Asia Center, 1996), 262.

10. Fredrik Barth, *Ethnic Groups and Boundaries: The Social Organization of Culture Difference* (Prospect Heights, IL: Waveland Press, 1998), 10–11.

11. Barth, 13.

12. Fredrik Barth, "Enduring and Emerging Issues in the Analysis of Ethnicity," in *The Anthropology of Ethnicity: Beyond "Ethnic Groups and Boundaries,"* ed. Hans Vermeulen and Cora Govers (Amsterdam: Het Spinhuis, 1994).

13. The story of how Chinese Muslims came to be seen as an ethnic group is brilliantly told in Zeyneb Hale Eroglu, *The Muslim Transnational in Modern China: Debates on Hui Identity and Islamic Reform* (New York: Columbia University Press, 2025).

14. Gladney, *Muslim Chinese,* 262. Unfortunately, he does not reproduce the original Chinese for "Islamic."

15. Sachiko Murata, *Chinese Gleams of Sufi Light: Wang Tai-Yu's Great Learning of the Pure and Real and Liu Chih's Displaying the Concealment of the Real Realm. With a New Translation of Jami's Lawa'ih from the Persian by William C. Chittick* (Albany: State University of New York Press, 2000), 23.

16. Sachiko Murata, ed., *The First Islamic Classic in Chinese: Wang Daiyu's Real Commentary on the True Teaching* (Albany: State University of New York Press, 2017), 37.

17. Wang Daiyu 王岱輿, *Zhengjiao zhen lun 正教真詮* [Real commentary on the true teaching] ([China]: Qingzhen Tang, 1642), 2r–2v. Throughout this chapter I have used the translation of Murata, *First Islamic Classic in Chinese,* 39.

18. Devin DeWeese, *Islamization and Native Religion in the Golden Horde: Baba Tükles and Conversion to Islam in Historical and Epic Tradition* (University Park: Pennsylvania State University Press, 1994), 55–57. Ahmed also quotes this passage, at greater length and to different ends. Ahmed, *What Is Islam?,* 324.

19. Ahmed, *What Is Islam?,* 325.

20. Greg Dening, *The Death of William Gooch: A History's Anthropology* (Honolulu: University of Hawai'i Press, 1995), 14.

21. Chase Robinson, *Islamic Historiography* (Cambridge: Cambridge University Press, 2002); Marilyn Robinson Waldman, *Toward a Theory of Historical Narrative: A Case Study in Perso-Islamicate Historiography* (Columbus: Ohio State University Press, 1980).

22. Clifford Geertz partly built his understanding of Islam on this story. Clifford Geertz, *Islam Observed: Religious Development in Morocco and Indonesia* (Chicago: University of Chicago Press, 1971). Geertz's sketch is probably best read alongside the more fine-grained, manuscript-based work of Nancy K. Florida, especially *Babad Jaka Tingkir* (Durham, NC: Duke University Press, 1995).

23. Marshall Hodgson, *The Venture of Islam,* vol. 2 (Chicago: University of Chicago Press, 2009).

24. See, for example, Zareena Grewal, *Islam Is a Foreign Country: American Muslims and the Global Crisis of Authority* (New York: New York University Press, 2014), 6–7: "Muslim world . . . a global community of Muslim locals, both majorities and minorities who *belong* . . . and who, in their totality, exemplify the universality of Islam."

25. For example, among the Hadhrami diaspora. Engseng Ho, *The Graves of Tarim: Genealogy and Mobility Across the Indian Ocean* (Berkeley: University of California Press, 2006).

26. Mimi Hanaoka, *Authority and Identity in Medieval Islamic Historiography: Persian Histories from the Peripheries* (Cambridge: Cambridge University Press, 2016).

27. For example, the conversion narrative of Sultan Satuq Bughrakhan in Eastern Turkistan and the aforementioned stories of Sunan Kalijaga. Gunnar Jarring, *Literary Texts from Kashghar* (Lund: CWK Gleerup, 1980); Geertz, *Islam Observed.*

28. C. E. J. Whitting, "The Unprinted Indigenous Arabic Literature of Northern Nigeria," *Journal of the Royal Asiatic Society* 75, no. 1–2 (1943): 20–26; Rian Thum, *The Sacred Routes of Uyghur History* (Cambridge, MA: Harvard University Press, 2014).

29. I owe this useful phrase to Shahzad Bashir, personal communication.

30. Chen Bo 陳波, "The Making of 'China' out of 'Zhongguo': 1585–1690," *Journal of Asian History* 50, no. 1 (2016): 73.

31. From the Qing onward, many people of Zhongguo (i.e., Zhongguoren) have themselves embraced the term "China," as well as variants from the same history of transmission. Examples from the protagonists in this book include Ma Lianyuan

and Manṣūr Ma Xuexhi, both of whom referred to themselves by the Arabic form of "China": *al-Ṣīn.*

32. Guo Wu, "New Qing History: Dispute, Dialog, and Influence," *Chinese Historical Review* 23, no. 1 (2016): 60–61.

33. I use this term in the sense that Benedict Anderson originally intended it, not as a synonym for "nation" but instead as a broader phenomenon that includes dynastic realms and religious communities. Benedict Anderson, *Imagined Communities: Reflections on the Origin and Spread of Nationalism* (London: Verso, 1991).

34. Haun Saussy, *The Problem of a Chinese Aesthetic* (Stanford, CA: Stanford University Press, 1993).

35. Eroglu, *Muslim Transnational in Modern China.*

36. Bruno Latour, *Reassembling the Social: An Introduction to Actor-Network-Theory* (Oxford: Oxford University Press, 2007), 31.

Conclusion

1. I use the term "Chinafication" rather than "Sinicization" to reflect the fact that the Chinese-language term refers to the nation-state. Sinicization, on the other hand, usually refers to notions of Chinese culture or civilization.

2. Li Hongchun 李红春, "Li Hongchun fuyanjiuyuan yingyao canjia 'Ma Lianyuan yu Yisilanjiao Zhongguohua' xueshu huiyi 李红春副研究员应邀参加'马联元与伊斯兰教中国化' 学术会议 _云南省社会科学院" [Associate researcher Li Hongchun participated by invitation in the conference "Ma Lianyuan and the Chinafication of Islam"], 云南省社会科学院, 2018, https://web.archive.org/web/20200323200813/http:/www.sky.yn.gov.cn/dtxx/csdt/2271658201445552244.

3. "用中华优秀文化浸润我国伊斯兰教." Xi Jinping 习近平, "Guanyu jiaqiang he gaijin xin xingshi xia Yisilanjiao gongzuo de yijian 关于加强和改进新形势下 伊斯兰教工作的意" [On strengthening and improving Islam work in the new situation] (General Office of the Central Committee of the Communist Party of China and State Council Office, April 19, 2018), transcribed by Adrian Zenz and Mishel Kondi and available at https://uyghurtribunal.com/wp-content/uploads/2021/11/Transcript-Document-10.pdf.

4. Feng Jinyuan 冯今源, "Cong Zhongguo Yisilanjiao Hanwen yizhu kan Rujia sixiang dui Zhongguo Yisilanjiao de yingxiang he shentou 从中国伊斯兰教汉文译著看儒家思想对中国伊斯兰教的影响和渗透" [The influence and penetration of Confucian thought in Chinese Islam as seen in the Chinese Muslim Chinese-language translations and compositions], in *Yisilanjiao zai Zhongguo 伊斯兰教在中国,* ed. Gansu sheng minzu yanjiusuo 甘肃省民族研究所 (Yinchuan: Ningxia People's Press 宁夏人民出版社, 1982), 257–281. See Chapter 8 for a discussion of Feng's essay.

5. Ma Jia 马佳, "Yisilanjiao Zhongguohua de shijianzhe: Ma Lianyuan ji qi sixiang yaoyi 伊斯兰教中国化的实践者: 马联元及其思想要义" [A practitioner of the Chinafication of Islam: Ma Lianyuan and the essentials of his thought], *Beifang Minzu Daxue Xuebao: Zhexue Shehui Kexue Ban 北方民族大学学报: 哲学社会科学版,* no. 4 (2016): 82–86.

6. Xi Jinping, "Guanyu jiaqiang he gaijin xin xingshi xia Yisilanjiao gongzuo de yijian."

7. Hannah Theaker and David Stroup, "Making Islam Chinese: Religious Policy and Mosque Sinicisation in the Xi Era," November 1, 2024, available at SSRN, https://ssrn.com/abstract=5130111 or http://dx.doi.org/10.2139/ssrn.5130111.

8. Niklas Luhmann, *Art as a Social System* (Stanford, CA: Stanford University Press, 2000), as elaborated in Till Mostowlansky and Andrea Rota, "A Matter of Perspective? Disentangling the Emic–Etic Debate in the Scientific Study of Religion\s," *Method and Theory in the Study of Religion* 28, no. 4–5 (2016): 317–336.

9. Quentin Skinner put it succinctly: "We must classify in order to understand, and we can only classify the unfamiliar in terms of the familiar." Skinner, "Meaning and Understanding in the History of Ideas," *History and Theory* 8, no. 1 (1969): 6.

Selected Primary Sources

Arabic, Persian, and Turkic

ʿAbd al-Aḥad. *Manāqib al awliya* [al-manāqib al-Aḥmadiyyaaḥmadiyya]. N.p., n.d. [early twentieth century]. Duplicated manuscript.

ʿAbd al-Qādir Guanli Ye 關裡爺. *al-Rashḥat al-sharīfat* [The sublime dewdrop]. c. 1830. Facsimile of an 1887 manuscript in Guanli Ye 關裡爺, *Reshiha'er: Zhengui de lushu (wanzheng diancang Gansu ban—Yuanshi shougao kanbu. Xin yi. Zhushi. Jiaokan) 熱什哈爾: 珍貴的露珠（完整典藏甘肅版——原始手稿刊布．新譯．註釋. 校勘）* [Rashaha: Precious dewdrop (Complete classic, Gansu recension—Publication of the original manuscript. New translation. Annotation. Collation)]. Manuscript transcription and translation by Ma Xuehua 馬學華 and Zhang Chengzhi 張承志. Taipei: Net and Books Co., 2021.

ʿAbd al-Shukūr ibn Ibrāhīm. *al-Rashfa* [The sip]. N.p., 1920. Duplicated manuscript.

Amānatallah, Mawlawi. *Hidayut Ool Islam in Arabic and Hindoostanee.* Edited by John Borthwick Gilchrist. Calcutta: Hindoostanee Press, 1804.

Anonymous. *Aṣl al-īmān* [The root of faith]. Yongchang, 1907. Woodblock.

Anonymous. *Hawā-ye / Zifa chu cheng 字法初程* [The air of / Beginning rules of grammar]. Edited by Ma Lianyuan 馬聯元. Xinping, Yunnan: The families in and around the Xinping county center, 1895. Woodblock.

Anonymous. *Miftāḥ mirāḥ / Zi fa cuoyao 字法撮要* [The key of happiness / Synopsis of morphology]. Edited by Ma Lianyuan 馬聯元. Taoguoyuan, Yunnan: The coreligionists of Taoguoyuan, 1895. Woodblock.

Anonymous. *Rāhnamā-ye muwāfiq-i Imām Ja'far Ṣādiq* [The consistent guide to the path of Imām Ja'far Ṣādiq]. Early nineteenth century. Manuscript.

Anonymous. *Tawbah al-aghyār / Tawbah al-ʿajā'ib / Khwājah khatm / Barāt Shaʿbān* [The repentance of the other / The marvelous repentance / Khwājah recitation / Barāt Night]. Dabai, Yunnan: Muslims of Dabai Village, 1894. Woodblock.

Anonymous. *Taẕkirah'i ḥaẓrat haft Muḥammadān* [Tazkira of the seven Muḥammads]. In an untitled compilation of tazkirahs. Uncataloged, paginated manuscript in the Library of the Minzu Research Institute, Minzu University, Beijing.

Anonymous. *Taẕkirah'i Ḥaẓrat Khwāja Muḥammad Sharīf Buzurgwār* [Tazkirah of Ḥaẓrat Khwāja Muḥammad Sharīf Buzurgwār]. Jarring Collection, Lund University Library, manuscript number Prov. 327, 23a.

Anonymous. *Tazkirah of Ḥaẓrat Āfāq Khojam.* Manuscript # Prov. 369. Jarring Collection, Lund University Library. [c. 1900]. Manuscript.

Anonymous. *Zaxue 雜學* [Miscellany]. Chengdu: Ma Shanqing 馬善慶, 1870. Woodblock.

ʿAṭṭar, Farīd al-Dīn, and Reynold A. Nicholson. *Taẕkirat al-awliyā* [Tazkira of the saints]. [Thirteenth century]. London: Luzac and Company, 1905

Baoming Zhenjing 寶命真經 [The Qur'an]. [Dali, Yunnan]: Du Wenxiu, 1862. Woodblock.

Changde Huijiao jiaoyu fuzhu hui 常德回教教育輔助會. *Huiwen duben 回文讀本* [Arabic reader]. Vol. 8. N.p.: Changde Daqing Qingzhensi 常德大慶街清真寺, 1925.

Dīdāmarī, Muḥammad Aʿẓam, *Wāqiʿāt-i Kashmīr.* Oriental Research Library, Srinagar, manuscript #1843.

Dihlawī, ʿAbd al-ʿAzīz b. Ḥamīdullah. *ʿUmdat al-Islām: Qingzhen yu zhu 清真玉柱* [The pillar of Islam: The jade pillar of Islam]. Edited by Ma Lianyuan 馬聯元. Heyang, Yunnan: Teacher Li Guozhu and the Muslims of Heyang County, 1897. Woodblock.

Emin, Mehmet. *Majālis irshādiyyah* [Council of guidance]. Shanghai: Shanghai Believer's Classics Company 上海穆民經書公司, n.d. [c. 1940]. Offset printing?

Ḥasan Ẓiyāʾ al-Dīn Ma Anyi 馬安義. *Min sharḥ al-Wiqāyah al-masmi bi-al-tawḍīḥ: Al-juz' al-thānī* [Commentary on the Wiqāyah called the explication: Part two]. [Yunnan]: Yunnan Hongwen Shiyin Ju 雲南宏文石印局, 1924. Duplicated manuscript.

Huart, Clément. *Inscriptions arabes et persanes des mosquées chinoises de K'ai-fong-fou et de Si-ngan-fou.* Boston: Brill, 1905.

Ibn ʿAli, Khwāja Akhund. *Siyar al-mukhliṣīn* [Lives of the loyal]. Nineteenth century. BP189.7.N35.A23 1700z [misidentified as Jāmiʿ al-Maqāmāt]. Library of the University of California, Berkeley. Manuscript.

Jarring, Gunnar. *Literary Texts from Kashghar.* Lund: CWK Gleerup, 1980.

Kāshgharī, Muḥammad Ṣādiq. *Zubdat al-masāʾil wa-l-ʿaqāʾid* [The cream of the questions and the creed]. Istanbul: Ḥājjī ʿAbbās Āqā, 1897.

Khāl al-Dīn, Mīr. *Hidāyatnāma.* 1729 / 1730. OR 8162. British Library. Manuscript.

Ma Anyi 馬安義. *Taḥqīq al-īman* [The realization of faith]. [Yunnan]: Guang ji tang 廣濟堂, 1905. Woodblock.

[Ma Dexin 馬德新]. *Taḥqīq al-ṣalawat* [The realization of prayers]. [Yunnan]: n.p., 1863. Woodblock.

Maḥmūdī, ʿAbdallah al-. "Imām al-Muslimīn fī al-Ṣīn al-imam ʿAbdallah Ma Changh Chingh." *Rabṭah al-Ulama' al-Suriyyīn* (blog), July 19, 2018. https://web.archive.org/web/20220713021857/https://islamsyria.com/ar/التراجم/ينغ-انغ-ما-الله-عبد-الإمام-الصين-في-المسلمين-إمام.

Ma Lianyuan 馬聯元. "Fu: 'Bianshu Da Zaxue' Ma Zhiben zi xu Alabowen (yuan wen) 附：《编述大杂学》马致本自序 阿拉伯文（原文）" [Appendix: "Compilation of the great miscellany," Ma Zhiben's self-preface in the original Arabic]. [c. 1902]. In *Weishan Huizu wenshi ziliao 巍山回族文史资料* [Weishan Hui ethnicity historical materials], vol. 12, *Ma Lianyuan jingxue shijia 马联元经学世家* [The religious scholar family of Ma Lianyuan], edited by Ma Yunliang 马云良,

7–18. Kunming: Yunnan Ethnicities Publishing House, 2011. Manuscript facsimile.

——. *Ḥurūf al-hijā'* [Letters of the alphabet]. [Yunnan], 1891. Woodblock.

——. *Jawāmiʿ al-daʿawāt / Da zaxue 大杂学* [Gatherings of prayers / Grand miscellany]. [c. 1902]. Beijing: 宗教文化出版社 [Zongjiao wenhua chubanshe], 2017. Typeset edition.

——. *Sharḥ al-laṭā'if / Weiyan ji zhu 微言集註* [Commentary on *Laṭā'if* / Collected commentary on the precis]. Kunming: Guang Ji Tang 廣濟堂, 1898. Woodblock.

——. *Tabṭīl al-thathlīth wa tathbīt al-tawḥīd* [Invalidation of the trinity and proof of the oneness of God]. [Kunming]: Guang Ji Tang 廣濟堂, 1899. Woodblock.

——. *Tafṣīl al-īmān: al-Faṣl / Tianfang fen xin pian ji si pian yao dao 天方分信篇暨四篇要道* [Elements of faith: The chapter / Essay on the divisions of faith and four essential principles]. Kunming: Xing Shun He, 1894. Woodblock.

——. *Tianfang fen xin pian ji si pian yao dao 天方分信篇暨四篇要道* [Essay on the divisions of faith and four essential principles]. Yuxi, Yunnan: 哦山白吧清真寺 [Eshan bai ba qinzhensi], 2018.

——. *Tianfang xingli awen zhujie 天方性理阿文注解* [Arabic commentary on the precis]. Shanghai: 寫真製版印刷 [Xie zhen zhiban yinshua], [c. 1930s]. Manuscript.

Ma Lianyuan, ed. *al-Qur'ān kalām Allah / Baoming Zhenjing 寳命真經* [The Qur'an, the word of God] / The true classic of the precious command]. Kunming: Xing Shun He Company 興順和號, 1895. Woodblock.

[Ma Lianyuan 馬聯元] Muḥammad Nūr al-Ḥaqq ibn Sayyid Luqmān. *Sharḥ al-Laṭā'if* [Commentary on *Laṭā'if*]. Kanpur: ʿAlī Maḥmūd, 1902. Lithograph.

[Ma Lianyuan 馬聯元] Muḥammad Nūr al-Ḥaqq ibn Sayyid Luqmān. *Min sharḥ al-Wiqāyah al-masmi bi-al-tawḍīḥ* [Commentary on the Wiqāyah called the Explication]. Kanpur: Maḥmūd al-Maṭābi', 1903. Lithograph.

Ma Lianyuan 馬聯元 and Abū Naṣr Muḥammad ibn Wadʿān. *Khutab: Zhisheng baolun 至聖寳論* [Sermons: Precious discourses of the Prophet]. Kunming: Xifa Company 喜發號, 1894.

Ma Lianyuan 馬聯元 and al-Nasafī. *Mukhtaṣar sharḥ al-ʿaqā'id / 天方释难要言* [Abridged commentary on the creed / Essentials of the explanation of the difficulties of Islam]. Kunming: Xing Shun He Company 興順和號, 1893. Woodblock.

Manṣūrallah, Burhān al-Dīn Ma Xuezhi 马学智, Ibrāhīm, and Muḥammad ʿAbd al-Ḥakīm. *Risālah aqṣarayyah li-bayān al-silsilah al-Jahriyya* [The briefest treatise on the Jahriyya chain of transmission]. [Jinjipu, Ningxia]: undated facsimile publication circa 2010 under the title *Zheherenye shi 哲合忍耶史*, 1983. Duplicated manuscript.

Muḥammad Tawāḍuʿ (Pang Shiqian 龐士謙). *Al-Ṣīn wa al-Islām* [China and Islam]. Cairo: Society of the Muslim Brothers Press, 1945.

Muḥammad Yūsuf. *Nuzhat al-qulūb* [Delights of the hearts]. 1272 AH [1856 / 1857]. Duplicated manuscript.

Sirhindī, Aḥmad. *Maktūbāt-i Imām Rabbānī* [The letters of Imām Rabbānī]. Istanbul: Hakikat Kitabevi, 1977.

Tumurtāshi, Muḥammad b. ʿAbdallah. *Tanwīr al-abṣār* [The enlightenment of perception]. Edited by Ma Lianyuan 馬聯元. Kunming: Nan Guo'an 男國安, 1895. Woodblock.

Turkistānī, Mūsa. *Ūlūgh Turkistān fāji ʿasi* [The tragedy of great Turkistan]. Madina: Maṭābiʿ al-Rashīd, 1979.

Chinese, Including Translations from Arabic and Persian

ʿAbduh, Muḥammad. *Huijiao renyi lun 回教認一論* [Treatise on tawhid in Islam]. Translated by Ma Ruitu 馬瑞圖. Shanghai: Zhonghua Shuju, 1937.

Abū al-Imān ʿAbd al-Qādir Guanli Ye 关里爷. *Reshihaer 热什哈尔*. Translated by Yang Wanbao 杨万宝, Ma Xuekai 马学凯, and Zhang Yongzhi 张永志. Beijing: Shenghuo Dushu Xinzhi Sanlian Shudian, 1993.

Abudunla Alei 阿布顿拉 阿雷. *Musilin bidu 穆斯林必读* [Required readings for Muslims]. N.p., 2010.

Anonymous. *Baiqi Guo shi zupu 白奇郭氏族谱* [Genealogy of the Baiqi Guo clan]. N.p., 1987.

Anonymous. *Huihui yuanlai 回回原來* [The origins of the Huihui]. Laizhou, Shandong: n.p., 1894.

Anonymous. *Jiu pin chengchuan 九品乘传* [The ninth-ranked transmission]. Hong Kong: Lan Yue Chubanshe, 2013.

Anonymous. *Sheng mi zhenyuan 省迷眞原* [Avoiding perplexity about the real origin]. Beijing: Beijing Fu Hua Yinshuasuo, 1914.

Democratic Committee of the Islamic Xianmen Shrine of Xining, Qinghai. "Qinghai sheng Xining shi Yisilan jiao Xianmen Gongbei lishi 青海省西宁市伊斯兰教鲜门拱北历史" [History of the Islamic Xianmen Shrine of Xining, Qinghai]. Xining, 2010.

Ding Shijun 丁士俊. "Kangle Dingmen Ding Shijun jishu Dingmen lishi 康乐丁门丁士俊记述丁门历史" [Written account of the history of the Dingmen by Ding Shijun of Lintan]. In *Zhongguo Sufei xuepai dianji 中国苏菲学派典籍* [Sources on Chinese Sufi denominations], edited by Ma Tong 马通 and Ma Haibin 马海滨, 542–544. N.p., 2010.

Ding Zhengwu 丁正武 and Ma Fuchun 马富春. "Lintan Ding Zhengwu koushu Dingmen lishi 临潭丁正武口述丁门历史" [Oral narration on the history of the Dingmen by Ding Zhengwu of Lintan]. In *Zhongguo Sufei xuepai dianji 中国苏菲学派典籍* [Sources on Chinese Sufi denominations], edited by Ma Tong 马通 and Ma Haibin 马海滨, 539–541. N.p., 2010.

General Office of the Central Committee of the Communist Party of China and General Office of the State Council. "Guanyu jiaqiang he gaijin xin xingshi xia Yisilan jiao gongzuo de yijian 关于加强和改进新形势下 伊斯兰教工作的意见" [Suggestion on the strengthening and improvement of work on Islam under the new circumstances]. 2018. Transcribed by Adrian Zenz and Mishel Kondi. *Uyghur Tribunal,* 2021. https://uyghurtribunal.com/wp-content/uploads/2021/11/Transcript-Document-10.pdf.

Guo Zhichao 郭志超. "Taiwan Baiqi Guo Huizu ji qi Dalu zujia de jiaowang 台湾白奇郭回族及其与大陆祖家的交往" [Contacts Between the Taiwan Baiqi Guo Hui and their ancestral home on the Mainland]. *Huizu Yanjiiu 回族研究,* no. 2 (1996): 20–22.

Jin Hanqing 金漢青. *Zhiben Ma Laofuzi liu xun shou xu 至本馬老子六旬壽序* [Preface for Teacher Ma Zhiben's sixtieth birthday]. [Yunnan]: n.p., 1900.

Jin Tianzhu 金天柱. *Qingzhen shiyi 清真釋疑* [Clearing up doubts about Islam]. Edited by Hai Zhengzhong 海正忠. Beijing: Zongjiao wenhua chubanshe 宗教文化出版社, 2020.

Kairawani, Rahmatallah. *Huiye bian zhen 回耶辨真.* Translated by Wang Jingzhai 王静斋. Peking: Qingzhen Shu Bao Shi 清真書報社, 1922.

Lan Xu 藍煦. *Tianfang zhengxue 天方正學* [Correct learning of Islam]. Beijing: Qingzhen Shu Bao Shi 清真書報社, 1925.

Li Hongchun 李红春. "Li Hongchun Fuyanjiuyuan yingyao canjia 'Ma Lianyuan yu Yisilanjiao Zhongguohua' xueshu huiyi 李红春副研究员应邀参加'马联元与伊斯兰教中国化' 学术会议_云南省社会科学院" [Associate researcher Li Hongchun participated by invitation in the conference "Ma Lianyuan and the Chinafication of Islam"]. 云南省社会科学院, 2018. https://web.archive.org/web/20200323200813/http:/www.sky.yn.gov.cn/dtxx/csdt/2271658201445552244.

Liu Zhi 劉智. *Tianfang san zi you yi 天方三字幼義* [Islamic three-character classic]. [Kunming], [c. 1890s].

——. *Tianfang Zhisheng shilu nianpu 天方至聖實錄年譜* [Chronological veritable record of the Ultimate Sage of Islam]. Chengdu: Bao Zhen Tang 寶真堂, 1872.

Li Zhongtang 李忠堂. "Minguo sishiqi nian fang wen Lugang jishi 民國四十七年訪問鹿港紀實" [Record of a visit to Lukang in the year of the republic forty-seven]. *Zhongguo Huijiao Xiehui Huibao 中國回教協會會報* 74 (1960).

Ma Da'en 馬大恩. "Chongke Qingzhen zhinan xu 重刻清真指南叙" [Preface to the reprinting of *Compass of Islam*]. In *Qingzhen zhinan 清真指南* [Compass of Islam], by Ma Zhu 馬注, 1r–3r. Guangzhou: Hao Pan Street Mosque, 1870.

Ma Dexin 馬德新. *Chaojin tuji 朝覲途記* [Account of the Hajj route]. Translated by Ma Anli 馬安禮. Yunnan: n.p., 1861.

Ma Jianzhi 馬健之. *Huijiao gangyao 回教綱要* [Essentials of Islam]. Kunming: Mu Guang Shu Dian 穆光書店, 1948.

Ma Jun 马军. *Yisilan xinyang wenda 伊斯兰信仰问答* [Questions and answers on Islamic faith]. Gansu: Gansu minzu chubanshe, 2011.

[Ma Jun 馬俊 et al.]. *Huijiao bizun 回教必遵* [Requirements of Islam]. N.p.: Ma Bufang, 1939.

Ma Lianyuan 馬聯元. *Bian li ming zheng yulu 辨理明正語録* [Quotations discriminating the truth with clear proof]. Kunming: Nancheng Mosque, 1899.

——. "編述大雜學序" [Bianshu Da Zaxue Zu]. Translated by Ma Yulong [Ma Ruitu]. *Tianfang xueli yuekan 天方學理月刊* 9, no. 4 (1932): 12–14.

——. *Qingzhen yuzhu 请真玉柱* [Jade pillar of Islam]. Translated by Li Xiurong 李秀荣 and Liu Hongkuan 刘宏宽. N.p., 2003.

Ma Lianyuan 马联元 and Liu Zhi 劉智. *Tianfang xingli benjing zhushi 天方性里本经注释* [Explanation of the original classic of nature and principle in Islam]. Translated by Ruan Bin 阮斌. [Beijing]: Zhongguo Minzhu Tongmeng [China Democratic League], 1983.

Ma Qirong 馬啓榮. *Xi lai zongpu 西来宗谱* [Genealogy of the arrival from the west]. Guangzhou: Huaisheng Mosque, 1877.

Ma Xuezhi 马学智. *Daotong shi zhuan 道统史传* [History of the transmission of the Way]. Translated by Ma Yi 马义. Xiji, Ningxia: Xiji xian Beidasi, 1997.

Ma Zaiyuan 马在渊. *Sufei you men: Gui Zhen zong yi li de mimi 苏菲有门：归真总义里的秘密* [Sufi's gateway: The secret in general meaning of the return to the True One]. Hong Kong: Huai feng shushe, 2016.

Ma Zhu 馬注. *Qingzhen zhinan 清真指南* [Compass of Islam]. Guangzhou: Hao Pan Street Mosque, 1870.

———. "Qingzhen zhinan 清真指南" [Compass of Islam]. In *Huizu he Zhongguo Yisilanjiao guji ziliao hui bian 回族和中国伊斯兰教古籍资料汇编,* edited by Ningxia shaoshu minzu guji zhengli chuban guihua xiaozu bangongshi 宁夏少数民族古籍整理出版规划小组办公室编, vol. 1 辑 7 函. Tianjin: Tianjin guji chubanshe 天津古籍出版社, 1987.

Ma Zhu 馬注 and anonymous. "Saidianchi jiapu 賽典赤家譜" [Genealogy of Saidianchi]. N.d. In *Yunnan Huizu guji diancang 云南回族古籍典藏* [Collection of ancient texts of the Hui nationality of Yunnan], vol. 11, edited by Yao Jide 姚继德. Kunming: Yunnan Chuban Jituan 云南出版集团, 2019.

[Qi Mingde 祁明德] and [Qi Jiequan 祁介泉]. *Long Ahong 聋阿訇* [The Deaf Cleric]. Linxia: Gansu sheng Linxia shi Mingde Qingzhensi 甘肃省临夏市明德清真寺, 2004.

Riḍā, Muḥammad Rashīd. *Muhanmode de moshi 穆罕默德的默示* [The revelation of Muhammad]. Translated by Ma Ruitu 馬瑞圖. Shanghai: Zhonghua Shuju, 1946.

Wang Daiyu 王岱輿. *Zhengjiao zhen lun 正教真詮* [Real commentary on the true teaching]. [China]: Qingzhen Tang, 1642.

Wang Dayuan 汪大淵. *Daoyi zhilüe 島夷誌略* [Record of the island barbarians]. Edited by Su Jiqing 苏继廎. Beijing: Zhonghua Shuju, 1981.

Wang Shouqian 王守謙. "Liyan 例言" [Preface]. In Lan Xu 藍煦, *Tianfang zhengxue 天方正學* [Correct learning of Islam], 1–5. Beijing: Qingzhen Shu Bao Shi 清真書報社, 1925.

Xinhua.net. "Yang Faming: Zhagen Zhonghua wenhua wotu jianchi woguo Yisilanjiao Zhongguohua fangxin 杨发明: 扎根中华文化沃土 坚持我国伊斯兰教中国化方向" [Yang Faming: Taking root in the fertile soil of Chinese civilization: Persevere in the Chinafication of our country's Islam]. March 10, 2018. https://web.archive.org/web/20200808074958/http://www.xinhuanet.com/politics/2018lh/2018-03/10/c_1122516862.htm.

Xu Zhiming 徐之銘. "Chaojin tuji xu 朝覲途記序" [Preface to "Account of the Hajj route"]. In 馬德新 Ma Dexin, *Chaojin tuji 朝覲途記* [Account of the Hajj route]. Yunnan: n.p., 1861.

Zhang Shizhong 張時中. "'Kelimu' jie qimeng qianshuo '克里默'解启蒙浅说" [Explanatory primer on the kalima]. *中国穆斯林,* no. 2 (1983): 4–8.

Zhang Shizhong 張時中, trans. *Si pian yao dao 四篇要道譯解* [Four essential principles in translation]. Chengdu: 王占超, 1872.

Zhang Shizhong 張時中 and Ashige 阿世格. *Gui zhen zong yi 歸真總義* [General meaning of the return to the True One]. [Sichuan]: [Baozhentang], 1878.

Zhao Can 趙燦 and She Yunshan 舍蘊善. "Jingxue xichuan pu 經學系傳普" [Genealogy of the transmission and lineage of classical learning]. 1714.

——. *Jingxue xichuan pu 经学系传普* [Genealogy of the transmission and lineage of classical learning]. Edited by Chen Hui 陈晖. Beijing: Zongjiao wenhua chubanshe, 2022.

Multilingual

Attaqwa Mosque. *Taiguo qingmai Yisilan jingzhen qingzhensi ershier xuexiao shiwu zhounian jinian kan 泰国清迈伊斯兰敬真清真寺二十二学校十五周年纪念刊* [Commemorative publication for the twenty-second anniversary of the Islamic "Venerating the Real" Mosque of Chiang Mai, Thailand, and the fifteenth anniversary of its school]. Chiang Mai, 1988.

Hu Songshan 虎嵩山. *Lughāt tafsīr Ḥusaynī: Housaini dacidian 侯賽尼大辭典* [Dictionary of the *Tafsīr Ḥusaynī*]. [China]: n.p., 1951.

Liu Zhi 劉智. *Laṭā'if* [Subtleties] *Xingli Weiyan 性理微言* [Precis of metaphysics]. Translated by Ma Lianyuan 馬聯元. Kunming: Ma Zilian 馬子廉, 1898. Woodblock.

Ma Lianyuan 马联元. *Haiting jie yi 赫聽解譯* [Explanatory translation of the *Khatm*]. [Kunming]: Guang Ji Tang 廣濟堂, 1900. Woodblock.

——. *Qingzhen yuzhu A Han duizhao 请真玉柱 阿汉对照* [Jade pillar of Islam: Arabic Chinese comparison]. Translated by Muhammad Ramadan 穆罕默德来迈丹. N.p., 1981.

Acknowledgments

All books are group projects, and this one is no exception. I would first like to acknowledge the important contribution of the caretakers, especially the mosque personnel, booksellers, and antique dealers, who generously provided me access to so many of the sources for this study. Their primary purposes in preserving books were often something other than sharing them with a non-Muslim historian from the other side of the planet. Without their generous welcome and willingness to put aside their own business for a few hours or days, this project would have been impossible. My research in such collections within the People's Republic of China (PRC) ended prematurely in December of 2017, when a stark rise in repressive policies toward Muslims made continued visits untenable. For the same reason, I refrain from thanking these archivists and caretakers individually. Outside of China, I am grateful to the librarians at the Attaqwa and Ban Haw mosques in Chiangmai, the Patkapur Mosque in Kanpur, Darul Uloom Nadwatul Ulama in Lucknow, Toyo Bunko in Tokyo, Tenri University Library, Osaka University Library, Institut National des Langues et Civilisations Orientales in Paris, and King Abdulaziz University in Jeddah.

Several institutions have placed great trust in this project by funding my research and writing. This began with small travel grants from Loyola University New Orleans. The research those grants enabled was critical for framing the project and seeking further support. It was at the National Humanities Center, which supported my first sabbatical, that I began the writing process, informed and inspired by brilliant colleagues and the legendary NHC staff. Research in Saudi Arabia was funded by the Muhammad Alagil Chair at the Asia Research Institute, University of Singapore, and can be credited for broadening my interests in the diasporic stories of Islamic China. The Nottingham Research Fellowship funded further time and travel, particularly to the diasporic archives analyzed in this book. And I would not have been able to complete this book without the funding provided by the Philip Leverhulme

Prize, one of the exceedingly rare sources of research support that is not tied to a specific proposed project.

I was fortunate to have two generous and astute peer reviewers, and I am grateful to them for contributing critiques that sharpened the work substantially. My research and writing of this book was considerably slowed when the PRC atrocities in the Uyghur region emerged in late 2017, diverting much of my research energies to the documentation of state policies toward Muslims. I thank my former editor, Kathleen McDermott, for her patience and understanding, and my new editor, Joseph Pomp, for moving the book from draft to publication with unusual speed and nuanced feedback. Thank you to Christine Dahlin for striking the perfect balance of intervention and restraint in the copyedits, and to John Donohue of Westchester Publishing Services for his efficient management of the final stages of production.

I am indebted to Jonathan Lipman for ongoing conversations, advice on matters scholarly and otherwise, comments on the manuscript, and emergency scans of sources. Jonathan's impact on the field of Islam / China has been enormous not just for his publications, but also due to his work building community and supporting new members.

Thank you to my colleague Huda Abdul Ghafour Amin Kashgary, who jointly collected oral histories with me in Saudi Arabia, for opening doors and teaching me about the Turkistani community. Thank you also to my research assistants at the University of Nottingham who wrote summaries and draft translations of selected sources, namely Youssra Hasan (Arabic) and Chloe Ma (Chinese).

Muhammad al-Sudairi, Noriko Unno, Waleed Ziad, David Brophy, William Chittick, Eric Schluessel, Isa Youshe, Joshua Freeman, and John Chen all generously shared sources with me, for which I am deeply grateful. Shahzad Bashir made invaluable comments on Chapter 9. The ideas and information in this book were shaped by conversations with many other colleagues, including Chris Washington, Janice Jeong, David Gilmartin, Hale Eroglu, Nakanishi Tatsuya, Dror Weil, Ha Guangtian, Zvi Ben-Dor Benite, Eric Schluessel, Hannah Theaker, Leila Chérif-Chebbi, Oded Abt, David Atwill, Ulrich Brandenburg, James Frankel, Nancy Florida, Aaron Glasserman, Isa Youshe, Florian Sobieroj, David Stroup, Ed Pulford, Hai Peng, Xin Zhaokun, C. Patterson Giersch, and Jim Millward. Many other colleagues I leave unnamed due to current political circumstances, but I am equally if not more grateful to them for their insights. All errors in this book are of course my own.

Special thanks are due to Mark Elliott and Engseng Ho, who have supported my work as mentors and colleagues for two decades now, providing feedback and encouragement, nurturing scholarly communities, sharing panels, and writing letters of recommendation. In a similar vein I would like to thank Jeff Wasserstrom for his enduring advocacy and support.

Parts of Chapters 3 and 6 are reprinted from “The Naqshbandiyya Mujaddidiyya in China,” *Journal of the Royal Asiatic Society* 34, no. 2 (2024). A portion of Chapter 7 is reprinted from Rian Thum and Huda Abdul Ghafour Amin Kashgary, “The Turkistanis of Mecca: Community Histories of Periphery and Center,” *Asian Ethnicity* 22, no. 1 (2021). Much of the text of “What Is Islamic History,” *History and Theory* 58, no. 4 (2019), is reprinted in Chapter 9. The Conclusion builds on ideas I first presented in “Surviving in a ‘Society’-Centric World: Comments on Engseng Ho’s ‘Inter-Asian Concepts for Mobile Societies,’” *Journal of Asian Studies* 76, no. 4 (2017).

Thank you to my neighbors in New Orleans for their patience with the ever-present book project that repeatedly dragged me away from important cocktail hours.

And thanks to Laura Murphy for encouragement, patience, and deep critical engagement with my ideas and interests.

Index